Making Law Work:
Environmental Compliance
&
Sustainable Development

Volume 2

DZ

For Barbara, Cassidy, Hannah, & David

DK

For Mrs. Tabitha W. Kaniaru and our children, for their support and encouragement

EK

For my parents, and colleagues at the Institute for Environmental Policy, for their support and patience

And from all

For Jo Gerardu, a tireless champion of INECE and the public good

Making Law Work:
Environmental Compliance
&
Sustainable Development

Volume 2

Edited by
Durwood Zaelke
Donald Kaniaru
&
Eva Kružíková

CAMERON
MAY
INTERNATIONAL LAW & POLICY

"A vital and important book that will become required reading for all who share our concern about the Earth's environment and who know that enforcement and compliance are the bedrock of the rule of law and sustainable development."

Gus Speth,
Dean,
Yale School of Forestry & Environmental Studies

"This book provides important lessons for treaty negotiators, parliamentarians, regulators, prosecutors, judges, and NGOs. An indispensable tool for all who are concerned with using law to protect the Earth's vital ecosystems and to promote sustainable development."

Charles Di Leva,
Chief Counsel, ESSD & Int'l Law,
World Bank

"This book may be the difference between making environmental law work and finding ourselves falling over the precipice…. Read it and join the battle…."

Greg Wetstone,
Director of Advocacy,
Natural Resources Defense Council

"This important work comes just in time to help the world understand what we need to do to improve enforcement and compliance."

José Sarney Filho,
Former Minister of the Environment,
Brazil

TABLE OF CONTENTS

VOLUME 1

3.2 MEA Case Studies

3.3 Case Studies of State Implementation of MEAs

3.4 Guidelines on MEA Compliance

VOLUME 2

Chapter Seven

Information Regulation

Introduction

This chapter introduces a selection of the best literature on the public's right to government information and information held by private firms. Environmental compliance and enforcement have for some time benefited from information disclosure laws that address information *under the control of government agencies*. The public's right to government-held information is a human right,[1] and is now further operationalized through the Aarhus Convention and an increasing number of national laws.[2] Citizens and NGOs have used this right both as an accountability mechanism for government programs and as part of their strategy to pressure private polluters or those otherwise harming the environment.

More recently, new information rights have been established providing citizens and NGOs with access to information *held by private sector firms*. Regulation by information alerts the public to the environmental track records of businesses and industries, particularly those that deal in hazardous chemicals.[3] This type of regulation aims to empower civil

---

[1] The right to information is a human right, as well as an environmental right. *See* DAVID HUNTER, JAMES SALZMAN, & DURWOOD ZAELKE, INTERNATIONAL ENVIRONMENTAL LAW AND POLICY, 1316-1317 (2nd ed. 2002) (referencing in particular, Article 19 of the Universal Declaration of Human Rights, Article 19 of the International Covenant on Civil and Political Rights, Article 10(1) of the European Convention, and Article 13 of the American Convention).

[2] *See* Svitlana Kravchenko, *Strengthening Implementation of MEAs: The Innovative Aarhus Compliance Mechanism*, excerpted in Chapter Three: Multilateral Environmental Agreements in Action.

[3] One of the first such forms of information regulation was the Emergency Planning and Community Right To Know Act (EPCRA), 42 U.S.C. 11001, et. seq., which was also known as the "Bhopal Bill" when it was passed by the U.S. Congress in 1986 to reduce the likelihood that the Union Carbide chemical disaster that killed thousands in Bhopal, India, in 1984 would be repeated in the U.S. Among other things, the EPCRA requires the regulator to publish an inventory (Toxics Release Inventory, or TRI) of certain chemicals released by certain firms. *See Joseph A. Davis, Bye Bye TRI? Reform or Revolution in the Mother of Environmental Databases (2003), available at* http://environmentwriter.org/resources/articles/0904_tri.htm. *See also* Bradley C. Karkkainen, *Information as Environmental Regulation: TRI and Performance Benchmarking, Precursor to a New Paradigm*, 89 GEO. L.J. 257 (2001).

society, enlisting their resources and creativity to press for improved environmental performance.[4] In an age where environmental agencies in both developed and developing countries face limited budgets and constrained resources that hinder their effectiveness, information regulation represents the latest in a series of strategies to enlist external forces to pressure polluters to change their behavior.

Information regulation may be defined as the disclosure of a polluter's environmental performance to the general public, to be used by consumers, shareholders, workers, competitors, NGOs, and the media. The disclosure of a polluter's poor environmental performance can act as a sanction, especially when it empowers third parties to take action against the polluter.[5] This is the cornerstone of "information regulation."[6] The disclosure of environmental performance data functions by harnessing social and market forces to pressure polluters to change their behavior. For example, armed with environmental information about a firm's compliance record, consumers may choose not to buy the firm's products. Moreover, disclosure of such information may adversely impact a firm's business-to-business sales, stock value, and its ability to hire or retain employees. In addition, NGOs can use the disclosed information to pursue polluters in court through tort suits and citizen-enforcement actions, to organize boycotts, and to galvanize support for stricter emissions standards and higher penalties.

Disclosure can take a variety of forms. The government, either through voluntary or mandatory programs, can collect and disseminate information. For instance, the U.S. Environmental Protection Agency's Toxics Release Inventory (TRI) requires the disclosure of specified chemical emissions by private firms under threat of stiff fines.[7] Other

---

[4] *See* Chapter Six: NGO Compliance Strategies.

[5] It can also act as a reward, where affirmative information about a firm's environmental performance can draw positive attention, including from consumers. Environmentally sensitive consumers are the heart of the $226.8 billion U.S. market for goods and services that appeal to consumers who value health, the environment, social justice, personal development, and sustainable living. LOHAS stands for Lifestyles of Health and Sustainability and includes approximately 30 percent of adults, or 63 million consumers, in the U.S. *See* The Lohas Journal, *at* http://www.lohasjournal.com. *See also* STEPHEN O. ANDERSEN & DURWOOD ZAELKE, INDUSTRY GENIUS: INVENTIONS AND PEOPLE PROTECTING THE CLIMATE AND FRAGILE OZONE LAYER (2003) (discussing the U.S. EPA's EnergyStar certification program that identifies energy-efficient household appliances). *See* related discussion on certification systems in Chapter Nine: Compliance Assistance and "Beyond Compliance".

[6] David W. Case, *The Law and Economics of Environmental Information as Regulation*, 31 ELR 10773 (citing Tom Tietenberg, *Disclosure Strategies for Pollution Control*, 11 ENVTL. & RES. ECON. 587 (1998)). *See also* Daniel C. Esty, *Environmental Protection in the Information Age*, 79

continued

mandatory government programs include efforts in Indonesia and China to rate industrial facilities according to their level of environmental performance, with low-rated facilities given one year to improve before their rating is released to the public. Regulators also can encourage the media to report negative environmental news, such as industrial accidents, governmental investigations, and fines.

Environmental management systems (EMS) represent another strategy that utilizes information to help firms manage their environmental performance. The International Organization for Standardization's ISO 14000 program is a leading example. EMS programs do not necessarily result in the public disclosure of environmental performance information, but rather signal that a firm is following specified environmental management practices.[8]

This chapter begins with an article by Peter H. Sand describing initiatives to establish the public's "right to know" through mandatory disclosure of industry-held environmental risk data.[9]

In the next article, Annette Killmer discusses methods to design and implement mandatory disclosure policies to maximize effective civil society participation.[10] Jérôme Foulon, Paul Lanoie, and Benoît Laplante, in an article published by the World Bank, then discuss the impact of public disclosure programs compared to traditional monitoring and enforcement practices.[11]

N.Y.U. L. Rev. 115 (2004); Neil Gunningham, Martin Phillipson & Peter Grabosky, *Harnessing Third Parties as Surrogate Regulators: Achieving Environmental Outcomes by Alternative Means*, 8 Bus. Strategy & Env't 211 (1999) (focusing on the "need to design innovative strategies ... [that are] complementary to that of government regulation").

[7] Firms that fail to disclose required information face fines of up to US$27,500 per day for each substance requiring disclosure. *See* EPCRA Section 313 Questions and Answers, *at* http://www.epa.gov/tri/guide_docs/1998/1998qa.pdf.

[8] Similarly, regulators can encourage the media to report superior performance that goes beyond compliance. *See* discussion of certification systems, audits, and EMS in Chapter Nine: Compliance Assistance & "Beyond Compliance".

[9] Peter H. Sand, *The Right to Know: Environmental Information Disclosure by Government and Industry*, Revised version of a paper presented to the 2nd Transatlantic Dialogue on "The Reality of Precaution: Comparing Approaches to Risk and Regulation" (Warrenton/VA, June 15, 2002) and the Conference on "Human Dimensions of Global Environmental Change: Knowledge for the Sustainability Transition" (Berlin, December 7, 2002).

[10] Annette B. Killmer, *Designing Mandatory Disclosure to Promote Synergies Between Public and Private Enforcement*, INECE 7th International Conference Proceedings (forthcoming 2005).

[11] Jérôme Foulon, Paul Lanoie, and Benoît Laplante, *Incentives for Pollution Control: Regulation or Information?* 44 J. Envtl Econ. & Mgmt, 169 (2002).

In another World Bank article, Shakeb Afsah, Benoit Laplante, and David Wheeler describe Indonesia's information regulation program.[12] The fifth article in this chapter, by Hua Wang, Jinnan Bi, David Wheeler, Jinnan Wang, Dong Cao, Genfa Lu, and Yuan Wang describes a similar program implemented in China that publicly discloses environmental performance of industrial firms.[13] Finally, Susmita Dasgupta and Benoit Laplante discuss how capital markets in Argentina, Chile, Mexico, and the Philippines react to announcements of environmental events, including good news such as superior environmental performance and bad news such as citizen complaints.[14]

---

[12] Shakeb Afsah, Benoit Laplante, & David Wheeler, *Regulation in the Information Age: Indonesian Public Information Program for Environmental Management* (1997), *available at* http://www.worldbank.org/nipr/work_paper/govern/.

[13] Hua Wang, Jinnan Bi, David Wheeler, Jinnan Wang, Dong Cao, Genfa Lu, and Yuan Wang, *Public Ratings of Industry's Environmental Performance: China's Greenwatch Program*, INECE 6th International Conference Proceedings, vol. 2 (2002), *available at* http://www.inece.org.

[14] Susmita Dasgupta and Benoit Laplante, *Pollution and Capital Markets in Developing Countries*, 42 J. ENVTL ECON. & MGMT, 310 (2001).

The Right to Know: Environmental Information Disclosure by Government and Industry

Peter H. Sand

Revised version of a paper presented to the 2nd Transatlantic Dialogue on "The Reality of Precaution: Comparing Approaches to Risk and Regulation" (Warrenton/VA, 15 June 2002) and the Conference on "Human Dimensions of Global Environmental Change: Knowledge for the Sustainability Transition" (Berlin, 7 December 2002).

Global knowledge management is crucially dependent on public access to information – in particular, information on environmental risks. Yet most existing systems of governance favour administrative or corporate secrecy, thereby monopolizing environmental information in the hands of governmental authorities or private stakeholders. This paper describes innovative initiatives to establish civil society's 'right to know', by mandatory disclosure of government-held information (from the 1966 US *Freedom of Information Act* to the 1998 UN/ECE *Aarhus Convention*) and of industry-held environmental risk data (through the worldwide spread of *Pollutant Release and Transfer Registers*, and through court-enforced access to 'privileged' documentation – for example, on tobacco-related health risks). These disclosure strategies have triggered a 'third wave' of environmental regulation, replacing or supplementing traditional command-and-control and market-based instruments. However, the paper also highlights continuing transparency deficits (sometimes resulting in 'manufactured uncertainty') with regard to risk-sensitive information of common concern.

Environmental governance is plagued by uncertainty, with regard both to bio-geophysical processes and to socio-economic costs and benefits (Arrow & Fisher 1974; Iida 1993; Harremoës 2000; Stewart 2002). Some of those uncertainties are exogenous, often incalculable, and we simply have to cope with them as risks and unknowns (Knight 1921, 19; Jaeger *et al.* 2001; Funtowicz & Ravetz 2001; Engel *et al.* 2002).[1] Other information deficits, however, are manifestly endogenous, home-made – "manufactured uncertainty" (Beck 1998, 9) or "smokescreen uncertainty" (Lewis 1998). The sad reality is that we are all too often kept in the dark – through neglect or by design, by public officials or private stakeholders (Stiglitz 1999; Eigen 2003). The purpose of this paper is to take a closer look at instruments which different legal systems have developed to cope with the problem of undisclosed or concealed risk information; *i.e.*, citizen access to publicly-held and privately-held data on environmental risks, the knowledge or ignorance of which may be decisive for precautionary action.

I.   *Public Data Disclosure*

Historically, there have been significant differences between and among national administrative laws with regard to government-held information. While most European countries (including Britain, France, and Germany) have had a notorious tradition of secrecy with regard to a broad range of data kept by public authorities (Rowat 1966, 1979; Schwan 1984; Rose-Ackerman 1995, 114; Vahle 1999) – partly out of a legitimate concern with effective governance (Dahl 1994; Rowan-Robinson *et al.* 1996), – the one major exception was Sweden: Starting with the *Freedom of the Press Act* of 1766, Swedish citizens have had a right of access to public data, unmatched in any other legal system (Andersen 1973; Holstad 1979; Petrén 1987). Other Nordic countries followed much later: Finland's *Publicity of Documents Act* in 1951; Denmark's *Public Access Act* in 1970 (*Offentlighedslov* 1970; Holm 1975). Even so, the Scandinavian approach to government-held information remained unusual among the prevailing pattern of 'arcane administration' in Europe, where access to files by citizens was long viewed as incompatible with the principle of representative – as distinct from 'direct' – democracy (Bullinger 1979, 217).

---

[1] Paradoxically, the 'veil of uncertainty' (Brennan & Buchanan 1985, 30) may even facilitate collective response and decision-making (Helm 1998; Kolstad 2002)

Against that background, the US *Freedom of Information Act* of 1966 (FOIA 1966; Foerstel 1999) – already foreshadowed by the Federal *Administrative Procedure Act* (APA 1946, §3; Cross 1953), and at the state level by California's 1952 'Brown Act' (Singer 1979, 310) – and the avalanche of 'sunshine statutes'[2] following in their wake all over North America and in other common law countries (GSA 1976; Duncan 1999; McDonagh 2000; Smyth 2000; Roberts 2002) radically changed the global map of comparative administrative law, and may actually have changed the universal catalogue of constitutional rights (South Africa 1996, §32/1/b; South Africa 2000, §3; Calland & Tilley 2002; Banisar 2002; Bullinger 1985, 106).

Initially, European countries other than those in Scandinavia were slow to follow suit. Among the first examples in continental Europe was the Dutch *Administrative Transparency Act* of 1978 (Netherlands 1978; Luebbe-Wolff 1980; Rutteman 2001). More than ten years later, after considerable debate in the European Commission and Parliament, Council Directive No. 313 of 1990 on *Freedom of Access to Information on the Environment* mandated the enactment of transparency legislation in all EU member countries (EU 1990; Winter 1990; Krämer 1991; Pallemaerts 1991; von Schwanenflügel 1991; Engel 1993; Fluck 1993; Fluck & Theuer 1994; Prieur 1997).

Even though 'green' politicians and academics in Europe had long hailed FOIA as "the new *Magna Carta* of ecological democracy" (Fischer 1989, 152) and as evidence of a new "structural pluralism" (Giddens 2000, 55; Roberts 2001), reactions at the governmental level were anything but enthusiastic. Several member states missed the prescribed deadline for the new statutory enactments and administrative reforms required, and the Commission had to resort to judicial actions to make Germany comply (ECJ 1999; EU 2000b; Schoch 2002). Implementation of the 1990 Directive – now superseded by EU Parliament/Council Directive 2003/4/EC (Wilsher 2001; Jahnke 2003; EU 2003) – is still far from perfect (Hallo 1996; Kimber & Ekardt 1999; EU 2000a). It seems as though old administrative habits, and especially the entrenched reluctance of civil service departments to conduct their business in the open, are hard to break indeed.

---

[2] The term goes back to the US Supreme Court Justice Louis D. Brandeis, who recommended "publicity … as a remedy for social and industrial diseases. Sunlight is said to be the best of disinfectants" (Brandeis 1932, 92).

Things began to change in the wake of the 1992 Rio Conference – starting with the Convention for the Protection of the Marine Environment in the North-East Atlantic (OSPAR 1992, article 9; Sands 1995, 619), opening public access to government-held information regarding that particular maritime sub-region, which extends beyond the EU. Next was the Council of Europe, with the Convention on Environmental Liability (Lugano 1993, article 15; Ebbeson 1997, 90) providing access to information held not only by governments, but also by "bodies with public responsibilities for the environment and under the control of a public authority". Finally, the process of reform reached the still wider geographical framework of the United Nations Economic Commission for Europe (UN/ECE), which includes not only the Nordic countries but also the United States and Canada, and especially the countries of Central and Eastern Europe. Freedom of access to environmental information – under the catchword of *glasnost* – had long been one of the political demands of civil-society opposition groups in the former socialist countries, preceding and indeed precipitating the fall of the Berlin Wall (Stec 1998). Not surprisingly therefore, it was an alliance of Northern and Eastern European NGOs which played a key role in the preparation and negotiation of the 1995 UN/ECE *Sofia Guidelines* on access to information and public participation in environmental decision-making (Wates 1996). They led to the adoption of the *Aarhus Convention* on 25 June 1998 (UN/ECE 1998; Scheyli 2000; Petkova & Veit 2000; Zschiesche 2001; Rose-Ackerman & Halpaap 2002; Bruch & Czebiniak 2002), one of whose 'three pillars' now is public access to environmental information – including so-called 'passive access' (the right to seek information from public authorities, under article 4); and the duty of governments to collect, disclose and disseminate such information regardless of specific requests ('active access', under article 5; Stec *et al.* 2000, 6).

From a comparative perspective, it is probably fair to say that Europe has begun to catch up with North America, but still has a lot to learn in this regard (Coliver *et al.* 1999; Öberg 2000; Wilcox 2001). It would certainly be worthwhile to study both the trans-cultural and psychological implications of that learning process, and its impact on civic and administrative attitudes towards environmental risks (Wiener & Rogers 2002) and on the perceived balance of openness versus security (Geiger 2000; Gassner & Pisani 2001). Even though some information-based policies – such as environmental impact assessments, and 'prior informed consent' procedures – are now globally accepted (Sand 1990, 25; Kern *et al.* 1999; Farber & Morrison 2000; Wiener 2001), 'context-related' instruments for information rights and duties are still far from mainstream in EU environmental governance (Burkert 1998; Holzinger *et al.* 2002). One of the most difficult sub-tasks was to persuade the European Union itself (*i.e.*, the bureaucracy in Brussels) that it, too, had a problem with information disclosure: It took years of litigation (ECFI 1997, 1998, 1999; ECJ 2001) to establish public access to EU Parliament, Council and Commission documents (Kunzlik 1997; O'Neill 1998; Monediaire 1999; Travers 2000; Wägenbaur 2001; Broberg 2002), now guaranteed by the 'Transparency Regulation' of 30 May 2001 (EU 2001).[3] If that is any consolation – some other inter-governmental bureaucracies like the World Bank had to go through a similar learning curve as regards information disclosure to the public (Shihata 1994, 28; Udall 1998, 404).[4]

II.   Private Data Disclosure

The Atlantic divide looms larger still when it comes to questions of access to privately-held environmental data, especially information on environmental and health-related risks. The turning point for North American regulatory history was the Bhopal accident in December 1984, which occurred at the local affiliate of a US chemical company in India and killed more than 2,400 people (Desai 1993; Lapierre & Moro 2001). In the face of the magnitude of that tragedy – and also because it was followed in 1985 by another, albeit less catastrophic, accident in West Virginia (in a plant owned by the same corporation; Abrams & Ward 1990, 143) which illustrated the risk of similar disasters at home – legislative reaction in the United States was swift, and truly innovative.

The *Toxics Release Inventory (TRI)* established in 1986 by the federal *Emergency Planning and Community Right-to-Know Act* (EPCRA 1986; Weeks 1998; Greenwood & Sachdev 1999) requires mandatory reporting of toxic industrial emissions. The information is then made publicly available (on-line) via a computerized database operated by the U.S. Environmental Protection Agency (EPA) <http://www.epa.gov/tri>, and

---

[3] Given that the EU is a signatory to the 1998 Aarhus Convention, its own institutions will, upon ratification, become 'public authorities' subject to the convention's disclosure requirements (Davies 2001; Rodenhoff 2002, 350). See also art. 42 (access to documents), EU Charter of Fundamental Rights (Nice 2000; Goldsmith 2001)

[4] See World Bank Procedures 17.50 on *Disclosure of Operational Information* (September 1993, revised in June 2002 <http://www1.worldbank.org/operations/disclosure/policy.html>). On similar initiatives in the African, Asian and Inter-American Development Banks, the European Bank for Reconstruction and Development, the International Finance Corporation and the Multilateral Investment Guarantee Agency, see *Yearbook of International Environmental Law* **5**, 296 (1994); **7**, 262 (1996); **9**, 340 (1998); Handl 2001, 47; Saul 2002; and the website of the NGO Bank Information Center, <http://www.bicusa.org>

also via nation-wide non-governmental networks and special NGO websites, such as the "Chemical Scorecard" <http://www.scorecard.org> kept by *Environmental Defense* and the "Right-to-Know Network" <http://www.rtknet.org> operated by *OMB Watch* (Bass & MacLean 1993). As a result, anybody can download standardized, site-specific, up-to-date and user-friendly data on specified toxic emissions from all facilities covered by *TRI*. At the state level, California's 1986 *Safe Drinking Water and Toxic Enforcement Act* (known as '*Proposition 65*', <http://www.oehha.ca.gov/prop65.html>) imposed additional warning and disclosure requirements for toxic chemicals – as interpreted and applied by the courts (Lungren case 1996; Rechtschaffen 1996, 1999; Freund 1997) – unless emitters can show that the level of exposure is low enough to pose 'no significant risk' (§25249.10.c).

Although there had been earlier toxic-emission disclosure laws at the state and local level since the 1970s – mainly in response to demands by labour leaders to alert employees to workplace risks (McGarity & Shapiro 1980; Chess 1984; Hadden 1989) – the near-instant success of *TRI* and *Proposition 65* seems to have taken everyone by surprise (Wolf 1996; Konar & Cohen 1997; Stephan 2002). Both statutes began taking effect in 1988. The most recent data available – for the 10-year period from 1988 to 1997 – show that atmospheric emissions of some 260 known carcinogens and reproductive toxins from *TRI*-reporting facilities have been reduced by approximately 85% in the state of California, and by some 42% in the rest of the country (*i.e.*, for all chemicals listed in California as known to cause either cancer or reproductive toxicity *and* reported as air emissions under *TRI*; Roe 2002, 10233/figure 1).

Attempts at explaining this "accidental success story" (Fung & O'Rourke 2000, 116) variously emphasize the innovative use made of (a) electronic communications via the Internet, by *TRI* (Jobe 1999); (b) reversal of the burden of proof for exemptions, by *Proposition 65* (Barsa 1997); (c) enforcement by citizen suits, under both schemes (Grant 1997; Green 1999; Graf 2001, 669); (d) standardized data, facilitating comparison and 'performance benchmarking' (Karkkainen 2001); and (e) the 'reputational' effects of such competitive ranking on a firm's behaviour (Graham 2001, 8; Graham & Miller 2001). While it will, of course, be important to learn the right lessons from all of this, the outcome is unlikely to be attributable to a set of isolated causes, let alone mono-causal. There certainly are a number of plausible external driving forces, and 'success' more often than not rests on the right combination of information and regulation. Be that as it may, a number of observers view the advent of 'informational regulation' (Magat & Viscusi 1992; Kleindorfer & Orts 1998; Sage 1999; Sunstein 1999; Stewart 2001; Case 2001), 'smart regulation' (Gunningham *et al.* 1998, 63), or 'regulation by revelation' (Florini 1998), as a viable alternative to the stalemate of traditional environmental law-making and the kind of regulatory fatigue it seems to have spread (Lyndon 1989; Pedersen 2001; Cohen 2001). Scientists advocate "mutual transparency as a useful means to ensure accountability" (Brin 1998, 149); international lawyers and political scientists refer to 'sunshine methods' as effective new strategies to induce compliance with environmental treaties (Weiss & Jacobson 2000, 549); and economists hail disclosure strategies as the 'third wave' in pollution control (Tietenberg 1998), after command-and-control (emission standards and fines) and market-based approaches (emission charges, tradable permits).

'Right-to-know' laws have since been enacted in at least 25 U.S. states and in Canada (Zimmermann *et al.* 1995; Duncan 1998, 188; CEC 2001; Harrison & Antweiler 2003). Not surprisingly, the North American pilot experience had its ripple effects elsewhere, the new buzz-word being *Pollutant Release and Transfer Registers (PRTR)*: in Australia and Japan, prompted in part by guidelines developed in the Organisation for Economic Cooperation and Development (OECD 1996, 1998, <http://www.oecd.org/ehs/ehsmono/#PRTRS>) in response to a recommendation of the 1992 Rio Conference on Environment and Development (*Agenda 21*, §19.61.c); in Brazil, Indonesia, and a number of other developing countries, through technical assistance projects organized by the World Bank (Wheeler 1997; Afsah *et al.* 2000; World Bank 2000). Further initiatives for worldwide dissemination of the concept have been launched by the UN Environment Programme (UNEP, <http://www.chem.unep.ch/prtr>); the UN Institute for Training and Research (UNITAR 2000); the *Inter-Organization Programme for the Sound Management of Chemicals* (IOMC 2001); and private-sector networks such as the *International Right-to-Know Campaign*, <http://www.irtk.org> (Casey-Lefkowitz 2001), and the *Global Reporting Initiative*, <http://www.globalreporting.org> (GRI 2002).

The European Union decided, in July 2000, to establish a mandatory *European Pollutant Emission Register* (EPER 2000), to be operated by the European Environment Agency (EEA) 'on top' of national inventories currently under preparation in several member countries, with the first national data to be delivered to the EEA by 2003. The first operational system in Europe was introduced in 1974 by the Netherlands Ministry of Housing, Spatial Planning and the Environment (*VROM*), on a voluntary basis. A mandatory system followed in Norway, with data accessible to the public though not actively disseminated. Sweden has started mandatory reporting (after voluntary pilot studies since 1994) under a new *PRTR* system operated by the Environmental Protection Agency in cooperation with the Chemical Inspectorate. The United Kingdom currently has a multi-register system operating in England and Wales only. Other countries planning to have integrated national systems in operation by 2003 include Austria, Belgium, the Czech Republic, Denmark, Finland, Germany, Hungary, and Ireland (UN/ECE 2000, Annex I).

Perhaps the most promising regional activity currently underway in Europe is the new *Protocol on Pollutant Release and Transfer Registers,* to be signed in the framework of the *Aarhus Convention* at the forthcoming Ministerial Conference on 'Environment for Europe' in Kiev, 21-23 May 2003 (UN/ECE 2002, decision I/3). Once adopted and ratified in the legal context of the convention, public access to emission data along *TRI* lines may become an actionable right – hence potentially subject to supranational judicial review by the European Court of Human Rights in Strasbourg (Guerra case 1998; McGinley case 1998; Weber 1990; Gavouneli 2000; Fievet 2001, 173) – well beyond the EU, and especially in the countries of Central and Eastern Europe. As mentioned before, people in those countries are acutely sensitive to information on environmental risks, which was denied to them in the past, and which they do not wish to see monopolized again, whether by public or by private knowledge-holders and "knowledge brokers" (Litfin 1994, 4).

The PRTR Task Force/Working Group has held eight meetings to date, and a draft text has been finalized for adoption at the Kiev Conference (UN/ECE 2003).[5] The main purpose of the Protocol is to require all member countries to establish "publicly accessible national pollutant release and transfer registers" for pollutants and source categories to be listed in annexes and expected to be expanded over time, possibly also including 'diffuse sources' such as agriculture and traffic (draft article 2/ 11). A net effect therefore will be to bring important environmental data held by the private sector into the public domain.

---

[5] Note that the protocol will be open to all UN member states (draft article 26) regardless of their membership in the UN/ECE or the Aarhus Convention. At the November 2002 session, however, the US delegation declared that it would not participate in a negotiating capacity but would "continue to follow this and other international processes dealing with the issue of PRTRs" (UN/ECE Doc. MP.PP/AC.1/2002/2, paragraph 19)

III.   Outlook

Let us remember, however, that this is only the tip of the iceberg. There is a huge mass of privately-held environmental and health risk information that is woefully 'asymmetric' – to use a somewhat euphemistic term coined by Kenneth Arrow (Arrow 1963; Cranor 1999) – yet is not covered by the *Aarhus Convention* at all, and where Europe still lags years behind North America in terms of public access rules. A striking illustration is disclosure of the tobacco industry's 'privileged' documents under the 1998 Minnesota settlement (Humphrey case 1998; Ciresi *et al.* 1999; Little 2001): It is only now, after court-enforced electronic access to those corporate files, that a research team from the University of California was able to document the multinationals' well-planned and highly successful sabotage of EU tobacco advertising legislation (Bitton *et al.* 2002; Neuman *et al.* 2002), culminating in the annulment of a 1998 Council Directive (EU 1998; Simma *et al.* 1999) by the European Court of Justice in October 2000 (ECJ 2000; Schroeder 2001; Tridimas & Tridimas 2002).[6] The documentation shows, in gruesome detail and transparency, how 'captured' governments and top politicians (with Germany up-front)[7] were used and – to put it bluntly – corrupted in a game that will have massive and measurable negative effects on environmental health for years to come.[8]

More transparency might also help in some of the academic analysis concerned. For example, a recent collection of legal opinions on the EU

---

[6] The EU Commission has since proposed a new *Directive on the approximation of the laws, regulations and administrative provisions of the Member States relating to the advertising and sponsorship of tobacco products* (30 May 2001). The EU Council, at its meeting on 2 December 2002, agreed (against German opposition) to adopt the draft directive as amended by the European Parliament on 20 November 2002. The German Government, under pressure from economic lobbyists and the conservative opposition party, now plans to take the new directive to the European Court in Luxembourg once again (Lechner 2002; Didzoleit 2002)

[7] Simpson 2002. On 17 October 2002, Germany earned the infamous 'Marlboro Man Award' from the NGO *Network for Accountability of Tobacco Transnationals* <http://www.infact.org/101702mm.html>, for the country's stalwart diplomatic efforts – in coalition with the USA and Japan – to block a global ban on tobacco advertising, promotion and sponsorship under draft article 13 of the World Health Organization's *Framework Convention on Tobacco Control*, finalized in Geneva on 1 March 2003 for adoption by the 56th World Health Assembly in May 2003 (FCTC 2003). Germany has announced her refusal to accept the treaty, while the United States now insists on a "general reservation clause" that would allow countries to opt out of any provision they find objectionable (Tobacco Lite 2003)

[8] Stochastic mortality estimates in the EU Commission's 'Explanatory Memorandum' to its proposed new Directive of 30 May 2001, COM (2001) 283/final, p. 9 (§7.3.2). For legislative and economic background see Kevekordes 1994; Donner 1999; Chaloupka & Warner 2000

ban on tobacco advertising, by a respectable German publisher (Schneider & Stein 1999), demonstrated – according to the editors' preface – "striking conformity and unanimity" among the experts, to the effect that the ban had indeed been *ultra vires*. However, readers had to proceed as far as page 55 to discover (Kleine 2000) that the learned book had been solicited and sponsored by the *Confederation of European Community Cigarette Manufacturers (CECCM)*. Given this abundance of 'manufactured uncertainty' (and a good deal of pseudo-certainty, too), there clearly is a need for new disclosure rules – to be applied not only to government and industry, but also to scientific writers and law professors. Pending that, all I can recommend is a high degree of precaution when approaching German legal publications on this topic.

Far more serious, however, are recent developments triggered by the tragic events of September 11, 2001. In the face of terrorist bombing threats against the most vulnerable targets – for example, major chemical factories, – a large part of industrial risk data in the United States is now in the process of being re-classified as 'critical infrastructure information' (Cha 2002; Davis 2002; Cohen 2002). Not surprisingly, economic pressure groups which had always resisted the disclosure of environmental risks to the public – such as the *American Chemistry Council (ACC*, formerly the *Chemical Manufacturers Association, CMA)*, the *Coalition for Effective Environmental Information (CEEI)*, and the *Center for Regulatory Effectiveness (CRE)* – are lending enthusiastic support to the Bush Administration's efforts at restricting access to such information (Greenwood 1999). They scored a first tactical victory with the 'data quality rider' attached to the U.S. Treasury Department's annual appropriation bill in December 2001 (DQA 2001; Adler 2001; Logomasini 2002; Conrad 2002), which directed the Office of Management and Budget (OMB) to develop new *"Guidelines for Ensuring and Maximizing the Quality, Objectivity, Utility, and Integrity of Information Disseminated by Federal Agencies"* (OMB 2002; EPA 2002). Substantive and procedural restrictions on environmental information disclosure have since been imposed by the *Homeland Security Act* of 25 November 2002 (HSA 2002; Gidiere & Forrester 2002; Blanton 2002; O'Reilly 2002; Echeverria & Kaplan 2002; Steinzor 2002; McDermott 2002). Further setbacks for public access to chemical risk information are to be expected from section 202 of the *Domestic Security Enhancement Act* now in preparation (DSEA 2003, also known as "Patriot Act II").

Right up to the 2002 Johannesburg *World Summit on Sustainable Development*, the United States – no matter how much fault critics may have found with its environmental record in other areas – had remained the undisputed champion of citizen access to environmental data, public or private. Indeed, in his message to the summit, Secretary of State Colin Powell highlighted the 'access initiative' by 26 civil society organizations in nine countries to assess how well governments are providing access to risk information (Powell 2002, 10; Petkova *et al.* 2002; WRI 2002). Starting from Principle 10 of the 1992 *Rio Declaration*, the 'Plan of Implementation' adopted by the summit re-affirmed the need "to ensure access, at the national level, to environmental information", and in particular, "to encourage development of coherent and integrated information on chemicals, such as through national pollutant release and transfer registers" (Johannesburg Report 2002; Gray 2003).[9] However, at the Nairobi session of the UNEP Governing Council in February 2003, a follow-up proposal for global guidelines on the application of Rio Principle 10 – including more specific rules on information access – ran into opposition from the United States in coalition with the Group of 77/ China, and was deferred to the next (2005) session.[10]

Are we about to come full circle, then? The very principle of transparency, alas, will risk a severe backlash as the public's hard-won 'right to know' suddenly confronts the ugly claw of a zombie, resurrected from the dark ages of European administrative law: Government's 'hiding hand'.

References

Abrams, Robert, and Douglas H. Ward. 1990. Prospects for Safer Communities: Emergency Response, Community Right-to-Know, and Prevention of Chemical Accidents. *Harvard Environmental Law Review* 14,

Adler, John. 2001. How EPA Helps Terrorists. *National Review* (27 September 2001)

---

[9] Sections 23(f) and 128. See also the Johannesburg Declaration's call on private sector corporations "to enforce corporate accountability, which should take place within a transparent and stable regulatory environment"

[10] (Report p. 4, article 29); and the call for "public access to relevant information" in the work programme to implement the 'Johannesburg Principles on the Role of Law and Sustainable Development', adopted by the Global Judges Symposium on 20 August 2002; *Environmental Policy and Law* 32, 236-238 (Rehbinder 2003). "Enhancing the Application of Principle 10 of the Rio Declaration on Environment and Development", UN Doc. UNEP/ GC.22/3/Add.2/B (2002), and decision UNEP/GC.22/L.3/Add.1 (2003) directing the Executive Director to submit a report for review in 2005; *Earth Negotiations Bulletin* 16:30, 9 (10 February 2003); see also the U.S. State Department's current position on PRTRs, note 5 above.

Afsah, Shakeb, Allen Blackman, and Damayanti Ratunanda. 2000. *How Do Public Disclosure Pollution Control Programs Work? Evidence from Indonesia*. Washington/DC: Resources for the Fut ure (Discussion Paper 00-44)

Agenda 21 = Action Programme adopted by the United Nations Conference on Environment and Development (Rio de Janeiro, 3-14 June 1992). New York: UN Doc. A/CONF.151/26/Rev.1 (1993) 1, 9

Andersen, Stanley V. 1973. Public Access to Government Files in Sweden. *American Journal of Comparative Law* 21, 419-473

APA 1946 = Administrative Procedure Act. *U.S. Code* 5, §501 (1946, as amended)

Arrow, Kenneth. 1963. Uncertainty and the Welfare Economics of Medical Care. *American Economic Review* 53, 941-973

Arrow, Kenneth, and Anthony C. Fisher. 1974. Environmental Preservation, Uncertainty, and Irreversibility. *Quarterly Journal of Economics* 88, 312-319

Banisar, David, editor. 2002. *Freedom of Information and Access to Government Records Around the World*. London: Privacy International

Barsa, Michael. 1997. California's Proposition 65 and the Limits of Information Economics. *Stanford Law Review* 49, 1223-1247

Bass, Gary D., and Alair MacLean. 1993. Enhancing the Public's Right-to-Know About Environmental Issues. *Villanova Environmental Law Journal* 4, 287-310

Beck, Ulrich. 1998. Politics of Risk Society. In *The Politics of Risk Society*, edited by Jane Franklin. Cambridge: Polity Press, 9-22

Bennett, Robert, and John Kyl. 2001. *Critical Infrastructure Information Security Act*. U.S. Senate Bill 107-1456

Bitton, Asaf, Mark David Neuman, and Stanton A. Glantz. 2002. *Tobacco Industry Attempts to Subvert European Union Tobacco Advertising Legislation*. San Francisco: University of California Center for Tobacco Control Research and Education

Blanton, Thomas. 2002. The World's Right to Know. *Foreign Policy* (July/August 2002), 50-58

Brandeis, Louis D. 1932. Other People's Money. 2nd ed. New York: Stockes

Brennan, Geoffrey, and James M. Buchanan. 1985. *The Reason of Rules: Constitutional Political Economy.* Cambridge: Cambridge University Press

Brin, David. 1998. *The Transparent Society: Will Technology Force Us to Choose Between Privacy and Freedom ?* Reading/MA: Addison-Wesley

Broberg, Morten. 2002. Access to Documents: A General Principle of Community Law? *European Law Review* 27, 194-205

Bruch, Carl, and Roman Czebiniak. 2002, Globalizing Environmental Governance: Making the Leap from Regional Initiatives on Transparency, Participation, and Accountability in Environmental Matters. *Environmental Law Reporter* 32, 10428-10453

Bullinger, Martin 1979. Western Germany. In Rowat 1979, 217-236

Bullinger, Martin 1985. Freedom of Expression and Information: An Essential Element of Democracy. *German Yearbook of International Law* 28, 88-143

Burkert, Herbert 1998. Informationszugang als Element einer europäischen Informationsrechtsordnung? Gegenwärtige und zukünftige Entwicklungen. In *Globalisierung und informationelle Rechtskultur in Europa,* edited by Siegfried Lamnek and Marie T. Tinnefeld. Baden-Baden: Nomos, 113-135

Calland, Richard, and Alison Tilley, editors. 2002. *The Right to Know, the Right to Live: Access to Information and Socio-Economic Justice.* Cape Town: Open Democracy Advice Center

Case, David W. 2001. The Law and Economics of Environmental Information as Regulation. *Environmental Law Reporter* 31, 10773-10789

Casey-Lefkowitz, Susan. 2001, *International Right-to-Know: Strategies to Increase Corporate Accountability in the Midst of Globalization.* Washington/DC: Natural Resources Defense Council

CEC 2001 = North American Commission for Environmental Cooperation. *Taking Stock: North American Pollutant Releases and Transfers 1998*. Montréal/Québec: CEC

Cha, Ariana E. 2002. Risks Prompt U.S. to Limit Access to Data. *Washington Post* (24 February 2002), A-1

Chaloupka, Frank J., and Kenneth E. Warner. 2000. The Economics of Smoking. In *The Handbook of Health Economics*, edited by Joseph P. Newhouse and Anthony J. Culyer. Amsterdam: North Holland, 1541-1647

Chess, Caron. 1984. *Winning the Right to Know: A Handbook for Toxics Activists*. Philadelphia: Delaware Valley Toxics Coalition

Ciresi, Michael V., Roberta B. Walburn, and Tara D. Sutton. 1999. Decades of Deceit: Document Discovery in the Minnesota Tobacco Litigation. *William Mitchell Law Review* 25, 477-566

Cohen, Mark A. 2001. Information as a Policy Instrument in Protecting the Environment: What Have We Learned? *Environmental Law Reporter* 31, 10425-10431

Cohen, Mark A. 2002. Transparency after 9/11: Balancing the "Right-to-Know" with the Need for Security. *Corporate Environmental Strategy* 9, 368-374

Coliver, Sandra, Paul Hoffman, Joan Fitzpatrick, and Stephen Bowen, editors. 1999. *Secrecy and Liberty: National Security, Freedom of Expression and Access to Information*. The Hague: Nijhoff

Conrad, James W. Jr. (ACC). 2002. The Information Quality Act : Antiregulatory Costs of Mythic Proportions? *Kansas Journal of Law and Public Policy* 12, 521-557

Cranor, Carl. 1999. Asymmetric Information, the Precautionary Principle, and Burdens of Proof. In *Protecting Public Health and the Environment: Implementing the Precautionary Principle*, edited by Carolyn Raffensperger and Joel Tickner. Washington/DC: Island Press, 74-99

Cross, Harold L. 1953. *The People's Right to Know: Legal Access to Public Records and Proceedings*. New York: Columbia University Press

Dahl, Robert A. 1994. A Democratic Dilemma: System Effectiveness versus Citizen Participation. *Political Science Quarterly* 109, 23-34

Davies, Peter. 2001. Public Participation, the Aarhus Convention and the European Community. In *Human Rights in Natural Resource Development*, edited by Donald M. Zillmann, Alastair Lucas and George Pring. Oxford: Oxford University Press, 155-185

Davis, Ann. 2002, New Alarms Heat Up Debate on Publicizing Chemical Risks. *Wall Street Journal* (30 May 2002)

Desai, Bharat H. 1993. The Bhopal Gas Leak Disaster Litigation: An Overview. *Asian Yearbook of International Law* 3, 163-179

Didzoleit, Winfried. 2002. Tabakwerbung: Nagel im Sarg. *Spiegel* (9 December 2002), 40

Donner, Andreas. 1999. *Tabakwerbung und Europa*. Berlin: Berliner Wissenschafts-Verlag

DQA 2001 = Data Quality (Information Quality) Act. Consolidated Appropriations Act: Fiscal Year 2001 of 2000. U.S. Public Law 106-554

DSEA 2003 = Domestic Security Enhancement Act of 2003. Draft by U.S. Department of Justice (9 January 2003). <http://www.publicintegrity.org/dtaweb/report.asp?ReportID=502&l1=10&L2=10&L3=0&l4=0&L5=0>

Duncan, Linda F., editor. 1999. Public Access to Government -Held Environmental Information: Report on North American Law, Policy and Practice. In *North American Environmental Law and Policy*, Cowansville/Québec: Commission for Environmental Cooperation, 57-197

Ebbeson, Jonas 1997. The Notion of Public Participation in International Environmental Law. *Yearbook of International Environmental Law* 8, 51-97

Echeverria, John D., and Julie B. Kaplan. 2002. Poisonous Procedural "Reform": In Defence of Environmental Right to Know. *Kansas Journal of Law and Public Policy* 12, 579-649

ECFI 1997 = Judgment by the European Court of First Instance of 5 March 1997 (T-105/95, WWF UK vs. Commission, *European Court Reports* [1997] II, 313

ECFI 1998 = Judgment by the European Court of First Instance of 6 February 1998 (T-124/96, Interporc II vs. Commission, *European Court Reports* [1998] II, 231

ECFI 1999 = Judgment by the European Court of First Instance of 14 October 1999 (T-309/97, Bavarian Lager Co.Ltd. vs. Commission, *European Court Reports* [1999] II, 3217

ECJ 1999 = Judgment by the European Court of Justice of 9 September 1999 (C-217/97, Commission vs. Germany, *European Court Reports* [1999] I, 5087), declaring the 1994 German Environmental Information Act (*Umweltinformationsgesetz / UIG, BGBl* I, 1490) inadequate for compliance with EU Directive 90/313/EEC

ECJ 2000 = Judgment by the European Court of Justice of 5 October 2000 (C-376/98, Germany vs. European Parliament and Council: Tobacco Advertising), *European Court Reports* [2000] I, 8419; and Order of the Court of 3 April 2000 regarding removal of documents, *European Court Reports* [2000] I, 2247

ECJ 2001 = Judgment by the European Court of Justice of 6 December 2001 (C-353/99 P, Council vs. Heidi Hautala *et al.*), *Official Journal of the European Communities* [2002] C 84, 8

Eigen, Peter, editor. 2003. *Access to Information: Global Corruption Report 2003*. Berlin: Transparency International

Engel, Rüdiger 1993. *Akteneinsicht und Recht auf Informationen über umweltbezogene Daten: die Informationsrichtlinie der EG im Vergleich zur bundesdeutschen Rechtslage*. Pfaffenweiler: Centaurus

Engel, Christoph, Jost Halfmann, and Martin Schulte, editors. 2002. *Wissen, Nichtwissen, unsicheres Wissen*. Baden-Baden: Nomos

EPA 2002 = U.S. Environmental Protection Agency. Draft Guidelines for Ensuring and Maximizing the Quality, Objectivity, Utility, and Integrity of Information Disseminated by the Environmental Protection Agency. <http://www.epa.gov/OEI/qualityguidelines>

EPCRA 1986 = Emergency Planning and Community Right-to-Know Act. *United States Code* 42, §11001, enacted as Title III of the Superfund Amendments and Re-authorization Act, U.S. Public Law 99-499, as amended and supplemented (e.g., by the Pollution Prevention Act of 1990)

EPER 2000 = Implementation of a European Pollutant Emission Register (EPER): Decision by the European Commission (2000/479/EC, 17 July 2000). *Official Journal of the European Communities* [2000] L 192, 36

EU 1990 = Directive on Freedom of Access to Information on the Environment: Council of the European Communities (90/313/EEC, 7 June 1990). *Official Journal of the European Communities* [1990] L 158, 56

EU 1998 = Directive on the Approximation of the Laws, Regulations and Administrative Provisions of the Member States relating to the Advertising and Sponsorship of Tobacco Products: Council of the European Communities (98/43/EC, 6 July 1998). *Official Journal of the European Communities* [1998] L 213, 9

EU 2000a = Report by the European Commission on the Experience Gained in the Application of Council Directive 90/313/EEC. EU Doc. COM (2000) 400/final (26 June 2000)

EU 2000b = Action for financial penalties, brought by the European Commission in the European Court of Justice on 8 November 2000 (C-408/00, Commission vs. Germany , *Official Journal of the European Communities* [2001] C 28, 13) for non-compliance with several EU Directives; after new legislation was enacted by Germany in 2001 (*UIG, BGBl* I, 2218), the case was removed from the Court's register on 22 February 2002

EU 2001 = Regulation (EC) 1049/2001. *Official Journal of the European Communities* [2001] L 145, 43 (effective 31 December 2001); prior to the regulation, the matter had been covered by a "code of conduct" (implemented by Council Decision 93/731 and Commission Decision 94/90)

EU 2003 = Directive on Public Access to Environmental Information, and Repealing Council Directive 90/313/EEC: European Parliament and Council of the European Communities (2003/4/EC, 28 January 2003). *Official Journal of the European Communities* [2003] L 41, 26; the earlier directive will be repealed as from 14 February 2005 (article 11)

FCTC 2003 = World Health Organization. *Draft WHO Framework Convention on Tobacco Control.* Geneva: WHO Doc. A/FCTC/INB6/5 (3 March 2003)

Farber, Daniel A., and Fred L. Morrison. 2000. Access to Environmental Information. In *International, Regional and National Environmental Law,* edited by Fred L. Morrison and Rüdiger Wolfrum. The Hague: Kluwer Law International, 845-860 Fievet, Gilles. 2001, Réflexions sur le concept de développement durable : Prétention économique, principes stratégiques et protection des droits fondamentaux, *Revue Belge de Droit International* 34, 128-184

Fischer, Joschka. 1989. *Der Umbau der Industriegesellschaft: Plädoyer wider die herrschende Umweltlüge,* Frankfurt: Eichborn; English translation in *Ecological Enlightenment: Essays on the Politics of Risk Society,* edited by Ulrich Beck. 1995. Atlantic Highlands/NJ: Humanity Press

Florini, Ann. 1998. The End of Secrecy. *Foreign Policy* 111, 50-63

Fluck, Jürgen, editor. 1993. *Freier Zugang zu Umweltinformationen,* Heidelberg: Müller

Fluck, Jürgen, and Andreas Theuer, editors. 1994-. *Informationsfreiheitsrecht mit Umweltinformations-und Verbraucherinformationsrecht.* Heidelberg: Müller (loose-leaf collection)

Foerstel, Herbert N. 1999. *Freedom of Information and the Right to Know: The Origins and Applications of the Freedom of Information Act.* Westport/ CT: Greenwood Press

FOIA 1966 = Freedom of Information Act of 4 July 1966. *U.S. Code* 5, §552 (1966, as amended/supplemented; e.g., by the Electronic Freedom of Information Act of 1996)

Freund, Michael. 1997. Proposition 65 Enforcement: Reducing Lead Emissions in California. *Tulane Environmental Law Journal* 10, 333-370

Fung, Archon, and Dara O'Rourke. 2000. Reinventing Environmental Regulation from the Grassroots Up: Explaining and Expanding the Success of the Toxics Release Inventory. *Environmental Management* 25, 115127

Funtowicz, Silvio O., and Jerry R. Ravetz. 2001. Global Risk, Uncertainty, and Ignorance, In *Global Environmental Risk*, edited by Jeanne X. and Roger E. Kasperson. Tokyo: United Nations University Press, 173194

Gassner, Ulrich, and Christian Pisani. 2001. Umweltinformationsanspruch und Geheimnisschutz: Zukunftsperspektiven, *Natur und Recht* 23, 506-512

Gavouneli, Maria. 2000. Access to Environmental Information: Delimitation of a Right. *Tulane Environmental Law Journal* 13, 303-327

Geiger, Gebhard, editor. 2000. *Sicherheit der Informationsgesellschaft: Gefährdung und Schutz informationsabhängiger Infrastrukturen*, Baden-Baden: Nomos

Giddens, Anthony. 2000. *The Third Way and Its Critics* . Cambridge: Polity Press

Gidiere, Stephen, and Jason Forrester. 2002. Balancing Homeland Security and Freedom of Information. *Natural Resources and Environment* 16, 139-145

Goldsmith, Lord. 2001. A Charter of Rights, Freedoms and Principles. *Common Market Law Review* 38, 12011216

Graf, Michael W. 2001. Regulating Pesticide Pollution in California Under the 1986 Safe Drinking Water and Toxic Exposure Act (Proposition 65). *Ecology Law Quarterly* 28, 663-754

Graham, Mary. 2001, *Information as Risk Regulation: Lessons From Experience*, Cambridge/MA: Harvard University, Innovations in American Government Program (OPS-10-01)

Graham, Mary, and Catherine Miller. 2001. Disclosure of Toxic Releases in the United States. *Environment* 43:8, 8-20

Grant, Don S. II. 1997. Allowing Citizen Participation in Environmental Regulation: An Empirical Analysis of the Effect of Right-to-Sue and Right-to-Know Provisions on Industry's Toxic Emissions. *Social Science Quarterly* 78, 859-873

Gray, Kevin. 2003. World Summit on Sustainable Development: Accomplishments and New Directions ? *International and Comparative Law Quarterly* 52, 256-268

Green, Krista. 1999. An Analysis of the Supreme Court's Resolution of the Emergency Planning and Community Right-to-Know Act Citizen Suit Debate. *Boston College Environmental Affairs Law Review* 26, 387-434

Greenwood, Mark A. 1999. *White Paper from Industry Coalition to EPA on Concerns Over Information Program.* Washington/DC: Coalition for Effective Environmental Information; reprinted in Bureau of National Affairs, *Daily Environment Reporter* (4 May 1999), E-1

Greenwood, Mark A., and Amit K. Sachdev. 1999. *A Regulatory History of the Emergency Planning and Community Right to Know Act of 1986: Toxics Release Inventory.* Washington/DC: Chemical Manufacturers Association

GRI 2002 = Global Reporting Initiative. *Sustainability Reporting Guidelines.* Boston: GRI

GSA 1976 = Government in the Sunshine Act. U.S. Public Law 94-409 (1976), *U.S. Code* 5, §552b (1977)

Guerra case 1998 = Judgment by the European Court of Human Rights of 29 February 1998 (App. No. 14967/89, Anna Maria Guerra *et al.* vs. Italy). *European Human Rights Reports* 26, 357

Gunningham, Neil, Peter Grabosky, and Darren Sinclair. 1998. *Smart Regulation: Designing Environmental Policy.* Oxford: Clarendon

Hadden, Susan G. 1989. *A Citizen's Right-to-Know: Risk Communication and Public Policy.* Boulder: Westview

Hallo, Ralph E., editor. 1996. *Access to Environmental Information in Europe: The Implementation and Implications of Directive 90/313/EEC.* London: Kluwer Law International

Hallo, Ralph E. 2001. *Proposal for a New Directive on Public Access to Environmental Information: An Analysis.* Brussels: European Environmental Bureau (EEB Doc. 2001/004)

Handl, Günther. 2001. *Multilateral Development Banking: Environmental Principles and Concepts Reflecting General International Law and Public Policy.* London: Kluwer Law International & Asian Development Bank

Harremoës, Poul. 2000, *Scientific Incertitude in Environmental Analysis and Decision Making* (Heineken Lecture), The Hague: Royal Netherlands Academy of Arts and Sciences

Harrison, Kathryn, and Werner Antweiler. 2003. Environmental Regulation vs. Environmental Information: Canada's National Pollutant Release Inventory. *Journal of Policy Analysis and Management* 22 (forthcoming)

Helm, Carsten. 1998. International Cooperation Behind the Veil of Uncertainty. *Environmental and Resource Economics* 12, 185-201

Holm, Nils E. 1975. The Danish System of Open Files in Public Administration. *Scandinavian Studies in Law* 19, 153-177

Holstad, Sigvard. 1979, Sweden, in: Rowat 1979, 29-50

Holzinger, Katharina, Christoph Knill, and Ansgar Schäfer. 2002. *Steuerungswechsel in der europäischen Umweltpolitik? / European Environmental Governance in Transition?* Bonn: Max Planck Project Group on Common Goods (Law, Politics and Economics), Preprint 2002/29

HSA 2002 = Homeland Security Act of 25 November 2002. U.S. Public Law 107-296

Humphrey case 1998 = Settlement Agreement and Stipulation for Entry of Consent Judgment, State *ex rel.* Humphrey v. Philip Morris Inc., No. C1-94-8565, 1998 WL 394331 (Minn. Dist. Ct., 8 May 1998)

Iida, Keisuke. 1993, Analytic Uncertainty and International Cooperation: Theory and Application to International Economic Policy Considerations, *International Studies Quarterly* 37, 431-457

IOMC 2001 = Inter-Organization Programme for the Sound Management of Chemicals, Summary Record of the 7th Meeting of the IOMC PRTR Coordinating Group (Paris, June 2001), Geneva: World Health Organization

Jaeger, Carlo, Ortwin Renn, Eugene A. Rosa, and Thomas Webler. 2001. *Risk, Uncertainty and Rational Action*. London: Earthscan

Jahnke, Marlene 2003. Right to Environmental Information. *Environmental Policy and Law* 33, 37

Jobe, Margaret M. 1999. The Power of Information: The Example of the US Toxics Release Inventory. *Journal of Government Information* 26, 287-295

Johannesburg Report 2002 = Report of the World Summit on Sustainable Development (Johannesburg, South Africa, 26 August – 4 September 2002). New York: UN Doc. A/CONF.199/20

Karkkainen, Bradley C. 2001. Information as Environmental Regulation: TRI and Performance Benchmarking, Precursor to a New Paradigm? *Georgetown Law Journal* 89, 257-370

Kern, Kristine, Helge Jörgens, and Martin Jänicke. 1999. *Die Diffusion umweltpolitischer Innovationen: Ein Beitrag zur Globalisierung von Umweltpolitik*, FFU-Report 99-11. Berlin: Free University

Kevekordes, Daniel. 1994. *Tabakwerbung und Tabaketikettierung im deutschen und europäischen Recht*. Cologne: Heymanns

Kimber, Cliona J.M., and Felix Ekardt. 1999. Zugang zu Umweltinformationen in Grossbritannien und Deutschland. *Natur und Recht* 21, 262-268

Kleindorfer, Paul R., and Eric W. Orts. 1998, Informational Regulation of Environmental Risks, *Risk Analysis* 18, 155-170

Kleine, Maxim. 2000. Book Review of Schneider and Stein 1999. *Zeitschrift für ausländisches öffentliches Recht und Völkerrecht (Heidelberg Journal of International Law)* 60, 277-278

Knight, Frank H. 1921 (reprinted 1985). *Risk, Uncertainty and Profit*. Chicago: University of Chicago Press

Kolstad, Charles D. 2002. International Environmental Agreements and the Veil of Uncertainty. Paper presented at the Conference on *Risk and*

Uncertainty in Environmental and Resource Economics , Wageningen/NL (June 2002)

Konar, Shameek, and Mark A. Cohen. 1997. Information as Regulation: The Effect of Community Right-to-Know Laws on Toxic Emissions. *Journal of Environmental Economics and Management* 32, 109-124

Krämer, Ludwig, 1991. La directive 90/313/CEE sur l'accès à l'information en matière d'environnement : genèse et perspectives d'application. *Revue du Marché Commun*, 866

Kunzlik, Peter. 1997. Access to the Commission's Documents in Environmental Cases: Confidentiality and Public Confidence. *Journal of Environmental Law* 9, 321-344

Lapierre, Dominique, and Javier Moro. 2001. *Il était minuit cinq à Bhopal: récit*. Paris: Laffont; English translation 2002: *Five Past Midnight in Bhopal*, London: Scribner

Lechner, Kurt. 2002. CDU-Rechtsexperte kritisiert EU-Mitgliedsstaaten. (2 December 2002) <http://www.kurt-lechner.de/tabakwerbeverbot.php>

Lewis, Sanford J. 1998. *The Precautionary Principle and Corporate Disclosure*. Los Angeles: Good Neighbor Project <http://gnp.enviroweb.org/precaution.htm>

Litfin, Karen T. 1994. *Ozone Discourse: Science and Politics in Global Environmental Cooperation*. New York: Columbia University Press

Little, Margaret A. 2001, A Most Dangerous Indiscretion: The Legal, Economic, and Political Legacy of the Government's Tobacco Litigation, *Connecticut Law Review* 33, 1143-1205

Logomasini, Angela. 2002. Toxic Road Map for Terrorists. *The Washington Post*(4 September 2002)

Luebbe-Wolff, Gertrude. 1980, Das niederländische Gesetz über die Verwaltungsöffentlichkeit. *Die Verwaltung* 13, 339-355

Lugano 1993 = Convention on Civil Liability for Damage Resulting form Activities Dangerous to the Environment, adopted by the Council of

Europe (Lugano, 21 June 1993, not yet in force). *International Legal Materials* 32, 1228

Lungren case 1996 = Judgment by the California Supreme Court in People *ex rel.* Lungren vs. Superior Court (American Standard Inc.). California Reports: 4th Series 14 (1996), 294

Lyndon, Mary L. 1989. Information Economics and Chemical Toxicity: Designing Laws to Produce and Use Data. *Michigan Law Review* 87, 1795-1861

Magat, Wesley A., and W. Kip Viscusi. 1992 *Informational Approaches to Regulation*, Cambridge/MA: MIT Press; reprinted in *Foundations for Environmental Law and Policy*, edited by Richard L. Revesz. 1997. Oxford: Oxford University Press, 149

Marsh, Norman S., editor. 1987. *Public Access to Government-Held Information*. London: Stevens

McDermott, Patrice. 2002. Withhold and Control: Information in the Bush Administration. *Kansas Journal of Law and Public Policy* 12, 671-692

McDonagh, Maeve. 2000. Freedom of Information in Common Law Jurisdictions: The Experience and the Challenge. *Multimedia und Recht* 3, 251-256

McGarity, Thomas O., and Sidney A. Shapiro. 1980. The Trade Secret Status of Health and Safety Testing Information: Reforming Agency Disclosure Policies. *Harvard Law Review* 93, 837-888

McGinley case 1998 = Judgment by the European Court of Human Rights of 9 June 1998 (App. No. 21825/93, 23414/94, McGinley and Egan vs. United Kingdom). *European Human Rights Reports* 27, 1

Monediaire, Gérard. 1999. Les droits à l'information et à la participation du public auprès de l'Union européenne. *Revue Européenne de Droit de l'Environnement* 3, 129-156

Netherlands 1978 = *Wet Openbaarheid van Bestuur* (Administrative Transparency Act) of 9 November 1978. Netherlands *Staatsblad* [1978] 581, in force 1 May 1980

Neuman, Mark A., Asaf Bitton, and Stanton Glantz. 2002. Tobacco Industry Strategies for Influencing European Community Tobacco Advertising Legislation. *The Lancet* 359: 9314, 1323-1330 (13 April 2002)

Nice 2000 = European Union Charter of Fundamental Rights, proclaimed at Nice on 7 December 2000, *Official Journal of the European Communities* [2001] C 80, 1

Öberg, Ulf 2000. EU Citizens' Right to Know: The Improbable Adoption of a European Freedom of Information Act. *Cambridge Yearbook of European Legal Studies* 2, 303-328

OECD 1996 = Organisation for Economic Cooperation and Development. *Pollutant Release and Transfer Registers (PRTRs): A Tool for Environmental Policy and Sustainable Development.* Guidance Manual for Governments, OECD Doc. GD(96)32. Paris: OECD

OECD 1998 = Organisation for Economic Cooperation and Development. *Proceedings of the OECD International Conference on PRTRs: National and Global Responsibility (Tokyo, 9-11 September 1998).* OECD Environmental Health and Safety Series on PRTRs No.1. Paris: OECD

Offentlighedslov 1970 = Public Access to Documents in Administrative Files. Danish Act No. 280 of 10 June 1970, in force 1 January 1971

OMB 2002 = U.S. Office of Management and Budget. Guidelines for Ensuring and Maximizing the Quality, Objectivity, Utility, and Integrity of Information disseminated by Federal Agencies: Republication (February 2002). *Federal Register* 67, 8452-8460

O'Neill, Michael. 1998. The Right of Access to Community-Held Documentation as a General Principle of EC Law. *European Public Law* 4, 403-432

O'Reilly, James T. 2002. "Access to Records" Versus "Access to Evil:" Should Disclosure Laws Consider Motives as a Barrier to Records Release? *Kansas Journal of Law and Public Policy* 12, 559-578

OSPAR 1992 = Convention for the Protection of the Marine Environment of the North-East Atlantic, adopted at Paris on 22 September 1992 (revising and consolidating the earlier 1972 Oslo and 1974 Paris Conventions). *International Legal Materials* 32, 1068

Pallemaerts, Marc, editor. 1991. *Het recht op informatie inzake leefmilieu/ Le droit à l'information en matière d'environnement/ The Right to Environmental Information*, Brussels : Story -Scientia

Pedersen, William F. Jr. 2001. Regulation and Information Disclosure: Parallel Universes and Beyond. *Harvard Environmental Law Review* 25, 151-211

Petkova, Elena, and Peter Veit. 2000. *Environmental Accountability Beyond the Nation State: The Implications of the Aarhus Convention*. Washington/ DC: World Resources Institute

Petkova, Elena, Crescencia Maurer, Norbert Henninger, and Fran Irwin. 2002. *Closing the Gap: Information, Participation, and Justice in Decision-Making for the Environment*. Washington/DC: World Resources Institute

Petrén, Gösta. 1987. Access to Government-Held Information in Sweden. In Marsh 1987, 35-54

Powell, Colin L. 2002. Only One Earth. *Our Planet* 13:2, 8-10

Prieur, Michel, editor. 1997. *Le droit à l'information en matière d'environnement dans les pays de l'Union européenne*. Limoges : PULIM

"Proposition 65" = Safe Drinking Water and Toxic Enforcement Act (1986). *California Health and Safety Code* §25249.5-25249.13

Rechtschaffen, Clifford. 1996. The Warning Game: Evaluation Warnings Under California's Proposition 65. *Ecology Law Quarterly* 23, 303-368

Rechtschaffen, Clifford. 1999. How to Reduce Lead Exposures with One Simple Statute: The Experience of Proposition 65. *Environmental Law Reporter* 29, 10581

Rehbinder, Eckard. 2003. World Summit on Sustainable Development. Environmental Law Network International: *ELNI Review* No.1, 1-3

Rio Declaration 1992 = Rio Declaration on Environment and Development, adopted by the United Nations Conference on Environment and Development (Rio de Janeiro, 3-14 June 1992). New York: UN Doc. A/ CONF.151/26/Rev.1, 1, 3; reprinted in *International Legal Materials* 31, 874

Roberts, Alasdair. 2001. Structural Pluralism and the Right to Information. *University of Toronto Law Journal* 51, 243-271

Roberts, Alasdair. 2002. New Strategies for Enforcement of the Access to Information Act. *Queen's Law Journal* 27, 647-682

Rodenhoff, Vera. 2002. The Aarhus Convention and its Implications for the 'Institutions' of the European Community. *Review of European Community and International Environmental Law* 11, 343-357

Roe, David. 2002. Toxic Chemical Control Policy: Three Unabsorbed Facts. *Environmental Law Reporter* 32, 10232-10239

Rose-Ackerman, Susan. 1995. *Controlling Environmental Policy: The Limits of Public Law in Germany and the United States*. New Haven/CT: Yale University Press; German translation 1995: *Umweltrecht und –politik in den Vereinigten Staaten und der Bundesrepublik Deutschland*. Baden-Baden: Nomos

Rose-Ackerman, Susan, and Achim A. Halpaap. 2002. The Aarhus Convention and the Politics of Process: The Political Economy of Procedural Environmental Rights. *Research in Law and Economics* 20, 27-64

Rowan-Robinson, Jeremy, Andrea Ross, William Walton, and Julie Rothnie. 1996. Public Access to Environmental Information: A Means to What End ? *Journal of Environmental Law* 8, 19-42

Rowat, Donald C. 1966. The Problem of Administrative Secrecy. *International Review of Administrative Sciences* 32, 99-106

Rowat, Donald C., editor. 1979. *Administrative Secrecy in Developed Countries*. New York: Columbia University Press

Rutteman, Joost. 2001. The Netherlands. In *Implementing Rio Principles in Europe: Participation and Precaution*. Brussels: European Environmental Bureau, 68-72

Sage, William M. 1999. Regulating Through Information: Disclosure Laws and American Health Care. *Columbia Law Review* 99, 1701-1825

Sand, Peter H. 1990. *Lessons Learned in Global Environmental Governance.* Washington/DC: World Resources Institute

Sands, Philippe J. 1995. *Principles of International Environmental Law.* Manchester: Manchester University Press

Saul, Graham. 2002. Transparency and Accountability in International Financial Institutions. In Calland and Tilley, 127-137

Scheyli, Martin. 2000. Die Aarhus-Konvention über Informationszugang, Öffentlichkeitsbeteiligung und Rechtsschutz in Umweltbelangen. *Archiv des Völkerrechts* 38, 217-252

Schneider, Hans P., and Torsten Stein, editors. 1999. *The European Ban on Tobacco Advertising: Studies Concerning Its Compatibility with European Law.* Baden-Baden: Nomos

Schoch, Friedrich K. 2002. Informationsfreiheitsgesetz für die Bundesrepublik Deutschland. *Die Verwaltung* 35, 149-157

Schroeder, Werner. 2001. Vom Brüsseler Kampf gegen den Tabakrauch: 2. Teil. *Europäische Zeitschrift für Wirtschaftsrecht* 12, 489-495

Schwan, Eggert. 1984. *Amtsgeheimnis oder Aktenöffentlichkeit.* Munich: Schweitzer

Schwanenflügel, Matthias von. 1991. Das Öffentlichkeitsprinzip des EG-Umweltrechts. *Deutsches Verwaltungsblatt* 106, 93-104

Shihata, Ibrahim F.I. 1994. *The World Bank Inspection Panel.* Oxford: Oxford University Press

Simma, Bruno, Joseph H.H. Weiler, and Markus C. Zöckler. 1999. *Kompetenzen und Grundrechte: Beschränkungen der Tabakwerbung aus der Sicht des Europarechts.* Berlin: Duncker & Humblot

Simpson, David. 2002, Germany: How Did It Get Like This? *Tobacco Control* 11, 291-293

Singer, Michael J. 1979. USA. In Rowat 1979, 309-356 Smyth, Gerry. 2000. Freedom of Information: Changing the Culture of Official Secrecy in Ireland. *Law Librarian* 31, 140-146

South Africa 1996 = Constitution of the Republic of South Africa Act, 1996

South Africa 2000 = Promotion of Access to Information Act, 2000

Stec, Stephen 1998. Ecological Rights Advancing the Rule of Law in Eastern Europe. *Journal of Environmental Law and Litigation* 13, 275-358

Stec, Stephen, Susan Casey-Lefkowitz, and Jerzy Jendroska. 2000. *The Aarhus Convention: An Implementation Guide*. Geneva: United Nations Economic Commission for Europe

Steinzor, Rena. 2002. "Democracies Die Behind Closed Doors:" The Homeland Security Act and Corporate Accountability. *Kansas Journal of Law and Public Policy* 12, 641-670

Stephan, Mark 2002. Environmental Information Disclosure Programs: They Work, But Why? *Social Science Quarterly* 83, 190-205

Stewart, Richard B. 2001. A New Generation of Environmental Regulation? *Capital University Law Review* 29, 21-141

Stewart, Richard B. 2002. Environmental Regulatory Decision Making Under Uncertainty. *Research in Law and Economics* 20, 71-126

Stiglitz, Joseph. 1999. *On Liberty, the Right to Know, and Public Discourse: The Role of Transparency in Public Life*. Oxford: Oxford Amnesty Lecture (27 January 1999)

Sunstein, Cass R. 1999. Informational Regulation and Informational Standing: *Akins* and Beyond. *University of Pennsylvania Law Review* 147, 613-675

Tietenberg, Tom. 1998. Disclosure Strategies for Pollution Control. *Environmental and Resource Economics* 11, 587-602

Tobacco Lite 2003 = Editorial, *The Washington Post* (5 May 2003), A-20

Travers, Noel. 2000. Access to Documents in Community Law: On the Road to a European Participatory Democracy. *The Irish Jurist* 35, 164-237

Tridimas, George, and Takis Tridimas. 2002. The European Court of Justice and the Annulment of the Tobacco Advertisement Directive: Friend of National Sovereignty or Foe of Public Health? *European Journal of Law and Economics* 14, 171-183

Udall, Lori. 1998. The World Bank and Public Accountability: Has Anything Changed? In *The Struggle for Accountability: The World Bank, NGOs, and Grassroots Movements* , edited by Jonathan A. Fox and L. David Brown. Cambridge/MA: MIT Press, 391-436

UN/ECE 1998 = United Nations Economic Commission for Europe. *Convention on Access to Information, Public Participation in Decision-Making and Access to Justice in Environmental Matters,* adopted at the 4th UN/ECE Ministerial Conference on "Environment and Europe" in Aarhus/ Denmark (23-25 June 1998, in force 30 October 2001). Geneva: UN Doc. ECE/CEP/43; reprinted in *International Legal Materials* 38, 517

UN/ECE 2000 = United Nations Economic Commission for Europe: Committee on Environmental Policy. *Pollutant Release and Transfer Registers: Report on the First Meeting of the Task Force (Prague 21-23 February 2000).* Geneva: UN Doc. CEP/WG.5/2000/5

UN/ECE 2002 = United Nations Economic Commission for Europe. *First Meeting of the Parties to the Convention on Access to Information, Public Participation in Decision-Making and Access to Justice in Environmental Matters (Lucca, 21-23 October 2002).* Geneva: <http://www.unece.org/cep>

UN/ECE 2003 = United Nations Economic Commission for Europe: Working Group on Pollutant Release and Transfer Registers. *Draft Protocol on Pollutant Release and Transfer Registers.* Geneva: UN Doc. MP.PP/2003/ 1 (3 March 2003)

UNEP 2002 = United Nations Environment Programme. Report on the Implementation of the Programme for the Development and Periodic Review of Environmental Law for the First Decade of the Twenty-First Century (Montevideo Programme III). Nairobi: UN Doc. UNEP/GC.22/ 3/Add.2 (11 November 2002)

UNITAR 2000 = United Nations Institute for Training and Research. *Designing and Implementing National Pollutant Release and Transfer Registers: A Compilation of Resource Documents.* Geneva: UNITAR (CD-Rom)

Vahle, Jürgen. 1999. Informationsrechte des Bürgers contra „Amtsgeheimnis". *Deutsche Verwaltungspraxis* 50, 102-106

Wägenbaur, Bertrand. 2001. Der Zugang zu EU-Dokumenten: Transparenz zum Anfassen. *Europäische Zeitschrift für Wirtschaftsrecht* 12, 680-685

Wates, Jeremy. 1996. *Access to Environmental Information and Public Participation in Environmental Decision-Making: UN ECE Guidelines From Theory to Practice.* Brussels: European Environmental Bureau

Weber, Stefan. 1990. Environmental Information and the European Convention on Human Rights. *Human Rights Law Journal* 12, 177-185

Weeks, Rebecca S. 1998. The Bumpy Road to Community Preparedness: The Emergency Planning and Community Right-to-Know Act. *Environmental Law* 4, 827-889

Weiss, Edith B., and Harald K. Jacobson. 2000. *Engaging Countries: Strengthening Compliance with International Environmental Accords.* Cambridge/MA: MIT Press

Wheeler, David. 1997. Information in Pollution Management: The New Model. In *Brazil: Managing Pollution Problems*, World Bank Report 16513-BR. Washington/DC: World Bank

Wiener, Jonathan B. 2001. Something Borrowed for Something Blue: Legal Transplants and the Evolution of Global Environmental Law. *Ecology Law Quarterly* 27, 1295-1371

Wiener, Jonathan B., and Michael D. Rogers. 2002. Comparing Precaution in the United States and Europe. *Journal of Risk Research* 5, 317-349

Wilcox, William A.Jr. 2001. Access to Environmental Information in the United States and the United Kingdom. *Loyola of Los Angeles International and Comparative Law Review* 23, 121-247

Wilsher, Daniel. 2001. Freedom of Environmental Information: Recent Developments and Future Prospects. *European Public Law* 25, 671-697

Winter, Gerd, editor. 1990. *Öffentlichkeit von Umweltinformationen: Europäische und nordamerikanische Rechte und Erfahrungen*. Baden-Baden: Nomos

Wolf, Sidney M. 1996. Fear and Loathing About the Public Right-to-Know: The Surprising Success of the Emergency Planning and Community Right-to-Know Act. *Journal of Land Use and Environmental Law* 11, 217-313

World Bank 2000. *Greening Industry: New Roles for Communities, Markets, and Governments* . Washington/DC

WRI 2002 = World Resources Institute. Partnership for Principle 10. Washington/DC: <http://www.pp10.org>

Zimmermann, Nils, Michael M'Gonigle, and Andrew Day. 1995. Community Right to Know: Improving Public Information About Toxic Chemicals. *Journal of Environmental Law and Practice* 5, 95-139

Zschiesche, Michael. 2001. Die Aarhus-Konvention: mehr Bürgerbeteiligung durch umweltrechtliche Standards? *Zeitschrift für Umweltrecht* 12, 177-183; English transl. The Aarhus Convention: More Citizens' Participation by Setting Out Environmental Standards? Environmental Law Network International: *ELNI Newsletter* No. 1, 21-29

Designing Mandatory Disclosure To Promote Synergies Between Public And Private Enforcement

Annette B. Killmer

7ᵀᴴ INECE CONFERENCE PROCEEDINGS (FORTHCOMING 2005)

1   Introduction

The task of reducing process pollution in a community setting, where emissions from the manufacture of products negatively affect the larger community, presents a particular challenge to environmental practitioners, since there tends to be a lack of formal relationships between the polluter and those affected by the pollution (Tietenberg & Wheeler, 1998). This is especially true when industrial activity affects larger segments of society or even the global environment, as is, for example, the case with the emissions of greenhouse gases. Yet, even under a 'sustainable development scenario' of the future, it is likely that the global level of industrial production will increase relative to current levels. As the World Development Report 2003 points out, improving the quality of life for current and future generations in developing countries will require a "substantial growth in income and productivity" (World Bank, 2003, p. xiii). This growth is desirable, because industrial production has a valuable, positive impact on society through the manufacture of consumable goods and the provision of employment. However, pollution intensity has to decline at a rate commensurate with the growth of industrial output to prevent a net increase in pollution (World Bank, 2000). Thus, environmental practitioners are faced with the challenge of reducing the negative impacts of industrial production – to the point of altogether preventing the most harmful emissions and wastes – so that they do not entirely offset the positive impacts.

The traditional approach to controlling pollution is through command-and-control regulation that stipulates a fixed, uniformly applicable environmental target, as well as rules for monitoring and, if necessary, enforcing[1] compliance with this requirement (U.S. Congress, 1995). Command-and-control regulation can be very powerful and is often employed when strict adherence to a standard is required to prevent deleterious consequences to human health. Yet, as several scholars have pointed out, in both developed and developing countries, regulatory agencies charged with monitoring and enforcing these policies frequently operate under the constraints of limited budgets and restricted maximum financial penalties, which limits the effectiveness of command-and-control regulation (Dasgupta, Laplante, & Mamingi, 2001; Foulon, Lanoie, & Laplante, 2002; Gunningham, Philipson, & Grabosky, 1999; Harrington, 1988; Hentschel & Randall, 2000; Heyes, 2000; Laplante & Rilstone, 1996; World Bank, 2000). Moreover, from an economic development perspective, uniform standards are considered inefficient if abatement cost functions differ between the regulated firms (Lübbe-Wolff, 2001; Office of Technology Assessment, 1995). To remedy these limitations, environmental practitioners and scholars have explored a variety of court-based and market-based instruments, as well as – more recently – information-disclosure approaches[2]. This last type of approach, as a supplement to traditional command-and-control regulation, is the focus of the current paper.

Mandatory information disclosure approaches to pollution prevention have acquired the reputation of a promising policy instrument in developed and developing countries (Stephan, 2002; Tietenberg, 1998; World Bank, 2000, and references therein). In contrast to other environmental policy instruments, information disclosure approaches are not designed to influence pollution levels directly, but rather require firms to regularly disclose certain environmentally relevant information about their processes or products to the general public (Anderson & Lohof, 1997). This disclosure can have considerable negative or positive consequences for the disclosing firms, because civil society may choose

---

[1] Monitoring is here defined as the process of verifying a firm's emission data and compliance with the standard, and enforcement as the undertaking of actions (e.g. imposing a penalty) to compel a non-compliant firm into reducing its emissions. Both public and private actors can enforce compliance, yet governmental regulatory agencies are bound by any enforcement rules specified in the associated regulations for the standard.

[2] As used in this paper, *court-based instruments* include tort law cases, citizen suits and statutory liability claims, *market-based instruments* include pollution charges and taxes, as well as tradable permits and pollution credits, and *information disclosure approaches* refer to policies that require the systematic disclosure of information by firms. Thus, the latter term does not include voluntary or ad hoc publications of information, such as may occur through participation in voluntary eco-labeling schemes, corporate reports, court cases or 'leaks' to the press.

against or in favor of a firm's products based on the information provided. Similarly, the disclosure may change a firm's market valuation if it gives rise to concerns over future liabilities or indicates precautions against such liabilities through good environmental management (Anderson & Lohof, 1997; Barth & McNichols, 1994; Blacconiere & Northcut, 1997; Garber & Hammitt, 1998; Konar & Cohen, 1997, 2001; World Bank, 2000). Empirical evidence from the U.S. Toxic Release Inventory (TRI), Indonesia's Program for Pollution Control, Evaluation and Rating (PROPER) and other disclosure programs reveals significant improvements in the participating firms' environmental performances, in some cases beyond compliance requirements, and the U.S. TRI has even resulted in proactive initiatives by heavily polluting industries (Afsah & Vincent, 1997; Arora & Cason, 1995; Kappas, 1998; Khanna & Damon, 1999; Konar & Cohen, 1997; Tietenberg & Wheeler, 1998; World Bank, 2000). Judging by these examples, mandatory information disclosures, or more specifically the private efforts to enforce pollution reductions that result from this disclosure, hold the promise of reducing the need for costly regulatory enforcement – which is clearly an appealing prospect given the aforementioned restricted regulatory budgets.

The challenge at this point, though, is that the empirical evidence on mandatory information disclosure in the reduction of process pollution comes primarily from two cases (the U.S. TRI and Indonesia's PROPER), and the dynamics introduced by the involvement of civil society have received only limited analytic attention (Gunningham et al., 1999; Heyes, 2000; Stephan, 2002). As such, our understanding of the circumstances in which public and private efforts to reduce pollution are indeed complementary, or "additive" (Heyes, 1998, p. 59), is insufficient to confidently generalize from the experiences of TRI and PROPER. To improve our understanding of these dynamics, a recent research study considers the conditions under which the regulator's and civil society's efforts to enforce pollution reductions are complementary, and how the regulator can foster this positive interplay (Killmer, 2004). The present paper draws on the key arguments and findings from this larger study to derive a set of recommendations that are pivotal to designing mandatory disclosure approaches in ways that promote synergies between public and private enforcement.

Specifically, a systematic analysis of the dynamics introduced by the involvement of civil society in pollution prevention enforcement suggests that the design and implementation of a mandatory disclosure policy should:

- Involve careful consideration of (a) what information is presented, (b) how it is presented and distributed, (c) how civil society can be assisted in its use of the information through capacity building and other education initiatives, and (d) whether the existing legal and institutional context permits the level of civil society involvement that the disclosure policy is supposed to encourage.

- Take into account that the effectiveness of different avenues for civil society involvement varies with the regulatory context as well as with the nature and number of polluting firms.

- Make provisions to allow for a greater flexibility in the regulator's behavior than is generally accommodated by traditional command-and-control regulations.

The next section introduces the analytical model that was developed by Killmer (2004) to investigate the dynamics of interest here. Section 3 presents the key insights provided by the model with respect to conditions that promote or hinder the effective involvement of civil society in the enforcement process. The final section of this paper discusses the policy implications that follow from these insights – particularly those that reveal counter-productive dynamics – and thereby arrives at the recommendations listed above.

2   An Analytical Model of Civil Society Involvement

The standard theory with respect to imperfectly enforceable regulations is one of choice under uncertainty (Heyes, 1998). Much of the literature in environmental enforcement traces its roots to the classic economic analysis of crime by Becker (1968), which suggests that an individual or entity will weigh the certain cost of compliance against the expected penalty for non-compliance (Cohen, 1998; Heyes, 1998, 2000). A corollary of this theory is the principle of marginal deterrence (Shavell, 1992; Stigler, 1970), according to which the decision to comply or not depends on the *absolute* expected penalty, whereas the decision about the *extent* of non-compliance depends on the *marginal* expected penalty. In the context of reducing process pollution, these two theories predict that a rational firm will comply with a performance standard if and only if its cost of reducing emissions to the level of the standard is equal to or less than the expected penalty. The theories further predict that non-compliant firms will emit at the level where the increase in the expected penalty associated with emitting one more unit of pollution equals the abatement costs foregone by emitting that extra unit. Under this traditional economic model of compliance and enforcement, the firm's objective with respect to a particular pollutant can be generically expressed as shown in Eq. 1, where *Abatement Cost[x]* is the expense incurred to achieve pollution level x, the *Penalty* is a function of the difference between actual emissions, x, and the legal pollution standard, s, and the likelihood of having to pay the penalty is dependent on the probabilities of monitoring and enforcement (which, in more complex models, are often specified to depend on x and/or s).

$$\min_x \text{ Total} = \text{Abatement} + p(monitor) * p(enforce) * \text{Penalty}[x-s] \qquad \text{(Eq. 1)}$$
$$\text{Cost} \qquad \text{Cost}[x]$$

The theories do not specify the source of the penalty, but the theoretic models in the pollution control literature have largely focused on regulatory fines associated with command-and-control regulation and on taxes or permit costs associated with economic incentive instruments (see overview by Cohen, 1998 and reference cited therein). In these models, the regulator chooses certain parameters (e.g. the amount of the fine or tax), and these choices influence the level of compliance and hence the level of system-wide pollution abatement.

$$\min_x \text{ Total} = \text{Abatement} + p(monitor)\{ p(enforce)*\text{Penalty}[x-s] + p(levyfine)*\text{Fine}[x-d]\} \dots$$
$$\text{Cost} \qquad \text{Cost}[x]$$

$$+ \{1 - p(monitor)\}*\text{Penalty}[d-s] + p(target)*\text{CivilFine}[d] \qquad \text{(Eq. 2)}$$

However, over the past decade, civil society has noticeably entered into the picture – though by and large not into the equation of analytical enforcement models – as a second source of pressure toward pollution reductions. The systematic publication of environmental data in a readily accessible format (such as the internet-accessible TRI database in the U.S.) has greatly assisted public participation in the enforcement process by virtually eliminating the direct cost to civil society of collecting the necessary information. As such, public disclosure provides the victims of process pollution with the data needed to create incentives for polluters to control their emissions (Tietenberg & Wheeler, 1998), and hence considerably lowers the transaction costs of achieving a more efficient outcome (Coase, 1960). In short, mandatory information disclosure introduces civil society as a third party into the traditional firm-regulator dyad – a change that alters the firm's cost function in several important ways, as shown in the generic objective function for firms given by Eq. 2.

The first alteration compared to Eq. 1 is that the regulator is now monitoring two aspects of a firm's performance, namely compliance with the pollution standard (as before) *and* accurate disclosure. If, during monitoring, the regulator finds that disclosed emissions, d, are below actual emissions, x, the firm would be fined for under-disclosure with a certain probability[3], which translates into an additional expected cost of p(*monitor*)*p(*levyfine*)*Fine[x-d] for the firm. Second, a firm can choose to self-disclose a violation of magnitude [d-s] and incur the associated penalty for non-compliance. This behavior has an expected cost of {1 - p(*monitor*)}*Penalty[d-s]. The third additional cost is any financial pressure brought directly by civil society (CivilFine) against polluting firms. The expected cost from such pressure is a function of disclosed emissions, d, since that is the information civil society acts on, and of p(*target*), the probability of civil society being successful in targeting a certain firm and bringing direct financial pressure to bear. Thus, combining a traditional pollution standard with a mandatory disclosure requirement can result in three additional sources for increasing costs of non-compliance to firms and hence for inducing them to abate their levels of pollution.

In making their decision, it is also crucial that firms take into account the behavioral flexibility of civil society. Unlike the regulator, whose actions are circumscribed by statutes and rules, civil society can exert pressure toward pollution reductions through various behaviors. For the purpose of this discussion, six common types of intervention are considered:

  i. *No Action*: Civil society receives information, but does not act on it

  ii. *Market Pressure*: Civil society exerts direct pressure on firms through markets

  iii. *Suits Against Firms*: Civil society brings suits against certain non-compliant firms

---

[3] Small infractions are unlikely to be pursued, but, for example, the U.S. EPA can levy up to US$27,500 per violation for failure to report the mandated information for the TRI on time.

iv.   *Suit Against Agency*: Civil society brings legal actions against the regulator to increase the agency's monitoring and enforcement efforts

v.   *Suit Against Agency & Market Pressure*: A combination of interventions (i) and (iv)

vi.   *Suits Against Agency & Firms*: A combination of interventions (ii) and (iv)

The No Action case is included here not only because it provides the comparison case to traditional models that do not include civil society, but also because it serves as a reminder that the mere wide-spread publication of data does not automatically translate into private actions. For the other intervention behaviors, it is assumed that they are carried out with the intention to have an overall positive effect on pollution reductions.

Depending on which intervention behavior civil society chooses, the firm will face a slightly different objective function. For example, the CivilFine term is likely to be significant when civil society exerts market pressure or brings suits against firms (either alone or in combination with a judicial action against the regulator), but is equal to zero in the 'No Action' case and in the pure 'Suit Against Agency' case. The latter case differs from the No Action case, in that civil society can influence the firm indirectly through a successful judicial action by inducing the regulator to increase p(*monitor*), p(*enforce*) or p(*levyfine*). Thus, firms face different objective functions depending on the behavior of civil society. Moreover, firms have only limited ability to foretell how civil society will intervene in the process, unless civil society is *a priori* restricted in its choices (for example, a country's legislation may not give its citizens the necessary legal standing to bring judiciary actions). In this way, private involvement in the enforcement process reduces the predictability of interactions within the system compared to the traditional, highly codified interactions between firms and the enforcement agency.

An important question from the perspective of environmental decision makers is whether – despite or because of this reduced predictability – civil society's involvement in the enforcement process is ultimately effective[4] in achieving pollution reductions beyond those that could be achieved by the regulator alone. This question has been addressed in some detail by Killmer (2004) through analytically solving the particular objective functions firms would face under various sets of enforcement conditions, whereby the sets of conditions differ from each other in the type of intervention chosen by civil society, the regulator's enforcement strategy, and the financial constraints imposed on the regulator and/or civil society. Comparing the solutions across the various sets of conditions reveals a number of important dynamics that policy makers should take into consideration when designing mandatory disclosure policies.

3   Key Findings Reveal Potential Conflicts And Synergies

With regard to the effectiveness of civil society involvement in enforcing pollution prevention policies, the comparison of environmental outcomes under various enforcement conditions offers four key insights.

> **Finding 1**: Under certain conditions, *excluding* civil society from the enforcement process through enforcing solely the performance standard (and expending no resources on enforcing the disclosure policy) leads to the most effective environmental outcome.

The dynamic described by Finding 1 can be observed when civil society exerts pressure directly on firms, through the market or legal suits, but has only limited resources at its disposal to do so. The finding is even more clearly illustrated in the No Action case, where an exclusive enforcement of the performance standard is the most effective and cost-effective[5] strategy for a budget-constrained regulator. Thus, if civil society does not have or chooses not to expend the resources to participate meaningfully in the enforcement process, excluding civil society by not enforcing the disclosure requirement allows the regulator to focus all its resources on achieving lower pollution levels.

It is important to note, however, that Finding 1 refers to reducing pollution in an effective manner. Foregoing the monitoring and enforcement of an existing disclosure requirement is clearly not the most desirable strategy from a public access perspective. Thus, Finding 1 also serves to illustrate

---

[4] *Effectiveness* in the current context refers to the amount of pollution reduced, specifically the difference between the total amount of pollution in the absence of the policy (counter-factual case) and the total amount of pollution actually emitted by the firms in the system under a certain set of enforcement conditions.

[5] *Cost-effectiveness* is here defined as the amount of financial resources expended per unit of pollution reduced.

that achieving the most effective pollution reduction and the best public access to information are not invariably compatible objectives, even though both are generally considered socially desirable.

The dynamics just described indicate that the effectiveness of civil society's involvement depends on its resources for such an involvement. In addition, civil society's effectiveness depends either directly or indirectly on the regulator's resources. The direct link is apparent in the dynamics associated with legal actions against the regulatory agency:

> **Finding 2**: Suits brought by civil society against a social-cost-minimizing regulator, either solely or in combination with direct pressure on polluting firms, will increase the effectiveness of enforcement if and only if the regulator is not bound by a budget constraint.

Finding 2 emphasizes that civil society actions against a social-cost-minimizing regulator do not have a positive effect *unless* the regulator is able to increase enforcement efforts in response to those actions[6]. In this latter case, civil society intervention can lead to more effective pollution control because judicial actions can induce the regulator to enforce pollution abatement beyond the social-cost minimizing level. (It is worth noting that, while abating pollution beyond the social-cost minimizing level may be effective, it is not, economically speaking, efficient.) On the other hand, if the regulator is unable to increase its enforcement effort due to a binding budget constraint, judicial actions that prescribe a change in regulatory behavior invariably mean that the available resources have to be reallocated, for example to an increase in enforcement at the expense of monitoring. Yet, a social-cost-minimizing regulator would be expected to choose the highest level of pollution control feasible within the binding budget constraint, and hence a reallocation of resources would not lead to a more effective outcome. Moreover, bringing legal actions against a budget-constraint regulator is likely to reduce overall cost-effectiveness compared to the No Action alternative, since the same amount or less pollution is reduced but at a higher cost, due to the cost incurred by civil society.

---

[6] This finding applies in the short- to medium-term. In the medium- to long-term, successful judiciary actions may be used by the regulator to make its enforcement processes more efficient, to lobby for an increase in its budget or to leverage the pressure from civil society into obtaining other additional resources.

An indirect link between civil society's effectiveness and the regulator's budget resources is illustrated by the third finding:

Finding 3: Private enforcement through market pressure creates a disincentive for firms to disclose, particularly for firms with high levels of emissions.

Under a combined performance standard/disclosure policy, the firm is faced not only with penalties from the regulator for non-compliance with the policy requirements, but also with the possibility that civil society will penalize it for any disclosed emissions. Firms can evade the pressure from civil society to some extent by under-reporting their emissions[7]. As modeled for the purposes of the present analysis, the mandatory disclosure policy anticipates this behavior and includes a regulatory fine on under-reporting, but (consistent with reality) this fine is not levied with certainty. Thus, in making their disclosure decision, firms have to weigh the expected cost of inaccurate disclosure against the cost of revealing their true emissions, which consist of the regulatory fine for non-compliance with the standard *and* the penalty from civil society. Since this combined penalty from regulator and civil society tends to increase with a greater extent of non-compliance, firms that know themselves to emit above the standard have an increasing incentive to under-report the higher their levels of emissions.

At the same time, civil society's interventions are based on the disclosed information, and it is reasonable to assume that civil society is particularly interested in reducing pollution from firms that are emitting considerably above the standard. Hence, by creating incentives for firms to under-disclose, civil society inadvertently limits its own involvement in the enforcement process – *unless* the regulator counteracts the deterioration in data quality through more stringent enforcement of the disclosure requirement[8]. This in turn requires the availability of regulatory resources and hence establishes an indirect link between civil society's effectiveness and the regulator's budget.

It is important to note that an increasing demand on regulatory resources as a result of civil society involvement is diametrically opposed to one of

[7] Incidentally, the model used in this analysis assumes that civil society can exert some market pressure on targeted firms even in the absence of information, mirroring, for example, reputational effects on firms in 'dirty industries'.

[8] In the United States, the regulator often has access to self-reporting or monitoring-based data through other sources, but this situation is atypical, particularly in developing countries.

the commonly cited benefits of involving civil society in the enforcement process, namely that it reduces the need for costly regulatory enforcement. Finding 3 illustrates that mandatory disclosure requires some form of enforcement to ensure that the requested information is disclosed – and disclosed accurately. Yet, it is in large part the paucity of good information about actual emissions that limits the regulator's ability to enforce pollution standards and other traditional command-and-control regulations that demand continuous compliance. Moreover, it is similarly difficult for the regulator to gain access to complete and accurate pollution data, regardless of whether the data are used to satisfy a performance standard or a disclosure requirement. Thus, mandatory information disclosure does not circumvent the acquisition of reliable information on which to act – and hence does not resolve one of the fundamental problems the regulator faces in enforcing pollution control.

Yet, despite the countervailing dynamics mentioned in conjunction with the first three findings, the regulator's and civil society's enforcement efforts can work synergistically under certain conditions and lead to more effective pollution control than could be achieved by the regulator alone.

> **Finding 4**: Public and private enforcement is most likely to be complementary when the regulatory budget is binding and civil society exerts a reasonable level of direct pressure on firms, either through markets or through citizen suits.

Given a binding regulatory budget, the enforcement agency by itself is not in a position to induce firms to reduce pollution to the social-cost-minimizing level. However, if civil society has the necessary resources to create incentives for firms to reduce pollution (see also Finding 1), the regulator's best strategy is to focus on enforcing the disclosure requirement and hence provide civil society with good-quality information about actual emissions, which are then best used to exert direct pressure on firms through the market or through citizen suits (see also Finding 2). The regulator's task of obtaining reliable information will be slightly complicated by the fact that civil society levies a penalty on disclosing information about pollution, rather than on the pollution itself, when it exerts pressure on the disclosing firms (see also Finding 3). Nevertheless, under these conditions, the positive effects of civil society's involvement can be sufficiently large to outweigh any counter-productive changes in firms' behaviors as well as the constraints imposed on the regulator through its budget. Judging by the empirical evidence available, this situation is in fact given in the context of both the U.S. TRI and Indonesia's PROPER, and it is presumably the situation envisioned for similar programs, such as the ones in Canada, Mexico, the European Union, and the Philippines (Environment Canada, 2005; European Commission, 2004; Nauman, 2003; Presencia Ciudadana, 2004; World Bank, 2000).

4   Recommendations for Effective Disclosure Policies Revisited

The analysis of the economic model reveals three countervailing dynamics that suggest, at least in theory, that the success of the TRI and PROPER may be the exception rather than the rule. However, as revealed by the fourth finding, these countervailing dynamics do not occur invariably – indeed, they can be largely avoided by paying due attention to their possible occurrence during policy design and implementation.

As such, the findings presented here have three major policy implications. First, it is important to establish that there is a demand from civil society for the information provided, and that civil society has the ability to become meaningfully involved in the enforcement process. (Establishing demand accurately is unlikely to be feasible, but already active participation by the intended target audience in the design and implementation of the policy will be very helpful in gauging demand.) While non-governmental organizations, shareholders and competing firms in various countries are adept at leveraging funds and taking advantage of legal provisions that grant them access to the environmental policy process, neither the demand for information, nor the skills or legal provisions necessary to act on it can be taken for granted. Therefore, the design and implementation of a mandatory disclosure policy should involve careful consideration of (a) what information is presented, (b) how it is presented and distributed, (c) how civil society can be assisted in its use of the information through capacity building and other education initiatives, and (d) whether the existing legal and institutional context permits the level of civil society involvement that the disclosure policy is supposed to encourage.

Second, not all avenues for civil society involvement are equally effective in a given context. For example, while judicial actions against the regulatory can certainly be effective to achieve certain goals, Finding 2 illustrates that they can also be ineffective or even counter-productive in some contexts. Similarly, citizen suits against firms tend to be limited by the existing pollution standard, since they usually require evidence that a firm is out of compliance with an existing regulation. Nor can it be presumed that it is always feasible for shareholders, consumers or competitors to exert effective market pressure; a small number of polluters, publicly-traded firms, and those that produce products or services which are directly traded to consumers are more easily targeted effectively through stock markets or consumer boycotts then large numbers of polluters, privately-held firms, or those that produce raw materials or intermediate goods. Therefore, the design and implementation of a mandatory disclosure policy should take into account that the effectiveness of different avenues for civil society involvement varies with the regulatory context as well as with the nature and number of polluting firms.

Third, introducing a mandatory disclosure approach (and hence civil society as a third party to the traditional regulator-firm dyad) fundamentally changes the role of the regulator. In this new context, the regulator is not only charged with maximizing compliance by the polluting firms within the usual budget and maximum-penalty constraints. The regulator also has to strategically respond to changes in firms' behaviors arising from civil society's involvement (which itself may vary in type and intensity), as well as operate under any constraints imposed through legal actions against the enforcement agency. Therefore, the design and implementation of a mandatory disclosure policy should make provisions to allow for a certain flexibility in the regulator's behavior. Given such flexibility, the regulator will be in a better position to effectively adapt its behavior to these new demands.

Thus, systematic analysis of the dynamics introduced by civil society involvement in the enforcement of pollution prevention polices reveals important countervailing dynamics. Yet, these dynamics can be forestalled through circumspect policy design and implementation, and environmental practitioners can thereby foster a positive interplay between the regulator's and civil society's efforts to enforce pollution reductions.

5   References

Afsah, S., & Vincent, J. (1997). *Putting Pressure on Polluters: Indonesia's PROPER Program* (Case Study for the HIID 1997 Asia Environmental Economics Policy Seminar). Cambridge, MA: Harvard Institute for International Development.

Anderson, R. C., & Lohof, A. Q. (1997). *The United States Experience with Economic Incentives in Environmental Pollution Control Policy* (Policy Evaluation Report No. EE-0216A). Washington, D.C.: Environmental Law Institute (in cooperation with U.S. EPA).

Arora, S., & Cason, T. N. (1995). An experiment in voluntary environmental regulation: Participation in EPA's 33/50 program. *Journal of Environmental Economics and Management, 28*(3), 271-286.

Barth, M. E., & McNichols, M. F. (1994). Estimation and market valuation of environmental liabilities relating to Superfund sites. *Journal of Accounting Research, 32*(Suppl.), 177-209.

Becker, G. (1968). Crime and punishment: An economic approach. *Journal of Political Economy, 78*, 169-217.

Blacconiere, W. G., & Northcut, W. D. (1997). Environmental information and market reactions to environmental legislation. *Journal of Accounting, Auditing and Finance, 12*(2), 149-178.

Coase, R. H. (1960). The problem of social cost. *Journal of Law and Economics, 3*(1), 1-44.

Cohen, M. A. (1998). *Monitoring and Enforcement of Environmental Policy* (Working Paper). Nashville, TN: Owen Graduate School of Management, Vanderbilt University.

Dasgupta, S., Laplante, B., & Mamingi, N. (2001). Pollution and capital markets in developing countries. *Journal of Environmental Economics and Management, 42*, 310-335.

Environment Canada. (2005). *National Pollutant Release Inventory* [Web database]. Retrieved on 18.02.05, from http://www.ec.gc.ca/pdb/npri/npri_home_e.cfm

European Commission. (2004). *The European Pollutant Emission Register* [Web database]. Retrieved on 18.02.05, from http://europa.eu.int/comm/environment/ippc/eper/

Foulon, J., Lanoie, P., & Laplante, B. (2002). Incentives for pollution control: Regulation or information? *Journal of Environmental Economics and Management, 44*, 169-187.

Garber, S., & Hammitt, J. K. (1998). Risk premiums for environmental liabilities: Superfund and the cost of capital. *Journal of Environmental Economics and Management, 36*, 267-294.

Gunningham, N., Philipson, M., & Grabosky, P. (1999). Harnessing third parties as surrogate regulators: Achieving environmental outcomes by alternative means. *Business Strategy and the Environment, 8*, 211-224.

Harrington, W. (1988). Enforcement leverage when penalties are restricted. *Journal of Public Economics, 37*, 29-53.

Hentschel, E., & Randall, A. (2000). An integrated strategy to reduce monitoring and enforcement costs. *Environmental and Resource Economics, 15*, 57-74.

Heyes, A. G. (1998). Making things stick: Enforcement and compliance. *Oxford Review of Economic Policy, 14*(4), 50-63.

Heyes, A. G. (2000). Implementing environmental regulation: Enforcement and compliance. *Journal of Regulatory Economics, 17*(2), 107-129.

Kappas, P. (1998). *Industry Self-regulation and Environmental Protection.* Unpublished Dissertation, University of California, Los Angeles.

Khanna, M., & Damon, L. (1999). EPA's Voluntary 33/50 Program: Impacts on Toxic Releases and Economic Performance of Firms. *Journal of Environmental Economics and Management, 37*(1), 1-25.

Killmer, A. B. (2004). *The Effect of Civil Society Involvement on Regulatory Enforcement & Environmental Outcomes under a Mixed Pollution Prevention Policy.* Unpublished Dissertation, University of California, Santa Barbara.

Konar, S., & Cohen, M. A. (1997). Information as regulation: The effect of community right to know laws on toxic emissions. *Journal of Environmental Economics and Management, 32*, 109-124.

Konar, S., & Cohen, M. A. (2001). Does the market value environmental performance? *Review of Economics and Statistics, 83*(2), 281-309.

Laplante, B., & Rilstone, P. (1996). Environmental inspections and emissions of the pulp and paper industry in Quebec. *Journal of Environmental Economics and Management, 31*, 19-36.

Lübbe-Wolff, G. (2001). Efficient environmental legislation - on different philosophies of pollution control in Europe. *Journal of Environmental Law, 13*(1), 79-87.

Nauman, T. (2003). *El movimiento mexicano a favor del Derecho a la Información* [Web publication]. Retrieved on 18.02.05, from http://www.americaspolicy.org/citizen-action/series/sp-04-rtk.html

Office of Technology Assessment. (1995). *Environmental Policy Tools: A User's Guide* [Web publication]. Retrieved on 18.02.05, from http://www.wws.princeton.edu/~ota/ns20/year_f.html

Presencia Ciudadana. (2004). *Derecho a la Información* [Web site]. Retrieved on 13.02.04, from http://www.presenciaciudadana.org.mx/medio/medio.htm

Shavell, S. (1992). A note on marginal deterrence. *International Review of Law and Economics, 12*(Sept.), 345-355.

Stephan, M. (2002). Environmental information disclosure programs: They work, but why? *Social Science Quarterly, 83*(1), 190-205.

Stigler, G. J. (1970). The optimum enforcement of laws. *Journal of Political Economy, 78*, 526-536.

Tietenberg, T. (1998). Disclosure strategies for pollution control. *Environmental and Resource Economics, 11*(3-4), 587-602.

Tietenberg, T., & Wheeler, D. (1998). *Empowering the Community: Information Strategies for Pollution Control* (Paper presentation). Airlie House, Virginia: Frontiers of Environmental Economics Conference.

U.S. Congress. (1995). *Environmental Policy Tools: A User's Guide* (Report No. OTA-ENV-634). Washington, D.C.: U.S. Government Printing Office.

World Bank. (2000). *Greening Industry: New Roles for Communities, Markets, and Governments.* New York: Oxford University Press.

World Bank. (2003). *World Development Report 2003: Sustainable Development in a Dynamic World.* New York: World Bank and Oxford University Press.

Incentives for Pollution Control: Regulation or Information?

Jérôme Foulon, Paul Lanoie, and Benoît Laplante

44 Journal of Environmental Economics and Management 169 (2002)

1. INTRODUCTION

It has long been recognized that the implementation of environmental laws, regulations, and standards has suffered from a lack of resources to undertake appropriate monitoring activities and reluctance to use stringent enforcement actions toward those recalcitrant polluters.[2] In view of those difficulties, an increasing number of environmental regulators around the world have sought to complement or supplement traditional enforcement actions (fines and penalties) with the adoption of *structured* information programs (or public disclosure programs) by which the environmental performance of polluters is revealed.[3]...

Since July 1990, the Ministry of Environment, Lands, and Parks of British Columbia, Canada (henceforth MOE), publishes twice a year a list of firms that either do not comply with the existing regulation or whose environmental performance is of concern to the MOE. The publication of these lists has in fact been noticed by the community and the market.

---

[2] We define monitoring as the process of verifying the firm's status of environmental performance (e.g., compliance with standards) and enforcement as the undertaking of actions (e.g., fines and penalties) to bring the firm to improve its environmental performance.

[3] Examples of such programs now abound in both developed (e.g., the Toxics Release Inventory in the United States) and developing countries (e.g., the ECOWATCH program in the Philippines).

Lanoie *et al.* [21] present evidence that firms appearing on the lists have seen their stock value significantly reduced after the announcement. Simultaneously, however, the Ministry continues to undertake legal action for those violating the regulation. These unique features allow us to analyze the relative contribution of both types of enforcement actions on the performance of polluters. To do so, we focus on the environmental performance of the pulp and paper plants appearing on the list. Our results provide some evidence that the public disclosure strategy adopted by the province of British Columbia has a larger impact on both emissions levels and compliance status than orders, fines, and penalties traditionally imposed by the MOE and courts. Hence, important reductions in pollution emissions can be obtained at little additional costs: by releasing the information instead of keeping the same information in the sole hands of the environmental regulators. ... Our results ... show that the adoption of stricter standards and higher penalties had a significant impact on emissions levels.

2.   CONTEXT AND MODEL

2.1.   *Context*

Industry and regulatory context. Canada is the largest producer of pulp and paper in the world with approximately 33% of world production. Within Canada, the 23 pulp and paper plants located in British Columbia account for approximately 30% of the Canadian production, with 6.5 million tons of pulp and 1.5 million tons of paper produced in 1992. ...The washing and bleaching steps of the [pulp] production process are important sources of pollution: washing produces large amount of biological oxygen demand (BOD) and total suspended solids (TSS), while bleaching further produces dioxins and furans.[9]...

British Columbia's list of polluters. On July 13, 1990, the MOE released for the first time (in British Columbia and in Canada) a list of industrial operations (and municipalities) which were either not complying with their waste management permits (Part I) or deemed by the Ministry to be a potential pollution concern (Part II). ...

In order to be listed in the *non-compliance* section of the list, a firm must be *significantly* out of compliance with its permit requirements and

---

[9] See Environment Canada [10] for more details.

standards. Typical entries (reasons) in this section of the list are of the following nature:

- exceeded permit limits for TSS in July, August, and September;

- exceeded permit limits for maximum and average total suspended solids in October, for BOD 3 of 13 days in November, and for pH 2 days in December;

- incomplete submission of monitoring data....

3.   ESTIMATION STRATEGY AND DATA SET

For the purpose of our empirical analysis, we use plant-level annual data from the pulp and paper industry since this industry has a long history of environmental regulation and generally offers the best availability of emissions data.[18]

Over the period 1987–1996, 24 pulp and paper plants were in operation in British Columbia. After discussion with the MOE, 4 plants were excluded since their manufacturing processes were hardly comparable with those of the other plants. Five other plants were dropped since MOE's files were incomplete, especially over the period 1987–1990. ...

The analysis is performed for both BOD and TSS. For each of them, we use two different ways of defining the dependent variable: the absolute level of pollution (ABSBOD, ABSTSS) and a measure of the level of compliance with the emissions standards (COMPBOD, COMPTSS), defined as

(actual emissions – allowable emissions)/allowable emissions.[19]

Observe in Fig. 2 that emissions levels fell considerably over the period of analysis and that compliance rate significantly improved. ...

---

[18] Magat and Viscusi [24], Laplante and Rilstone [23], Nadeau [26], Dion *et al.* [8], and Lanoie *et al.* [22] also use the pulp and paper industry for a similar reason.
[19] Allowable emissions (kg/day) are calculated as emissions standards (kg/ton) times daily production (ton/day).

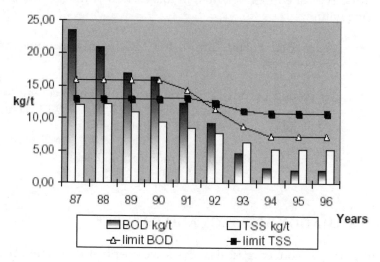

FIG. 2. Actual emissions and limits.

4. EMPIRICAL RESULTS

...

The significance of the contemporaneous *out of compliance* variable and not of the lagged variable is not necessarily surprising given that two lists are published each year (in some years, the first list was published in January). The appearance on the list under the heading of concern seems to have no impact on pollution (except for the TSS compliance rate when the contemporaneous of concern variable is used), which may suggest that the MOE was correct to eliminate this category in 1994.

The variable capturing the major change in regulation regul90 is almost everywhere negative and significant. The impact of this new regulation is strong: improvement in the compliance rate of around 0.160 for BOD and 0.08 for TSS and reduction of the level of emissions in the range of 3600–4640 kg/day for BOD and 1330–1945 kg/day for TSS.

As discussed earlier, the introduction of lower (more stringent) emissions standards leads to an increase in the expected probability of being caught in noncompliance with the negative consequences that may follow for firms. This, with a significant increase in the maximum penalty, partly explain the plants' reaction to the new regulation. As shown in Fig. 2, plants had a better rate of compliance at the end of the period with stricter limits than at the beginning of the period where limits were less stringent. As discussed above, with the new limits, all firms had to be equipped with "state-of-the-art" abatement technologies (secondary treatment).

Prosecutions have no impact on either types of pollutants, while fines (both contemporaneous and lagged) lead to an improvement in the BOD absolute levels in the range of 1600–1900 kg/day.[24] It is instructive to compare the magnitude of the impact of fines versus the impact of the lists. Three observations can be made.

First, the appearance on the out of compliance list seems to have an impact on both types of pollutants, each one of them expressed either in absolute terms or in terms of compliance rate. On the other hand, fines have an effect only on the BOD absolute levels. Second, when the coefficients are comparable (in the BOD absolute levels equations using contemporaneous policy variables ...), the coefficients on the FINE variable are larger than those of the out of compliance, but not significantly... . Third, the fact that it is only the contemporaneous out of compliance variable that is significant (not the lagged) may suggest that the lists of polluters can provide a stronger incentive than conventional enforcement measures for a quick response to correct a damageable situation. Firms may thus give greater weight to the potential financial impact of a negative public image than fines. Altogether, these three observations suggest that MOE's lists could have had a relatively stronger impact than the fines as they were applied. ...

The production level has a positive impact on the absolute level of TSS emissions. ... However, this effect is not appearing with BOD; in fact, it turns out that production has a negative impact on the BOD compliance rate. ... This result suggests that larger firms may be able to comply more easily with the BOD regulation for reasons like the existence of economies of scale in the abatement technology.[26]

The *localization* variables are rarely significant for BOD, while many of them are significant in the regressions related to TSS. Last, the coefficients

---

[24] Note that this result is significant at 10% in specifications (5) and (6) where the contemporaneous variable is used. In the TSS equations, only lagged fine is significant in the last specification (16).

[26] Similar results were observed in Lanoie et al. [22].

of our process variable are everywhere positive, and they tend to be more significant in the BOD regressions than in the TSS. This shows that, as expected, the use of the kraft process leads to lower compliance rates and higher absolute levels of emissions.

5. CONCLUSION

This paper has examined the relative impact of both traditional enforcement practices and information strategies on pollution levels and rates of compliance. The analysis was performed in the context of British Columbia where the MOE publishes, since 1990, a list of firms that either do not comply with the existing regulation or are of concern to the MOE, and where simultaneously the Ministry continues to undertake legal action for those violating the regulation. The empirical investigation was based on a sample covering 15 plants in the pulp and paper industry over the period 1987–1996. Two types of pollutants were considered: BOD and TSS. Our results showed that a tightening up of the standards in 1990 had a very significant impact on plants' environmental performance and that appearances on polluters' list led plants to improve their environmental performance. Furthermore, we provided some evidence that the impact of appearing on the polluters' list was relatively stronger than that of fines.

Our analysis suggests that, although useful, information strategies cannot necessarily replace traditional enforcement practices in the area of environmental protection. In fact, these two approaches can be perhaps better used as complementary policy instruments in order to achieve improvements in firms' environmental performance. This way of proceeding presents the advantage of putting different types of pressure (reputational, financial, judiciary) on firms, increasing the likelihood that they will undertake actions in line with environmental protection.

While it is not feasible to assess completely the costs and benefits of the public disclosure program, it is important to note that the information presented in the lists published in British Columbia is information that is currently collected in the context of the existing monitoring program. Hence, the lists do not necessitate the collection of additional information, but simply require that the same information be used differently: instead of being solely in the hands of the environmental regulator, the information is disclosed. The results obtained in this paper suggest that the incremental cost of making this information public is in all likelihood small relative to the benefits brought upon by the reduction in pollution emissions obtained from such disclosure.

From a policy-making perspective, our analysis thus offers two important results. First, the presence of clear and strong standards accompanied with a significant and credible penalty system does send appropriate signals to the regulated community, which then responds with a lowering of pollution emissions. Second, the public disclosure of environmental performance does create *additional* and *strong* incentives for pollution control. These results do suggest that both traditional enforcement activities *and* information belong to the regulator's arsenal.

REFERENCES

8. C. Dion, P. Lanoie, and B. Laplante, Monitoring of pollution regulation: Do local conditions matter, *J. Regulatory Econ.* **13**, 5–18 (1998).

10. Environment Canada, "The Basic Technology of the Pulp and Paper Industry and Its Environment Protection Practices", Government of Canada, Ottawa (1993)

21. P. Lanoie, B. Laplante, and M. Roy, Can capital markets create incentives for pollution control? *Ecol. Econom.* **26**, 31–41 (1998).

22. P. Lanoie, M. Thomas, and J. Fearnley, Firms responses to effluent regulations: Pulp and paper in Ontario, 1985–1989, *J. Regulatory Econ.* **13**, 103–120 (1998).

23. B. Laplante and P. Rilstone, Environmental inspections and emissions of the pulp and paper industry in Quebec, *J. Environ. Econom. Management* **31**, 19–36 (1996).

24. W. A. Magat and W. K. Viscusi, Effectiveness of the EPA's regulatory enforcement: The case of industrial effluent standards, *J. Law Econ.* **33**, 331–360 (1990).

26. L. W. Nadeau, EPA effectiveness at reducing the duration of plant-level non-compliance, *J. Environ. Econom. Management* **34**, 54–78 (1997).

Regulation in the Information Age: Indonesian Public Information Program for Environmental Management

Shakeb Afsah, Benoît Laplante and David Wheeler

World Bank, New Ideas in Pollution Regulation, (1997).

I. INTRODUCTION

The forces of the "information age" are expected to change our lives, but in ways that are as yet difficult to predict. A salient feature of the new age is far greater capacity to collect, process and disseminate information. This technological change is effectively disintegrating many geographical, political, and organizational boundaries, creating fertile ground for new forms of human organization.

In this paper, we argue that regulation should change fundamentally in the new information age. Governments should allocate fewer resources to setting rules that impose standards of behavior, and more to collecting and disseminating appropriate information. Such information will enable individuals, communities, market agents and regulators to interact in ways which promote socially desirable patterns of production and consumption. This new view of regulation ... puts much more weight on the *process* that leads to efficient levels of consumption and production.

How can this new approach be operationalized? One promising approach is a Public Performance Audit (PPA) System, which analyzes, rates, and publicly discloses the performance of government agencies, public utilities or private firms. Performance indicators, once publicly disclosed, can provide powerful incentives for reducing negative externalities from private activities. Public scrutiny and review also encourage public managers to improve the performance of their agencies. PPA systems can increase both the transparency and accountability of public institutions, and make it feasible for the public to assess the government's use of their taxes.

A well-designed PPA can increase the efficiency of resource allocation by mobilizing the power of reputation to reduce transactions costs and encourage socially-desirable behavior. It can induce improvements from poor performers which would otherwise require costly litigation. Moreover, public recognition can encourage performance which exceeds legally-required standards.

In this paper, we illustrate the PPA concept with a system recently adopted by Indonesia's Environmental Impact Management Agency (BAPEDAL) for controlling industrial pollution. ...

II.   TRADITIONAL REGULATION AND ITS PROBLEMS

...

The debate over *command-and-control* regulation and *market-based instruments* (such as pollution taxes or tradable permits) concerns the proper instrument to achieve the determined target. While regulators have generally preferred the imposition of uniform standards for subgroups of polluters that share certain characteristics, [Note 2] economists have typically advocated instruments which use market forces to induce pollution abatement. Both approaches, however, share a common problem of implementation. *Monitoring* the behavior of polluters and *enforcing* compliance with regulations have proven very difficult in both developed and developing countries. [Note 3] For example, O'Connor (1994) cites the experience of East Asia:

> In several ... countries ... ,[Note 4] the monitoring problem is compounded by weak enforcement. In short, when violators of standards are detected, if penalised at all they often face only weak sanctions. (…) polluters are exempted from fines either on grounds of financial hardship or because the violators wield undue political influence. Perhaps the most pervasive problem is that, even when fines are levied, they are frequently so low in real terms that they have little if any deterrent value.(p.94)

...

III. PUBLIC INFORMATION AND REGULATION

...

While information is posed to play a much broader role than might have been expected even a decade ago, its appearance onstage raises a number of new questions: about the *process* that generates the information used by the regulator to assess environmental performance; the *reliability* of the information that is revealed; and the *nature of the revelation mechanism*. In the next section, we discuss these issues in the context of Indonesia's public disclosure program, which is called PROPER PROKASIH.

IV. PROPER PROKASIH

The monitoring and enforcement of formal regulation in Indonesia is currently weak, and the modest size of BAPEDAL's budget assures that this weakness will persist in the near future. However, manufacturing is growing at over 10% annually, and the Indonesian Government recognizes the mounting risk of severe pollution damage. Under these conditions, the Environment Ministry has decided that a large-scale public disclosure program may induce significant pollution abatement while the formal regulatory system is further developed and strengthened. BAPEDAL hopes that pressure on factories from public disclosure will provide a low-cost substitute for formal enforcement of the regulations, and create incentives for the adoption of cleaner technologies.

NATURE OF THE REVELATION MECHANISM

Since the purpose of PROPER PROKASIH is to publicly reveal the environmental performance of a variety of polluters, the revelation mechanism has been a primary focus of attention. When the program was developed, certain problems had to be confronted. *First*, the grading system adopted by the Agency should accommodate polluters with widely different characteristics. *Second*, the grading system should be simple and its implications easily understood by the public. A few commonly understood categories are easy to process, so it quickly became clear that grading should have a modest number of dimensions. In this context, continuous numerical ratings in many dimensions are generally suboptimal, both because they may not be clearly understood and because their incremental precision does not add value commensurate with the extra costs of providing it. Moreover, categorical ratings (grades) are easily understood because they are omnipresent in public and private evaluation systems. Some grading systems are dichotomous (e.g. pass / fail) while others have several categories (e.g. A, B, C, D, F). *Third*, the grading system should discriminate between firms in compliance with the regulations and those out of compliance. *Finally*, it should provide incentives for firms to comply with the regulations, but also inducements for them to exceed the regulatory requirements. In late 1993, BAPEDAL settled on the five-color scheme shown in Table 1.

Table 1: PROPER PROKASIH's five-color Scheme

Compliance Status	Color Rating	Performance Criteria
Not in Compliance	Black	Polluter makes no effort to control pollution and causes serious environmental damage
	Red	Polluter makes no effort to control pollution but not sufficiently to achieve compliance
In Compliance	Blue	Polluter applies effort sufficient only to meet the standard
	Green	Pollution level is significantly lower than the discharge standards. Polluter also ensures proper disposal of sludge: good housekeeping; accurate pollution records and good maintenance of the waste water treatment system
	Gold	All requirements of Green, plus similar levels of pollution control for air and hazardous waste. Polluter reaches high international standards by making extensive use of clean technology, waste minimization pollution prevention, recycling, etc.

THE EVALUATION PROCESS AND THE RELIABILITY OF INFORMATION

Existing environmental regulations in Indonesia cover hazardous wastes as well as air and water pollution. Their compliance requirements vary by type of polluter, generally classified as industrial or non-industrial, stationary or mobile, and point or non-point source. Regulation of hazardous waste and air pollution is very recent, with a Presidential Decree issued in 1994 for hazardous waste and a 1995 Ministerial Decree specifying air emissions standards for stationary sources. Regulation of water pollution has a significantly longer record of development and implementation experience. A 1991 Ministerial Decree (KEP/MEN/03/

1991) specifies discharge standards, based on pollution loads for fourteen industries. For the remaining industries, Decree KEP/MEN/03/1991 specifies pollution concentration standards which vary according to water quality objectives in the receiving rivers.

Given its relative depth of experience with regulation of water pollution, BAPEDAL decided to focus on compliance with water regulations in the first phase of PROPER. While it had very limited information on air pollution or hazardous waste, the agency had considerable information on industrial water pollution from two sources: its Clean River Program (PROKASIH), which was introduced in 1989, and its regulatory monitoring and enforcement activity (JAGATIRTA) under KEP/MEN/03/1991. Combined with self-monitoring reports from polluters, these information sources were in most cases judged sufficient for a careful compliance assessment in Phase I of PROPER. ... [E]xisting information on polluters was complemented with a survey questionnaire sent to selected polluters, and with an inspection program by BAPEDAL to verify the validity of the data *on site*.

IMPACT OF PROPER PROKASIH

The program was introduced in June 1995 and was extensively covered in the national as well as the international press. In June 1995, five factories were publicly awarded the Green rating (no factories were rated Gold). Since it was the first time that a program of this nature was implemented in Indonesia, the reaction of neighboring communities towards those plants rated Black or Red was unknown. It was therefore decided in June 1995 that only the distribution of the 182 plants across the color scheme would be publicly disclosed. Plants rated Black or Red were privately notified of their ratings and were given until December 1995 to improve their performance before their name and rating be publicly disclosed. As shown in Table 2, the threat of disclosure was sufficient to prompt a group of 10 factories to invest in pollution abatement sufficiently to improve their rating to Red or Blue. We believe that the primary driving force behind these improvements are reputational incentives based on the expectations of strong responses from communities and markets.

Table 2: Impact of PROPER PROKASIH

RATINGS	SHORT-TERM IMPACT			MEDIUM-TERM IMPACT	
	JUN 1995	DEC 1995	% Change	DEC 1995	SEP 1986
Gold	--	--	--	--	--
Green	5	4	--	--	1
Blue	61	72	+ 18%	--	33
Red	115	108	-6%	115	80
Black	6	3	-50%	5	6

In December 1995, 120 factories were rated Black or Red. As shown in Table 2, by September 1996, 34 of these factories had progressed to Blue or Green increasing the compliance rate by nearly 29%. The reaction of plants between June 1995 and September 1996 provides strong evidence that PROPER is creating incentives for pollution control in Indonesia. While reputational incentives are obviously at work, it is interesting to note that in several cases, PROPER became the means by which owners of factories became aware of the environmental performance of their factories. Direct consultations that BAPEDAL had with owners of factories revealed that PROPER has an educational function by increasing the awareness level of employees and employers' about the regulations and their environmental performance.

It is also very interesting to note that the number of factories that volunteered their participation in PROPER increased from 11 in June 1995 to 23 by December 1995. As would be expected, we find that volunteers have on average a superior environmental performance than nonvolunteers. Clearly, these factories saw some positive values from their environmental performance being publicly disclosed. Finally, we have anecdotal evidence that financial markets may create incentives for pollution control. In mid-1995, a factory wanted its shares to be traded on the stock market but was deeply concerned about the impact of its poor rating on the value of its shares. Within a period of 3 months, the firm invested in pollution control equipment, achieved a Blue rating, and then went public.

PROPER also has an important impact on BAPEDAL itself. In particular, the need for accuracy in the ratings has compelled BAPEDAL to increase the number of inspections it is conducting, and improve the quality and reliability of the data it is collecting. Moreover, the database provided through PROPER is currently used to identify priorities of action. The information collected trough PROPER also provides BAPEDAL with solid evidence of a factory's compliance status and can support stronger enforcement actions if desired.

V. CONCLUSIONS

A new approach to regulation in Indonesia is showing that local communities and market forces can be powerful allies in the struggle against excessive industrial pollution. PROPER's ratings are designed to reward good performance and call public attention to polluters who are not in compliance with the regulations. Armed with this information, local communities can negotiate better environmental arrangements with neighboring factories; firms with good performance can advertise their status and earn market rewards from their performance; investors can accurately assess environmental liabilities; and regulators can focus their limited resources on the worst performers. Moreover, transparency is increased because the environmental agency itself is opened to public scrutiny. By committing itself to a public disclosure strategy, it chooses to reveal its own ability to process information reliably and enforce the existing regulations.

During its first two years of operation, PROPER has proven quite effective in moving poor performers toward compliance, and motivating some firms to pursue higher ratings by abating beyond the requirements and investing in pollution prevention. Undeniably, public information is having an important impact on industrial pollution control in Indonesia. Inspired by this example of public information in action, the governments of Philippines, Colombia, Mexico and Brazil are now moving rapidly toward developing their own public disclosure programs.

To conclude, we must rethink the regulator's role in pollution management once we recognize that local communities, consumers, and investors may all provide incentives for pollution control if empowered to do so. In the information age, the regulator's role is no longer confined to producing and policing rules and standards. Instead, the regulator can gain important leverage through programs such as public disclosure, which harness the power of communities and markets. A broader implication is that one size no longer "fits all" for regulatory policy design. Optimal combinations of regulatory tools, including new information strategies, will depend on country specific social, economic and institutional conditions.

REFERENCES

Afsah, S. and D. Wheeler (1996), "Indonesia's new pollution control program: using public pressure to get compliance", **East Asian Executive Reports**, 18, 6, 9-12.

Canada (1988), Prosecutions Under the Pollution Control and Habitat Protection Provisions of the Fisheries Act, Fisheries pollution reports, Volume 4, Environment Canada and Fisheries and Oceans Canada, Ottawa, Ontario.

Deily, M.E. and W.B. Gray (1991), "Enforcement of pollution regulations in a declining industry", **Journal of Environmental Economics and Management**, 21, 260-274.

Environmental Protection Agency (1991), "Environmental education", **EPA Journal**, 17, 4.

Hamilton, J.T. (1995), "Pollution as news: media and stock market reactions to the Toxic Release Inventory data", **Journal of Environmental Economics and Management**, 98-103.

Hettige, M. and D. Witzel (1996), *Pollution Control Priorities for Mexico*, World Bank, Policy Research Department, Washington, D.C. (mimeo).

Hettige, M., Pargal, S., Singh, M. and D. Wheeler (1996) *Formal and Informal Regulation of Industrial Pollution: Comparative Evidence from Indonesia and the US*, World Bank, Policy Research Department, Washington, D.C. (mimeo).

Konar, S. and M. A. Cohen (1997), "Information as regulation: the effect of community right to know laws on toxic emissions", **Journal of Environmental Economics and Management**, 32, 1, 109-124.

Lanoie, P. and B. Laplante (1994), "The market response to environmental incidents in Canada: a theoretical and empirical analysis", **Southern Economic Journal**, 60, 657-672.

Lanoie, P., Laplante, B. and M. Roy (1997), *Can Capital Markets Create Incentives for Pollution Control?*, World Bank, Policy Research Department, Washington D.C. (mimeo).

Magat, W.A. and W.K. Viscusi (1990), "Effectiveness of the EPA's regulatory enforcement: The case of industrial effluent standards", **Journal of Law & Economics**, 33, 331-60.

Muoghalu, Michael I., Robison, H. David and John L. Glascock (1990), "Hazardous waste lawsuits, stockholder returns, and deterrence", **Southern Economic Journal**, October 1990, 357-70.

O'Connor, D. (1994), *Managing the Environment with Rapid Industrialisation: Lessons from the East Asian Experience*, Development Centre of the Organisation for Economic Cooperation and Development, Paris.

Pargal, S., and D. Wheeler (1996), "Informal regulation in developing countries: evidence from Indonesia," **Journal of Political Economy, December**

Russell, Clifford S. (1990), "Monitoring and enforcement", in *Public Policies for Environmental Protection*, edited by P. R. Portney, Washington D.C.: Resources for the Future, pp. 243-74.

Wheeler, D. and D. Witzel (1996), *Development, Regulation and the Fate of Sepetiba Bay*, World Bank, Policy Research Department, Washington, D.C. (mimeo).

END NOTES

[Note 2] For example, pollution standards are typically defined for a group of plants belonging to the same industrial sector.

[Note 3] We define monitoring as the set of activities aimed at verifying the regulatory compliance of a specific polluter. Among others, these activities include inspections of a polluter's facilities and effluent sampling (see Magat and Viscusi (1990) for a description of the various types of inspections undertaken by the US Environmental Protection Agency). We define enforcement as the set of actions which penalize non-compliance with regulations. Monitoring and enforcement together determine a polluter's expected penalty for non-compliance. A profit-maximizing firm will compare this expected penalty with the expected cost of abating pollution to determine the most profitable level of pollution control.

[Note 4] The countries studied are Japan, Korea, Taiwan, Thailand, and Indonesia.

Public Ratings of Industry's Environmental Performance: China's Greenwatch Program

Hua Wang, Jinnan Bi, David Wheeler, Jinnan Wang, Dong Cao, Genfa Lu, and Yuan Wang

6TH INECE CONFERENCE PROCEEDINGS, VOL. 2 (2002).

...

2. PUBLIC DISCLOSURE: THE "THIRD WAVE" OF ENVIRONMENTAL REGULATION

[R]ecent research suggests that public information about polluters can operate effectively through community and market channels that compliment the effect of formal regulation. During the past decade, a number of regulatory initiatives have attempted to exploit this potential to reduce pollution. In many cases, such programs have focused on toxic pollutants that are not covered by conventional regulation. Examples include the US Toxic Release Inventory; Canada's National Pollutant Release Inventory; the UK's Pollutant Inventory; Australia's National Pollutant Inventory (Tietenberg and Wheeler, 2001); and UN-sponsored Pollutant Release and Transfer Registers in Mexico, Egypt and the Czech Republic. Recently the public disclosure approach has also been applied to water pollutants in Canada, Indonesia and Philippines, with similar programs planned in India, Thailand and Vietnam. China's pilot disclosure programs are unique in breadth, since they cover all major air, water and toxic pollutants.

3. INDUSTRIAL POLLUTION CONTROL IN CHINA

3.1 China's Industrial Pollution Problem

China's industrial growth has been extremely rapid during the period of economic reform. In the 1990's, the output of the country's millions of industrial enterprises has increased by more than 15% annually. Industry, China's largest productive sector, accounted for 47% of its gross domestic product and employed 17% of the country's total labor force in 1995. While industry has helped lift tens of millions of people out of poverty, its polluting emissions have also produced serious environmental damage. Recent research (Bolt, et al., 2001) suggests that China's air pollution problem is the worst in the world ... . With over 300,000 premature deaths per year, China accounts for over 40% of the total for the developing world, more than twice the number for South Asia, which has a comparable population. Similar percentages characterize other measures of health damage. ...

Chinese industry is a primary source of this problem. China's State Environmental Protection Administration (SEPA) estimates that in 1995, industrial pollution accounted for over 70% of the national total, including 70% for organic water pollution (COD, or chemical oxygen demand); 72% for sulfur dioxide emissions; and 75% for flue dust (a major component of suspended particulates).[3] For this reason, SEPA has declared control of industrial pollution to be a top priority for Chinese regulators. During the past decade, conventional regulation has probably saved millions of lives by holding the growth rate of total emissions well below the growth rate of industry (Dasgupta, Wang and Wheeler, 1997). However, the continuing severity of pollution has led the Chinese government to experiment with public pollution disclosure as a possible compliment to existing measures.

3.2   The Role of Public Disclosure in Chinese Environmental Management

Public disclosure has two potentially important roles to play in China's system of regulating industrial pollution: strengthening of regulatory institutions and encouragement of public participation in regulation. In many cases, Chinese regulators already have the information needed for public rating of environmental performance. Many agencies receive regular, facility-level reports on EIA status, emissions, pollution control investments, field inspections and accidents. Some measures are explicitly tied to public participation. For example, EIA reports must include strong evidence of participation in project assessment by affected local communities. However, public disclosure also significantly raises the ante by pressuring regulators toward more accurate and timely record keeping. With its credibility on the line in a disclosure program, a regulatory agency has a strong incentive to maintain high internal standards. This is particularly true for emissions monitoring, which provides the foundation for an environmental performance rating system.

Performance-based ratings also provide a valuable environmental management tool for enterprises, which in many cases have never undertaken a comprehensive assessment of their environmental performance.

The experiences of Hohhot Municipality and Zhenjiang City suggest that disclosure also changes the balance of environmental initiative between the private and public sectors. Prior to disclosure, enterprises in both areas generally resisted regulators' attempts to monitor them more closely. After disclosure attracted wide-spread publicity through the news media, however, companies perceived an impact on their public image and the market image of their products. Enterprises that improved their performance immediately requested new monitoring reports so that their public ratings could be improved as well. Enterprises with poor ratings shifted from passive resistance to active solicitation of inspections, as a means of improving their performance ratings. At the same time, enterprises with good ratings felt continued pressure to maintain their environmental performance to avoid complaints from the public about backsliding. ...

4. PUBLIC DISCLOSURE IN ZHENJIANG

4.1   *Program Design*

Zhenjiang is a city located in Jiangsu Province, a southeast province and one of the richest areas in China. Zhenjiang's disclosure program reflects design principles that have proven successful in previous disclosure programs in Indonesia and the Philippines. First, the performance rating system should be simple and its implications easily understand and accepted by the public. Second, it should provide information on both superior and inferior performance. Finally, the ratings should be published in a form that is easily communicated by the broadcast and print media. All three principles are respected by the 5-color rating system ... of the Zhenjiang Environmental Information Disclosure Program. The system divides industrial firms' environmental performance into five symmetric categorical ratings, with two (black, red) denoting inferior performance; one (yellow) denoting compliance with national regulations but failure to comply with stricter local requirements; and two ratings (blue, green) denoting superior performance. Because it recognizes three performance levels for firms that comply with national regulations, the system provides incentives for continuous improvement. Even for non-compliant firms, the system rewards efforts to improve by recognizing two levels of performance. ...

4.2   Ratings Dimensions

The program's color-coded ratings are generated by a detailed accounting of environmental performance … . The ratings system draws on four principle sources of information: reports on industrial firms' polluting emissions; inspection reports on their environmental management; records of public complaints, regulatory actions and penalties; and surveys that record characteristics of the firms that are relevant for rating environmental performance.

4.2.1   <u>Compliance with Regulations</u>

The rating system incorporates six dimensions of environmental pollution: water, air, noise, solid waste, electromagnetic radiation, and radioactive contamination. It includes emissions information for 13 regulated air and water pollutants: chemical oxygen demand, suspended solids, oil, volatile hydroxybenzene, chromium, cyanide, lead, arsenic, mercury, cadmium, flue dust, industrial dust and sulfur dioxide. Pollutant discharges are rated by total quantity and concentration. Solid wastes are rated in three dimensions: production, disposal, and recycling.

4.2.2   <u>Management behavior</u>

This element involves a detailed accounting of behavior in several dimensions. Environmental management effort is graded with respect to: timely payment of pollution discharge fees; implementation of the national Pollutant Discharge Reporting and Registering Program, the Standardized Waste Management Measure, and the Three Synchronizations Program[4]; and variables related to internal environmental monitoring, staff training, and internal document preparation. In addition, the rating system considers the firm's efficiency of resource use; its technological level (e.g., implementation of the national Cleaner Production Audit Program"); and the quality of its environmental management system.

4.2.3   <u>Social impact</u>

Indicators in this category include the firm's record with respect to public complaints, pollution accidents, illegal pollution, and administrative penalties.

4.3   Ratings Construction

The Zhenjiang rating system uses a series of yes/no questions to translate its multidimensional performance indicators into 5 color codes. ... The first stage of the process involves selection of industrial firms for rating. Plants that volunteer are automatically included, while the rest are firms classified as large on the basis of plant size, production value and reported pollution discharge load. In the second stage, the Zhenjiang Environmental Protection Bureau uses its own records to develop information on the firms' polluting emissions. The Environmental Protection Bureau also surveys the firms to gather information for the indicators of management behavior and social impacts.

A distinctive feature of the ratings process is its "Inform-Respond-Check-Disclose" reciprocal mechanism, in which industrial firms can exchange comments about their ratings with the Environmental Protection Bureau prior to disclosure. By reconsidering and rechecking at the firms request, the Environmental Protection Bureau encourages (but is not required to gain) their acceptance of the final ratings, as well as promoting a more detailed environmental accounting by the firms themselves. After setting the ratings, the Environmental Protection Bureau sends them to the program's Steering Board for final checking and ratification prior to public disclosure. The deputy mayor in charge of environmental protection leads the Steering Board, and its members come from the Environmental Protection Bureau and other relevant administrative departments and institutions. Its main responsibility is to ratify the ratings and transmit them to the firms and the news media. To ensure accurate press reports, the Environmental Protection Bureau invites reporters to a detailed presentation of the program, including an explanation of the rating system and a demonstration of the computer program that is used for ratings development.

4.4   The Experience of Public Disclosure in Zhenjiang

4.4.1   Pilot Disclosure

The pilot program began in June, 1999, with selection and rating of 101 firms drawn from several industry sectors ... . During the pilot phase, the Zhenjiang Environmental Protection Bureau regularly reported its progress to the municipal government and the media. The firms were informed of their pilot ratings in 1998. Ten firms were delisted during this initial period because of data quality, leaving 91 firms for disclosure.

The latter accounted for 95% of polluting emissions in Zhenjiang, as well as 65% of the city's economic output.

Their pilot ratings … indicated widespread deficiencies, with 69% of the firms rated as Yellow, Red or Black. However, 31% demonstrated superior performance even in the pilot disclosure period, and a few even earned the highest (Green) rating.

4.4.2   Public Disclosure

In May, 2000, the Zhenjiang municipal government officially recognized the program and issued a formal "Notice of Implementation of the Environmental Information Program in Zhenjiang City." The municipal government also presided over the first disclosure at a press conference on July 26th, 2000. Other participants included representatives of all 91 rated firms, the Program Steering Board, and deputies from the Jiangsu Province Environmental Protection Bureau and the Environmental Protection Bureaus of other cities in Jiangsu. The Steering Board publicly released the ratings, and the firms' representatives accepted and commented on them. For several days after the press conference, local newspapers and TV stations continually reported the event, the results of the first disclosure, and promises by poorly-rated firms to improve their environmental performance.

The results show that many firms chose to improve their environmental performance during the one-year grace period between pilot disclosure and public disclosure. The number of superior performers doubled, from 31% of the rated firms to 62% … . The pressure from public disclosure clearly reinforced another program, "One Control and Double Attainments (OCDA)", that was implemented in Zhenjiang during the period 1998-2000. The objectives of the latter program were total emissions within permitted limits and full compliance with local and national standards by enterprises in Zhenjiang City

Industrial environmental performance in Zhenjiang improved significantly after combined implementation of OCDA and public disclosure. As a result, the disclosure program Steering Board announced its support for annual disclosures.

5. PUBLIC DISCLOSURE IN HOHHOT

5.1   Program Design

Hohhot is a city located in Inner Mongolia Autonomous District, a northern and poor area of China. The Hohhot public disclosure program focused on firms that met three criteria: major contributions to local pollution; management with some independence of action; and possible susceptibility to public pressure for improvement. To maximize the incentive effects of disclosure, the ratings standards were set to reveal a broad distribution of relative environmental performance in Hohhot.

5.2   Ratings Dimensions

Hohhot chose the same color rating categories as Zhenjiang, ranging from green (best performance) through blue, yellow and red, to black (worst performance). ...

5.3   Ratings Construction

In Hohhot, development of the ratings system proceeded in parallel with a series of meetings to build support for the concept from government agencies, the general public and the affected industry sectors. The assessment work utilized the data collected by the Environmental Supervision Station of Hohhot City for the year 1999. Ratings were developed during the period December, 1998 to December, 1999, and several review meetings were conducted prior to official disclosure in March, 2000. As in Zhenjiang, a pilot ratings exercise was undertaken in consultation with affected enterprises before the ratings were disclosed to the public.

5.4   The Experience of Public Disclosure in Hohhot

On March 24, 2000, the Hohhot City government convened a news conference to disclose the environmental performance ratings to the public. Participants included the program development team, other government agencies, representatives from China's State Environmental Protection Administration (SEPA), and representatives from the 56 industrial enterprises and 51 other institutions that were rated. Media participants included Inner Mongolia TV, Hohhot City Economic TV, The Hohhot Daily, The Inner Mongolia Daily, The Hohhot Evening News, Hohhot People's Radio, and the Hohhot Journalist Station for China's

Environmental Daily. Broadcast news programs featured stories about the disclosure for several days after the event.

As in the case of Zhenjiang, the evidence suggests that many polluters responded to the combined effect of pilot and public disclosure. After public disclosure, large, persistent polluters such as the Hohhot Power Plant and the Hohhot Cement Mill repeatedly sent deputies to the Hohhot Environmental Protection Bureaus to promise that they would increase pollution control to improve their ratings. [T]he 56 industrial enterprises rated in Hohhot greatly improved their environmental performance during the period 1999-2000. Enterprises rated Good or better increased from 24% to 62%, and enterprises in the worst (Black) category decreased from 11% to 5%. As in Zhenjiang, this improvement undoubtedly reflects pressure from both the OCDA and public disclosure programs.

6. LESSONS LEARNED

Experiments with public pollution disclosure continue to expand in China. After observing the results in Hohhot and Zhenjiang, the Environmental Protection Bureau of Jiangsu Province has decided to implement disclosure in its 13 municipalities in the next a couple of years. The evidence to date suggests that public disclosure of environmental performance will be an important new component of China's system for regulating pollution. Implementation should be feasible in most of China, because technical and design issues are not overly complex. The knowledge and expertise needed for a disclosure program are available in almost every city of China. With support from a national coordination center, there should be no technical barriers to implementation of disclosure in the entire country. The case studies suggest that the costs of design and implementation are not high in China, since most of the necessary information already exists in the records of provincial and local Environmental Protection Bureaus. However, it might well be appropriate for China's highly-varied regions to institute ratings criteria and procedures that reflect their special circumstances.

The Zhenjiang and Hohhot experiences have suggested a number of important lessons for successful implementation of disclosure. The first is that government support and involvement at all levels are critical. The case studies suggest that involvement of local government leaders is particularly important. Since most urban enterprises in China are still state-owned, successful disclosure depends on strong administrative and legal support. In the two case studies, city mayors supported the program after lobbying from the local Environmental Protection Bureau and expressions of support from the central government. Support from the local media was critical, as well as public pressure for a better environment.

Timing is also very important in this context. In both cities, the experience of pilot disclosure suggests that many enterprises will improve their performance prior to public disclosure if they are informed of their ratings and given sufficient time to invest in pollution control. For public disclosure itself, intervals of one year between public ratings may a reasonable balance between the loss of public pressure over longer intervals and the higher cost of developing new ratings over shorter intervals. Public disclosure clearly places unprecedented demands on environmental agencies' management information systems. Although there are substantial start-up costs, the agencies realize large long-run gains from much more flexible, current and well-documented information systems. In this dimension, the pressure for improved information management under public disclosure also yields substantial benefits for the information requirements of conventional regulation.

REFERENCES & NOTES

1. While the authors helped design the Greenwatch program in China, those environmental officers in China's State Environmental Protection Administration (SEPA), the Zhenjiang Municipal Environmental Protection Bureau, and the Hohhot Municipal Environmental Protection Bureau played the key roles. Particular thanks are due to SEPA administrator Mr Xie Zhenghua and to colleagues in China including Zhang Liwei, Yu Fei, Zou Shoumin, Zhang Cingfeng, Zhou Guomei, Gao Dong, Yang Jintian, Wang Yuan, Chu Guimin, Cu Xinhua, Yang Yingfeng and Fan Yongying for their support and collaboration. The World Bank's InfoDev Program provided partial financial support for this work. The usual disclaimers apply.
2. For evidence on toxic emissions reduction in the US, see Konar and Cohen (1996) and Tietenberg and Wheeler (2001). The impact of disclosure on two water pollutants (biochemical oxygen demand and suspended solids) has been analyzed for Canada (Foulon, Lanoie and Laplante, 2000), Indonesia (Afsah and Vincent, 1997) and Philippines (World Bank, 1999).

3. Source: Environmental Yearbooks, China's State Environmental Protection Administration.

4. This program's purpose is to ensure that new construction projects include pollution abatement facilities that meet state emission and effluent standards. Under the program, a new industrial enterprise or one that wishes to expand or change its production process must register its plans with the local environmental protection bureau and design (first synchronization), construct (second synchronization), and begin to operate (third synchronization) pollution control facilities simultaneously with the principal part of the enterprise's production activities. S. Afsah, S. and B. Laplante, 1996,"Program-Based Pollution Control Management: The Indonesia Prokasih Program," World Bank, Policy Research Department Working Paper, No. 1602, May.

6. Afsah, S., B. Laplante and D. Wheeler, 1996, "Controlling Industrial Pollution: A New Paradigm", World Bank, Policy Research Working Paper #1672.

7. Afsah, S. and J. Vincent, 1997, "Putting Pressure on Polluters: Indonesia's PROPER Program, A Case Study for the HIID 1997 Asia Environmental Economics Policy Seminar" Harvard Institute for International Development, March.

8. Arbeláez, 1, 5. Dasgupta, B. Laplante and D. Wheeler, 1998, "Colombia's Pollution Charge System: Implementation, Impact and Implications," World Bank, Development Research Group, April.

9. Blackman, A. and G. Bannister, 1998, "Community pressure and clean technology in the informal sector: An econometric analysis of the adoption of propane by traditional Mexican brick makers," Journal of Environmental Economics and Management, 35 (1), 1-21.

10. Blackman, A., S. Afsah and D. Ratunanda, 2000, "How Do Public Disclosure Pollution Control Programs Work? Evidence from Indonesia," Resources for the Future Discussion Paper No. 00-44, October.

11. Bolt, K., S. Dasgupta, K. Pandey and D.Wheeler 2001, "Cleaning the Air in Developing Countries," Forum For Applied Research and Public Policy 2001, Vol. 16, No. 3, Fall.

12. Chow, G., 1983, Econometrics (New York: McGraw-Hill).

13. Coase, R., 1960, "The Problem of Social Cost," The Journal of Law and Economics 3(October), 1-44.

14. Dasgupta, S., M. Huq, D. Wheeler and C. Zhang, "Water Pollution Abatement by Chinese Industry: Cost Estimates and Policy Implications," 2001, Applied Economics, Vol. 33 (4).

15. Dasgupta, S., H. Wang and D. Wheeler 1997, "Surviving Success: Policy Reform and the Future of Industrial Pollution in China," World Bank Policy Research Department Working Paper No. 1856, October

16. Dasgupta, S. and D. Wheeler 1997, "Citizen Complaints as Environmental Indicators: Evidence from China World Bank, Policy Research Department Working Paper No. 1704, January.

17. Dasgupta, S., B. Laplante, H. Wang and D. Wheeler 2001, "Confronting the Environmental Kuznets Curve," Journal of Economic Perspectives, Vol. 15, No.4, Fall.

18. Dasgupta., S., B. Laplante and N. Mamingi, 2001, "Pollution and Capital Markets in Developing Countries," Journal of Environmental Economics and Management, 0 (0), 1-26.

19. Dasgupta, S., B. Laplante, N. Mamingi and H. Wang, 2000, "Industrial Environmental Performance in China: The Impact of Inspections," World Bank Development Research Group Working Paper No. 2285, February.

20. Foulon, J., R Lanoie and B. Laplante, 2000, "Incentives for Pollution Control: Regulation and (?) or (?) Information," World Bank Development Research Group Working Paper No. 2291, February.

21. Hahn, R., 1989, "Economic Prescriptions for Environmental Problems: How the Patient Followed the Doctor's Orders," The Journal of Economic Perspectives, 3(2), 95-114.

22. Hamilton, J., 1995, "Pollution as News: Media   and   Stock market Reactions to the Toxics Release Data," Journal of Environmental Economics and Management, 28(1), 98-113.

23. Hartman, R., D. Wheeler and M. Singh, 1997, "The Cost of Air Pollution Abatement," Applied Economics, 29(6), 759-774.

24. Hartman, R., M. Huq and D. Wheeler 1997, "Why Paper Mills Clean Up: Determinants of Pollution Abatement in Four Asian Countries," World Bank, Policy Research Department Working Paper No. 1710.

25. Hettige, H., M. Huq, S. Pargal and D. Wheeler 1996, "Determinants of Pollution Abatement in Developing Countries: Evidence from South and Southeast Asia," World Development 24 (12), 1891-1904.

26. Hettige, H., S. Dasgupta and D. Wheeler 2000, "What Improves Environmental Compliance? Evidence from Mexican Industry," Journal of Environmental Economics and Management," 39 (1), 39-66.

27. Huq, M. and D. Wheeler 1992, "Pollution Reduction Without Formal Regulation: Evidence from Bangladesh," World Bank Environment Department Working Paper No. 1993- 39.

28. Jha, V., A. Markandya, and R. Vossenaar 1999, Reconciling Trade and the Environment. Lessons from Case Studies in Developing Countries, (Edward Elgar: Cheltenham, UK and Lyme, US).

29. Khalid, R., and J. Braden, 1993, "Welfare Effects of Environmental Regulation in an Open Economy: The Case of Malaysian Palm Oil," Journal of Agricultural Economics, 44, 25-37.

30. Klassen, R. and C. McLaughlin, 1996, "The Impact of Environmental Management on Firm Performance,"Management Science, 42(8), 1199-1214.

31. Konar S. and M. Cohen, 1996, "Information as regulation: The effect of community right to know laws on toxic emission," Journal of Environmental Economics and Management, 32, 109-124.

32. Lanoie, R and B. Laplante, 1994, "The Market Response to Environmental Incidents in Canada: a Theoretical and Empirical Analysis," Southern Economic Journal, Vol. 60.

33. Lanoie, R, B. Laplante and M. Roy, 1997, "Can Capital Markets Create Incentives for Pollution Control?" Ecological Economics, 26, 31-41.

34. Martin, R, H. Hettige, M. Singh and D. Wheeler 1995, "The Industrial Pollution Projection System," World Bank Policy Research Department Working Paper No. 1431, March.

35. Muoghalu, M., D. Robison and J. Glascock, 1990, "Hazardous waste lawsuits, stockholder returns, and deterrence," Southern Economic Journal, 57, 357-70.

36. OECD, 1989, Economic Instruments for Environmental Protection, Paris, Organization for Economic Cooperation and Development.

37. OECD, 1994, Applying Economic Instruments to Environmental Policies in OECD and Dynamic Non-Member Countries, Paris, Organization for Economic Co-operation and Development.

38. OECD, 1995, Environmental Taxes in OECD Countries, Paris, Organization for Economic Co-operation and Development.

39. Pargal, S. and D. Wheeler 1996, "Informal Regulation of Industrial Pollution in Developing Countries: Evidence from Indonesia," Journal of Political Economy, 104(6), 1314+.

40. Tietenberg, I and D. Wheeler 2001, "Empowering the Community: Information Strategies for Pollution Control," in Henk Folmer (ed.), Frontiers of Environmental Economics (Edward Elgar: Cheltenham, UK and Lyme, US).

41. Tietenberg, 1,1998, "Disclosure Strategies for Pollution Control," Environmental and Resource Economics, 11, 587-602.

42. Tietenberg, 1,1990, "Using Economic Incentives to Maintain Our Environment," Challenge, 33(2), 42-46.

43. Tietenberg, 1,1985, Emissions Trading: An Exercise in Reforming Pollution Policy, Washington, DC, Resources for the Future.
44. Vincent, J., 1993, "Reducing Effluent While Raising Affluence: Water Pollution Abatement in Malaysia,"Harvard Institute for International Development, Spring.
45. Wang, Hua, 2000, "Information Approach to Industrial Pollution Control and Its Application in China," China Environmental Sciences, June, 2000.
46. Wang, H. and D. Wheeler 2000, "Endogenous Enforcement and the Effectiveness of China's Pollution Levy System," World Bank, Development Research Group Working Paper No. 2336, May
47. World Bank, 1999, Greening Industry: New Roles for Communities, Markets and Governments, (New York: Oxford/World Bank).

Pollution and Capital Markets in Developing Countries

Susmita Dasgupta, Benoit Laplante and Nlandu Mamingi

42 JOURNAL OF ENVIRONMENTAL ECONOMICS AND MANAGEMENT 310 (2001)

...

1. INTRODUCTION

Though environmental regulations have been in use now for approximately 30 years, it is generally recognized that their efficacy in controlling pollution emissions has been dampened by a lack of appropriate monitoring and enforcement.[3]

Resources devoted to the monitoring of standards have typically been characterized as insufficient.[4] Moreover, when compliance with the standards is found to be lacking, it is generally acknowledged that fines and penalties are too low to act as effective deterrents. In a recent study of environmental regulations in East Asian countries, O'Connor (19) writes:

> In several of the countries studied here,[5] the monitoring problem is compounded by weak enforcement. In short, when violators of standards are detected, if penalised at

---

[3] We define monitoring as the process of verifying the firm's status of environmental performance (e.g., compliance), and enforcement as the undertaking of actions (e.g., fines) to bring the firm to improve its environmental performance (e.g., comply with environmental standards).

[4] See Russell 22 . On the impact of monitoring on environmental performance, see 14, 16, and 18.

[5] The countries studied are Japan, Korea, Taiwan, Thailand, and Indonesia.

> all they often face only weak sanctions. (...) polluters are exempted from fines either on grounds of financial hardship or because the violators wield undue political influence. Perhaps the most pervasive problem is that, even when fines are levied, they are frequently so low in real terms that they have little if any deterrent value. In virtually all the countries studied, there remains considerable room for improvement on the enforcement front. (p. 94)

It is indeed generally said that firms in developing countries do not have incentives to invest in pollution control effort because of weak implementation of environmental regulation: compliance costs exceed expected benefits. However, this argument assumes that the environmental regulator is the only agent that can penalize firms lacking pollution control effort. Recent research indicates that local communities may exercise considerable leverage to pressure firms to improve their environmental performance.[6] The argument also ignores that capital markets may react *negatively* to the announcement of adverse environmental incidents (such as violation of permits, spills, court actions, complaints) or *positively* to the announcement of superior environmental performance. When accounting solely for regulators' fines and penalties and ignoring the costs that may be imposed by communities and markets, the expected costs associated with poor environmental performance may be significantly underestimated. Hence, the inability of formal institutions, especially in developing countries, to provide incentives for pollution control effort via the traditional channel of fines and penalties may not be as serious an impediment to pollution control as is generally argued. Communities and capital markets, if properly informed, may in specific circumstances provide the appropriate reputational and financial incentives.

A limited number of papers have analyzed the reaction of capital markets to environmental news in Canada and the United States. These studies have generally shown that firms suffer from a decline in market value upon announcement of adverse environmental news.[7] The impact of firm-

---

[6] See [1], [2], and [20].

[7] In the United States, these studies include, among others, analysis of the reaction of markets to releases of the *Toxics Release Inventory* [6], [11]. Lanoie and Laplante [12] analyze the reaction of capital markets to environmental news in Canada. For a survey of these studies, see [13].

specific environmental news on market value may work its way through various channels: a high level of pollution intensity may signal to investors the inefficiency of a firm's production process; it may invite stricter scrutiny by environmental groups and/or facility neighbors; or it may result in the loss of reputation, goodwill, and the like. On the other hand, the announcement of a good environmental performance or of the investment in cleaner technologies may have the opposite effect: lesser scrutiny by regulators and communities (including the financial community) and greater access to international markets, among other things.[8]

In this paper, we assess whether or not capital markets in Argentina, Chile, Mexico, and the Philippines react to the announcement of firm-specific environmental news. To our knowledge, the current analysis is the first of this nature performed in developing countries. This is potentially important from a policy perspective since it is not immediately clear that capital markets in these countries are developed enough to replicate the results observed in Canada and the United States. We show that capital markets react negatively (decrease in firms' value) to citizens' complaints targeted at specific firms. We also show that markets react positively (increase in firms' market value) to the announcement of rewards and explicit recognition of superior environmental performance. A policy implication from the current analysis is that environmental regulators in developing countries may explicitly harness those market forces by introducing structured programs of information release on firms' environmental performance, and empower communities and stakeholders through environmental education programs.[9]

These results may also shed some new light on the pollution haven hypothesis. A number of studies have examined the impact of environmental regulations on international competitiveness.[10] Many of these have concluded that pollution-intensive firms have not relocated in developing countries to benefit from lower environmental standards and/or poor enforcement of environmental regulations. Hettige *et al.* [8] observe that "one possibility is that the expected profitability of investment in pollution-intensive sectors has also been affected by

---

[8] See [21] and [11] for a more detailed discussion.
[9] We know of at least two such programs currently in place in developing countries: in Indonesia (PROPER Prokasih) and the Philippines (Ecowatch). Similar programs are currently being developed in Mexico and Colombia.
[10] See [9] and references therein.

growing concern over legal liability or reputational damage" (p. 480). Our results suggest that at least in the specific cases of publicly traded companies, the benefits associated with poor traditional enforcement of environmental compliance may have been significantly overestimated. In the next section, we describe our dataset. In Section 3, we briefly describe the event-study methodology used to measure the reaction of capital markets to environmental news (both positive and negative news). Results are presented in Section 4. We conclude in Section 5.

2.   DATASET

For each country retained in this analysis – Argentina, Chile, Mexico, and the Philippines – we selected a newspaper which has a large circulation and is of particular interest to the business community.[11] Environmental news was collected in each of the countries over the period 1990-1994 inclusively. Once these news items were collected, we identified those involving firms traded in local capital markets. ... The number of environmental news (i.e., newsclips) collected in each country is relatively large (a total of 7354 environmental news was collected over the period 1990-1994), with Mexico alone representing 47.5% of the total number of news. The number of environmental news events slightly declined over the period of analysis.[12] Approximately 20% of the news involves specific firms, traded and nontraded. As expected, the number of news involving publicly traded companies is relatively small in all countries, though large relative to their number in the economy. This may be explained by their generally greater visibility.

Environmental news was divided into two groups: positive (e.g., rewards, investment in pollution control), and negative (e.g., spills, complaints, warnings). The sample set is described in Table II. As can be observed, Chile registered 53 events (environmental news) involving 17 publicly

---

[11] In the United States, the Wall Street Journal is generally the preferred source of information for conducting event-study analyses. In Argentina, environmental news was collected from the newspaper *La Nacion* (daily circulation of approximately 250,000; ranks 3rd in Buenos Aires); in Chile, we used *El Mercurio* (daily circulation of approximately 200,000; ranks 3rd in Santiago); in Mexico City, we used *Excelsior* (daily circulation of 200,000; ranks 7th in Mexico City); finally, in the Philippines, news was collected from the *Manila Bulletin* (daily circulation of 300,000; ranks 3rd in Manila). These four daily newspapers were reviewed one by one, most in microfiche format, for the entire period of analysis. All newspapers were available from the Library of Congress. Information from missing issues was obtained directly from the publishers of the papers in the respective countries.
[12] For a thorough description of these environmental news, see [4].

traded firms over the period 1990-1994; 20 of those events were positive while 33 were negative. Argentina registered 20 events (5 positive and 15 negative) involving 11 firms. The *Manila Bulletin* reported 18 events (10 positive and 8 negative) with 10 firms. Finally, the Mexican sample consists of 35 events (of which only 4) were positive involving 10 publicly traded firms. ... [T]he number of events ... is smaller than the number of news (with name of publicly traded companies) ... . This is the case since a significant number of newsclips are simply a repetition or follow-up on an initial event and do not provide any additional information to what is already known. In most cases, we have included in our dataset only the announcement of the initial event unless subsequent announcements provided significantly different or additional information about the event.[13]...

4.   EMPIRICAL ANALYSIS

We apply the event-study methodology to the environmental events collected in each of the country over the period 1990-1994.[20] The size of the event window was determined empirically, as the theory pertaining to the appropriate size of the event window is not very instructive. We thus searched over a period of 10 days before and 10 days after the event for the event window yielding the best statistically significant results. This search indicates that an event window of 11 days (5 days prior to the announcement, the day of the announcement, and 5 days after) yields the best results.

---

[13] For example, especially in the case of environmental accidents such as a spill, the nature and impact of the accident may be covered in two or three consecutive issues of the newspaper. In such situations, only the initial announcement is treated as an event. On the other hand, for example, it is sometimes the case that a firm announces the investment in a pollution control project, and months later the firm is rewarded publicly for its effort to control pollution. These two announcements pertain to the same effort undertaken by the plant but nonetheless provide information of a different nature, and were thus treated as two different events. To this extent, we do not examine the potential cumulative impact of a sequence of announcements pertaining to a single event. We treat each announcement as an event and measure whether or not capital markets react to this type of information.
[20] A potential issue is raised with events occurring in early 1990 in that they may be a follow-up of initial events taking place in 1989. Three such events hold our attention: January 9 (Chilgener) and March 21 and 23 (Benguet). For each of these events, a further newspaper search was made from September to December 1989. It failed to reveal any other news that could have been related to the events described here. We have thus opted to retain these events in our dataset.

With respect to positive news, ... [there were] ... statistically significant increases in market values for 20 events out of 39. It is of further interest to note that 9 of these 20 statistically significant events involve the report of an agreement with the regulator or the *explicit* recognition by the regulator of a superior environmental performance. Markets appear to react to the explicit recognition of an investment in pollution control or superior environmental performance by the authorities. For those events, market values increase by more than 20% over the entire event window.

As indicated earlier, one may pool together events and test for the statistical significance of the average abnormal return for the events thus pooled. Given the results obtained on individual stock markets, it is of relevance to test if events reporting the explicit recognition of superior performance as a whole are statistically significant. ... As can be observed, explicit recognition events as a whole are strongly statistically significant on Days -4 and +1. Moreover, the difference between government actions and other positive events is statistically significant at Day -4 and Day +1.

With respect to negative events, ... there are 33 events out of 85 for which statistically significant decreases in market values are recorded. Of these 33 events, 17 events are related to some form of government or citizens' complaints.

Given the nature of these results, we have pooled together government and citizens' complaints and tested whether or not they had a statistically significant differential impact on market values when compared to all other negative events. Results ... indicate that government and citizens complaints as a whole are statistically significant at Day -1. Moreover, they have a statistically differential impact on market values when compared to all other negative events at Day -1.

We may interpret this result by noting that the filing of a complaint can provide *unanticipated* news to markets leading them to expect further actions, yet unknown, to be undertaken. Reductions in market values for events pertaining to complaints range from 4 to 15%. ... [T]hese losses are much greater in magnitude than any losses observed in previous studies conducted in Canada and the United States. This may be explained by a greater volatility of capital markets in developing countries as well as by a greater premium to information which otherwise may generally not be as readily available as in more developed markets.[21]

---

[21] On capital markets volatility in developing countries, see [3].

5.   CONCLUSION

In this paper, we have shown that despite a generally acknowledged poor enforcement of environmental regulations, capital markets in Argentina, Chile, Mexico, and the Philippines appear to react to the announcement of specific positive and negative environmental events. While fines and penalties used by the environmental agencies of these countries may have fallen short of creating incentives for pollution control, capital markets have penalized firms which are the objects of citizens' complaints, and rewarded firms which have obtained the explicit recognition of superior environmental performance.

These results need to be interpreted with care, and a number of caveats are in order including the following three. First, we are certainly not arguing that strong enforcement of regulations should be abandoned and that markets (firms, consumers, communities) be left to themselves to negotiate and induce pollution abatement from polluters. Indeed, not all firms may be responsive to the public release of their environmental performance, nor would all communities be able to use the revealed information appropriately or capital markets react to such information. In a recent paper, Foulon *et al.* [5] have shown that public disclosure may indeed complement a strong enforcement of environmental regulation. However, these results do suggest that in a number of circumstances, market forces (even in developing countries) have not remained idle upon receiving signals of the environmental performance of firms and have penalized (complaints) or rewarded (recognition of superior environmental performance) the owners of the firm through changes in market values. This is the result of interest in this paper. Further research in this area will indicate whether or not our findings can be generalized, and will provide a greater understanding of the mechanisms which underpin the reaction of capital markets.

Second, whether or not firms have "voluntarily" undertaken pollution abatement activities for obtaining a reward, and whether or not adverse market reaction has led firms to subsequently invest in pollution control is a further issue of investigation, especially in developing countries.[22] It is currently beyond the realm of our possibilities to comprehensively address this issue as it requires a vast amount of firm-level data that are not readily available for the countries studied here. From an anecdotal

---

[22] Konar and Cohen 11 have shown that firms that have suffered the largest reduction in

point of view, however, it is interesting to note, among others, that after Chilgener (Chile) had released a cloud of toxic air pollution over Santiago and suffered a loss of 5% of its market value in April 1992, it announced on September 25, 1992, an investment of 115 million dollars to control air pollution.

Finally, we do not know whether or not information will lead firms to behave in a socially optimal way. However, nor do we know if environmental standards are socially optimal. In this sense, it may be unfair to criticize the role of information as a policy tool on the basis that firms *may* react in a way that is not socially optimal (e.g., overinvesting in pollution abatement). Perhaps a better element of comparison is the following: in order to achieve a *given* level of desired environmental performance, would the traditional approach of fines, penalties, court actions, and the like (with its large transaction costs) or information provision prove to be more efficient (i.e., least costly)? We believe that in all likelihood the latter will prove to be more efficient. However, this is *not* to say that information provision will induce the desired behavior in each and every case. Nor do we argue that more information is always necessarily better. The specific circumstances under which information provision may work best has been the object of some research (e.g., Hamilton [6]) and will continue to do so. Further research should provide greater insight as to the exact role and impact that communities and markets may have on firms' environmental performance, and thereby on the evolving role of the regulator.

REFERENCES

1. S. Afsah, B. Laplante, and D. Wheeler, "Controlling Industrial Pollution: A New Paradigm," Policy Research Working Paper 1672, Development Research Group, The World Bank, 1996.

2. A. Blackman and G. J. Bannister, Community pressure and clean technology in the informal sector: An econometric analysis of the adoption of propane by traditional Mexican brickmakers, J. Environ. Econom. Management 35 1 , 1-21 1998 .

3. S. Claessens, S. Dasgupta, and J. Glen, Return behavior in emerging stock markets, World Bank Econom. Rev 9, 131-151 1995.

4. S. Dasgupta, B. Laplante, and C. Meisner, Environmental news in Argentina, Chile, Mexico, and Philippines, Local Environment, forthcoming.

5. J. Foulon, P. Lanoie, and B. Laplante, "Incentives for Pollution Control: Regulation or Information," Policy Research Working Paper 2291, Development Research Group, The World Bank 1999 .

6. T. Hamilton, Pollution as news: Media and stock market reaction to the Toxics Release Inventory data, J. Environ. Econom. Management 28, 98_113 1995 .

7. G. V. Henderson, Problems and solutions in conducting events studies, J. Risk Insurance 42, 282_306 1990 .

8. H. Hettige, R. E. Lucas, and D. Wheeler, The toxic intensity of industrial production: Global patterns, trends, and trade policy, Amer. Econ. Re_. 82, 478_481 1992 .

9. A. B. Jaffe, S. R. Peterson, P. R. Portney, and R. Stavins, Environmental regulation and the competitiveness of U.S. Manufacturing, J. Econom. Lit. 33, 132_163 1995 .

10. R. D. Klassen and C. P. McLaughlin, The impact of environmental management on firm performance, Management Sci. 42, 1199-1214 1996 .

11. S. Konar and M. A. Cohen, Information as regulation: The effect of community right to know laws on toxic emissions, J. Environ. Econom. Management 32, 109_124 1997 .

12. P. Lanoie and B. Laplante, The market response to environmental incidents in Canada: A theoretical and empirical analysis, Southern Econom. J. 60, 657-672 1994 .

13. P. Lanoie, B. Laplante, and M. Roy, Can capital markets create incentives for pollution control? Ecol. Econ. 26, 31-41 1998 .

14. B. Laplante and P. Rilstone, Environmental inspections and emissions of the pulp and paper industry in Quebec, J. Environ. Econom. Management 31, 19-36 1996 .

15. A. C. MacKinlay, Event studies in economics and finance, J. Econom. Lit. 35, 13_39 1997 .

16. W. A. Magat and W. K. Viscusi, Effectiveness of the EPA's regulatory enforcement: The case of industrial effluent standards, J. Law Econ. 33, 331-360, 1990 .

17. M. I. Muoghalu, H. Robison, and J. L. Glascock, Hazardous waste lawsuits, stockholder returns, and deterrence, Southern Econom. J. 357-370 1990 .

18. L. W. Nadeau, EPA effectiveness at reducing the duration of plant-level noncompliance, J. Environ. Econom. Management 34, 54-78 1997.

19. D. O'Connor, "Managing the Environment with Rapid Industrialisation: Lessons from the East Asian Experience," OECD, Paris, 1995 .

20. S. Pargal and D. Wheeler, Informal regulation of industrial pollution in developing countries: Evidence from Indonesia, J. Polit. Econ. 104, 1314_1327 1996 .

21. M. E. Porter and C. van der Linde, Toward a new conception of the Environment-Competitiveness Relationship, J. Econom. Perspectives 9, 97_118 1995 .

22. C. S. Russell, Monitoring and Enforcement, in "Public Policies for Environmental Protection" P. R. Portney, Ed. , Resources for the Future, Washington DC 1990 .

Chapter Eight

Emissions Trading Compliance

Introduction

This chapter introduces the topic of compliance with emissions trading schemes. Emissions trading is a market-based mechanism designed to allow firms to choose the least expensive strategy to meet environmental standards and has been successfully used in Europe and the U.S. to reduce acid-rain-causing sulfur dioxide emissions. As more and more countries accept the need to address climate change on a priority basis, emissions trading will play an increasingly significant role as an approach that not only creates incentives for firms to cut greenhouse gas emissions (GHG) but also spurs needed technological innovation that ensures that this is done at the lowest cost.[1] Understanding how to strengthen compliance with these kinds of market-based mechanisms is a priority for many policy-makers in both developed and developing countries.

Emissions trading schemes require strict compliance to succeed. High compliance is a "prerequisite of investor confidence."[2] Low or even

---

[1] *See* Henrik Hasselknippe, *Systems for carbon trading: an overview*, Climate Policy Special Supplement on Defining and Trading Emission Targets, 3 suppl. 2, 43-57 (2003) (describing the increasing number of regional, national, and international systems for trading and transfer of GHG emission allowances, focusing on the International Emissions Trading Association (IETA) Trading Schemes Database, developed by Point Carbon.). *See also* Joe Kruger, Katherine Grover, & Jeremy Schreifels, *Building Institutions to Address Air Pollution in Developing Countries: The Cap and Trade Approach* (2003), *available at* http://www.oecd.org/dataoecd/11/25/2957736.pdf (discussing the viability of emissions trading schemes in countries that lack the resources to use high-technology monitoring systems). For more on technological innovation and sustainable development, *see* Chapter Thirteen: Compliance & Competitiveness: The Porter Hypothesis.

[2] Rupert Edwards, *Effective Enforcement and Compliance in the EU ETS: A View from the Financial Sector*, *available at* http://inece.org/emissions/edwards.pdf ("[T]he rules must be credible or the investor community will not play or will heavily discount the price, thus undermining the policy goals."). *See generally*, the website for the International Conference on Copmliance and Enforcement of Trading Schemes in Environmental Protection 16-18 March 2004 (Worcester College, Oxford University, England), *available at* http://inece.org/emissions.

moderate levels of compliance can destroy markets and undermine the financial incentives that drive emissions trading.

Emissions trading schemes have been successful where monitoring and compliance were high. National level programs in Europe and the U.S. have benefited from sophisticated monitoring technology that allows regulators to track the emissions of participating firms. For example, the U.S. EPA has experienced nearly 100 percent compliance with its Sulfur Dioxide Allowance Trading Program in part due to its use of continuous emissions monitoring technology (CEM).[3] Participating facilities are required to install continuous emissions monitoring systems, which allows the EPA to maintain an accurate tally of SO_2 emissions. The EPA has described the CEM data as "the gold standard to back up the paper currency of emissions allowances" by "verifying the existence and value of the traded allowance."[4] The success of the SO_2 program indicates that, with high compliance, emissions trading schemes can succeed in identifying cost-effective methods to reduce emissions. But it is important to note that CO_2 emissions and other greenhouse gases are ubiquitous, and monitoring and compliance present difficult challenges, requiring different approaches and technologies.[5]

At the international level, emissions trading systems have been proposed as part of the Kyoto Protocol to the United Nations Framework Convention on Climate Change,[6] and in January 2005 the European Union instituted the world's first mandatory international trading scheme.[7] The

---

[3] Part of the Acid Rain Program in Title IV of the 1990 Clean Air Act Amendments, the trading scheme succeeded in 2003 in reducing SO_2 emissions by 38 percent of 1980 levels. *See* U.S. EPA's Acid Rain Program 2003 Progress Report, *available at* http://www.epa.gov/airmarkets/cmprpt/arp03/summary.html.

[4] U.S. EPA, "Continuous Emissions Monitoring Fact Sheet," http://www.epa.gov/airmarkets/monitoring/factsheet.html.

[5] For a discussion on monitoring greenhouse gas emissions in the EU ETS, *see* Joseph Kruger and William A. Pizer, *The EU Emissions Trading Directive: Opportunities and Potential Pitfalls*, Resources for the Future, Discussions Paper 04-24, April 2004 ("[T]he EU has more regulated sources and covers more industrial sectors. Some of the sectors ... have more varied sources of emissions, for which emissions measurement is not as straight forward as the utility and industrial boilers that make up the bulk of the U.S. programs. The EU ETS could also include multiple greenhouse gases in the second phase of the program and is likely to include a mixture of cap-and-trade and offset provisions.").

[6] The Kyoto Protocol's programs include: the national systems to estimate GHG emissions and removals (Article 5(1)); the reporting of GHG emissions (Article 7(1)); and the rules for the Protocol's three market-based mechanisms — joint implementation (JI), the clean development mechanism (CDM), and international emissions trading (Articles 6, 12, and 17).

[7] Terje Berntsen, Jan Fuglestvedt & Frode Stordal, *Reporting and Verification of Emissions*
continued

European Union Trading System (ETS) was devised to help EU countries meet their obligations under Kyoto. In its first phase, the ETS will involve more than 12,000 installations in the 25 Member States and account for approximately 45 percent of the EU's total CO_2 emissions.[8] The ETS aims to reduce GHG emissions to 8 percent of 1990 levels by 2012.[9]

The mandatory monitoring and reporting requirements under the ETS have forced companies to establish CO_2 budgets and carbon management systems for the first time.[10] The carbon market created by the scheme has spawned a new industry comprised of carbon traders, carbon finance specialists, carbon management specialists, and carbon auditors.[11] New businesses such as Climate Change Capital in the U.K., and the Chicago Climate Exchange in the U.S., are poised to benefit from the ETS.[12] In addition to driving practically an entirely new sector of the economy, the scheme is expected to allow the EU to achieve its Kyoto target at a cost of between €2.9 and €3.7 billion annually – less than 0.1 % of the EU's GDP. Without the scheme, compliance costs could reach up to €6.8 billion a year.[13]

The excerpt in this chapter, by John K. Stranlund, Carlos A. Chavez, and Barry C. Field, highlights the crucial role enforcement and compliance

and Removals of Greenhouse Gases, in IMPLEMENTING THE CLIMATE REGIME: INTERNATIONAL COMPLIANCE (Olav Schram Stokke, Jon Hovi & Geir Ulfstein eds., 2005).

[8] The scheme is based on Directive 2003/87/EC. The first phase, from 2005 to 2007, covers only selected industries and emissions, but will likely expand in its coverage in later phases (such as to transportation), as well as possibly link with other emissions trading schemes that may arise under Kyoto or other agreements.

[9] European Commission, *EU Emissions Trading: An Open Scheme Promoting Global Innovation To Combat Climate Change* (2004), *available at* http://europa.eu.int/comm/environment/climat/ pdf/emission_trading2_en.pdf (The EU scheme allows companies to use credits from Kyoto mechanisms, which provides cost-effective means for EU firms to cut emissions and creates additional incentives for firms to invest in emission-reduction projects abroad, such as in developing countries).

[10] *Id.*

[11] *Id.*

[12] Climate Change Capital is an independent merchant bank in the UK offering financial consulting to clients affected by climate change and energy policies, developing risk management and other financial markets that help develop new markets, and conducting a variety of research and transactional services related to carbon markets. *See* http:// www.climatechangecapital.com. Chicago Climate Exchange is a multi-national and multi-sector market for reducing and trading GHG emissions. *See* http:// www.chicagoclimatex.com/.

[13] *European Commission, supra* note 9. Similarly, a report by the Natural Resources Defense Council on the impacts on employment in the U.S. as a result of the proposed McCain-Lieberman Climate Stewardship Act indicated that the "jobs created outweigh jobs lost by a factor of five by 2015, rising nearly to seven to one by 2025." James Barrett *et al., Jobs*

continued

play in effective emissions trading schemes and then focuses on the problem of how emissions trading schemes should be enforced to achieve broad, cost-effective compliance.[14] The article describes two successful emissions trading schemes: the Sulfur Dioxide Allowance Trading program and the Regional Clean Air Incentives Market (RECLAIM) program.

---

and the Climate Stewardship Act: How Curbing Global Warming Can Increase Employment (2005), *available at* http://www.nrdc.org/globalWarming/csa/CSAjobs.pdf.

[14] John K. Stranlund, Carlos A. Chavez & Barry C. Field, *Enforcing Emissions Trading Programs: Theory, Practice, and Performance,* 30(3) Pol'y Studies J., 343 (2002).

Enforcing Emissions Trading Programs: Theory, Practice, And Performance

John K. Stranlund, Carlos A. Chavez and Barry C. Field

30(3) Policy Studies Journal Urbana 343 (2002)

...

1.   Introduction

Emission trading programs (also referred to as transferable or tradable pollution rights, and cap-and-trade policies) are an innovative approach to controlling pollution that continues to gather support from policy makers and members of the regulated community. Conceptually, emissions trading programs are quite simple, yet have very powerful implications. The typical design of a market-based system requires first that an environmental authority decide upon an acceptable level of overall emissions. Permits consistent with that target, each of which confer the right to release a certain amount of pollution over some period of time, are then issued to polluting firms. Facilities may apply these permits to their own emissions, sell excess permits to other pollution sources, or purchase permits from other firms if their emissions exceed their permit holdings. If the coverage of the system is extensive enough and there are no serious institutional barriers to trading, an active market in emissions permits is established. By exploiting the power of a market to allocate pollution control responsibilities, and by freeing facilities to choose the cheapest way to reduce their emissions, well-designed trading programs promise to achieve environmental quality goals more cheaply than traditional command-and-control regulations.[1]

---

[1] The idea that market-based pollution control policies can achieve environmental quality goals in a less expensive way than traditional command-and-control policies originates

continued

113

Despite the perceived advantages of market-based environmental policies over traditional command-and control approaches, a number of authors have made it clear that the efficiency gains realized by emissions trading programs will depend on rates of compliance, which in turn will depend on the enforcement processes and activities pursued by those running the programs. Although this literature has gone a long way toward elucidating the consequences of ill-enforced emissions trading program, much less effort has been devoted to the problem of how these systems should be enforced to achieve high rates of compliance in a cost-effective manner.[2]

Over the years, regulatory agencies have built administrative and legal systems to enforce the conventional command-and-control type of environmental regulation. Enforcement in a command-and-control world works by detecting and sanctioning performance that fails to meet the established standards. If a polluter has emissions in excess of the legal standard, the only way to move toward compliance is to reduce emissions toward the standard. How vigorously they move in this direction presumably depends in large part on the probability that violators will be detected and then sanctioned by authorities. But a polluter in an emissions trading program has another option. If they have emissions in excess of their permit holdings they can do two things to come into compliance: reduce emissions, or purchase more permits.

In an emissions trading system, therefore, regulators face a somewhat more complex enforcement problem. They must now focus both on emissions, and on the behavior of firms in terms of their participation in emission permit markets. Which is to say that successful enforcement must now be undertaken in coordination with the permit markets. There

---

with Crocker (1966) and Dales (1968). Montgomery (1972) provided the first rigorous theoretical justification for the use of market-based polices. This work spurred a very large theoretical literature on the design of these policies. A typical list of citations in this literature might include Hahn (1984), Krupnick, *et. al.* (1980), Malueg (1990), McGartland and Oates (1985), and Stavins (1995). A number of economists have sought to turn the theoretical literature into practical guides for policymakers [e.g., Brady (1983), Hahn (1989), Hahn and Noll (1982), Tietenberg (1985), and Tripp and Dudek (1989)].

[2] Malik's (1990) and vanEgteren and Weber's (1996) analyses are primarily predictive models of the compliance choices of firms in transferable permit systems. Keeler (1991), Malik (1992), and Hahn and Axtell (1995) all chose to focus on comparing the performance of transferable permit systems to command-and-control policies when firms may be non-compliant. Beavis and Walker (1983), Stranlund and Dhanda (1999), and Stranlund and Chavez (2000) provide conceptual notions of how emissions permit programs should be enforced, but say very little about how these systems are actually enforced.

are essentially three parts to the regulatory oversight required: (1) to keep track of trades so that, at any point in time, it is known how many permits each firm possesses; (2) to monitor every firm's emissions to make sure that they do not exceed the level allowed by the number of permits the firm holds; and (3) to penalize firms whose emissions exceed their permit holdings.

In this paper we combine a conceptual model of compliance incentives in emissions trading programs with the practice of enforcing actual emissions trading programs to develop practical guidelines for enforcing emissions trading programs. The paper proceeds as follows: We first present a model of the compliance incentives of firms in an emissions trading program. In section 3 we turn to a[n] account of the enforcement strategies employed in the two most prominent market-based systems: the Sulfur Dioxide Allowance Trading program (SO_2) and the Regional Clean Air Incentives Market (RECLAIM) program. These programs have been described and discussed extensively, but to our knowledge, no one has focused as clearly on their enforcement provisions. Armed with a conceptual understanding of the compliance incentives in emissions trading programs and knowledge of … how the SO_2 and RECLAIM programs are enforced, we evaluate the compliance performance of these two programs thus far. Taken altogether – theory, practice, and performance – we are able to develop several practical guidelines for enforcing emissions trading programs, which we lay out in our concluding section.

2.   Compliance Incentives in a Transferable Emissions Permit System

We begin with an examination of the structure of the compliance incentives faced by firms in a transferable emissions permit system. To do this we will first set the context with brief reviews of the basic structures of the SO_2 and RECLAIM programs.

2.1   Basics of the SO_2 and RECLAIM programs

The EPA's Sulfur Dioxide Allowance Trading Program, which is part of the U.S. Acid Rain Program implemented under Title IV of the 1990 Clean Air Act Amendments, was designed to reduce annual SO_2 emissions from fossil-fueled electric utility units by almost 10 million tons, nearly 50%

of the 1980 emissions levels.[3] The SO_2 program was designed to run in two phases. Phase I operations began in 1995, affecting a total of 445 units.[4] Phase II of the program, which began in the year 2000, extended the coverage of the program to include about 2100 units fired by coal, oil, and gas [U.S. EPA (2000)]. Units are allocated emissions allowances, each one of which authorizes its owner to emit one ton of SO_2 during a given year or any year thereafter. Overall emissions reductions are achieved by limiting the number of allowances in circulation. SO_2 allowances are fully marketable commodities; they can be bought and sold, or held for compliance purposes in future years. Sources cannot, however, borrow against future allocations for present compliance purposes.

The Regional Clean Air Incentives Market [RECLAIM] program contributes to the South Coast Air Quality Management District's [AQMD] efforts to achieve federal ambient standards for ozone and particulate matter in the Los Angeles airshed. RECLAIM was designed to reduce emissions of two pollutants, Nitrogen Oxides (NOx) and Sulfur Oxide (SO_x), from stationary sources that released more than four tons of either pollutant in any year since 1990.[5] By the end of the 1999 compliance year, RECLAIM covered 354 facilities. [South Coast Air Quality Management District (2001)].[6] The RECLAIM program started operations in October of 1993. By the year 2003 the program is expected to achieve reductions of 71% and 60% for NO_x and SO_x by affected sources from 1994 levels.[7]

---

[3] A wealth of information about the U.S. Acid Rain Program, including the SO_2 Allowance Trading Program can be found on the internet at http://www.epa.gov/airmarkets/arp/.

[4] This included 263 units at 110 mostly coal-burning electric utility plants, 175 units that voluntarily joined Phase I of the program as "substitution" units, and additional 7 units that joined Phase I as "compensating" units. See Ellerman, et. al. (1997) and Montero (1999) for descriptions of these voluntary opt-in provisions.

[5] Facilities that are not automatically subject to RECLAIM regulations have the option of voluntarily entering the program. Certain types of facilities were excluded from RECLAIM including, among others, dry cleaners, restaurants, and police and fire fighting facilities. For details on the exemptions to the general inclusion criteria see Regulation XX-RECLAIM, Rule 2002, (i) and (f); http://www.aqmd.gov/rules/html.

[6] Facilities under RECLAIM are divided into two cycles with compliance schedules that are staggered by six months. Compliance years for Cycle 1 facilities run from January 1 through December 31 and Cycle 2 compliance years are from July 1 through June 30. Overall the RECLAIM compliance year runs from January 1 of that year to June 30 of the next.

[7] RECLAIM sources represent only a small portion of the overall emissions inventory in this region; about 10 % of the total NOx emissions inventory in 1990 and 20% of the total SOx inventory [Schwarze and Zapfel (2000)].

RECLAIM facilities are allocated RECLAIM Trading Credits [credits] for each year until 2010.[8] Overall reductions in NO_x and SO_x emissions are achieved by reducing allocations of credits over time. Each credit allows the release of one pound of NO_x or SO_x during a specified compliance year. Facilities may use their allocations for compliance purposes, or sell or buy credits as they see fit.[9] No banking is allowed in the RECLAIM program–facilities cannot borrow credits from future allocations and, in contrast to the SO_2 program, they are not allowed to save credits for use or sale in future compliance years.

Although the RECLAIM program is an emissions trading program, it also includes emissions taxes (fees).[10] Assessment of emissions fees is based on each facility's total emissions, and the applicable unit fees for both NO_x and SO_x emissions increase with a facilities' level of emissions. Economists usually think of emissions taxes as an alternative method of incentive-based pollution control. In practice, however, emissions taxes tend to be used to raise revenue. The same is true for the RECLAIM taxes: the emissions fees were clearly not intended to provide incentives for pollution control, but rather are used to help finance the program. However, as we will discuss shortly, these taxes probably have an impact on facilities' compliance incentives.

2.2 *Compliance incentives in a transferable permit system*

An important feature of the SO_2 and RECLAIM programs is that they rely heavily on self-reporting of emissions from the facilities themselves.[11]

---

[8] February 1997 amendments to RECLAIM rules, Regulation XX-RECLAIM, extended the program indefinitely beyond 2010.

[9] There is a single spatial restriction on trading credits. Specifically, a facility in Zone 1 (the coastal zone) may only obtain credits from other Zone 1 facilities, while a facility in Zone 2 (the inland zone) may obtain credits from either Zone 1 or 2 [Regulation XX-RECLAIM, Rule 2005, (e); http://www.aqmd.gov/rules/html.].

[10] The various fees paid by RECLAIM facilities are described in South Coast Air Quality Managment District, "Rule 301 permitting and Associated Fees, http://www.aqmd.gov/rules/html/r301.html.

[11] A more rigorous development of the results in this section can be found in Stranlund and Chavez (2000), which examines the role of self-reporting in the enforcement of market-based environmental policies. Despite the prevalence of self-reporting requirements in the enforcement of environmental policies, only a few other authors have examined the role of these requirements, and all have done so in the context of enforcing standards. Harford (1987) provides a positive analysis of firm behavior in this setting, while Malik (1993), Kaplow and Shavell (1994), and Livernois and McKenna (1998) all examine the use and value of self-reporting in the design of optimal strategies for enforcing standards.

Much effort was devoted to designing monitoring systems for these programs by which sources can both collect and transmit emissions data. There are, then, two main ways in which a firm could be non-compliant: (1) by transmitting erroneous emissions data and (2) by having emissions in excess of allowance holdings. From the standpoint of the regulating authorities there are basically three things under its control: (1) the monitoring of performance to identify incidences of non-compliance, (2) possible penalties for reporting violations, and (3) penalties for emissions in excess of permit holdings.

Under these conditions firms will choose how much pollution they will emit, how much they will report emitting, and how many permits to hold. We may suppose that firms will make these decisions to minimize their expected costs, which consist of emissions control costs, receipts or expenditures from permit market transactions, and expected penalties from reporting and emissions violations. For simplicity and because the existing literature on enforcing market-based environmental programs has not yet been extended to dynamic environments, we will also assume throughout that emissions permits cannot be banked for future use or sale.[12]

Let us suppose that emissions permits are traded in a reasonably competitive environment; specifically, assume that no single facility can exercise power in the market for emissions permits, and transactions costs associated with trading permits are minimal. We also assume that facilities do not bear emissions fees as in the RECLAIM program. The enforcement strategy required to maintain complete emissions compliance in this setting has two parts, both of which tie the enforcement variables to the prevailing permit price. Denote the following variables:

p: market price of permits;

π: probability that a source will get audited, which is assumed to be sufficient to discover a violation if one exists;[13]

f: the per unit fine levied for emissions violators, and

---

[12] Future work that examines how dynamic choices involving permit banking, longer-term investments in production and pollution control technologies, and ongoing relationships between facilities and enforcers affect firms' compliance incentives would probably reveal ways in which enforcement strategies can be refined to exploit the effects of these dynamic elements.

[13] Like nearly all of the economic literature on enforcement, we conveniently sidestep the problem of monitoring accuracy. Clearly, however, obtaining reasonably accurate accounts of firms' emissions will be a critical component of any market-based environmental policy. This is another important issue that future research should address.

g: the per unit fine for under-reported emissions.

We assume that the penalties are applied automatically when violations are discovered. If the authorities wish to have complete compliance, there are two conditions that must be satisfied:

(1) $p < \pi \times [f + g]$;
(2) $p < f$.

The first condition provides firms with the proper incentive to submit truthful reports of their emissions, and is also necessary to guarantee that each firm will choose to be completely compliant. The second condition guarantees that each will hold enough permits to cover their emissions.

The intuition of why these simple conditions will guarantee complete compliance is straightforward. First, note that the permit price is the marginal benefit of non-compliance – it is the unit cost that is avoided when a firm chooses not to hold enough permits to cover its emissions. To understand why an enforcement strategy that satisfies $p < \pi \times [f + g]$ will provide the proper incentives to facilities so that they choose to submit truthful reports of their emissions, note that if a firm misrepresents its emissions it is because it is motivated to cover up an emissions violation rather than purchasing enough permits to be in compliance. Therefore, the marginal benefit of misrepresenting a violation is the foregone cost of being in compliance, which is the permit price. If a firm's emissions and reporting violations are discovered, it faces the per unit penalty f for its emissions violation and the per unit penalty g for its reporting violation. The expected marginal penalty of falsifying an emissions report is therefore the product of the probability that the violations are discovered and the sum of the per unit penalties for its emissions and reporting violations, $\pi \times [f + g]$. Hence, a firm will provide a truthful report of its emissions if the marginal benefit of under-reporting its emissions, p, is not greater than the expected marginal cost, $\pi \times [f + g]$.

Notice that the unit penalty for a reporting violation is not required to make sure that a facility has the proper incentive to submit accurate emissions reports. In fact, the SO_2 and RECLAIM regulations do not include explicit penalties for submitting false emissions reports.

Guaranteeing accurate emissions reporting is only useful insofar as it serves the primary goal of achieving complete emissions compliance where every firm holds enough permits to cover its emissions. In fact, firms will not hold enough permits to cover their emissions unless they have the correct incentive to submit truthful emissions reports. To understand why this is so, suppose that $p > \pi \times [f + g]$ so that a firm is not motivated to provide a truthful report of its emissions. Obviously, if $p > \pi \times [f + g]$, then $p > \pi \times f$. The permit price p represents a firm's marginal benefit of not holding enough permits to cover its emissions, while $\pi \times f$ represents the firm's expected marginal cost of holding too few permits, which consists of the unit penalty for this emissions violation times the probability that the violation will be discovered. Since the marginal benefit of the emissions violation outweighs its expected marginal cost, the firm will choose to hold fewer permits than it needs to cover its emissions. This is one of the most important lessons conveyed by this model of compliance incentives – facilities in a transferable permit system will not have the proper incentive to be compliant unless the enforcement strategy they face also removes the incentive to submit falsified emissions reports.

Although obtaining accurate emissions reports is necessary to induce compliance, it is not sufficient: an enforcement strategy must also satisfy $p \leq f$. Given the proper incentive to provide a truthful emissions report, a firm that is in violation will report the extent of its violation and will then be assessed the per unit penalty f. Therefore, if the price of being compliant – the permit price – is less than or equal to the certain marginal penalty for emissions violations, each firm will choose complete emissions compliance. If not, each firm will emit more pollution than the number of permits it holds allows.

This model of compliance incentives stresses the importance of the prevailing permit price. In a reasonably competitive environment the prevailing permit price completely summarizes each facility's marginal benefit of non-compliance. Thus, the effectiveness of any enforcement strategy will depend critically on the going permit price.

Clearly, a firm's compliance incentives in a competitive emissions trading program do not depend on anything specific about itself; including its initial allocation of permits, its scale of operations, or details about its production and emissions-control technologies.[14] Since firm-specific

---

[14] In contrast, the latter information can be valuable in the enforcement of command-and-control standards. When facing an emissions standard, for example, the benefit to a firm of emitting more than the standard allows is the costs it would have to incur to reduce its

continued

details are not important components of their compliance incentives, there is no reason for an enforcement authority to target its enforcement effort because it suspects that some facilities may be more likely to be non-compliant than others. This is important because sources in a market-based pollution control program will often be very different in ways that one might expect would influence their compliance incentives. For example, although all firms in the SO_2 program are fossil-fueled electric utilities, they vary greatly in terms of the scale of their operations, the fuel they use (high and low sulfur coal, as well as blends of fuels with different sulfur content), and their emissions control technologies, particularly whether they use a flue gas desulfurization (scrubber) technology or not. Because coverage of the RECLAIM program is not limited to a single industry, RECLAIM sources may be even more heterogeneous. Surprisingly, from the perspective of compliance incentives in competitive emissions trading programs, this heterogeneity simply does not matter.

In imperfectly competitive environments, however, prevailing prices may not convey all the necessary information about facilities' marginal benefits of non-compliance. Chavez (2000) shows that when a firm can exercise power in a permit market, its compliance incentives also depend on the degree to which the firm can manipulate permit prices. He also shows that significant transaction costs may also cause firms' marginal benefits of non-compliance to deviate from prevailing permit prices.

It is likely that the emissions fees faced by RECLAIM facilities will have the same impact. Recall that these are taxes per unit of emissions that increase with a facility's level of emissions. When faced with an emissions tax, a facility in an emissions trading system has two reasons to be non-compliant; to avoid the cost of holding enough permits to cover its emissions, the marginal benefit of which is the market price of permits, and to avoid paying the emissions tax, the marginal benefit of which is the tax rate. Thus, a facility's marginal benefit of noncompliance is the prevailing permit price *plus* the emissions tax rate. This suggests two aspects of the RECLAIM taxes that are important to keep in mind. First, when evaluating the compliance incentives of RECLAIM facilities, we must realize that the emissions tax they pay is an additional incentive to be non-compliant. Second, the differentiated tax rates suggests

---

emissions to satisfy the standard. Therefore, a firm's marginal control costs exactly indicate its marginal benefit of non-compliance to the standard. This will clearly depend on details of a firm's operations including its level of output, its choice of inputs, and the emissions-control technology it employs [Garvie and Keeler (1994)].

differentiated compliance incentives–since the larger sources of emissions pay higher fees, they have a greater incentive to be non-compliant.

Non-competitive complications and RECLAIM-like emissions fees aside, a firm's compliance incentives suggests an important principle for setting penalties in competitive emissions trading programs. Instead of choosing fixed unit penalties as we assumed, it may be more effective to tie penalties to the prevailing permit price. A particularly attractive feature of competitive emissions trading programs is that they are expected to adjust more easily to a variety of changes than other emissions-control policies. Technological advance, industrial growth and decline, and inflationary pressures are accommodated automatically by an emissions trading program through changes in the permit price.[15] However, since an effective enforcement strategy for a competitive trading system calls for setting $p \leq \pi \times [f + g]$, fixed unit penalties would require that monitoring (as captured by the audit probability π) must keep pace with fluctuations in the prevailing permit price. This may be a difficult task for enforcement authorities working with limited budgets.

Tying marginal penalties directly to the prevailing permit price can stabilize the monitoring requirement in the face of permit price fluctuations. For example, suppose that the marginal penalty for a reporting violation is chosen to be $g = \gamma \pi$, where $\gamma > 0$, and the marginal penalty for an emissions violation is $f = \emptyset p$, where $\emptyset > 1$ to satisfy the requirement that $p < f$. From the requirement that $p < \pi \times [f + g]$, a constant audit probability $\pi > 1/(\gamma + \emptyset)$ will guarantee complete emissions compliance, and is independent of fluctuations of the permit price.[16]

This recommendation corresponds well with suggestions that penalties for violations of environmental regulations be based on the economic gain of the violation to the offender [Wasserman (1992); for a discussion see Cohen (1999), section 3.5]. The prevailing permit price captures the

---

[15] In contrast, emissions taxes and standards that are designed to meet an aggregate emissions target must be adjusted constantly in response to these changes. [Hanley, Shogren and White (1997), pp. 94-95; Baumol and Oates (1988), pg. 178].

[16] This suggestion may be somewhat simplistic, because permit prices will fluctuate to some degree during a compliance period. In practice, penalties could be tied to some average price during the compliance period. If there is a reconciliation period following each compliance year as in the SO_2 and RECLAIM programs, marginal penalties could be tied to the average price during this grace period because this will be the final chance for firms to reconcile their permit holdings to their emissions of the previous year.

marginal gain from being non-compliant: therefore, using a gain-based criterion to set penalties suggests that they be tied to the prevailing permit price. Obviously, the information requirement is not severe; the enforcement authority need only observe the going permit price.[17]

3. Enforcing the SO$_2$ and RECLAIM Programs

We now turn to the actual practice of enforcing emissions trading programs. At the simplest level, enforcement of any law is characterized by two components; monitoring to detect violations and the assessment of sanctions if a violation is found. In this section we describe these components of the SO$_2$ and RECLAIM programs.

3.1 Monitoring in the SO$_2$ and RECLAIM programs

Since the goal of enforcing an emissions trading program is basically to reconcile a facility's permit holdings with its total emissions over some compliance period, monitoring to accomplish this goal involves keeping track of permit holdings and monitoring each source's emissions. In their essentials, the monitoring strategies of the SO$_2$ and RECLAIM programs are quite similar. Both programs have systems in place to track permit holdings. Emissions monitoring in both programs relies heavily on data generated and reported by the facilities themselves. To monitor emissions accurately and to minimize the opportunities facilities may have to falsify reports of their emissions, both programs impose rather stringent technological and process requirements on all facilities.

Keeping track of allowances in the SO$_2$ program is accomplished with the Allowance Tracking System (ATS). As the name suggests the ATS tracks the issuance of allowances, the holding of allowances in various accounts, the deduction of allowances for compliance purposes, and the transfer of allowances between accounts. The ATS is organized into two types of accounts, unit accounts and general accounts. Unit accounts are used by facilities for compliance purposes, while general accounts are used to hold or trade allowances and are not subject to allowance deductions to cover emissions.[18]

---

[17] In contrast, gain-based penalties applied to enforcing emissions standards require that authorities estimate the violators' marginal control costs on a case-by-case basis.

[18] Information about the structure of the Allowance Tracking System can be found at U.S. EPA, "Allowance Tracking Fact Sheet", http://www.epa.gov/airmarkets/tracking/factsheet.html.

All facilities in the SO_2 program are required to install continuous emissions monitoring systems [CEMS], or an equivalent device, to monitor their emissions of SO_2. These systems are capable of providing a nearly continuous and very accurate account of the volume of emissions leaving a facility.[19] All CEMS must be in continuous operation and must be able to sample, analyze, and record data at least every 15 minutes and then reduce the data to 1-hour averages. A unit's CEMS sends the emissions data to the utility's Data Acquisition and Handling System (DAHS), which collects and records the necessary measurements and formats the information electronically into a quarterly report. These quarterly reports are submitted to the EPA electronically.[20] The process for generating emissions reports and submitting them to the EPA is fully automated, thereby minimizing the opportunities for tampering with the emissions data.

Monitoring by EPA officials is focused largely on the facilities' emissions reports, as well as their testing and maintenance reports. The EPA subjects every emission report from SO_2 facilities to a series of reviews to verify their accuracy and determine compliance. Audits appear to be primarily of the source's reports rather than site visits, although the EPA may conduct site audits to inspect CEMS devices and review on-site operations and CEMS quality assurance records.[21]

As in the SO_2 program, RECLAIM authorities spent a great deal of effort designing a monitoring system that focuses on obtaining accurate reports of emissions from the facilities themselves. RECLAIM facilities are also required to install and maintain specific monitoring and reporting equipment, but these requirements differ among types of sources. Specifically, NO_x sources are classified into four categories depending

---

[19] These systems are not cheap. Ellerman, et. al. (1997) estimated the average cost of installing a CEMS for electric generating facilities covered under Phase I of the SO_2 program to be around $700,000, with average annual operating costs of about $47,000.

[20] Other requirements to support monitoring and reporting are related to initial equipment certification procedures, periodic quality assurance and quality control procedures, and procedures for filling in missing data. The approach for estimating emissions when monitoring equipment is not working properly is designed to over-estimate emissions. This biased approach is meant to provide incentive to sources to keep downtime of the monitoring systems to a minimum. See U.S. EPA, "Continuous Emissions Monitoring Fact Sheet", http://www.epa.gov/airmarkets/monitoring/factsheet.html, and "Emissions Tracking Fact Sheet," http://www.epa.gov/airmarkets/reporting/etsfactsheet.html.

[21] For details see U.S. EPA "Quarterly Report Review Process for Determining Final Annual Data", http://www.epa.gov/airmarkets/reporting/arp/closure2001.html.

upon emissions levels: major sources, large sources, process units, and equipment. SO_x sources are classified into three categories; major sources, process units, and equipment.[22]

Continuous Emissions Monitoring Systems are required for all NO_x and SO_x major sources.[23] Facilities in other source-categories are required to install monitoring systems that are cheaper than CEMS, and that are correspondingly less accurate. NO_x large sources must install a device called a fuel flow meter, also known as continuous process monitoring system. Process units and equipment categories for both NO_x and SO_x sources are required to use fuel flow meters or timers (engine hour meters) for emissions monitoring purposes. These devices are intended to produce periodic usage reports (amount of fuel or time of utilization) which, combined with equipment emission standards, are used to produce emissions reports [South Coast Air Quality Management District (1991)].[24]

Estimated emissions must be reported to the AQMD with additional equipment and specific software. Major sources must use a Remote Terminal Unit [RTU] to telecommunicate data to the AQMD Central Station. The RTU collects data, performs calculations, generates the appropriate data files, and transmits the data to the Central Station. Data for large sources and process units may be transmitted via RTU; alternatively, they may compile the data manually and transmit them to the Central Station via modem.

At the end of each compliance year, RECLAIM authorities initiate audits for the previous year. Evaluations of reported data focus on ensuring the accuracy of the data and to check for incidences of noncompliance. Every single emissions report is audited in every single year. Each of

---

[22] For a detailed description of the types of sources in each category see Regulation XX-RECLAIM, Rule 2011 (c), (d) and (e), and Rule 2012 (c) and (d). A 1996 audit of emissions revealed that major NOx sources were responsible for 84% of RECLAIM NOx emissions, while major SOx sources represented almost 98% of total RECLAIM SOx emissions [South Coast Air Quality Management District (1998)].

[23] The costs of CEMS are highly variable; however, in general they are quite expensive. The South Coast Air Quality Management District (1998) estimates the average installed cost of CEMS for RECLAIM facilities to be around $264,000, with an industry minimum of about $37,000 and a maximum of around $675,000. RECLAIM allows major sources to use alternatives to CEMS that are equivalent in terms of relative accuracy, reliability, reproducibility, and timeliness.

[24] Maintenance and testing procedures for all monitoring equipment are required for each year. As in the SO_2 program, RECLAIM rules also include an upwardly biased approach for estimating emissions when monitoring equipment is not working properly.

these reviews apparently includes site visits to inspect equipment, monitoring devices and operation records [South Coast Air Quality Management District (1998, 1999, 2000, 2001)].

The most difficult task of enforcing an emissions trading program is obtaining a reasonably accurate and continuous measure of the emissions leaving each facility. The production of accurate, or at least consistent, emissions data is the most important technical barrier to the widespread use of emissions trading programs [Russell and Powell (1996)]. Considering how much effort has gone into designing and maintaining the monitoring and reporting requirement in the SO_2 and RECLAIM programs, it is clear that policy makers are well aware of this.[25]

Regardless of how emissions are estimated, these data must be transmitted to enforcement authorities so that they can make a determination of compliance. Our model of compliance incentives in emissions trading programs and the reporting requirements of the SO_2 and RECLAIM programs stress the importance of removing firms' incentives or opportunities to submit falsified emissions reports. The model of compliance incentives suggests that this can be accomplished by providing the correct incentives for truthful reporting, while the SO_2 and RECLAIM programs accomplish this with very stringent technology and process requirements. Either way, it is clear that enforcement of any emissions trading program will be effective only if enforcers are able to obtain truthful reports of emissions from regulated facilities.

3.2   Sanctions in the SO_2 and RECLAIM programs

To provide a deterrent against non-compliance in a transferable permit system, facilities whose emissions exceed their permit holdings for some compliance period must face sanctions for these violations. The use of financial sanctions to punish non-compliance in the SO2 program is quite

---

[25] Reasonably accurate monitoring is possible in these contexts because technologies exist that are able to measure emissions leaving distinct discharge points from stationary pollution sources. Furthermore, SO_2 and RECLAIM facilities are large enough to bear the expense of sophisticated monitoring systems without too much difficulty. If emission trading programs are to move beyond their current applications, they must be adaptable to contexts in which emissions monitoring is much more difficult. These will include problems involving: (1) small stationary sources of pollution for which the expense of sophisticated emissions monitoring systems may not be justifiable; (2) mobile-sources of pollution for which feasible monitoring technologies do not yet exist; and (3) non-point source pollution problems such as agricultural run-off where polluters lack distinct discharge points.

close to the way penalties are applied in the model of compliance incentives in the previous section. The unit penalties in the SO_2 program are unique in the fact that they are applied automatically. The penalty was set at $2,000 per ton of excess emissions in 1990, and is indexed to inflation. Consequently, in 1998 the penalty was $2,581 per ton of excess emissions. In addition to the monetary penalty, a non-compliant utility must offset the excess SO_2 emissions from its allowance allocation in some future year.[26]

The most significant difference between the enforcement strategies of the SO_2 and RECLAIM programs is the way sanctions for emissions violations are applied. Whenever an audit reveals a RECLAIM facility to have emissions in excess of its credit holdings, the facility is provided an opportunity to review the audit and to present additional data to further refine the audit results. If, after that review, the facility is judged to be non-compliant, the facility's allocation for the subsequent compliance year is automatically reduced by the total amount of excess emissions. In addition, the RECLAIM authorities may seek to impose administrative financial penalties. Non-compliant facilities may face penalties of up to $500 for every 1,000-pound exceedance for every day the exceedance persists. Perhaps recognizing the greater incentive to be non-compliant when credit prices are high, if the annual average price of credits per ton of emissions reaches $8,000, then the $500 penalty can be applied to every 500 pounds of excess emissions, effectively doubling the available penalty. Application of the $500 penalty is not automatic. Imposition of the penalty depends on the facts of a particular case, including the extent of excess emissions, apparent reason for the exceedance, and the vigor with which a source moves to correct its violation.[27]

---

[26] To help facilities avoid these sanctions, facilities in the SO_2 program have 60 days at the end of each compliance year to acquire additional allowances if they have a shortfall, or to sell or save allowances if they hold more than they need. For additional information see U.S. EPA, "Annual Reconciliation Factsheet", http://www.epa.gov/airmarkets/arp/reconcil/index.html. RECLAIM facilities also enjoy a 60-day reconciliation period at the end of each compliance year. There are also 30-day reconciliation periods after each of the first three quarters of the compliance year. The purpose of these reconciliation periods is to make sure that RECLAIM facilities reconcile the number of credits they hold to their emissions on a more frequent basis than just once a year. See Regulation XX-RECLAIM, Rule 2004 (b) and (c); http://www.aqmd.gov/rules/html.

[27] See Regulation XX RECLAIM, Rule 2004 (d) for the definition of violations, and Rule 2010 (c) for procedures for assessing administrative penalties. The burden of proof for determining the number of days a violation persists falls on the facility. If the facility is unable to show the number of days its violation lasted to the AQMD's satisfaction, it can be assessed the financial penalty for every day of the entire compliance year [Regulation
continued

It is clear that any application of financial penalties in the RECLAIM program will be made on a case-by-case basis, rather than applied automatically as in the SO_2 program. Because of the resulting uncertainty that facilities must have about the consequences they will face if they are non-compliant, it is difficult to judge the deterrence value of the RECLAIM sanctions. We do know, however, that these sanctions provide less of an incentive to avoid emissions violations than if they were fixed and applied automatically as in the SO_2 program. This is true because facilities will not base their compliance decisions on the stated maximum penalty, but on their expectations of what penalty may actually be applied, which, of course, will be some lower value than the available penalty.

4. Compliance in the SO_2 and RECLAIM Programs

The enforcement strategies used in the SO_2 and RECLAIM programs have been quite successful to this point. The SO_2 program has apparently achieved a perfect compliance record. Compliance rates in the RECLAIM program have ranged between 85% and 95%.

Compliance in the SO_2 program

The perfect compliance record of the SO_2 program is quite remarkable when compared to other environmental policies.[28] However, when viewed from the perspective of our conceptual understanding of the compliance incentives in emissions trading programs, it is clear why SO_2 facilities have always chosen to be fully compliant.

One of the most important messages conveyed by our understanding of compliance incentives is that they depend critically on prevailing permit prices. The reason is simple: the prevailing permit price in a well-

---

XX RECLAIM, Rule 2004 (d), and Rule 2010 (c)]. The AQMD may also impose additional permit conditions to prevent further violations [Regulation XX-RECLAIM, Rule 2010 (b), 1 and 2; http://www.aqmd.gov/rules/html.].

[28] Even more remarkable is the rate of aggregate over-compliance achieved by SO_2 facilities. During Phase 1 of the SO_2 program, aggregate emissions were nearly 40% lower than the allocation of allowances in 1995; about 35% lower in 1996, 23% and 24% lower in 1997 and 1998, and about 29% lower in 1999. More dramatically, as a percentage of allowable emissions – the current allocation of allowances plus allowances saved from previous compliance years – aggregate emissions fell to only 30% in 1999. [U.S. EPA (1996-2000)] This is due to the fact that rapid increase in the stock of banked allowances has far outpaced the more modest decrease in the aggregate allocations of allowances.

functioning permit system is a facility's marginal cost of acquiring enough permits to cover its emissions. When permit prices are high, facilities have a greater incentive to be non-compliant, and when they are low, facilities are more likely to be compliant.

Although price data from before the beginning of Phase 1 of the SO_2 program in 1995 suggests highly variable trading prices, by early in the first year of the program, SO_2 allowance prices had converged so that allowances were trading at roughly the same prices [Joskow, et. al. (1998)].[29] In the second compliance year, 1996, average current allowance prices fell to a low of $68 per ton.[30] Since that date, however, current vintage prices have steadily increased; by the end of 1996, prices went up to $90, and then to $115 early in 1997. In 1998, the average price of a current vintage allowance increased from $100 at the beginning of the year to nearly $200 by the end of the year. By June of 1999, the monthly average price for current vintage allowances was in the range $210-$212, but again fell below $200 in the latter half of 1999.[31] During 2000 allowance prices fluctuated quite closely around $150.

The marginal penalty for emissions violations in the SO_2 Trading program has always been many times higher that prevailing allowance prices. This implies that the probability of detecting a violation necessary to achieve complete emissions compliance π, which is determined from $p \leq \pi \times [f + g]$, can be very low. For example, in 1998, prices for allowances ranged between $100 and $200 per allowance. In the same year the monetary penalty for excess emissions was $2,581 per unit. In addition, any excess emissions would have been offset in 1999, suggesting an additional per unit penalty for forfeited 1999 allowances equal to the present value of these allowances. Assuming that this value was roughly equal to 1998 permit prices, the effective marginal penalty for an emissions violation would have been in the neighborhood of $2,650 to $2,750. With a probability of detecting a violation as low as 0.08, $p < \pi \times [f + g]$ would be satisfied (even without a penalty for reporting violations) and sources

---

[29] Updated information on allowance prices and transactions can be found at U.S. EPA, "Monthly Average Prices of Sulfur Dioxide Allowances", http://www.epa.gov/airmarkets/trading/so2market/prices.html. Reported average prices differ slightly among the brokerage firms supplying price data.

[30] The current vintage is defined as those allowances that can be used to cover current emissions. In other words it includes allowances allocated for the current period plus banked allowances from previous compliance years.

[31] One of the surprises of the SO_2 program is that allowance prices have been much lower than they were expected to be before allowance trading began. Explaining this has been a major focus of the literature [see for example Burtraw (1996), Ellerman and Montero (1998), and Ellerman, et. al. (1997), especially section VI].

would have the correct incentive to provide accurate emissions reports. Given the effort expended on monitoring and the stringency of the reporting requirements in the SO_2 program, the actual probability of detecting reporting and emissions violations is probably much higher.

We have noted that as long as $p < \pi \times [f + g]$ is satisfied, emissions compliance is a simple matter of comparing the prevailing allowance price p to the certain unit penalty for emissions violations f. In the 1998 compliance year, for example, $p < f$ was easily satisfied because the unit value of the SO_2 sanctions was between 13 and 27 times higher than prevailing allowance prices.

Our understanding of compliance incentives in emissions trading programs confirms Becker's (1968) seminal insight about the substitutability between monitoring for compliance and penalties for non-compliance. He pointed out that if monitoring is costly but setting penalties is not, the enforcement costs of maintaining compliance can be minimized by setting marginal penalties at arbitrarily high levels so that monitoring probabilities can be made arbitrarily small. There are very sound theoretical and ethical reasons for why this strategy is not very practical and, perhaps for these reasons, the strategy is not observed in actual practice.[32] However, relative to prices for SO_2 allowances, the marginal penalty for emissions violations in the SO_2 program is very high. Thus, there is at least some precedence for setting penalties for emissions violations that are many times greater than prevailing permit prices. Within practical limits, therefore, the tradeoff between monitoring and penalties can be exploited to reduce monitoring effort, or to increase the deterrence value of a particular monitoring strategy.

Because SO_2 sources can also trade allowances dated for the future, we also have some indication of future allowance prices, and hence, future compliance incentives. Consider for example the results from the "7-year advance" auctions by the U.S. EPA[33]. The clearing prices for these

---

[32] See Cohen (1999, section 3) and Macauley and Brennan (1998, section 3.3.2) for discussions of the limits to setting arbitrarily high penalties, both with particular reference to enforcing environmental policies.

[33] Information on the results of annual auctions can be found at U.S. EPA, "Acid Rain Program Allowance Auctions", http://www.epa.gov/airmarkets/auctions/index.html. As the name suggests, "7-years advance" allowances can first be used for compliance purposes seven years into the future. A "6-years advance" auction was also conducted between 1994 and 1997.

auctions were about $168 a ton in 1999, $55 per ton in 2000, and $105 a ton in 2001. For the same years the clearing prices in the spot auctions were about $201, $126, and $174, respectively. This information suggests that allowance prices in the near future are likely to be similar to current prices (perhaps somewhat lower in real terms). Thus, as long as allowance prices remain well below the penalty for excess emissions, it seems likely that the perfect compliance record of the SO_2 program will persist.

Compliance in the RECLAIM program

The RECLAIM program has experienced non-compliant firms from its inception. In the early years much of the non-compliance was attributed to misunderstandings of the required protocols [South Coast Air Quality Management District (1998)]. In recent years there has been a substantial amount of classic non-compliance, that is, firms failing to purchase sufficient credits to cover their emissions. In the 1998 compliance year, 27 out 329 firms were non-compliant in NO_x emissions, while 31 out of 361 were non-compliant in 1999. In both years, all firms were compliant in SO_x emissions.[34]

Simple mistakes early on are easily explained as stemming from lack of experience with the RECLAIM rules. Explaining the more willful violations is not as straightforward. However, using the incentive approach that we've taken, a plausible explanation may start from the fact that effective prices for RECLAIM credits are high and increasing.[35] Average prices for a ton of NO_x emissions during the first four calendar years of the program were always below $250, but rose to $451 during the 1998 calendar year, and to $1,827 in 1999.[36] Average prices per ton of SO_x were under $150 during the first four years of the program, but rose

---

[34] In aggregate, RECLAIM facilities have been significantly over-compliant. Aggregate emissions of SOx as a percentage of allowable emissions given by the aggregate allocation of SOx credits were about 70% in 1994, rose steadily to about 90% in 1998, and are expected to be around 92% for the 1999 compliance year. Aggregate SOx emissions as a percentage of allowable emissions are similar. In 1994, aggregate SOx emissions were about 63% of allowable emissions, rising to 85% in 1998, and expected to be about 99% of allowable emissions in 1999 [South Coast Air Quality Management District (2001)].

[35] RECLAIM designers appear to have been aware of potential compliance problems they may face from high credit prices. They established a "backstop price" of $15,000 per ton, which if reached would trigger a complete reassessment of the program [Regulation XX-RECLAIM, Rule 2015, (b)-6; http://www.aqmd.gov/rules/html.]. Furthermore, recall that if credit prices reach $8,000 per ton, available monetary penalties for non-compliance are effectively doubled [Regulation XX-RECLAIM, Rule 2004, (d)-3; http://www.aqmd.gov/rules/html.].

[36] While credits are expressed in pounds, the AQMD reports prices per ton of emissions.

to about \$300 in 1998, and to \$780 per ton in 1999. In 2000, prices for NO_x credits rose dramatically: for compliance year 1999 NO_x credits traded in 2000 the average price rose to \$15,369 per ton, while for 2000 NO_x credits traded in 2000 the average price was \$45, 609. Average prices for 2000 SO_x credits traded in 2000 also increased, but to a more modest \$2,462 per ton [South Coast Air Quality Management District (2001)].[37]

In addition, because of the emissions fees that RECLAIM facilities face, effective prices for RECLAIM emissions credits in the first five years of the program, and therefore, facilities' marginal benefits of non-compliance in these years, were much higher than their market prices. Relative to RECLAIM credit prices from 1994 to 1998, the fees are not small. Furthermore, these fees vary with the amount of pollution released. For annual emissions between 4 and 25 tons per year, the fees are currently \$171.30 and \$203.10 per ton of NO_x and SO_x, respectively. When annual emissions are between 25 and 75 the fees are \$272.10 and \$328.30 per ton of NO_x and SO_x, respectively. Finally, for annual emissions greater than 75 tons, the fees are \$409.80 and \$492.90 per ton of NO_x and SO_x, respectively.[38] In 1998, the market price for credits for a ton of SO_x emissions was about \$300. Because of the SO_x emissions fee, however, a small source of SOx faced an effective price of SO_x emissions of just over \$500 per ton, while the effective price for a large source was nearly \$800 per ton, about 2.67 times higher than the prevailing credit price at the time. Of course, with current credit prices many times higher than they were in 1998, the impact of the emissions fees on RECLAIM facilities' compliance incentives has eroded substantially.

RECLAIM violations may also result from the fact that the monetary penalties for emissions violations are not fixed or automatic as they are in the SO_2 program. Recall that stated monetary penalties in the RECLAIM regulations are maximum administrative penalties and that actual financial sanctions are to be decided on a case-by-case basis. The resulting uncertainty that RECLAIM facilities must then have about the consequences of their violations lessens the deterrence value of these sanctions; that is, facilities' evaluations of their expected marginal costs

---

[37] Part of the explanation for increase in the prices NOX credits is apparently increased demand for credits by California power companies. High prices have led RECLAIM authorities to search for means to "stabilize" the NOx credit market. See the minutes of the RECLAIM board meeting of 1/19/2001, at www.agmd.gov/hb/010123a.html.

[38] Emissions fees, as well as other fees paid by RECLAIM facilities, appear not to be indexed to inflation. Therefore, they must be increased periodically so that their real values do not fall over time.

of non-compliance are probably substantially lower than if financial sanctions were fixed and applied automatically. Because of the relatively low expected marginal costs of non-compliance that stem from the uncertainty of the financial sanctions they may face, and the relatively high marginal benefits of non-compliance that are exacerbated by the RECLAIM emissions fees, it is quite possible that a number of RECLAIM facilities have decided that the incentives they face do not warrant their full compliance.

We are also somewhat pessimistic about the future compliance performance of the RECLAIM program. Not only will credit prices be quite high for the 2000 compliance year, they will remain high into the near future. The average price for 2003 NO_x credits traded in 2000 was about \$13,800, while the average price for 2003 SO_x credits traded in 2000 was nearly \$3,000 per ton [South Coast Air Quality Management District (2001)]. If there is no off-setting change in the RECLAIM enforcement strategy, the compliance problems the program has experienced thus far, though relatively few in number to this point in time, may very well increase in the future.

5. Conclusions: Principles for Enforcing Emissions Trading Programs

Taken together — a conceptual understanding of the compliance incentives faced by firms in an emissions trading program, the practice of enforcing the SO_2 and RECLAIM programs, and the compliance performance of SO_2 and RECLAIM facilities thus far — several guidelines for enforcing emissions trading programs emerge.

Our approach to examining compliance incentives in emissions trading programs stresses the importance of the prevailing permit price. In a reasonably competitive trading environment the prevailing permit price completely summarizes each facility's marginal benefit of noncompliance. A number of guiding principles follow from this simple observation. First, details about a firm's operations, like its production and emissions-control technologies, are not important components of their compliance incentives. Therefore, there is no reason for an enforcement authority to target its enforcement effort because it suspects that some facilities may be more likely to be non-compliant than others, even though they may be quite heterogeneous. There is no evidence that SO_2 and RECLAIM officials pursue some sort of targeted enforcement strategy.

Unfortunately, in non-competitive environments – those in which permit trades involve significant transaction costs, when a firm or group of firms can exercise power in a permit market, or when firms face differentiated emissions taxes as in the RECLAIM program – going permit prices may not convey all the necessary information about facilities' compliance incentives. Furthermore, these complications may produce differentiated compliance incentives.

Non-competitive elements aside, we have made several suggestions for setting penalties in emissions trading programs. First, since permit prices have such an important influence on compliance incentives, to stabilize compliance incentives and corresponding enforcement strategies in the face of permit price fluctuations, unit penalties for emissions violations should be tied directly to prevailing permit prices. This suggestion may be particularly useful in the RECLAIM program, where credit prices have risen rapidly over the last couple years. Unit penalties that follow credit prices would offset the increasing incentive toward non-compliance that comes with higher credit prices. In the RECLAIM context, this strategy must account for the emissions fees that RECLAIM facilities pay. Thus, our suggestion would be modified to tie penalties to prevailing credit prices *plus* the emissions tax rates.

Second, these penalties should be substantially higher than prevailing permit prices. Certainly, the perfect compliance record of facilities in the SO_2 program is due in large part to the fact that penalties in the SO_2 program have always been many times higher than going allowance prices.

Third, penalties should be applied automatically in cases of non-compliance. More generally, the application of penalties should not produce uncertainty for firms about the consequences of non-compliance. The fact that unit penalties in the SO_2 program are fixed and are intended to be applied automatically has probably been another contributing factor to the perfect compliance record of SO_2 facilities. On the other hand, we suspect that the determination of penalties on a case-by-case basis in the RECLAIM program produces uncertainty for facilities about the consequences of non-compliance, and thus weakens the deterrence value of the RECLAIM enforcement strategy.

On the other side of the enforcement equation – monitoring for compliance – it is clear that a well-functioning emissions trading program requires continuous and reasonably accurate estimates of the emissions leaving each facility. The designers of the enforcement components of the SO_2 and RECLAIM programs addressed this difficulty by requiring emissions sources to install and maintain advanced emissions monitoring systems.

The importance of accurate emissions monitoring in practice points to the fact that we lack a clear understanding of how monitoring accuracy is likely to affect the performance of emissions trading programs. The ability to obtain accurate data on facilities' emissions may be the most important factor limiting the widespread implementation of emissions trading programs.

But we really don't know what level of accuracy is required for a well-functioning program, how achieving reasonably accurate monitoring should be accomplished, or what constitutes efficient investments in monitoring accuracy. Future research that approaches this issue from the perspective of balancing the costs of obtaining greater accuracy against the benefits of doing so would go a long way toward illuminating the inherent trade-offs in the problem.

Our understanding of compliance incentives in emissions trading programs makes it clear, however, that accurate emissions data is only useful if facilities provide enforcement authorities with truthful reports of these emissions – the enforcement of any emissions trading program will be effective only if the incentive or opportunities for falsifying emissions reports are removed. As with generating accurate emissions data, the SO_2 and RECLAIM programs addressed this issue with very stringent technological and process requirements for submitting data to enforcement authorities.

While it is true that our understanding of the theory and practice of enforcing emissions trading programs adds new insight into the problem, it is equally true that this exercise reveals critical areas in which our knowledge is lacking. Future research that addresses issues concerning the dynamics of compliance, monitoring accuracy, and the enforcement problems associated with implementing emissions trading programs in a wider variety of environmental policy problems than at present is needed to help refine existing enforcement strategies and to design enforcement strategies for new market-based policies.

The practice and theory of market-based environmental control has progressed quite far since they were first proposed more than thirty year ago. However, too little attention has been given to understanding the nature of the compliance incentives inherent in these programs and to the manner in which these programs are actually enforced. It is our hope that this work will help to bridge the gap between the practice and theory of enforcing market-based environmental policies, and that it will help motivate policymakers and analysts alike to look for even more innovative ways to ensure that market-based policies can achieve environmental quality goals while conserving private and public resources.

References

Baumol, William and Wallace Oates. 1988. *The Theory of Environmental Policy*. New York: Cambridge University Press.

Beavis, Brian and Martin Walker. 1983. "Random Wastes, Imperfect Monitoring and Environmental Quality Standards." *Journal of Public Economics* 21: 377-387.

Becker, Gary S. 1968. "Crime and Punishment: An Economic Approach." *Journal of Political Economy* 76(2): 169-217.

Brady, Gordon.1983. "Emissions Trading in the United States: An Overview and Technical Requirements." *Journal of Environmental Management* 17(1), 63-79.

Burtraw, Dallas. 1996. "The SO_2 Emissions Trading Program: Cost Savings Without Allowance Trades." *Contemporary Economic Policy* 14: 79-94.

Chavez, Carlos A. 2000. *Enforcing Market-Based Environmental Policies*. Ph.D. Dissertation, Department of Resource Economics, University of Massachusetts-Amherst.

Cohen, Mark. 1999. "Monitoring and Enforcement of Environmental Policy." Forthcoming in *International Yearbook of Environmental and Resource Economics, Volume III*, edited by Tom Tietenberg and Henk Folmer. Brookfield Vermont: Edward Elgar Publishing.

Crocker, Tom. 1966. "Structuring of Atmospheric Pollution Control Systems." In *The Economics of Air Pollution*, H. Wolozin (ed.), W.W. Norton, New York.

Dales John. 1968. *Pollution, Property and Prices*. University of Toronto Press, Toronto.

Ellerman, A. Denny and Juan Pablo Montero. 1998. "The Declining Trend in Sulfur Dioxide Emissions: Implications for Allowance Prices." *Journal of Environmental Economics and Management* 36: 26-45.

Ellerman, A. Denny; Richard Schmalensee, Paul L. Joskow, Juan P. Montero, and Elizabeth M. Bailey. 1997. "Emissions Trading Under the U.S. Acid Rain Program: Evaluation of Compliance Costs and Allowance Market Performance." MIT Center of Energy and Environmental Policy, Cambridge, MA.

Garvie, Devon and Andrew Keeler. 1994. "Incomplete Enforcement with Endogenous Regulatory Choice." *Journal of Public Economics* 55: 141-162.

Hahn, Robert. 1984. "Market Power and Transferable Property Rights." *Quarterly Journal of Economics* 99: 753-65.

Hahn, Robert. 1989. *A Primer on Environmental Policy Design*. Harwood Academic Publishers, Chur, Switzerland.

Hahn, Robert and Robert Axtell. 1995. "Reevaluating the Relationship between Transferable Property Rights and Command-and-Control Regulation." *Journal of Regulatory Economics* 8(2): 125-48.

Hahn, Robert and Roger Noll. 1982. "Designing a Market for Tradeable Emissions Permits." In *Reform of Environmental Regulation*, Wesley Magat (ed.), Ballinger Publishing, Cambridge MA, 119-146.

Hanley, Nick; Jason Shogren, and Ben White. 1997. *Environmental Economics in Theory and Practice*. New York: Oxford University Press.

Harford, Jon. 1987. "Self-Reporting of Pollution and the Firm's Behavior Under Imperfectly Enforceable Regulations." *Journal of Environmental Economics and Management* 14: 293-303.

Joskow, Paul, Richard Schmalensee, and Elizabeth M. Bailey. 1998. "The Market for Sulfur Dioxide Emissions," *American Economic Review* 88(4), 669-685.

Kaplow, Louis and Steven Shavell. 1994. "Optimal Law Enforcement with Self-Reporting of Behavior." *Journal of Political Economy* 103(3): 583-606.

Keeler, Andrew. 1991. "Noncompliant Firms in Transferable Discharge Permit Markets: Some Extensions." *Journal of Environmental Economics and Management* 21: 180-189.

Krupnick, A., W. Oates and E. Van De Verg. 1980. "On Marketable Air Pollution Permits: The Case for a System of Pollution Offsets." *Journal of Environmental Economics and Management* 10, 233-47.

Livernois, John and C.J. McKenna. 1999. "Truth or Consequences: Enforcing Pollution Standards with Self-Reporting." *Journal of Public Economics* 73(3): 415-440.

Macauley, Molly and Timothy Brennan. 1998. "Enforcing Environmental Regulation: Implications of Remote Sensing Technology." RFF Discussion Paper 98-33. Washington DC: Resources for the Future.

Malik, Arun. 1990. "Markets for Pollution Control when Firms are Noncompliant." *Journal of Environmental Economics and Management* 18: 97-106.

Malik, Arun. 1992. "Enforcement Costs and the Choice of Policy Instruments for Pollution Control." *Economic Inquiry* 30: 714-721.

Malik, Arun. 1993. "Self-Reporting and the Design of Policies for Regulating Stochastic Pollution." *Journal of Environmental Economics and Management* 24: 241-257.

Malueg, David. 1990. "Welfare Consequences of Emissions Credit Trading Programs." *Journal of Environmental Economics and Management* 18(1), 66-77.

McGartland, A and W. Oates. 1985. "Marketable Permits for the Prevention of Environmental Deterioration." *Journal of Environmental Economics and Management* 12, 207-228.

Montero, Juan Pablo. 1999. "Voluntary Compliance with Market-Based Environmental Policy: Evidence from the U.S. Acid Rain Program." *Journal of Political Economy* 107(5): 998--1033.

Montgomery, W. David 1972. "Markets in Licenses and Efficient Pollution Control Programs." *Journal of Economic Theory* 5(3): 395-418.

Russell, Clifford S. and Philip T. Powell. 1996. "Choosing Environmental Policy Tools: Theoretical Cautions and Practical Considerations." Unpublished manuscript, Institute for Public Policy Studies, Vanderbilt University.

Schwarze, Reimund and Peter Zapfel. 2000. "Sulfur Allowance Trading and the Regional Clean Air Incentives Market: A Comparative Design Analysis of Two Major Cap-and-Trade Permit Programs." *Environmental & Resource Economics* 17(3), 279-98.

South Coast Air Quality Management District, Internet site, http://www.aqmd.gov.html. "Regulation XX – Regional Clean Air Incentives Market (RECLAIM)
http://www.aqmd.gov/rules/html.
"Rule 301. Permitting and Associated Fees http://www.aqmd.gov/rules/html/r301.html.

South Coast Air Quality Management District. 2001. "*Annual RECLAIM Audit Report for the 1999 Compliance Year.*" South Coast Air Quality Management District, Diamond Bar, CA.

South Coast Air Quality Management District. 2000. "*Annual RECLAIM Audit Report for the 1998 Compliance Year.*" South Coast Air Quality Management District, Diamond Bar, CA.

South Coast Air Quality Management District. 1998. "*RECLAIM Program Three-Year Audit and Progress Report.*" South Coast Air Quality Management District, Diamond Bar, CA.

South Coast Air Quality Management District. 1991. "*Marketable Permits Program: Enforcement – The Critical Element.*" Working Paper # 3. Office of Planning and Rules, South Coast Air Quality Management District, Diamond Bar, CA.

Stavins, Robert. 1995. "Transactions Costs and Tradeable Permits." *Journal of Environmental Economics and Management* 29: 133-148.

Stranlund, John K. and Carlos A. Chavez. 2000. "Effective Enforcement of a Transferable Emissions Permit System with a Self-Reporting Requirement." *Journal of Regulatory Economics* 18(2), 113-131.

Stranlund, John K. and Kanwalroop K. Dhanda. 1999. "Endogenous Monitoring and Enforcement of a Transferable Emissions Permit System." *Journal of Environmental Economics and Management* 38(3): 267-282.

Tietenberg, Tom. 1985. *Emissions Trading: An Exercise in Reforming Pollution Policy*. Resources for the Future, Washington DC.

Tripp, James and Daniel Dudek. 1989. "Institutional Guidelines for Designing Successful Transferable Rights Programs." *Yale Journal of Regulation* 6(2), 369-392.

U.S. Environmental Protection Agency, Acid Rain Program internet site, http://www.epa.gov/airmarkets/arp/.
   "Acid Rain Program Allowance Auctions, http://www.epa.gov/airmarkets/auctions/index.html.
   "Allowance Tracking Fact Sheet", http://www.epa.gov/airmarkets/tracking/factsheet.html
   "Annual Reconciliation Factsheet, http://www.epa.gov/airmarkets/arp/reconcil/index.html.
   "Continuous Emissions Monitoring Fact Sheet, http://www.epa.gov/airmarkets/monitoring/factsheet.html.
   "Emissions Tracking Fact Sheet, http://www.epa.gov/airmarkets/reporting/etsfactsheet.html.
   "Monthly Average Price of Sulfur Dioxide Allowances, http://www.epa.gov/airmarkets/trading/so2market/prices.html.
   "Quarterly Report Review Process for Determining Final Annual Data, http://www.epa.gov/airmarkets/reporting/arp/closure2001.html.

U.S. Environmental Protection Agency. 2000. *Acid Rain Program 1999 Compliance Report*. U.S. EPA Acid Rain Program, Washington DC.

U.S. Environmental Protection Agency. 1999. *Acid Rain Program 1998 Compliance Report*. U.S. EPA Acid Rain Program, Washington DC.

U.S. Environmental Protection Agency. 1998. *Acid Rain Program 1997 Compliance Report*. U.S. EPA Acid Rain Program, Washington DC.

U.S. Environmental Protection Agency. 1997. *Acid Rain Program 1996 Compliance Report*. U.S. EPA Acid Rain Program, Washington DC.

U.S. Environmental Protection Agency. 1996. *Acid Rain Program 1995 Compliance Report*. U.S. EPA Acid Rain Program, Washington DC.

vanEgteren, Henry and Marian Weber. 1996. "Marketable Permits, Market Power, and Cheating." *Journal of Environmental Economics and Management* 30: 161-173.

Wasserman, Cheryl. 1992. "Federal Enforcement: Theory and Practice." In *Innovation in Environmental Policy*, edited by Thomas Tietenberg. Brookfield Vermont: Edward Elgar Publishing.

CHAPTER NINE

COMPLIANCE ASSISTANCE & "BEYOND COMPLIANCE"

INTRODUCTION

This chapter introduces a selection of the best literature in the field of compliance assistance, including private sector efforts and "beyond compliance."[1] At their core, these efforts are about enabling and encouraging actors to voluntarily comply with laws that protect the environment and promote sustainable development. Under the rationalist theory of compliance, (described in Chapter Two: Complinace Theories), rational actors base their decision to comply on a self-interested calculation, balancing the costs and benefits of compliance against the costs and benefits of non-compliance.[2] But compliance at both the domestic and international level generally is a more complicated affair for a range of reasons.

At the domestic level, small and medium-sized firms often lack the capacity to comply. This may be due to a lack of capital, technical expertise, technology, or other necessary resources. Cooperative measures are therefore important to supplement deterrence-based strategies, as explained in the first excerpt in this chapter from Malcolm K. Sparrow's book *The Regulatory Craft*.[3]

At the international level, developing and transition countries often struggle to comply with Multilateral Environmental Agreements (MEAs) because of a lack of capacity. The Montreal Protocol is one of the few MEAs with a robust compliance assistance program to ensure broad

---

[1] Beyond compliance has been described as a "[v]oluntary overmeeting of environmental standards." *See* Seema Arora & Shubhashis Gangopadhyay, *Toward a theoretical model of voluntary overcompliance*, 28 J. ECON. BEHAVIOR & ORG., 289 (1995). *See also* BEYOND COMPLIANCE: A NEW INDUSTRY VIEW OF THE ENVIRONMENT (Bruce Smart ed., 1992).

[2] *See* Kal Raustiala, *Compliance & Effectiveness in International Regulatory Cooperation*, excerpted in Chapter Two: Compliance Theories.

[3] MALCOLM K. SPARROW, THE REGULATORY CRAFT: CONTROLLING RISKS, SOLVING PROBLEMS, AND MANAGING COMPLIANCE (2000).

compliance. Countries in non-compliance are eligible to receive financial and technical assistance designed to strengthen capacity and help implement and enforce domestic legislation required under the treaty.[4]

Additionally, the United Nations Environment Programme (UNEP), the United Nations Economic Council for Europe (UNECE), the Global Environment Facility (GEF),[5] and others have produced guidelines to facilitate implementation and compliance with certain MEAs.[6] The UNEP Guidelines, for instance, highlight several compliance assistance strategies, including sharing of experiences, evaluating the effectiveness of technology transfer, and drafting model legislation. But apart from these efforts, most MEAs do not have sufficient financial resources to provide significant compliance assistance.

At the regional level, the EU provides formidable financial and technical assistance to its Accession Countries to strengthen their institutional capacity to implement and ensure compliance with EU laws and regulations, as described in the second excerpt in this chapter, by Georges Kremlis and Jan Dusik.[7] The EU provides such support for the many years needed to approximate the *environmental acquis* and to build sufficient capacity before formal accession.[8]

At the domestic level, small- and medium-sized enterprises (SMEs) often lack the capacity to bring their businesses into compliance with environmental standards. A recent study in the U.K. noted that SMEs

---

[4] *See* K. Madhava Sarma, *Compliance with the Montreal Protocol*, excerpted in Chapter Three: Multilateral Environmental Agreements in Action (noting that from 1991-2004, the non-Article 5 Parties pledged nearly US$ 1.89 billion and paid nearly US$ 1.63 billion to the Multilateral Fund.). *See also* David G. Victor, *The Operation and Effectiveness of the Montreal Protocol's Non-Compliance Procedure*, *in* THE IMPLEMENTATION AND EFFECTIVENESS OF INTERNATIONAL ENVIRONMENTAL COMMITMENTS: THEORY AND PRACTICE (David G. Victor, Kal Raustiala, & Eugene B. Skolnikoff eds., 1998).

[5] The GEF helps developing countries fund projects and programs that protect the global environment. GEF grants support projects related to biodiversity, climate change, international waters, land degradation, the ozone layer, and persistent organic pollutants. *See* http://www.gefweb.org.

[6] *See* Elizabeth Mrema and Carl Bruch, *UNEP Guidelines and Manual on Compliance with and Enforcement of Multilateral Environmental Agreements (MEAs)*, excerpted in Chapter 3: Multilateral Environmental Agreements in Action (with Appendix, "A Survey of Other Guidance and Initiatives for Implementing MEAs").

[7] Georges Kremlis & Jan Dusik, *The Challenge of the Implementation of the Environmental Acquis Communautaire in the New Member States*, 7th INECE Conference Proceedings (forthcoming 2005).

[8] *See* ECOTEC, *The Benefits of Compliance with the Environmental Acquis for Candidate Countries*, *available at* http://europa.eu.int/comm/environment/enlarg/pdf/benefit_long.pdf.

comprise more than 99 percent of the 3.7 million businesses in the U.K. and generate about 60 percent of its commercial waste and as much as 80 percent of the pollution in England and Wales.[9] The study revealed that 82 percent of the SMEs could not name any environmental legislation unprompted, and 77 percent had not taken any measures aimed at reducing harm to the environment. Non-compliance rates among SMEs in developing and transition countries presumably are even higher.

Because environmental laws are often complex, compliance assistance is especially appropriate for SMEs.[10] For example, a study of dry cleaners in the Los Angeles area reported that there are more than 36,000 such businesses in the U.S., with 2,618 in California alone. Of the ones in California, the overwhelming majority were not in compliance.[11] In the third excerpt, Neil Gunningham and Darren Sinclair discuss compliance assistance programs for SMEs.[12] In the fourth excerpt, Paul Leinster, Jim Gray, Chris Howes, and Rosie Clark describe compliance assistance programs in the U.K.,[13] while in the fifth excerpt Ramani Ellepola describes compliance assistance in Sri Lanka.[14]

In addition to compliance assistance from the state, the private sector also provides a form of compliance assistance through certification programs, Environmental Management Systems, and self-auditing. In the sixth excerpt, Dara O'Rourke elaborates on these emerging

---

[9] The SME-nvironment 2003 survey was carried out by WS Atkins on behalf of NetRegs and covered 8,604 SMEs (defined as businesses with less than 250 employees) in 28 industries across the U.K. The survey found that only "23% of all respondents had implemented any measures aimed at reducing harm to the environment....". *See* http://www.environment-agency.gov.uk/commondata/acrobat/smenvironmnet_uk_2003.pdf.

[10] Michael P. Vandenberg, *Beyond Elegance: A Testable Typology of Social Norms in Corporate Environmental Compliance*, 22 STAN. ENVTL. L.J. 55, 83-84 (2003) ("[D]eterrence-based enforcement measures can undermine motivations to comply when directed at regulated entities that were motivated to comply but lacked the capacity to understand their obligations because of the complexity of the regulatory scheme."). *See also* Chapter Two: Compliance Theories.

[11] The rates of non-compliance were between 79% and 98%. See Timothy F. Malloy & Peter Sinsheimer, *Pollution Prevention as a Regulatory Tool in California: Breaking Barriers and Building Bridges* (2001), *available at* http://www1.law.ucla.edu/~erg/pubs/MalloyBuildingBridgesReport.pdf.

[12] NEIL GUNNINGHAM & DARREN SINCLAIR, LEADERS & LAGGARDS: NEXT-GENERATION ENVIRONMENTAL REGULATION, Chapter 2 (2002).

[13] Paul Leinster, Jim Gray, Chris Howes & Rosie Clark, *Compliance Promotion in the United Kingdom*, 7th INECE Conference Proceedings (forthcoming 2005).

[14] Ramani Ellepola, *Implementation of Industrial Pollution Control Programs in Sri Lanka*, 5th INECE Conference Proceedings, vol. 1 (1998), *available at* http://www.inece.org.

nongovernmental "regulations." Then Tim Bartley describes the evolution and value of certification systems.[15] A brief excerpt by Arnoldo Contreras-Hermosilla and Global Witness follows Bartley's piece, describing a certification program in Bolivia.[16] Clifford Rechtschaffen then outlines the value of mandatory audits and EMS programs for private firms.[17]

The incentives are different for firms that do have the capacity to achieve compliance. For these firms, there are other programs that encourage and reward activities that go "beyond compliance."[18] In the ninth excerpt in this chapter, Kathryn Harrison describes the workings of voluntary programs through four case studies in the U.S., Canada, the Netherlands, and Germany.[19] Then, in this chapter's final excerpt, the OECD describes a mixture of compliance assistance and voluntary compliance programs in Newly Independent States (NIS) .[20]

It is important to note that beyond compliance and voluntary compliance initiatives are most effective when they supplement deterrence-based strategies. As Chester Bowles said, "20 percent of the regulated population will automatically comply with any regulation, 5 percent will attempt to evade it, and the remaining 75 percent will comply as long as they think that the 5 percent will be caught and punished."[21] Every

---

[15] Dara O'Rourke, *Outsourcing Regulation: Analyzing Nongovernmental Systems of Labor Standards and Monitoring*, 31(1) Pol'y Studies J., 1 (2003); Tim Bartley, *Certifying Forests and Factories: States, Social Movements, and the Rise of Private Regulation in the Apparel and Forest Products Fields*, 31(3) Politics & Soc.,433 (2003).

[16] Arnoldo Contreras-Hermosilla & Global Witness, *Emerging Best Practices for Combating Illegal Activities in the Forest Sector* (2003).

[17] Clifford Rechtschaffen, *Deterrence vs. Cooperation and the Evolving Theory of Environmental Enforcement*, 71 S. Cal. L. Rev. 1181 (1998).

[18] *See supra* note 1. Another type of voluntary compliance includes programs that firms can opt into, such as voluntary emissions trading schemes. These types of voluntary programs may be useful to test new policy initiatives, but regulatory schemes that lack the threat of a sanction may not be as effective as those that do. *See* Daniel C. Esty, *Environmental Protection in the Information Age*, 79 N.Y.U. L. Rev. 115 (2004) ("It is important to note that not all "voluntary" actions are truly voluntary. Some such actions are taken in response to consumer demands and should be seen, therefore, as an institutional offshoot of the marketplace. Others represent efforts to forestall regulation, such as the EPA's 33/50 'voluntary' toxics reduction initiative."). *See also* Chapter Seven: Information Regulation; Chapter Thirteen: Compliance & Competitiveness: The Porter Hypothesis.

[19] Kathryn Harrison, *Talking with the Donkey: Cooperative Approaches to Environmental Protection*, 2(3) J. Indus. Ecology 51(1998).

[20] OECD, *Environmental Compliance and Enforcement in the NIS: A Survey of Current Practices of Environmental Inspectorates and Options for Improvements* (2000).

enforcement and compliance official has his or her own statistics to describe these categories, but they all recognize that deterrence remains vital for most compliance efforts. As the eminent jurist H.L.A. Hart explained: "[H]uman altruism is limited in range and intermittent ... 'Sanctions are therefore required not as the normal motive for obedience, but as a *guarantee* that those who would voluntarily obey shall not be scarified to those who would not. ... Given this standing danger, what reason demands is *voluntary* co-operation in a *coercive* system."[22] Experience demands assistance to those who lack the capacity to comply.

---

[21] CHESTER BOWLES, PROMISES TO KEEP: MY YEARS IN PUBLIC SERVICE, 1941-1969, 25 (1971). For further discussion on deterrence, *see* Chapter Four: Domestic Enforcement Strategies.

[22] H. L. A. Hart, THE CONCEPT OF LAW, 196-198 (2nd ed. 1994).

The Regulatory Craft: Controlling Risks, Solving Problems, and Managing Compliance

Malcolm K. Sparrow

Chapter 13 (2000)

... I hope this chapter succeeds in dismissing the ... misleading notion that enlightened regulatory practice necessarily rejects reactive tactics and embraces prevention. The two ideas - rejecting enforcement and rejecting reactive tactics - are related, of course, because of the strong association between enforcement methods and a reactive stance; so when regulators turn their backs on one, they most likely turn their backs on the other. The shortcomings of reactive strategies are well established and have been much written of. The introduction of my 1994 volume states:

> The traditional cultures of environmental protection, policing, and tax collection incorporate a classic enforcement mentality, built upon the fundamental assumption that a ruthless and efficient investigation and enforcement capability will produce compliance through the mechanism of deterrence. . . . In each of these three fields the traditional enforcement approach is under stress. There are too many violators, too many laws to be enforced, and not enough resources to get the job done.[1]

Later, in introducing the notion of problem solving more formally, I point out:

---

[1] Malcolm K. Sparrow, *Imposing Duties: Government's Changing Approach to Compliance* (Praeger, 1994), p. ix.

There is a certain foolishness in traditional enforcement approaches. They wait until the damage has been done, and then they react, case by case, incident by incident, failure by failure. Enforcement agencies accept the work *in the form and the order in which* it arrives, and, therefore, have tended to organize their activities around fail-ures rather than around opportunities for intervention.[2] ...

The Hard-Soft Dilemma and Its Surrogates

What I did not realize in 1994 was how quickly and easily rejection of reactive *strategies* leads to the decimation of reactive *capabilities*. The flawed logic that connects the two goes like this:

We recognize the limitations of a reactive strategy, with its too-late, incident-specific, heavy-handed enforcement orientation. We therefore *replace the reactive strategy with a preventive strategy,* moving resources from the back end to the front end, replacing investigators with educators and consultants to encourage and facilitate compliance. If prevention succeeds, we will need much less response and enforcement capacity, and we will be able to deemphasize those aspects of our work. This will come as an enormous relief given the thorny nature of enforcement, which does not sit well with our public commitment to customer service.

The reinvention movement has certainly signed onto this doctrine. David Osborne and Ted Gaebler include as one of their core reinvention themes, Anticipatory government: prevention rather than cure.[3] The National Performance Review's prescription for reform of the Internal Revenue Service states, as an underlying assumption, that compliance efforts should be moved upstream, because prevention is cheaper per case and

---

[2] *Ibid.*, p.33
[3] David Osborne and Ted Gaebler, *Reinventing Government: How the Entrepreneurial Spirit Is Transforming the Public Sector* (Addison-Wesley, 1992), pp. 219-49.

imposes less burden on taxpayers; whereas enforcement is more expensive per case and more intrusive.[4]

In fact, regulatory life is not quite that simple. Even if prevention is cheaper per case, preventive methods may involve a thousand times as many cases as those that would otherwise end up in enforcement. On the question of enforcement being more intrusive, scholars point out that the opposite is generally true, because preventive and proactive strategies involve engagement before any precipitating event has occurred. A desire to minimize intrusiveness normally pushes back the other way: "This reactive approach has some important advantages. It ensures that [regulators] do not intrude too deeply into social life, and that when they do intrude, there is an important reason for it."[5] The reinvention movement has certainly played a part in shaking regulators loose from their traditional, purely reactive, approaches. But as time progresses, and as the search for genuinely effective regulatory techniques matures, the regulatory field has to move beyond the simple idea that one simply switches everything from reaction to prevention. ...

A clear focus on the task of risk reduction, problem solving, or compliance management provides the escape route from these destructive tensions. The risk reduction mindset dismisses the inward-looking focus on tools and replaces it with an outward-looking focus on important risks. By picking important problems and organizing resources around each one, these strategies demand that the complete range of tools be available and considered with respect to each problem. The objective is to fashion an intervention that works, preferably for good, without any a priori preference over tools, style, or time of intervention. In designing a solution for a particular problem, enforcement tools should always be available but should never be assumed to be the most effective or the most resource efficient. Problem solving, recognizing the scarcity of the enforcement resource, will use enforcement surgically, incisively, and in the context of coherent control strategies. ...

---

[4] Customer Service Task Force, "Reinventing Service at the IRS," IRS Publication 2197, catalog no. 25006E (Department of the Treasury, 1998), p.69.
[5] Mark H. Moore and Darrel W. Stephens, *Beyond Command and Control: The Strategic Management of Police Departments* (Washington, D.C.: Police Executive Research Forum, 1991), p.31.

Reinterpreting Reaction and Prevention in the Context of Risk Control

Most regulators understand the limitations of reactive strategies. Indeed, most regulatory agencies have already made significant investments in methods designed to avert or minimize the need for detection, reaction, and enforcement. Having diversified their tool kits, those agencies now seek some rational strategic framework to make sense of their broader repertoire and to help staff understand what each tool is good for and how to use tools in combination. The temptation regulators face now is to switch from a reactive strategy (whose failings we know) to a preventive strategy (whose failings we have only recently begun to discover). Both are limiting, because both emphasize one set of tools at the expense of the other.

The strategic focus that regulators need is risk control (or risk reduction). A control strategy embraces all the tools and considers each stage in the chronology of any harm as a potential intervention point. Thus a control strategy brings no ideological or a priori preference for preventive or reactive tactics. Rather, per the art of problem solving, a control strategy respects the individual characteristics of each problem; seeks to identify its precursors, vital components, and methods of contagion; and from that analysis, picks the right points and moments to intervene.

Proactive Strategies

Some confuse proactive with preventive strategies or even use the terms interchangeably. Both appear in the regulatory lexicon as antidotes to the failings of a reactive strategy. But I think they address different failings. The choice between reactive or preventive stances has to do with the chronology of a harm and choosing the right point to intervene. It relates (in the list of reactive failings at the start of this chapter) to wrong tools and intervention that is too late. The choice between reactive or proactive stances has to do with passivity and with taking the world as it presents itself rather than determining how it really is. It relates to the idea that purely reactive strategies focus on the incidents that present themselves and assume the contents of the agency's collective in-baskets to represent all the important problems.

According to Chamber's *Twentieth Century Dictionary*, to be *proac-tive* means to act "*forward* or *forth* or *publicly*". Risk control, done well, will require regulators to become consciously and deliberately proactive in a number of senses, as follows.

Identifying Invisible or Underrepresented Problems

Regulators need to extend their view. To identify all the important problems, they have to look beyond existing workloads to uncover those problems represented only partially or not at all. That means investing deliberately in mechanisms for searching out issues that might not otherwise come to light, or that might not come to light soon enough for effective intervention.

The crime control field uses the term *invisible offenses* to refer to crimes that do not reveal themselves or that have extremely low reporting rates. They include extortion, gambling, prostitution, drug dealing, date rape, fraud, many other forms of white-collar crime, and crimes within the family such as incest and sexual or physical abuse.

To obtain the broader view, regulatory agencies need to create, or pay more attention to, techniques and systems for making the invisible visible and for spotting emerging problems early, before much harm is done. Relevant tools and techniques include proactive intelligence gathering, establishing information networks with related agencies, creative and exploratory data mining (using both internal and external data sources and cross matches), focus groups, questionnaires, victimization surveys, and canvassing external stakeholders. It is also important to include a random component in any inspection or audit program to reveal the true scope and nature of different risks. Inclusion of a random component reveals problems unlikely to be revealed by targeted activities, because the targeting is done based upon what the agency already thinks are the main problem areas. (Further discussion of these proactive information gathering methods appears in chapter 18.)

Giving Voice

Regulators also need to adopt a proactive stance in terms of teasing out opinions and perspectives that might not normally be heard and by giving voice to groups or interests that might otherwise remain voiceless. When defining or addressing problems, persisting in a reactive passivity might incline regulators to pay too much attention to the noisiest stake-holders, who often have very clear opinions about what the problem is and how it ought to be solved.

Engaging Others in Analysis and Decision making

Regulators also need to engage others quite deliberately during the analytic stages of problem solving or risk assessment. They need to present draft analyses and options outside the agency, engaging communities in weighing the pros and cons of each, and ferreting out potential contributors to a solution. Regulators should be able to gather and test ideas and perspectives from outsiders without offering them a veto or vote, without suffering the paralysis that results from trying to find unanimous consensus, and without negotiating away their capacity to take adverse actions against those they regulate.

The challenge of the implementation of the environmental acquis communautaire *in the new Member States*

Georges Kremlis and Jan Dusík

7ᵀᴴ INECE Conference Proceedings (forthcoming 2005)

1. Introduction

The greatest ever enlargement of the European Union has taken place on 1 May 2004, with the accession of ten new Member States, the extension of the EU territory by twenty-three percent and the increase of population by twenty per cent. Moreover, the accession of eight of the new Member States consolidated the fall of the iron curtain between Eastern and Western Europe which lasted for over 40 years after the Second World War.

A strong emphasis has been put on compliance by the applicants for EU membership with the *acquis communautaire*. ...

As a result, all new Member States are now presumed to have harmonized their legislation to the EU standards and to comply with the membership obligations. Of course, similarly to previous EU enlargements, a number of unilateral transitional periods have been granted to the new Members (including in the field of environment), and the EU has also "benefited" from a number of multilateral transitional periods (e.g. in free movement of workers or concerning the Schengen *acquis*); and it will take several years before the new countries meet the Maastricht criteria allowing them to participate in the Monetary Union. Another unique feature was the provision of pre-accession financing through ISPA, Phare and SAPARD; indeed around €3.5 billion are expected to be spent in the new Member States, Bulgaria and Romania for environment during 2000-6. However, all in all, this biggest ever EU enlargement is also believed to be the most carefully and timely prepared one. ...

2.   The deficit of implementation of the environmental *acquis* in the EU-15

The EU environmental policy and legislation has been gradually adopted since the 1970s and is traditionally fighting "for the place in the sun" with the economic policies, in particular with the single market ("growth and competitiveness versus environmental protection"). A number of important judgments of the European Court of Justice helped to identify the mutual position of the two streams of the EU policy: the most recent examples include the *Commission v. United Kingdom* case C-30/01 (judgment of 23 September 2003) on the application of single market legislation with environmental components for Gibraltar or the ongoing litigation in the case *Commission v. Austria* (C-320/03) concerning environmentally driven restrictions of transport over the Alps. Nevertheless, the environmental *acquis*[1] at present counts for 561 pieces of binding legislation[2], most importantly Directives, which the Member States are obliged to transpose, implement and enforce. And the field of environmental legislation is a dynamic one, with few new pieces of legislation adopted every year to review existing legislation or to cover new areas (e.g. the "Århus package"). ...

2.1.   Specificity of EC environmental legislation

There are some peculiarities embodied in environmental directives which distinguish these from other areas of Community law and which are important for realising the causes of the implementation deficit in the Member States.

First of all, EC environmental directives are characterised by a number of secondary obligations (i.e. obligations that have to be complied with at a later stage after the entry into application of a directive). Therefore, ensuring compliance is not limited to a straightforward exercise of transposition, as might be the case in some areas, but it is necessary to ensure at a later stage, e.g. adoption of plans and programmes, designations or establishment of protected zones and areas etc. Some of the secondary obligations also imply establishment of infrastructure and major investments (urban wastewater treatment, drinking water, landfills etc.).

---

[1] Based mainly on Article 175 of the EC Treaty, but also on Articles 95 and 308 of the EC Treaty

[2] Data from CELEX database, 19 May 2004; including all amendments and technical adaptations

Secondly, compliance with EC environmental law is often related to the use of EC funding (namely LIFE, Structural Funds, Cohesion Fund, TENs and the pre-accession funds) or to funding from loans of the European Investment Bank. When it is required to be informed of projects, the Commission carries out a scrutiny of the utilisation of EC funds to ensure that projects conform with Community legislation especially for environment, competition and public procurement – see Article 12 of Council Regulation (EC) No. 1260/99 laying down general provisions on Structural Funds[3], Article 8.1 of Council Regulation (EC) No 1164/94 establishing a Cohesion Fund[4], as amended, and for the TENs Article 7 on Compatibility of Council Regulation 2236/95 as amended[5]).

However, the cohesion policy is implemented in a decentralised way, and therefore the Commission is only made aware of the largest projects (Cohesion Fund and Large European Regional Development Fund (ERDF) projects).

Finally, many pieces of EC environmental legislation have a strong public participation component. This is now emphasized by the forthcoming ratification by the EC of the so-called Århus Convention (Convention on Access to Information, Public Participation in Decision-making and Access to Justice in Environmental Matters, adopted in Århus, Denmark, on 25 June 1998), whose three pillars require not only access of public to environmental information and public participation in decision-making involving environmental matters, but also access of the public to justice in this domain. Directives corresponding to the three pillars have been adopted or are expected to be adopted to implement the Århus Convention within the European Union legal order.

2.2. The extent and types of problems in application of EC environmental legislation

...

There are a number of sectors of the environmental legislation which cause more implementation problems than others[8]: nature protection, water and air quality, waste management and environmental impact assessment. In nature protection, the main problems include non-

---

[3] OJ L 161, 26/06/1999, p. 1
[4] OJ L 130, 25/05/1994, p. 1
[5] OJ L 228, 23/09/1995, p. 1
[8] For details, see Fourth Annual Survey on the implementation and enforcement of Community environmental law – 2002; Commission Staff Working Paper SEC(2003)804.

conformity of transposing legislation, insufficient designation of Natura 2000 sites, incorrect assessment of plans and projects affecting the protected sites and breaches of requirements for strict protection of species. The water quality issues mainly relate to secondary obligations, such as designations of protected zones, adoption of pollution reduction programmes or construction of sewerage and wastewater treatment systems, while drinking water problems occur in few areas of the EU. Most problems with the air quality, on the contrary, concern lack of transposition or reporting to the Commission. Non-conformity of legislation and lack of adoption of management plans are the most typical issues in the waste sector, together with the operation of illegal landfills in several Member States. Finally, concerns about environmental impact assessment stem mainly from complaints and are largely procedural, since Directive 85/337/EEC[9] is a procedural one; the material aspects would refer to obligations from the legislation in other sectors, such as the two major nature protection Directives[10]. ...

The available statistics demonstrate that compliance with EC environmental legislation still proves to be difficult in the EU-15 and the number of infringements per year does not seem to diminish. The Commission tries to take proactive measures to avoid starting full-bloodied infringement procedures, such as: package meetings, during which complaints or infringement cases are discussed with the authorities of the Member States; bilateral or multilateral proactive meetings to explain how Member States should comply with their obligations; various guidance documents; or reminder letters on adoption of new directives and deadlines for their transposition. The work of IMPEL, the informal network of Member States and the Commission for the implementation and enforcement of environmental law, has been also beneficial for ensuring consistent implementation and enforcement of the *acquis* throughout the Community, mainly through exchange of information, training of inspectors and development of best practice. Of course, the different breaches vary in gravity - and the aim of the Commission is to focus its attention in pursuing the infringements on serious breaches of a systematic character rather than on individual procedural omissions or isolated individual cases of bad application, which are often at centre of complaints from the citizens. An upstream approach which identifies the systemic shortcomings is preferred to a downstream one which tackles the symptoms. But in any case the deficit of implementation of

---

[9] OJ L 175, 05/07/1985, p. 40
[10] Directive 79/409/EEC, OJ L 103, 25/04/1979, p. 1, and Directive 92/43/EEC, OJ L 206, 22/07/1992, p. 7

the environmental *acquis* already in the EU of 15 Members is obvious and has to be tackled through a combination of both proactive and enforcement means.

3.   Challenges of implementation of the environmental *acquis* in the new Memberm States

We mentioned in the beginning of this article that this enlargement is argued to be the best prepared one ever, since the preparation for membership was monitored by the Commission some seven years prior to accession (starting with the Opinions on Application for Membership of the European Union of the candidate countries on July 1997). Publication of annual reports of the Commission on progress of individual applicant countries in harmonising legislation and practice with the EU was always high on the political agenda and criticisms of slow progress appeared on front pages of newspapers. The monitoring continued even after the signature of the Accession Treaty, with the possibility for the EU to impose safeguard measures should the pace of harmonisation not be maintained.

However, given the rather unsatisfactory record of compliance with EC environmental law by the EU-15, it can be expected that the new Member States will face similar problems. A number of factors, specific for these new countries, confirm such forecasts.

Even more than in the old EU Members, environment is low on the political agenda. This was apparent already in the pre-accession period when various political and economic lobbies were trying to bypass or at least delay adoption of legislation transposing EC environmental directives and budgetary allocations for environmental protection were decreasing.

A major challenge is obviously the financing of approximation. The costs of implementing the environmental *acquis* in the ten new Member States were estimated at € 50-80 billion and investments required from these countries were estimated at 2 to 3 per cent of GDP, higher than what is at present being allocated.[11]

The EU will significantly contribute to financing implementation by provision of resources from EU funds. € 21.7 billion will be made available to the new Member States from the Structural Funds and the Cohesion

---

[11] Communication from the Commission to the Council and the European Parliament on 2003 Environment Policy Review, COM(2003)745 final, page 38

Fund until the end of the current budgetary period (31.12.2006), out of which € 3 billion in the Cohesion Fund is earmarked for the environment, while other environmental projects can be supported from the main Structural Funds. These contributions, together with the pre-accession funding from Phare, ISPA and SAPARD instruments, should significantly contribute to financing implementation measures. The experience in the EU15 also shows that national budgets must also be set aside, and indeed should be more substantial.

Apart from finding sufficient financial resources to cover remaining investment needs and co-financing of EC-funded projects, two other challenges emerge in relation to EC funding. The first is the so-called conditionality, i.e. compliance of co-financed projects with EC environmental legislation and policy. Another issue, which is specific for the new Member States, is the establishment of adequate administrative capacity to prepare 'pipelines' of projects of sufficient quality and to properly manage the use of EC funds[12]. High attention to these issues has proven essential for maximising the utilisation of the EC funds by the beneficiary Member States and should be seen as a priority also by the new Members.

Well performing administrative structures will be necessary not only for administering EC funding, but also in ensuring correct implementation of the EC environmental law in general. Many environmental Directives require issuing of permits, monitoring of pollution and fulfilment of secondary obligations. A number of institutions, both horizontally and vertically, are typically involved in implementing these obligations and they need to be adequately staffed and well coordinated. A number of twinning projects under Phare have been carried out in the Central and Eastern Europe candidate countries prior to accession to strengthen their administrative capacity and to provide relevant training. Preparedness of administration to cope with obligations arising from EU membership has also been checked through peer reviews in 2002 and 2003, as part of the monitoring of accession preparations.

Other possible drawbacks are deficiencies in law enforcement and a lack of legal culture in the countries in transition. The disobedience of legislation is not primarily seen by the society as a negative feature, especially when it does not affect private individuals or property. Harm

---

[12] Communication from the Commission on the Challenge of environmental financing in the candidate countries, COM (2001)304 final, p. 3

to the state property or to a public interest is generally better accepted by the people. This may be particularly relevant for compliance with nature protection obligations, since it is more difficult to carry out monetary valuation of the damage caused to natural features. It is however fair to say that there are positive trends in these countries, and people start to discover the importance of non-material assets, such as clean rivers or biological wealth.

Finally, only slow progress is being made by the new Member States towards ensuring effective public participation in environmental decision-making. Of course the EC legislation (such as on the environmental impact assessment or access to information) directly related to participative democracy has been transposed into national legislation, but experience shows that practical application lags behind. Assaults on the basic principles of public participation were experienced when transposing legislation containing such provisions in the legislative process (such as the transposition of the nature directives in the Czech Republic's parliament). We may therefore expect a number of complaints by the citizens of the new Member States concerning access to environmental information and public participation in decision making.

4. Measures to face the challenges posed by enlargement

From 1 May 2004, the ten new Member States are subject to the same obligations as the EU-15. They have to comply with EC legislation, the national legislation transposing directives in force must be notified by that date and practical compliance must be ensured as well. Specific arrangements apply only in accordance with the transitional periods as agreed during the accession negotiations and spelled out in the Act of Accession[13]. Should the new Member States fail to comply with their obligations, the Commission may initiate the infringement procedure pursuant to Article 226 of the EC Treaty. Similarly, the Commission has a duty to investigate complaints lodged by EU citizens or NGOs against the new Member States.

The Act of Accession of the ten new Member States also foresees a number of intermediate targets within the agreed transitional periods. This is the first enlargement where such an arrangement has been made with

[13] Act concerning the conditions of accession of the Czech Republic, the Republic of Estonia, the Republic of Cyprus, the Republic of Latvia, the Republic of Lithuania, the Republic of Hungary, the Republic of Malta, the Republic of Poland, the Republic of Slovenia and the Slovak Republic and the adjustments to the Treaties on which the European Union is founded, OJ L 236, 23/09/2003, p. 33

the new Member States, with the aim to gradually fulfil the EC legal obligations rather than waiting until the (sometimes extensive) transitional periods elapse. The fulfilment of intermediate targets will be monitored as a matter of priority; non-compliance with these targets may trigger an infringement procedure.

A number of measures to eliminate possible opening of infringements immediately after accession have been undertaken both generally and in the environmental field. As concerns transposing legislation, the acceding countries were invited to use the pre-notification database for gradual storage of transposing legislation in an electronic version, aimed at avoiding a backlog of notifications on the date of accession. Most of the transposing legislation has been notified in this way and is now considered officially notified to the Commission.

Two systematic approaches have been undertaken as concerns ensuring compliance with environmental legislation by the Directorate-General for the Environment of the Commission. Shortly before the accession a series of environmental proactive meetings have been carried out in the new Member States, with the aim to explain to their national authorities responsible for compliance and enforcement how complaint and infringement procedures work in practice, how to prevent escalation of infringements and how to communicate effectively on these matters with the relevant Commission services. Those meetings have been highly appreciated by all new Member States, as they provided first-hand practical information and enabled contact with the Commission counterpart in the matters of compliance with EC environmental law. Such meetings can provide a solid basis not only for bringing infringements to an end in the most effective way, but can also be followed by package meetings and other specific meetings as currently organised with the existing Member States.

DG Environment of the Commission has also launched a systematic conformity check for the ten new Member States, building on a similar experience with the EU-15. The objective is to analyse, within the next two years, transposing legislation for the main Directives and remove any non-compliance in an early stage, in close collaboration between the Commission and the Member States concerned.

Concerning complaint and infringement procedures, the same priorities as the ones for the EU-15 will apply, in line with the White Paper on European Governance[14] and the Commission Communication on Better

Monitoring of Community Law[15]. The first priority will be the non-communication cases (in the absence of notification of transposing measures), followed by the cases of non-conformity (based on the conformity checking exercise) and horizontal bad application cases (secondary obligations, transitional periods contained in the Act of Accession including intermediate targets to be met and conditionality of EC funding). Of course this will not exclude handling of all received complaints, as required by the EC Treaty and by the Commission Communication to the European Parliament and the European Ombudsman on the Relations with the complainant in respect of infringements of Community law[16]. Such non-priority complaints can be handled through alternative means (e.g. package meetings) and the complainants should be encouraged to use the available national means of redress.

5.   Conclusions

In this article, the possible difficulties that the new Member States will very likely face to comply with their obligations under EC environmental legislation were tentatively addressed. The key messages could be summarized as follows.

1.   During the period prior to accession, the maximum possible was done, under close surveillance of the Commission. Therefore all obligations should in theory have been formally fulfilled by 1 May 2004. However, we can however expect that there will be failures, gaps and omissions.

2.   It is natural that there will be infringements and that the Commission will receive complaints from citizens from the new Member States; this has been the case for all previous EU enlargements. It is also likely that the number of cases will be growing gradually rather than in a single step. Experience with the EU-15 shows that the more public awareness you raise the more complaints are triggered by the citizens who know better their rights.

3.   The spectrum of problems, complaints and infringement cases against the new Member States is not expected to

[14] COM(2001)428 final, p. 25
[15] COM (2002)725 final, p. 11
[16] COM(2002)141 final

significantly differ from the situation in EU-15. It is also likely that they will concern similar issues, although there may be some specific aspects, such as the requirements to implement the investment heavy environmental *acquis*, inadequate administrative capacity or the lack of legal culture, which might cause some variations compared to the business-as-usual in the EU-15.

4. Limiting escalation of infringements will require effective use of proactive measures as described above, including bilateral meetings with the national authorities to discuss complaints, infringement cases or difficulties in implementation. The same is of course valid for the existing Member States.

5. The EC funding should be to the maximum possible extent prioritised for co-financing of measures bringing about compliance with obligations of the environmental *acquis*. Good project preparation will have to be ensured. In turn the *acquis* itself must also be respected for the construction and financing of infrastructure projects.

6. Finally, the performance of countries which just acceded to the European Union will be under strong scrutiny, since this is the biggest ever enlargement and the new Members are less developed compared to the EU-15 average. The success or failure of this enlargement will be crucial for deciding about potential future enlargements of the EU and it would also be the most suitable response to the recent escalation of anti-European trends both in the old and the new Member States.

LEADERS & LAGGARDS: NEXT-GENERATION ENVIRONMENTAL REGULATION

Neil Gunningham & Darren Sinclair

Chapter 2 (2002)

Chapter 2 "Regulating Small and Medium-Sized Enterprises"

Small and medium-sized enterprises (SMEs) represent a very high proportion of all enterprises in industrialised economies. In the UK, for example, over 99% of all enterprises fall within this category (defined for present purposes as those with fewer than 200 people),[1] with about 90% of these enterprises having fewer than ten employees. SMEs have different environmental performance characteristics from their larger counterparts. In particular, they commonly have a higher level of environmental impact per unit, and lower compliance rates with health, safety and environmental regulation (Bickerdyke and Lattimore 1997). Although their individual environmental impact may be small, their aggregate impact may, in some respects, exceed that of large enterprises. For example, collectively, they are claimed to be the source of around 70% of total environmental pollution in the UK (Groundwork 1998; KPMG 1997). In recent years, the environmental impact of SMEs may have been compounded by a substantial increase in the number of such enterprises.

The effective regulation of SMEs is a substantial policy challenge for environmental agencies in all jurisdictions, not least because this group has a number of unique characteristics which inhibit the application of conventional regulatory measures.[2] These include:

---

[1] There is no single generally accepted definition of an SME. Different definitions are adopted by different countries and for different purposes. See e.g. Hillary 2000a.

[2] For a general survey and documentation of the issues identified below, see the essays in Hillary 2000a.

- A lack of resources. This is exacerbated by higher compliance costs, a shortage of capital and economical marginality (Haines 1997).

- A lack of environmental awareness and expertise. Many are ignorant of their environmental impact, technological solutions to their environmental problems, or their regulatory obligations.

- A lack of exposure- including lower public profiles- which means that 'pressure groups gain none of the prestige, headlines and publicity by targeting SMEs that campaigns exposing the environmental misdemeanour of high profile multinational bring' (Hobbs 2000: 150).

- A lack of receptivity to environmental issues. Many SMEs have not integrated environmental issues into their business decisions, making it difficult to persuade them of economic benefits (Merritt 1998).

- The sheer numbers of such enterprises. This leads to infrequent inspections, and many businesses slip through the regulatory net and are untouched by environmental policy initiatives.

What motivates SMEs and their owners is also likely to be very different from what motivates large corporations. Most striking in this regard is not only their low level of environmental awareness but the substantial disparity between their environmental aspirations and their environmental performance. A 1999 study, for example, suggested that the typical owner-manager suffered a low standard of eco-literacy and poor environmental awareness (Tilley 1999: 241) and that while SMEs commonly expressed pro-environment attitudes they often experienced difficulties translating these ideals, aspirations and values into action (Tilley 1999; Hutchingson 1993).

The problems of ignorance and lack of awareness of regulation are even more severe in the case of *very* small enterprises or 'micro-businesses' (under five employees). In the closely related area of occupational health and safety (OHS) regulation, it was found that the vast majority of micro-businesses did not know that any legislation existed and were unaware of reliable advice sources. Most did not belong to any industry associations and were focused primarily on economic survival. Where it existed at all, concern about safety, health and the environment was limited to quite specific overt threats (Eakin 1992). Consistent with the above evidence, a Groundwork report (1998: ii) concluded that:

> a typical SME is ill informed and unwilling to take action unless threatened by strong external forces such as prosecution or customer demands. *Worse still, many foresee no threats or advantages to their companies from the environment* [emphasis added].

The policy challenge is made even more complex by the fact that SMEs are a very diverse group of enterprises, both within and across different sectoral groupings. And these variations may not only impact on the degree and type of environmental problems confronting a particular business and/or SME sector but also on the way in which an individual business and/or sector might be regulated or otherwise encouraged to improve its environmental performance. For example, despite the significant disadvantages of a lack of resources, information, economic security and external pressure, *some* types of SME are capable on occasion of responding with great flexibility and innovation.[3]

Recognising these problems, how can policy-makers overcome the considerable barriers to improving the environmental performance of SMEs, and design a strategy for their efficient and effective regulation? How can they bring the large majority of SMEs into compliance with environmental regulation? How can they persuade them to integrate environmental considerations into their core business activities? And, considering the diversity of SMEs, how can they develop policies that bring laggards up to the minimum legal standard while encouraging and rewarding leaders for going far beyond it? Unfortunately, SMEs are a particularly challenging subject for research. For example, one survey of 875 SMEs received only 15 responses, illustrating the understandable

---

[3] Two sectoral examples of this phenomenon are: SMEs working in innovative and fast-moving high-technology areas where high environmental performance may provide a competitive advantage; and those that perceive the risk of health, safety or environmental failures to be high. This latter group (for example, those working with high-risk chemicals) may be intrinsically motivated to improve without external prompting. However, these examples are likely to be the exception to the rule, with the very large majority of SMEs unlikely to respond voluntarily because they perceive no threats or advantages in doing so. For these firms, improvements are likely to come about only through the imposition of outside pressure (Wright 1998).

unwillingness of already under-resourced enterprises to co-operate in such research (Gunner 1994). In consequence, the existing literature on these issues is extremely sparse, and the fieldwork picture is extremely patchy.

Notwithstanding this disappointing track record, we believe it is possible to address the question of effective SME environmental performance, and at least provide provisional solutions to many of the regulatory challenges confronting SMEs. In doing so, it is important to recognise that, just as the motivations, attitudes and circumstances of SMEs may differ substantially from those of their larger counterparts, so also will the 'pressure points' that impact on enterprises' behaviour. Accordingly, an effective strategy must be tailored to their special characteristics.

This section ... has two principal goals. First, in this chapter we seek tospecify a series of instruments that are capable of substantially influencing the attitude and behaviour of SMEs and of engaging both leaders and laggards. ...

Second, recognising that one size does not fit all, and that different industry sectors have quite different characteristics and require different instruments and policy mixes, we seek to develop an industry-specific strategy for improving the environmental performance of SMEs. ...

In engaging in these tasks it must also be recognised that all instruments have both strengths and weaknesses and that none is likely to be wholly successful in achieving its environmental goals. As we have argued in our previous work (Gunningham and Sinclair 1999a; Gunningham and Grabosky 1998: Ch. 6), it is often the combinations of instruments, and the interactions of various institutional actors, including governments, commercial and non-commercial third parties, that determine the success of environmental regulation. This suggests a hierarchy of instruments. For example, some instruments are best used initially, and only to the extent that they fail will it be appropriate to invoke other, more interventionist, approaches. In contrast, in other circumstances, combinations of instruments should be used concurrently. A sequenced approach, gradually escalating from more co-operative to more interventionist instruments, may not only make the best use of scarce regulatory resources but also better motivate target groups. Finally, different industry sectors may have quite different characteristics and therefore may require different instrument mixes. This strengthens the case for developing industry specific strategies. ...

Education and training

Ignorance and a lack of capability are common explanations of poor environmental performance in SMEs.[4] Beyond a limited understanding of their regulatory obligations, the cleaner production literature suggests that SMEs are simply unaware of many financially attractive opportunities for environmental improvement. This is compounded by a shortage of technical and management expertise. One conclusion is that the large majority of SMEs simply 'do not possess the knowledge, skills or solutions necessary to allow them to fully integrate the environment into their business practices' (Tilley 1999).

These problems are exacerbated by a number of attitudinal obstacles on the part of SMEs to improving their environmental performance. These include: underestimating the impact of their activities on the environment; a narrow view of the relationship between business performance and the environment; the entrenched idea that protecting the environment is associated with technical complexity, burdens and costs; and a high resistance to organisational change (Gunningham and Sinclair 1997). Although these problems are not unique to SMEs, they are most prevalent within this group. Consequently, they have to be overcome before SMEs will be willing to improve environmental performance.

Unlike larger enterprises, most SMEs lack the internal resources and motivation to overcome the environmental challenges that confront them.[5] For this reason, there is a strong argument for providing information and education to SME executives and owners, tailored to their specific needs, which seek to modify their attitudes and behaviour. Although this proposition is not in serious dispute, achieving such change is problematic (UK Round Table on Sustainable Development 1999; KPMG 1997). While there is some limited evidence of SMEs switching from end-of-pipe to cleaner technology, many well intentioned efforts by governments and industry alike to promote the competitive advantages of cleaner production, for example, have had little impact on SME behaviour (Merritt 1998). The evidence suggests that there are considerable difficulties in persuading SMEs to act on environmental information, even when it is demonstrably in their own financial interest and/or backed by generous financial subsidies (Merritt 1998).

---

[4] Parts of the following analysis first appeared in Gunningham 1999.
[5] Indeed, it is arguable that regulators lack sufficient technical expertise to provide specific advice even to larger business.

For example, in the UK, the Department of Environment's Small Company Environmental and Energy Management Assistance Scheme (SCEEMAS) provides a 50% subsidy for the costs of consultancy fees in the implementation of the European Union's Ecomanagement and Audit Scheme (EMAS). Despite a comprehensive national advertising campaign, and supporting material such as case studies, guides, videos, newsletters and leaflets sent to thousands of SMEs, a subsequent review revealed that only 136 individual SMEs had participated in SCEEMAS (the scheme was subsequently abandoned) (ECOTEC 2000).

Yet not all education and informational initiatives have been unsuccessful, and much depends on how the information is presented and packaged, and on who presents it.[6] Drawing on what limited empirical literature is available, it would appear that a number of issues are crucial to successful policy implementation. These are:

- Capitalising on win-win solutions. The starting point for effective communication, information dissemination and education should be to focus on those circumstances where good environmental practice can also be good business practice[7] and to emphasise that what is good in environmental terms may also be good for the economic bottom line (APEC 1999).

- Developing industry-government partnerships. The aim of such partnerships is to actively engage an industry in the development of a cleaner production strategy that is tailored to its particular circumstances. This generates ownership, thus increasing awareness and the level of commitment to its implementation, and emphasises improved environmental management practices.

- The right people disseminating the information which must not only be transmitted, but also *received*. This is most likely to be achieved where there is face-to-face distribution from trusted sources (customers, suppliers and competitors,

---

[6] A recent survey points to EMS support schemes in Germany and the Cleaner Production Programme in the Netherlands as examples of successful initiatives that included substantial information-based components. See ECOTEC 2000.

[7] For example, it has been noted that adopting EMAS brought savings within only 14 months and that packaging reduction and re-use also saved considerable sums for many companies. See ECOTEC 2000.

industry peers, networks and associations) which emphasises practical solutions. Information should also be sector-specific, and delivered in a co-ordinated fashion. The various forms of information delivery must be effectively co-ordinated, preferably by government, to minimise duplication (Fanshawe 2000).

- Developing codes of practice. SMEs often require much more specific guidance on what is required of them than their larger counterparts. Codes of practice are an effective way to provide practical guidance on how to achieve compliance, and may be a valuable vehicle for promoting appropriate cleaner production benchmarks within an industrial sector.

- Exploiting third-party leverage. Most SMEs have frequent interaction with professionals (banks, lawyers, insurance companies) and larger enterprises along the supply chain, and rely on them as credible sources of information. This provides opportunities for using such professionals both to disseminate information and to exert pressure on SMEs to pursue opportunities for using environmental improvements to achieve greater business success. On the basis of enlightened self-interest (backed up by government persuasion), accountants might verify rudimentary environmental audits, banks might require an environmental checklist for loan approval, insurers might seek a statement of hazards identification and control, and larger enterprises may impose environmental management system (EMS) requirements (Hopkins 1995).

- Using more active 'hands-on support'. The ECOTEC report on SMEs emphasised the importance of providing continuing on-site help over months or years (rather than just 'self-help' information, limited training or brief environmental reviews), and noted that 'environmental graduates, through industrial placement schemes, can be used to provide extended support at low cost, bridging the gap between existing staff who have the company specific knowledge but no time, and the student who has the time and the generic environmental knowledge' (ECOTEC 2000).

- Integration with other strategies. Information and education cannot be relied on to influence SME behaviour in isolation (Merritt 1998). They must be seen as one component of a broader, integrated preventative strategy. What is needed is a hierarchy of controls, beginning with the facilitation of voluntary action through the dissemination of information and advice and support for cleaner production initiatives, escalating through the use of positive and negative incentives to encourage those who are otherwise constrained from taking preventative action through cost or other constraints, and culminating in the enforcement of command-and-control legislation for recalcitrants who are unpersuaded by less interventionist strategies. However, information and education are almost always a necessary base from which other, more interventionist, instruments can be launched. ...

Compliance Promotion in the United Kingdom

Paul Leinster, Jim Gray, Chris Howes & Rosie Clark

7ᵀᴴ INECE CONFERENCE PROCEEDINGS (FORTHCOMING 2005)

Society demands high environmental standards and expects companies, and individuals, to behave responsibly. The Environment Agency is the leading public body protecting and improving the environment in England and Wales. ...

Traditional regulatory approaches have achieved much to reduce environmental impacts. However, the nature of regulation has to change to keep pace with changes in the economy and society. The Environment Agency has responded to this challenge through its "Modernising Regulation Change Programme".

This article describes some of the approaches adopted by the Environment Agency to promote compliance with legal requirements and to encourage the environment to be at the centre of business thinking.

Principles of modern regulation

The Agency believes modern regulation focuses on outcomes and is risk based. ... Modern regulatory systems should encourage businesses and individuals to improve, rewarding good performers, while remaining tough on those who do not meet acceptable standards. In order to achieve this, modern regulation must be:

§ proportionate, allocating resources and implementing systems according to the risks involved;
§ transparent, with clear rules and processes for industry and local communities;
§ consistent, within and between sectors, and over time;

§ targeted on the environmental outcome to be achieved, taking into account environmental needs, best practice, sector specific and geographical circumstances;

§ cost effective.

This means that we will concentrate our resources where the risks to the environment are highest, including the highest hazards or the poorest performing operators. We will focus on systems to improve environmental quality. Consistent with this principle, we will adopt a proportionate approach where we see good performance. We have developed a screening method to assess risks to the environment in a quantitative fashion.

Transparency and trust are also vital aspects of our relationship with communities and society as a whole, and we must at all times be seen to maintain a neutral, open and fair stance. Accordingly, we make information on the environmental performance of business and our performance as a regulator widely available.

Tools for modern regulation

Adopting a risk-based approach to regulation, matching intervention measures to environmental performance, has implications for all involved in the regulatory process. ...

Direct regulation is the traditional approach to controlling emissions or abstractions, with permits specifying what a company can and cannot do at a particular site. As a modern regulator we are also developing risk based assessment methods and actively promote voluntary schemes. A number of these approaches are described below. ...

Operator Pollution and Risk Appraisal

The Agency aims to target its resources on those companies that pose the greatest risks to the environment. Two schemes for Operator and Pollution Risk Appraisal (OPRA) have been developed to assist the Agency in its regulation of the Integrated Pollution Control (IPC) regimes for major process industry and the Waste Management Licensing regime. With the implementation of two new European Community Directives in England and Wales,[8] elements of the waste industry and the large

---

[8] Integrated Pollution Prevention and Control (IPPC) and the Landfill Directive (LFD), introduced in England and Wales through regulations made under the Pollution Prevention and Control Act 1999

manufacturing sectors are brought under one regulatory regime for the first time.

In keeping with our aim to introduce common approaches to regulation across a range of regulatory regimes, the new Environmental Protection Operator and Pollution Risk Appraisal (EP OPRA) methodology has been developed as an important step in developing a unified approach to risk assessment across our regulatory regimes. The EP OPRA scheme fits within a recognised national framework for environmental risk assessment and management.[9] It incorporates an element of professional judgement, but the method itself is simple to apply and objective in nature and a public consultation on the scheme was held in 2002. Details of responses are on the Agency's web site.[10]

EP OPRA will help the Agency target its regulatory effort on those activities that present the greatest risk to the environment. Outputs from this scheme are being built into the proposed charging scheme for the PPC regulatory regime. As noted previously, charges for regulation are set to reflect the level of regulatory action required. EP OPRA has four attributes. Three reflect the environmental hazard of the operation and the fourth measures Operator performance. In general, the higher the score, the greater the regulatory level of activity required. ...

How the Agency promotes compliance

Companies need to accept responsibility for their actions and this should be reflected in business culture as well as in their operational targets. The principle of 'polluter pays' is now well accepted, whereby businesses should be held to be accountable for their actions. As noted previously, the Agency's OPRA system supports the polluter pays principle through a cost recovery charging framework which can provide a financial incentive to operators to reduce their environmental risks and impacts. By identifying, managing and reducing key risk areas, businesses can reduce their OPRA (risk) profile, which will then be reflected in lower compliance activities and, consequently, charges. In addition, businesses can benefit, in some circumstances, from cost savings in reduced waste and minimisation of resource use, and avoid costs associated with pollution incidents. Promoting corporate responsibility can improve

[9] Department for Environment Transport and the Regions, Environment Agency and the Institute of Environment and Health. Guidelines for Environmental Risk Assessment and Management.. Stationary Office, 2000
[10] http://www.environment-agency.gov.uk/yourenv/consultations

corporate image with an associated positive impact on shareholder value, as well as impacting for example on a Company's credit rating or insurance premium.

Optimising environmental improvement

The Environment Agency is developing sector plans and guidance, which address the specific issues associated with particular sectors. Sector plans relate to a coherent, recognisable, target group and define the national and local outcomes and risks that we believe should be addressed for that group. The sector may be a particular industry (such as nuclear or agriculture), or a recreational area (such as angling). This approach allows us to prioritise the regulatory workload between and within sectors. The overall objective is to optimise achieving environmental improvements.

Key to optimising environmental performance is to identify current good practice relevant to the sector, to educate and advise businesses and individuals and to communicate information to the public.

Identifying Good Practice

Good Practice includes reviewing techniques and experience from within the sector and across other sectors where similar environmental problems and processes may be encountered. Such reviews are not restricted to England and Wales and the Environment Agency is keen to learn from the experience of other countries. Good practice also includes the reduction of unnecessary bureaucracy which may inhibit the introduction of innovative solutions to poor environmental performance. In addition, we encourage full life cycle ('cradle to grave') analysis of processes to promote good environmental management throughout the whole supply chain.

Education

Businesses and individuals need to be more aware of how their actions impact on the environment and human health. Education and advice can help raise awareness of the issues by providing clear information relevant to specific audiences, demonstrating potential improvements (including cost savings) through case studies, and highlighting national, regional or sector initiatives. We also seek to raise awareness of regulatory requirements, so that businesses and individuals understand fully their responsibilities.

Education campaigns can be more resource effective than traditional regulation in situations of high volume low environmental risk. For example, the Agency runs targeted educational initiatives such as the "national tyres campaign" to promote recycling and minimise illegal tipping.

Information

We regularly publish environmental performance information for England and Wales, making use of communication tools such as our *Pollution Inventory, What's in Your Backyard* and *Spotlight on business environmental performance* to provide information about environmental performance to a wide audience. These publications are updated annually and are available on our website.[11] *"Spotlight"* both publicly praises good performers and names and shames poor performers. This we believe helps companies internalise their environmental performance. *What's in Your Backyard* publishes details of IPC OPRA and Waste OPRA scores for local facilities. ...

We also encourage individual businesses to make information on their environmental performance accessible to stakeholders, including local communities and investors, and we know that this information is used to guide investment decisions. ...

Compliance assessment

The Environment Agency has developed a range of tools which are being progressively implemented to help to assess risks. These include Compliance Assessment Plans (CAPs) and the Compliance Classification Scheme (CCS).

CAPs are used to ensure that compliance against all requirements of permits and other regulatory instruments are checked within a defined period. The CCS assesses the performance of a site against the conditions set in Agency issued permits. It is recognised that some non-compliances will present a greater environmental risk than others. The CCS is used to classify non-compliance with permit conditions according to potential impact on the environment and provides information to support consistent and proportionate responses to non-compliances. This also allows national profiling of sectors and companies. The potential risk

---

[11] http://www.environment-agency.gov.uk

categories used within the CCS are ranked from 1 (the highest potential risk arising from a non-compliance) to category 4 (where no immediate risk of harm to the environment is likely). These categories are then used to inform our enforcement activities, and are linked clearly to our Enforcement and Prosecution Policy.

Stakeholder involvement

Stakeholder involvement can take many forms, and embraces many types of stakeholders. Consultation at the outset of introducing new regulatory tools is perhaps the most obvious form of stakeholder involvement. Typically, we seek to identify affected businesses and local communities and other interested parties (industry or sector representative groups, non-governmental organisations, local liaison bodies, etc) and approach each of these individually. We also publish an invitation to provide comment on our web-site, with provision of a clear route to seek further information. For more broad ranging consultations we publish documents for national distribution.

The use of environmental information to guide investment decisions is also a form of stakeholder involvement and feedback suggests that companies, as well as environmental groups, respond positively to the opportunity to discuss issues with the regulators.

Performance review

Activities which potentially impact on the environment require monitoring so that the risk of adverse effects can be evaluated and appropriate action taken. The development of minimum criteria for environmental inspection is a Recommendation from the European Parliament which the UK has agreed to implement. This requires environmental inspections to be planned in advance and the Agency sees its policy of developing Compliance Assessment Plans as a means of fulfilling this obligation.

The role of the operator is to:
§   carry out monitoring and analysis to suitable standards;
§   assess and act upon the results within their own EMS;
§   make information available.

The role of the regulator is to:
- §   specify the standards for monitoring and analysis;
- §   ensure the operator complies with monitoring requirements;
- §   act upon the results in a proportionate manner;
- §   publish information on performance and response.

Through internal review, businesses should be encouraged to take responsibility for ensuring that they are not having an adverse impact on the environment, or on people.

Enforcement

Regulatory regimes need to be backed up by penalties or disincentives to non-compliance. Where businesses do not comply with legislation, the Environment Agency will use its enforcement powers firmly and fairly to prevent pollution or environmental damage, or to require remedial action. ...

Implementation of Industrial Pollution Control Programs in Sri Lanka

Ramani Ellepola

5ᴛʜ INECE CONFERENCE PROCEEDINGS, VOL.1 (1998)

...

1.3   Problems of Existing Industry versus New Industry

In reviewing the present status in Sri Lanka in relation to industrial effluents, it is clear that major pollution problems arise mainly from those industries which were established two to three decades ago, before the present Environmental Regulations came into force. As such, a clear demarcation has to be made between the so called 'existing' industries which are industries already in operation when the present environmental regulations came into force as opposed to 'new' industries which came into existence after environmental regulations came into force.

The Central Environmental Authority has been successful to a great extent in controlling pollution arising from new industries (i.e., industries established after 1990). It is a relatively easy task to control pollution from these 'new' industries, as action is taken by the industry at the planning stage itself to install the necessary pollution control systems.

The major problem lies in the control of pollution from the so called 'existing' industries. These are industries which were established twenty to thirty years ago before environmental regulations were in place. Many of these older industries often use outdated technology and have not given any thought to waste minimization or end of pipe treatment. Many of these industries are cash strapped, and find it difficult to adopt new technology or install end of pipe treatment systems as it may require considerable amounts of funds. Some of these industries also face problems such as the lack of physical space for the installation of the required end of pipe treatment systems. ...

The necessary legislative provisions are already in place for taking legal action against errant industrialists who are violating the norms and standards stipulated by the Central Environmental Authority. However, the Authorities have been fairly flexible in this regard particularly in relation to existing industries. These industries have been allowed sufficient time to meet the stipulated standards. In cases where the industry concerned does not make any attempt at all to abate the pollution from his industry the Central Environmental Authority proceeds with legal action. ...

3.   Programs To Assist Industry Comply with Environmental Norms

In Sri Lanka a mix of regulatory and incentive based strategies are adopted in order to control pollution arising from industries. There are many programs which have been initiated in recent times with a view to providing assistance to industries. Special emphasis has been given to the control of pollution from the so called "existing" industries which are older industries set up several years or decades ago before the present environmental regulations were in force. Some of these programs are briefly described below.

3.1   Pollution control and Abatement Fund (PCAF)

A 'Pollution Control and Abatement Fund' (PCAF) has been set up in order to provide interest free loans as well as free technical assistance to industries which have been established in the past and which have pollution problems at present.

Under this scheme industries are able to obtain funding on a concessionary basis for the installation of waste treatment systems and for the implementation of other pollution minimization measures. The funds are being disbursed through the major development banks. This is a boon to industries, in particular the small and medium scale industry who may lack the finances required for implementation of pollution control measures.

3.2   Common Waste Treatment Systems

In order to assist older industries in special areas with a high concentration of industries where the necessary space for the installation of treatment systems is not available, the Government, with World Bank assistance, is to set up common waste treatment systems for joint waste treatment. Industries in such areas will be expected to join the common waste treatment system or install waste treatment systems on their own. Two areas with a high concentration of industries have been identified, one to the North of Colombo the capital city, and the other to the south of Colombo, where such treatment systems are to be installed in the near future. The treated waste water from these two treatment systems will be disposed of into the ocean through pipelines after treatment.

3.3   Demonstration Waste Treatment Systems

There are several specific industrial sectors where the required pollution control technology is not available in the country at present. Demonstration waste treatment systems have been set up for such industrial sectors by the Government in order to assist similar industries to set up their own treatment systems with confidence.

3.4   Cleaner Technology/Waste Minimization Project

Another program which is being implemented in order to assist industries is a demonstration waste minimization project in selected industrial sectors. A UNIDO assisted waste minimization project is being implemented by the Central Environmental Authority covering three selected industrial sectors. These are the distillery, textile and metal finishing industrial sectors. Through this project, selected industries in these three industrial sectors have been shown ways and means of reducing waste generation quantities through simple process and raw material changes, as well as good house keeping practices. Demonstration waste minimization projects such as these help industries in meeting the required environmental standards while at the same time reducing end-of-pipe treatment costs.

3.5   Future Siting of Industry

In order to avoid the problems arising from inappropriate siting of industry, the Government has made a policy decision that in future, all effluent generating high polluting industry should be sited in industrial estates with treatment facilities. However, at present a sufficient number of such estates are not available for this purpose. The Ministry of industries is in the process of identifying and developing several industrial estates countrywide, in order to cater to this need. The plan is to develop these industrial estates on a Build Own and Operate or Build Own and Transfer basis. In addition to these, there are several industrial estates being developed by the private sector.

3.6   Relocation of Selected Industrial Sectors

Other programs which are ongoing is the relocation of industries which have similar processes, to one central location in order to facilitate sharing of costs for waste treatment and disposal. One example in this regard, is the relocation of tanneries situated in and around Colombo to a suitable location outside Colombo. The main reason for the relocation of these tanneries was that these tanneries which were established several decades ago were carrying out their operations in highly residential areas which had developed in and around these industries. The operation of these tanneries was causing a major nuisance to the nearby residents. In addition, although these tanneries many of which are involved in chrome tanning generate substantial quantities of waste water often containing chromium, in most of these locations there is not sufficient space for the installation of the necessary treatment systems. The relocation of the tanneries has given an opportunity to the industry to share the cost of waste treatment in addition to minimizing pollution/nuisance problems by moving out from the populated areas.

3.7   Management of hazardous industrial waste

Although the quantities of hazardous waste arising from industrial operations in Sri Lanka is not very substantial at the present time, it is envisaged that the problem is bound to become serious with increased industrialization. There are a few selected industrial sectors which are already facing a problem in relation to the disposal of hazardous waste. With an increasing number of industries installing treatment systems for the treatment of their waste water, a serious problem with regard to the disposal of sludge from such waste treatment systems has arisen. A recent survey carried out in Sri Lanka, has estimated that a total of 40,000 MT of hazardous waste is being generated within the country annually, of which almost fifty percent consists of waste oil. The proper disposal of this waste poses a serious problem, due to the non availability of a high temperature incinerator or a properly designed land fill site in the country. The government is in the process of identifying a suitable site to be developed as a hazardous waste land fill site. ...

3.8   Controls on the Import and Use of Toxic Chemicals

Chemicals classified as pesticides, fertilizers or pharmaceuticals are fairly well regulated in Sri Lanka, as legislation is already in place for the purpose. All pesticides, fertilizers and pharmaceuticals go through a registration process whereby aspects such as toxicity and environmental effects are looked into very carefully, as well as efficiency.

However, the use of toxic chemicals by industry is a fairly serious problem in Sri Lanka, as extremely toxic/hazardous chemicals are sometimes being imported into the country, for use in industry. At the present time there is no registration or permit scheme in place for the control of industrial chemicals.

A complete inventory of the chemicals in use within the country has been compiled by the Central Environmental Authority. Relevant data on nearly one thousand chemicals is now available in the Authority as a computerized data base. Chemical and trade names, acute and chronic toxicity data, environmental effects, disposal methods, and the legal status of these chemicals in other countries are available in this data base. In addition, international data basessuch as the Geneva based International Register of Potentially Toxic Chemicals (IRPTC) has made available their data bases to the Central Environmental Authority. ...

Outsourcing Regulation: Analyzing Non-Governmental Systems of Labor Standards and Monitoring

Dara O'Rourke

31(1) THE POLICY STUDIES JOURNAL 1 (2003)

[*Editor's Note:* One example of nongovernmental regulation and "privatized" regulation is certification systems, which is discussed in a subsequent article by Tim Bartley entitled *Certification of Forests and Factories: States, Social Movements and the Rise of Private Regulation in the Apparel and Forest Products Fields.*]

...

The Emergence of Nongovernmental Regulation

Much of the existing literature on "privatized" regulation explains nongovernmental regulation as a response to two connected trends: the weakening of national governments (due to globalization, neoliberal movements to shrink the state, or simply the failure of state bureaucracies) and the strengthening of multinational corporations (Strange, 1996; Evans, 1997; Schmidt, 1995; Cutler, Haufler, & Porter, 1999). States are turning to "market-based" and private voluntary strategies as an alternative or a supplement to traditional regulation (Haufler, 2001). Firms support this trend as a step towards enlightened "self-regulation."

Some governments clearly view nongovernmental regulatory strategies as more "flexible" and "responsive" regulatory mechanisms (Ayres & Braithwaite, 1992) that can supplement overworked and under-resourced state labor agencies (Nadvi & Wältring, 2001; Reinicke, 1998). Market-based mechanisms and public disclosure systems are also increasingly popular as methods of regulation (Braithwaite & Drahos, 2000). Non-state, market-driven systems (Cashore, 2002) are attractive to governments, as they can take up some of the demands placed on state agencies, an especially pressing concern in developing nations. By enlisting the energies of multinational firms, private sector auditors, and NGOs in monitoring labor performance, governments can potentially increase compliance without increasing state budgets or staff (Nadvi & Wältring, 2001).

Firms are "voluntarily" participating in or leading these programs because of significant new pressures to improve their labor, environmental, and social performance. Brand-sensitive firms are joining nongovernmental initiatives or creating their own codes of conduct and monitoring schemes in response to direct pressures and demands from activists. Codes and monitoring systems are viewed as a strategy to reduce reputational risks in the marketplace (Conroy, 2001). One bad supplier can significantly damage a firm's reputation and, in turn, its sales and stock value. Firms with suppliers in countries with weak enforcement systems or a poor track record on child labor are viewed with suspicion by informed stakeholders. These firms thus need independent means of establishing their "good" performance (Nadvi & Wältring, 2001, p. 28). Firms may also be advancing these programs as a strategy to preempt stricter state regulation and to undermine the legitimacy of the state and unions in regulating labor issues.

Codes of conduct and monitoring systems also offer several advantages over traditional regulatory regimes in the eyes of firms. These systems build on some of the central organizational principles of contemporary globalization—outsourcing production, monitoring, and continuous improvement—and so can advance a form of regulation that multinational firms find compatible with business strategies (Wach & Nadvi, 2000; Sabel, 1994). Supplier firms in developing countries increasingly see compliance with new labor standards as a prerequisite to entry into global supply chains. Today contractors have to perform not only to world-class standards on quality and price but also on labor and environmental standards. Meeting these new standards can mean greater market access, closer ties to global buyers, and in some cases price premiums (Conroy, 2001; Nadvi & Kazmi, 2001).

The development of nongovernmental regulatory systems, however, has also been motivated by public perceptions of the failures of state and intergovernmental regulation and by growing demands from civil society actors for new mechanisms of corporate accountability. One surprising trend in the emergence of nongovernmental regulation has been the role and support of NGOs that have historically been extremely suspicious of market mechanisms, weakening state roles, and privatized regulation. However, for groups interested in strengthening the enforcement of labor standards, nongovernmental regulation is attractive as a supplemental system of monitoring and enforcement. Increasingly influential NGOs are thus advancing market-oriented, nongovernmental standards and monitoring systems as a supplement to state regulation in countries where it is ineffective and as a new point of leverage over firms operating globally (Cashore, 2002; Conroy, 2001).

Consumers are in many ways at the root of these processes. Increasingly aware consumers are demanding more information on the products they buy and on systems to help them avoid "sweatshop" products. Elliott and Freeman (2001) report that over 80% of consumers polled in the United States are willing to pay more for products that are made under "good" conditions, over 75% report feeling a moral obligation to help improve workers' conditions, and over 90% agree that countries should be required to maintain minimum standards for working conditions. Consumers in particular seek to avoid "bad" companies, such as those implicated in "sweatshop" production. A recent poll by Environics International (1999) found that 51% of Americans reported "punishing" a firm for bad social performance in the previous year. Codes of conduct, monitoring systems, and labeling schemes have emerged as means to provide consumers with the information needed to buy their desired level of workplace conditions and to send market signals to firms to improve their performance (Liubicic, 1998; Freeman, 1994). ...

References

Ayres, I., & Braithwaite, J. (1992). *Responsive regulation: Transcending the deregulation debate.* Oxford, United Kingdom: Oxford University Press.

Braithwaite, J., & Drahos, P. (2000). *Global business regulation.* Cambridge, United Kingdom: Cambridge University Press.

Cashore, B. (2002). Legitimacy and the privatization of environmental governance: How non state market-driven (NSMD) governance systems gain rule making authority. *Governance,* 15(4), 503-529.

Conroy, M. (2001). *Can advocacy-led certification systems transform global corporate practices? Evidence and some theory* (Working Paper Series No. 21). Amherst, MA: Political Economy Research Institute, University of Massachusetts.

Cutler, C., Haufler, V., & Porter, T. (1999). *Private authority in international politics*. Albany: State University of New York Press.

Elliott, K., & Freeman, R. (2001, January). *White hats or Don Quixotes? Human rights vigilantes in the global economy* (NBER (National Bureau of Economic Research) Working Paper No. W8102). Cambridge, MA.

Environics International. (1999, May). *The millenium poll on corporate social responsibility*. Retrieved from www.environicsinternational.com

Evans, P. (1997). The eclipse of the state? Reflections on stateness in an era of globalization. *World Politics, 50, 1*.

Freeman, R. (1994). A hard-headed look at labour standards. In W. Sengenberger & D. Campbell (Eds.), *International Labour Standards and Economic Interdependence*. Geneva: International Labour Organization, 79-92.

Haufler, V. (2001). *A public role for the private sector: Industry self-regulation in a global economy*. Washington, DC: Carnegie Endowment for International Peace.

Liubicic, R. (1998). Corporate codes of conduct and product labeling schemes: The limits and possibilities of promoting international labor rights through private initiatives. *Law and Policy in International Business, 30*(1), 111-158.

Nadvi, K., & Wältring, F. (2001). *Making sense of global standards* (Draft IDS-INEP working paper). Sussex, United Kingdom: Institute for Development Studies.

Reinicke, W. (1998). *Global public policy: Governing without government?* Washington, DC: Brookings Institution Press.

Schmidt, V. (1995). The new world order incorporated: The rise of business and the decline of the nation state. *Daedalus, 124*(2), 75-106.

Strange, S. (1996). *The Retreat of the State*. Cambridge, United Kingdom: Cambridge University Press.

Wach, H., & Nadvi, K. (2000). *Global Labour and Social Standards and their Implications for Developing Country Producers: A Bibliographic Overview* (Working paper). Sussex: United Kingdom: Institute for Development Studies.

Certifying Forests and Factories: States, Social Movements, and the Rise of Private Regulation in the Apparel and Forest Products Fields

Tim Bartley

31(3) Politics & Society 433 (2003)

Recent decades have seen dramatic shifts in the regulation of industries away from traditional "command and control" strategies — based on fixed standards enforced by the state—and toward regulatory forms based on different social control strategies—like market mechanisms, the provision of information, and informal shaming processes.[1] Often, these are controlled by different types of actors as well—various types ofprivate groups rather than government agencies. One regulatory form that rose to prominence in the 1990s is the private certification association. Here, nongovernmental associations certify companies on the basis of their social or environmental performance. These associations embody a new regulatory form that uses certification and the provision of information to address the impact of industry operations. Large-scale certification programs emerged across two otherwise very different industry contexts in the 1990s —the apparel industry, where certification associations focus on labor conditions and the problem of sweatshops, and the forest products industry, where they focus on environmental conditions and deforestation. This not only supports the image of certification as a general regulatory form but also raises questions about why it has emerged at these particular places and times.

This article explains why remarkably similar systems of private regulation have emerged in the apparel and forest products fields in North America. I use a comparative case study approach to examine the processes by which this distinctive set of institutional arrangements for regulating corporate activity was created. By identifying similarities across the trajectories of the two cases, I find two dynamics that explain the rise of private certification systems. One set of dynamics resulted from social movement campaigns that targeted companies—from demonstrations against Nike's labor practices in Indonesia to protests of Home Depot's sales of tropical timber. The other set of processes is linked to an international institutional context of neo-liberalism and free trade, which led both state and nonstate actors to support private, rather than public, forms of regulation. Rather than seeing certification and other "corporate social responsibility" initiatives as merely reflections of larger trends, I show specific ways in which social movement strategies and neo-liberal institutional arrangements led to the formation of private regulatory associations, rather than other solutions—like intergovernmental regulatory structures. Through this, I develop some more general ideas about the links between globalization, institutions, and the emergence of new regulatory forms.

The Rise of Certification Associations

Private certification programs emerged in both the apparel and forest products fields in the 1990s ... Forest certification efforts took off somewhat more rapidly than labor standards certification, but both were rising to prominence in the mid-1990s.

By the end of the decade, there were three overarching forest certification programs and three overarching labor standards certification programs operating in North America.[3] The Forest Stewardship Council, Sustainable Forestry Initiative, and CSA-International address forest management, while the Fair Labor Association, Social Accountability International, and Worldwide Responsible Apparel Production focus on labor conditions. Through programs like the Forest Stewardship Council and the Sustainable Forestry Initiative, firms like Home Depot and International Paper have had timber sources certified as "sustainable." ...

While quality and technical certification have existed for a long time—through Underwriters Laboratory, the "Good Housekeeping Seal of Approval," and a variety of industry standards bodies—the use of certification to address the larger societal and ecological impacts of production processes is rather new. This form has emerged alongside a discourse of corporate social responsibility, a rise of partnerships between companies and nongovernmental organizations (NGOs), and a range of experiments with corporate codes of conduct, sustainability reporting, eco-labeling, social auditing, independent monitoring, and Fair Trade products. At first, these trends may seem to be little more than responses to consumer demand or public relations ploys. But with closer attention, both of these images are lacking as explanations for certification programs. First, in contrast to the notion that certification and labeling initiatives are merely responses to the rise of socially and environmentally responsible consumerism, research on these programs suggests that stable markets for certified products rarely exist before the programs are begun—at least not at a scale that would warrant the amount of effort being put into these programs. Instead, making markets for certified products is part of a larger institution-building project that occurs along with the construction of certification associations.[4] Second, while it is tempting to reduce certification programs to nothing more than empty, corporate-sponsored public relations rhetoric—and clearly this is the case for some initiatives—this does notfit easily with the active role that credible environmental, labor, and human rights NGOs have taken in creating some of the earliest certification programs. Clearly, the rise of certification is tied up with larger political dynamics and is worthy of careful study.

The research literature on certification programs—coming out of both academic and practitioner circles—overwhelmingly treats labor standards and forest certification separately.[5] Few have noticed the similarity in these two types of certification,[6] and none have systematically charted or explained that similarity. Yet labor standards certification and forest certification programs are remarkably alike—in form, function, and framing.

In both cases, certification associations are typically private, nonprofit organizations, made up of coalitions of companies and NGOs. For example, the board of the Fair Labor Association includes representatives ofLiz Claiborne and the Lawyers Committee for Human Rights. Social Accountability International includes Toys R Us and the International Textile, Garment, and Leather Workers' Federation. Home Depot and Greenpeace both participate in the Forest Stewardship Council, while Georgia-Pacific and Conservation International are affiliated with the Sustainable Forestry Initiative. These partnerships have led some observers to dub certification systems "the NGO-industrial complex."[7]

Environmental and labor standards certification associations also carry out very similar activities. In both cases, associations set standards, accredit other organizations to inspect production sites and check companies' compliance with those standards, and then lend the name ofthe association, in some way, to companies that are found to be in compliance—sometimes through a product label.

Beyond their activities, there are striking similarities in the discourse surrounding labor standards and forest certification—as shown in the two quotations below. These two speakers work in different fields and have very different professional backgrounds. One is talking about forest certification and the other about labor standards certification.

> You have to understand, this is a non-governmental approach to trying to solve a problem. And, to me, it's reflective of the complexities of doing business today ... and of the world economy—that a lot of these problems are difficult to address by government action by legislation. And ... something like [this association] is very interesting because it's a nongovernmental approach to solving what is really a public policy problem.[8]

> So much of trade is ... such a massive, complex, dense network ... that you could never set up a regulatory system that would cover it. ... Compliance would be almost impossible. ... There's no mechanism to establish that kind of international regulatory framework. So this is one that cut right to the chase and said "We're going to empower consumers to buy products that come from well-managed [sources]." And this tool was very direct and very powerful and it was kind of captured everyone's imagination.[9]

The first statement refers to labor standards, the second to forestry. Yet both talk about the purpose and significance of certification in similar ways—as a means for addressing problems posed by global supply chains that is more direct than government action.

In sum, quite similar systems of private regulation of have emerged in these two cases. This is surprising, considering that the politics of labor and the environment have historically tended to move on quite separate tracks. Furthermore, it suggests that something beyond industry-specific politics may be driving the rise ofprivate certification as a new regulatory form. If so, then it should be possible to identify factors and processes that are operating across industries and that have helped bring about the rise of certification.

Toward an Explanation

Insights from institutional theories and research frame this study. Although a variety of diferent "institutionalisms" exist, institutionalists of a cultural, historical, or rational choice bent tend to agree on the importance of understanding the processes and mechanisms by which institutional arrangements are generated and change.[10] The emergence of institutions is a "bumpy" process, subject to a variety of political and organizational problems.[11] Building new institutions requires collective action and is thus plagued by problems of free-riding and defection.[12] Furthermore, the organizations that push or carry institutionalization projects may themselves fail, especially when resources are scarce or battles for legitimacy are particularly fierce.[13] It is by no means certain that the "right" institutions will always emerge to address a particular problem. Thus, instead of explaining new forms of private regulation by invoking their possible consequences (e.g., buffering global capitalism, facilitating flexible accumulation, shielding companies from criticism, etc.), I seek to explicate the process by which individual and collective actors built particular types of private regulatory programs, paying attention to the problems they encountered along the way.

Yet it is also important to remember that new organizational, regulatory, or institutional forms rarely emerge on their own but rather out of competition between alternative sets of solutions and conflicts between actors backing these. ... While emerging institutions are indeed products of strategic problem-solving activity, as well as some ritualistic borrowing and mimesis, they are best conceptualized as sets of practices that are in competition to become dominant institutions, in a field shaped by power, interests, and preexisting institutional arrangements. ...

Case Background

No single set of actors is responsible for creating certfication initiatives. Instead, a number of actors—including states, social movements, NGOs, companies, and in the labor standards case, trade unions—have played roles at various moments.[23]

Forest certification emerged as a response to campaigns about tropical deforestation and has so far focused primarily on wood products. The first overarching forest certification body was the Forest Stewardship Council (FSC), founded in 1993. The initial impetus for this program came out of discussions in the early 1990s among the Woodworkers

Alliance for Rainforest Protection, individuals with experience in community forestry in South America, and a few organizations that had recently begun to perform their own certifications of forest products.[24] As the idea grew into an organization, environmental groups such as World Wide Fund for Nature—or World Wildlife Fund (WWF) in the United States—and Greenpeace got involved, followed by a few companies, like the British home improvement retailer B&Q and Home Depot.[25] After the founding of the FSC, several industry groups put together their own certification programs, and battles over how to do certification ensued. This article focuses only on the moments leading up to the creation of the FSC, not on later developments.[26]

[I]t is important to keep in mind some limits and potentials of these sorts of systems for fundamentally altering the conditions of workers and the natural environment. First, certification systems deal in reputation, which means they have the potential effect of "greenwashing" reality, or cleaning up corporate images without changing practices on the ground. In addition, these are privatized forms of regulation, so they potentially conflict with democratic ideals of openness and accountability. Since corporations typically play some role, whatever impacts these programs may have will likely be limited—although not necessarily unsubstantial. Furthermore, their impacts depend on the enforcement activity of external actors, like consumers, investors, suppliers, and so forth—without which they have little power. Yet even given these limitations, certification programs represent something significant on the global governance scene. At their best, they allow credible NGOs to "discipline" companies, temper corporate control of the certification process, and help solidify linkages between social movements/civil society in affluent countries and workers and forest-dependent communities in the global south. The emergence of private regulation may also eventually have unintended effects, for instance, by changing the structure of industries or shaping the strategies pursued by activist groups. ...

Social Movement Pressure on Companies

In both the apparel and forest products fields, certification systems emerged in a context of social movement activity and public controversy about the social or environmental dimensions of the industry. [A]ttention and discourse about tropical deforestation rose rapidly in the late 1980s and peaked around 1989. The graph shows mentions of the terms rainforests or deforestation in the *New York Times* and *Los Angeles Times*.[30] ...

Environmental organizations like Friends of the Earth, the Rainforest Action Network, Greenpeace, and WWF were largely responsible for focusing attention on tropical deforestation. During the 1980s, environmental groups in Europe, and particularly Friends of the Earth in the United Kingdom, built sizeable campaigns to boycott tropical timber.[31] Similar campaigns emerged in the United States somewhat later, led by the Rainforest Action Network. Beyond encouraging individual consumer boycotts, environmental activists put direct pressure on companies involved in the timber trade. While tropical timber companies are rather small and not well-known to the public, environmentalists found a target in large do-it-yourself stores like B&Q in the United Kingdom and later Home Depot in the United States. These campaigns often publicly embarrassed companies, for instance, by filling the parking lots of home improvement stores with inflatable chainsaws.[32]

In response to boycotts, tropical timber exporting companies began making claims about the supposed environmental friendliness of their forest operations and products. They sometimes labeled their products with authoritative-sounding claims about sustainability and environmental protection. For instance, one Malaysian company's "Certificate of Products from Sustained Yield Management" said, "The hardwood rainforest products supplied come from wellmanaged production forests in accordance with the principle of sustained yield management thus safeguarding the environment and the ecological balance."[33] Exporting governments sometimes made supporting statements. Ghana's statement is instructive: "We confirm that all Ghanaian tropical hardwoods supplied by [company name] come from forest resources which are being managed to ensure a sustained yield of timber and other forest products in perpetuity and to arrest forest depletion and environmental degradation."[34]

Company claims making and attempts at self-certification spurred further criticism from environmental groups. In 1991, the WWF-UK issued a report showing that the vast majority of tropical timber firms' claims about their environmental friendliness could not even begin to be substantiated and called claims made by tropical timber trade associations "a remarkable mix of fact, conjecture and allusion together with a smokescreen of diverting but wholly irrelevant information."[35] This report became the cornerstone of a series of credibility battles, resulting in what one participant called "a confusing deluge of claims and counterclaims."[36] As one forester noted, "You might find one label which says 'We plant 10 million trees for every tree we cut down.' And you think, well, is that a good thing or a bad thing? And then somebody else says 'We buy our timber from only sustainably managed forests.' Well, you know, which product should I buy?"[37] In the environmental community, another observer recalled, "The problem was defined as proliferation of dubious claims, confusion in the marketplace, and no reliable mechanisms to leverage improvement for forest management."[38] ...

Friends of the Earth in the United Kingdom ... began working on a system for recognizing environmentally preferable sources of timber. By 1988, this group had developed a"Good Wood Seal of Approval" and published its first Good Wood Guide.[40] (In the United States, the Rainforest Action Network followed a bit later, publishing the Wood User's Guide in 1991.) Yet soon the originators of these programs discovered that tracking wood products through complex supply chains was beyond their capacity.[41] Friends of the Earth discontinued the Good Wood Seal in 1990. Other groups, like the Rainforest Alliance and Scientific Certification Systems, were beginning to put together their own independent certification initiatives in the late 1980s as well, and several of these groups would later help build an overarching association to standardize and oversee certification—the Forest Stewardship Council.[42]

Tropical timber campaigns also led some wood products retailers to enter into partnerships with environmental NGOs. In 1990, WWF forged a partnership with the British home improvement retailer B&Q, and soon they were building a"buyers group," that is, a group of retailers that would commit to selling sustainably produced wood products.[43] By the next year, the "1995 Group" buyers group had formed, and approximately twelve members had committed to sell only "sustainable" wood products by 1995.[44] The important point here is that social movement pressure was spawning partnerships that put retailers like B&Q in a position to be potential supporters of a certification system that had yet to be developed.

In sum, as social movement organizations put pressure on tropical timber producers and retailers, this created a demand for a more overarching system for evaluating claims about forest management, harvesting practices, and the use of the infamously ambiguous term "sustainability." In fact, environmental groups and a few companies were both expressing some interest in a larger system that could establish the credibility of some claims and discredit others. ...

Tropical Timber Bans and the Impact of Free Trade Rules

In the 1980s and 1990s, a variety of legislative bodies, under pressure from environmental groups, passed policies intended to slow the rate of tropical deforestation. Hundreds of European cities, a few American cities and states, and several European countries moved to ban imports of tropical timber in the early 1990s.[57] This trend of legislative bans led to a pivotal moment in the regulation of international forestry.

This came in 1992, when the Austrian parliament voted to ban the import of tropical timber unless it could be labeled as sustainably produced.[58] Tropical timber exporting countries like Indonesia and Malaysia charged that this amounted to a nontariff barrier to trade and threatened to challenge the law under the Generalized Agreement on Tariffs and Trade (GATT). In 1993, the Austrian government backed down and revised the law.[59]

This had two very important effects. First, it established that governmental action on tropical timber imports was vulnerable to challenge under global free trade rules, thus discouraging other governments from taking this route. As Crossley argues, "Importing countries have generally taken heed of the pitfalls encountered by the Austrian approach and moved away from using mandatory, legislative means to address timber trade issues. It has become clear that they are likely to be GATT-illegal and subject to challenges under the World Trade Organization (WTO)."[60] Second, when the Austrian government backed away from requiring labels for tropical timber, it took the money allocated for that project and funneled it into a private labeling program—the emerging FSC. As one observer recalls, "WWF-Austria managed to persuade the Austrian government to use that project money to support FSC. ... That was a major area of funding [for the FSC] for certainly the first two years."[61] The Swiss, Dutch, British, and Mexican governments also made financial contributions early on, and government aid agencies have continued to provide some funding.[62] So this is a situation in which the interaction between state policy and free trade rules helped a private regulatory program get off the ground in very concrete ways. ...

International Forestry Campaigns and the Defeat of Governmental Solutions

Environmental groups had several specific experiences with failures and defeats in intergovernmental arenas. During the 1980s and 1990s, environmentalists made a number of attempts to embed forest management standards in existing international organizations. Yet as several notable campaigns got shut down, environmental groups recognized an increasingly dismal set of opportunities for inter-governmental action and began constructing nongovernmental regulatory programs.

In the late 1980s, Friends of the Earth in the United Kingdom proposed creating an international forest certification system under the auspices of the International Tropical Timber Organization (ITTO), a preexisting international trade organization, which had governments as members.[85] The environmental group convinced the UK Overseas Development Administration to submit the proposal to the ITTO at its 1989 meeting. Although it asked only for study of the issue, the proposal spurred a great deal of controversy and was attacked, particularly by timber-exporting countries.[86] As one Friends of the Earth campaigner said,

> We thought that the ITTO could at least—through the project that we proposed—investigate the feasibility of certification. And this might be a way of kind of gently easing into the ITTO system what was really quite an innovative and potentially quite contentious subject. And as it turned out, even the consideration of the feasibility of it turned out to be too contentious.[87]

Timber exporting countries argued that since similar organizations did not exist for nontropical forests (temperate or boreal), certification would constitute a trade barrier and would impinge on their sovereignty.[88] Discussions about the proposal were mired in North-South conflicts, industry resistance, and questions about the compatibility of certification with free trade agreements like GATT.[89]

In the face of this opposition, the UK government weakened the proposal, and the ITTO agreed to commission a study on the general topic of how market incentives could improve forest management.[90] For environmental groups like Friends of the Earth, this was already a defeat. One participant from the NGO community went on the record at the 1989 meeting to say that the results of the certification discussion had "reduced the original Pre-Project Proposal by United Kingdom on labeling systems to an insignificant study."[91] In the following years, the ITTO continued to study certification, and even endorsed it, but never again considered actually administering an inter-governmental certification system.[92]

The failure of the ITTO to act decisively on the enforcement and verification of forestry standards fueled the formation of a private certification system. The first meetings of what was to become the Forest Stewardship Council were occurring in late 1990, and in a 1991 report, the WWF explicitly framed the emerging FSC as an alternative to failed intergovernmental programs, referring to "leaving the ITTO behind."[93] As one FSC employee put it, "FSC was a response to the failure of international organizations that ought to have had the remit to enforce, to implement and develop good forestry standards—ITTO in particular. ... And FSC was set up to correct that failure."[94]

So the ITTO affair is an example of both a"road not taken" in the emergence of certification and an instance in which environmental groups got an object lesson of sorts on the politics of free trade and began to frame nongovernmental programs as alternatives.

Forestry campaigners' frustration with intergovernmental arenas intensified in the following years, after the 1992 United Nations Commission on Environment and Development (UNCED) "Earth Summit" in Rio de Janeiro. Going in to the meeting, some environmental groups thought the summit had the potential to produce a binding international agreement on forest management. But the idea of a global forest convention was crushed in preconference meetings, "initially vetoed by the Malaysian government but unmourned by many other states," including those worried about revenues that would be lost to forest conservation.[95] Instead of producing a binding international convention, the Earth Summit resulted in a vague set of non-binding guidelines, known as the Forest Principles, as well as an overall guidance document known as Agenda 21.[96]

Environmental groups viewed Rio as a nearly complete failure on forestry issues and began devoting even more of their energies and resources to private alternatives. One observer explained that environmentalists were especially disappointed because "there were expectations created. People were certainly upset before. ... But it reached heightened proportions, unprecedented proportions, post-Rio—because the expectations were so high."[97]

Some environmental groups became especially disenchanted with intergovernmental areas at this point, and seem to have interpreted Rio as one more piece of evidence that private rather than intergovernmental, initiatives were the place to focus their energies. This seems especially the case for WWF. One former WWF official explained that governments had proven too slow and intergovernmental arenas had proven too easily subject to veto.[98] In an influential 1993 report, Johnson and Cabarle reviewed attempts to work through institutions like the ITTO and UNCED and argued that

> these and other emerging "official" international forums are crucial for negotiating, designing, and enacting the land-use and economic policies needed to make forest management more sustainable and to get it practiced on an appreciable scale. However, if past experiences with international forestry efforts are any guide, these forums will offer little substantive guidance on how to define and implement more sustainable forest practices locally. The timber-certification movement is critical to filling that gap.[99]

After Rio, WWF put a great deal of time and money into an emerging private, nongovernmental program —the FSC. While the earliest work on the FSC came from other sources, by the October 1993 founding conference, a number of WWF representatives were involved, some in key leadership positions.[100] Representatives from WWF took a leading role in developing the FSC from a concept into an organization and contributed significant resources to the project. As one participant in this process said, "There were a lot of actors that played diferent roles at different times. But clearly WWF was front and center for all effective purposes. It was the incubator and the surrogate mother, so to speak, for the FSC."[101] ...

CONCLUSION

Why did the same regulatory form emerge in two otherwise quite different fields in the 1990s? The answer is that the fields experienced roughly similar dynamics of controversy, conflict, and innovation, resulting from a particular type of social movement strategy and a neo-liberal institutional context. Social movement campaigns that targeted companies for their labor or forestry practices led to spiraling debates about the credibility of corporate claims to social and environmental responsibility. A neo-liberal institutional context encouraged states and NGOs to build private regulatory associations, by limiting opportunities for governmental and intergovernmental regulation. In this context, states offered support for private regulatory initiatives, sometimes after being constrained in attempts to develop governmental or intergovernmental solutions. ... My analysis has identified two types of mechanisms driving the rise of private regulation—one about social movements, the other about free trade rules and regimes. ...

While I have focused on explaining the apparel and forest products cases, the analysis has uncovered a story that is potentially generalizable to other settings, given several conditions. If social movement pressure exists and is directed at companies that place value on theirbrand reputations, and if commodity chains in the industry are heavily international in scope, then I would expect processes in these fields to look similar to the apparel and forest products fields. Specifically, I would expect social movement campaigns and industry responses to generate demand for some overarching system to evaluate company claims. When international trade is involved, then institutional arrangements for securing free trade will mitigate against governments doing this directly, and we are more likely to see governments and other interested parties supporting private certification associations. On the other hand, certification can be carried out through governmental means, where intranational trade is more prominent.[112] As the research literature in this area advances and expands, additional research will be able to see if these mechanisms help explain the conditions under which private certification associations are likely to materialize.

More broadly, what can the cases analyzed here contribute to our understanding of how new regulatory forms and institutional arrangements emerge? First, my analysis points to the intersection of globalization and institutional emergence as an important area for theoretical elaboration. Over the past century, social scientists have shown quite decisively that institutions matter—that is, that market activity is embedded in and depends on particular institutional arrangements.[113]

But our theories of institutional emergence and change often assume a context in which production networks are primarily national in scope, firms are clearly bounded, and nation-states stand as the ultimate arbiter of rights and rules. These baseline conditions seem to be changing. Scholars from a variety of camps have argued that globalization disrupts existing institutions, alters the power of states, and gives rise to new forms of governance.[114] In addition to the effects of hypermobile capital, capitalist globalization has also meant the rise of institutions for defining and securing "free trade."[115] As my analysis illustrates, these institutions of globalization can have far-reaching implications for other institution-building projects.

Finally, this study tells a story about what can happen when social movements'"corporate campaign" strategies collide with corporations'"branding" strategies. As I have shown, once social movements attack companies and companies respond with claims about their social/environmental friendliness, the movement company interaction tends to take on the character of a spiraling debate over the credibility of claims on both sides. An interesting sort of politics of legitimacy and information ensues, along with pressures for institutions that can generate credibility and impersonal trust.[116] This dynamic is especially likely to take hold when companies have invested in creating brand images that are cognitively and emotionally significant in the minds of consumers and investors—and thus worth defending in the media and public arena. As social movements increasingly target companies—rather than or in addition to governments—and brands become sites of cultural and political struggle,[117] it may add a new layer to the politics of regulation in the twenty-first century.

NOTES

1. Ian Ayres and John Braithwaite, *Responsive Regulation: Transcending the Deregulation Debate* (New York: Oxford University Press, 1992); Neil Gunningham and Peter Graobosky, with Darren Sinclair, *Smart Regulation: Designing Environmental Policy* (Oxford: Clarendon Press,1998); and Sol and Picciotto and Ruth Mayne, eds., *Regulating International Business: Beyond Liberalization* (New York: St. Martin's, 1999).
3. Although similar processes have occurred in Europe, this study is restricted to programs operating in North America.
4. Jason McNichol, "Contesting Governance in the Global Marketplace: A Sociological Assessment of British Efforts to Build Markets for NGO-Certified Wood Products" (Berkeley: Center for Culture, Organization, and Politics, University of California, 2000).
5. Jill Esbenshade, *The Social Accountability Contract: Private Monitoring and Labor Relations in the Global Apparel Industry* (Ph.D. dissertation, University of California, Berkeley, 1999); Dara O'Rourke, "Outsourcing Regulation: Analyzing Non-Governmental Systems ofLabor Standards and Monitoring," *Policy Studies Journal* (forthcoming, 2003); Charles Sabel, Dara O'Rourke, and Archon Fung, "Ratcheting Labor Standards: Regulation for Continuous Improvement in the Global Workplace" (unpublished paper, 2001); Nina Ascoly, Joris Oldenziel, and Ineke Zeldenrust, "Overview of Recent Developments on Monitoring and Verification in the Garment and Sportswear Industry in Europe" (unpublished manuscript, SOMO, Centre for Research on Multinational

Corporations. 2001); Jason McNichol, "The Forest Stewardship Council as a New Para-Regulatory Social Form," in E. Meidinger, G. Elliot, and G. Oesten, eds., *The Social and Political Dimensions of Forest Certification* (Remagen-Oberwinter, Germany: Forstbuch, 2002); McNichol, "Contesting Governance in the Global Marketplace; Benjamin Cashore, "Non-State Global Governance: Is Forest Certification a Legitimate Alternative to a Global Forest Convention," (unpublished paper, Yale University, 2002); and Kristiina A. Vogt, Bruce C. Larson, John C. Gordon, Daniel J. Vogt, and Anna Fanzeres, *Forest Certification: Roots, Issues, Challenges, and Benefits* (Boca Raton, FL: CRC Press, 2000).

6. Gary Gereffi, Ronie Garcia-Johnson, and Erika Sasser, "The NGO-Industrial Complex" *Foreign Policy* (July/August 2001); and Virginia Haufler, *A Public Role for the Private Sector: Industry Self-Regulation in a Global Economy* (Washington, DC: Carnegie Endowment for International Peace, 2001).

7. Gereffi et al., "The NGO-Industrial Complex."

8. Interview no. 26.

9. Interview no. 15.

10. Elisabeth Clemens and James Cook, "Politics and Institutionalism: Explaining Durability and Change," *Annual Review of Sociology* 25 (1999): 441-66; and Robert Bates, Avner Grief, Margaret Levi, Jean Laurent Rosenthal, and Barry Weingast, eds., *Analytic Narratives* (Princeton, NJ: Princeton University Press, 1998).

11. Neil Fligstein, "Markets as Politics: A Political-Cultural Approach to Market Institutions," *American Sociological Review* 61 (1996): 656-73; Paul DiMaggio, "Constructing an Organizational Field as a Professional Project: U.S. Art Museums, 1920-1940," in W.W. Powell and P. DiMaggio, eds., *The New Institutionalism in Organizational Analysis* (Chicago: University of Chicago Press, 1991); and Hayagreeva Rao, "Caveat Emptor: The Construction of Nonprofit Consumer Watchdog Organizations," *American Journal of Sociology* 103 (1998): 912-61.

12. Michael Hechter, "The Emergence of Cooperative Social Institutions," in M. Hechter, K.D. Opp, and R. Wippler, eds., *Social Institutions: Their Emergence, Maintenance and Efects* (New York: Aldine de Gruyter, 1990); Elinor Ostrom, *Governing the Commons: The Evolution of Institutions for Collective Action* (New York: Cambridge University Press, 1990).

13. Rao, "Caveat Emptor"; and Michael T. Hannan and John Freeman, *Organizational Ecology* (Cambridge, MA: Harvard University Press, 1989).

23. While much of the critical discourse surrounding these initiatives has focused on corporate dominance of certification and monitoring, it is striking how few companies were involved in the early development of these programs. In fact, mass industry involvement did not occur until

later, as industry associations founded competing, weaker bodies. This by no means invalidates the corporate dominance critique, but reminds us that corporations were mainly late adopters rather than innovators.

24. Interview nos. 22, 29, 31.

25. Interview no. 34.

26. *See* Cashore, "Non-State Global Governance," and McNichol, "The Forest Stewardship Council," on the legitimation and marketing of forest certification.

30. These were coded using the Lexis-Nexus database and included alternate forms of the words (i.e., "rain forest" in addition to "rainforest").

31. Interview no. 35.

32. Interview nos. 15, 16.

33. Christopher Upton and Stephen Bass, *The Forest Certification Handbook* (Delray Beach, FL: St. Lucie Press, 1996), 139.

34. *Ibid.*, 139. Notice that both of these claims used the term sustained yield rather than just sustainable or sustainable development. Forest products producers have been appropriating sustainability rhetoric into rationales for increased production since the 1930s, and the term sustainability remains one of the most open and contested terms in environmental discourse.

35. World Wildlife Fund, *Truth or Trickery: Timber Labelling Past and Future* (London: World Wildlife Fund, UK,1994), 7. This report included results from a 1992 follow up study that still found a number of empty claims like "timber from managed forests," "sustained yield," and "for each tree felled, more are planted."

36. Simon Counsell, "Briefing: Timber: Eco-Labelling and Certification" (Friends of the Earth, www.foe.co.uk, 1995), 1.

37. Interview no. 16.

38. Interview no. 15.

40. Counsel, " Briefing: timber: Eco-Labelling and Certification"; Richard Donovan, "Role of NGOs", In Viana et al., Eds, *Certification of Forest Products* (Washington, DC: Island Press 1996, 93-110).

41. Interview no. 35.

42. Chris Maser and Walter Smith, *Forest Certification in Sustainable Development: Healing the Landscape* (Boca Raton, FL: Lewis Publishers, 2001).

43. Jason McNichol, "The Forest Stewardship Council," and "Contesting Governance."

44. Michael B. Jenkins and Emily T. Smith, *The Business of Sustainable Forestry* (Washington, DC: Island Press,1999). See McNichol, "Contesting Governance," for more on how loosely coordinated protests against retailers and the resulting buyers groups helped build a market for certified wood.

57. Johnson and Cabarle, *Surviving the Cut*; Conrad B. MacKerron and Douglas G. Cogan, *Business in the Rainforests: Corporations, Deforestation and Sustainability* (Washington, DC: Investor Responsibility Research Center, 1993).

58. Vogt et al., *Forest Certification*; Crossley, "A Review of Global Forest Management"; Dudley et al., *Bad Harvest?*; Christopher Elliott, *Forest Certification From a Policy Network Perspective* (Jakarta, Indonesia: Center for International Forestry Research, 2000).

59. Interview #18; Elliott, *Forest Certification from a Policy Network Perspective.*

60. Crossley, "A Review of Global Forest Management."

61. Interview no. 18.

62. Interview nos. 18, 34, 17.

85. Rachel Crossley, "A Review of Global Forest Management Certification Initiatives: Political and Institutional Aspects" (paper for the conference on Econonomic, Social and Political Issues in Certification of Forest Management, May 1996, Malaysia, UBCUPM).

86. Fred P. Gale, *The Tropical Timber Trade Regime* (New York: St. Martin's, 1998); Counsell, "Briefing: Timber: Eco-Labelling and Certification"; Vogt et al., *Forest Certification*; Elliott, *Forest Certification from a Policy Network Perspective*; and Steven Johnson, "ITTO's Role in Building the Foundations for Assessing and Certifying Sustainable Tropical Forest Management" (www.pfnq.com.au, 2000).

87. Interview no. 35.

88. Gale, *The Tropical Timber Trade Regime*. As Gale points out, while timber exporting countries were the most vehement critics, representatives from North American and European governments may have been willing accomplices in the derailment ofthe certification proposal.

89. *Ibid.*

90. Elliott, *Forest Certification From a Policy Network Perspective*; and Gale, *The Tropical Timber Trade Regime.*

91. International Tropical Timber Organization, "Report ofthe International Tropical Timber Council, 7th session, Yokohama, 30 October–7 November 1989" (Yokohama, Japan, 1989), 25.

92. In 1993, a report commissioned by the ITTO recommended country-level certification as a more workable alternative to product or forest certification (see Johnson, "ITTO's Role"). 93. Another report followed in 1994, which took a somewhat more optimistic view of forest certification.

93. Elliott, *Forest Certification from a Policy Network Perspective*, 48.

94. Interview no. 18.

95. Nigel Dudley, Jean-Paul Jean-Renaud, and Francis Sullivan, *Bad Harvest? The Timber Trade and the Degradation of the World's Forests* (London: Earthscan,1999),119; and Upton and Bass, *The Forest Certification Handbook*, 124.

96. Dudley et al., Bad Harvest; and Upton and Bass, *The Forest Certification Handbook*.

97. Interview no. 27.

98. *Ibid*.

99. Johnson and Cabarle, Surviving the Cut, 51.

100. "List of Participants," FSC conference, Toronto, 1992; and interview no. 18.

101. Interview no. 27.

111. I also used the pattern of referrals generated by my interviews to map a network of connections among key players (available from the author upon request). This map shows a striking, unbridged gap between individuals working on forest certification and those working on labor standards certification, which suggests that the two programs developed separately, not as a result of simple diffusion from one field to another.

112. The U.S. Department of Agriculture's recently finalized standards for organic agricultural products are an example of a governmental certification process, which only apply to producers outside the United States on a voluntary basis. See Mrill Ingram and Helen Ingram, "Creating Credible Edibles: The Alternative Agriculture Movement and Passage of U.S. Federal Organic Standards," in D. Meyer, V. Jenness, and H. Ingram, eds., *Routing the Opposition: Social Movements, Public Policy, and Democracy* (forthcoming).

113. Max Weber, *Economy and Society*, edited by Roth and Wittich (Berkeley: University of California Press, 1978); Randall Collins, "Weber's Last Theory of Capitalism: A Systematization," *American Sociological Review* 45 (1980): 925-42; Fligstein, "Markets as Politics"; and W. Richard Scott, *Institutions and Organizations* (Thousand Oaks, CA: Sage, 1995).

114. Saskia Sassen, *Losing Control? Sovereignty in an Age of Globalization* (New York: Columbia University Press, 1996); Philip G. Cerny, "Globalization and the Changing Logic of Collective Action," *International Organization* 49, no. 4(1995): 595-625; and Kenichi Omae, *The Borderless World* (New York: HarperCollins, 1990).

115. Peter Evans, "The Eclipse of the State? Reflections on Stateness in an Era of Globalization," *World Politics* 50 (1997): 62-87.

116. Susan Shapiro, "The Social Control of Impersonal Trust," *American Journal of Sociology* 93 (1987): 623-58. Shapiro talks about this process as the elaboration of higherorder "guardians of trust ." Interestingly, to the extent that state agencies are becoming limited in their ability to serve

this guardian role, we should expect to see an acceleration of this process, and the emergence ofmultiple layers ofinstitutions that attempt to secure trust or credibility in some form.

117. Naomi Klein, *No Logo: Taking Aim at the Brand Bullies* (New York: Picador, 1999).

Emerging Best Practices for Combating Illegal Activities in the Forest Sector

Arnoldo Contreras-Hermosilla and Global Witness

(DFID-World Bank-CIDA 2003)

...

Promoting certification as a tool to ensure greater law compliance. The Bolivian experience

Bolivia started a certification program in the late nineties that quickly mushroomed to about a million hectares certified in a few years.

Why is Bolivia adopting certification with such enthusiasm? First, once it was clear that the government was determined and that the legal obligation to implement sustainable forest management plans was there to stay, the relative coincidence between these plans and the requirements of certification appears to have contributed to the expansion of the area under certified forests.

Certification is desirable for entrepreneurs because certified forests are exempt from the government forest audit. Some concessionaires and entrepreneurs have indicated that they prefer to deal with an independent certifying firm rather than with the government bureaucracy.

Furthermore, entrepreneurs perceived certification as a way to obtain international market advantages and therefore were willing to take the additional steps to obtain it. Initially, entrepreneurs expected certified products to command higher market prices and better access to markets. This belief was fuelled by some analysts who believed that certified wood could command a price premium reaching some 5-15% in the international markets. This premium has yet to materialize in Bolivia. Consumers are not willing to pay higher prices for certified products.

However, the expectation that certification will contribute to defend market shares or even expand them, is strong. According to some entrepreneurs, many markets for Bolivian products would have closed in the absence of certification. These perceptions have proven to be true. Exports of certified products have shown great dynamism: in the year 2000, exports of certified forest products, the great majority made up of finished products, reached US$8.6 million (7% of forestry exports) which represents a 200% growth compared to the year before. ...

Deterrence vs. Cooperation and the Evolving Theory of Environmental Enforcement

Clifford Rechtschaffen

71 SOUTHERN CALIFORNIA LAW REVIEW 1181 (1998)

...

1. Mandatory, Publicly Disclosed Environmental Audits of Publicly Traded Companies

a. Existing policies for disclosure of violations detected by environmental audits:

As the term is generally used and defined by the EPA, an environmental audit is a "systematic, documented, periodic and objective review by regulated entities of facility operations and practices related to meeting environmental requirements."[261] Companies began conducting audits with some frequency in the mid-1980s due to increasingly aggressive activity by government and private citizens, including stepped-up criminal enforcement, as well as the recognition that audits could result in significant economic savings.[262] ...

---

[261] Environmental Auditing Policy Statement, OPPE-FRL-3046-6, 51 Fed. Reg. 25,004, at 25,006 (July 9, 1986) [hereinafter Environmental Auditing Policy Statement]. ...

[262] *See* [Mary Ellen Kris & Gail L. Vannelli, *Today's Criminal Environmental Enforcement Program: Why You May Be Vulnerable and Why You Should Guard Against Prosecution Through an Environmental Audit*, 16 Colum. J. Envtl. L. 227, 240 (1991); Lucia Ann Silecchia, *Ounces of Prevention and Pounds of Cure: Developing Sound Policies for Environmental Compliance Programs*, 7 Fordham Envtl. L.J. 583, 584-594 (1996)] and *infra* note 305.

b.   **The benefits of mandatory, publicly disclosed audits of publicly traded corporations:**

... Although not without limitations, environmental auditing is a very effective means for businesses to monitor their compliance with environmental requirements, which is precisely why many responsible corporations voluntarily conduct them. As discussed above, audits may be more extensive than agency inspections or carried out more frequently.[278] Such self-policing efforts, especially where results must be reported to governmental agencies, can be a highly effective tool for promoting compliance.[279] Ideally, all regulated firms should conduct audits. As a first step in this direction, audits should be required for all publicly traded corporations. Publicly traded corporations can best afford environmental audits, and many already conduct them.[280]

Environmental audits also should be disclosed to the public. There are strong utilitarian and entitlement rationales justifying public disclosure.[281] For example, disclosure of environmental audits, like disclosure of financial audits, helps promote the efficient functioning of securities markets. Securities law requires publicly held corporations to disclose independently audited financial statements to the public and potential investors on the theory that disclosure provides investors with the information they need to make intelligent decisions. Information in an environmental auditem - which is essentially a snapshot of a firm's environmental health is at least as relevant to some investors as a picture of a firm's financial well-being.[282] Likewise, audit disclosure can help

---

[278] *See supra* Part III.A.3. [in original version of article.]

[279] *See* Eric Bregman & Arthur Jacobson, *Environmental Performance Review: Self-Regulation in Environmental Law*, 16 Cardozo L. Rev. 465, 484 (1994) ... ; [Douglas C. Michael, *Cooperative Implementation of Federal Regulations*, 13 Yale J. on Reg. 535, 575 (1996)]. ...

[280] Moreover, publicly traded corporations are likely to be most sensitive to market pressure triggered by public disclosure of environmental audits since the audience of parties interested in the audits includes investors, consumers, and employees. Limiting an audit requirement to publicly traded corporations is admittedly an imperfect solution. Smaller, closely held companies clearly commit a substantial number of environmental violations. Moreover, some small public companies may not be in a better position to bear the costs of audits than private companies. Nonetheless, this incremental step is probably all that is politically feasible at this time.

[281] ... *See* John M. Mendeloff, *The Dilemma of Toxic Substance Regulation: How Overregulation Cures Underregulation at OSHA* 209-10 (1988).

[282] This is especially true as the socially responsible investment movement expands. [There is a growing socially responsible investment movement that evaluates the environmental record of companies as a basis for investment in the stock market. *See* Steven J. Bennett, Richard Freierman & Stephen George, *Corporate Realities & Environmental Truths Strategies for Leading Your Business in the Environmental Era* 13 (1993). ...]

consumers make better-informed decisions about whether to purchase a firm's products, and allows workers to negotiate for less hazardous working conditions or demand wage premiums for risky jobs.[283] Beyond the marketplace, disclosure furthers citizen power and advances democratic decisionmaking. It allows local residents and members of the public to participate more effectively in permit, land use, and other local political decisions involving the company. It enhances the public's ability to bargain with private corporations and exert pressure on companies to change their environmental practices.[284] It also enables citizens to enforce environmental laws, since "the public cannot participate in [the enforcement] process without having access to adequate information regarding a facility's compliance with environmental regulations."[285] In essence, disclosure has an important deterrent function and helps promote compliance by raising the firms' costs of violating environmental requirements.[286]

In addition to these utilitarian rationales, public disclosure is justified on entitlement grounds namely, that members of the public have a fundamental right to know what substances and risks they are exposed to by facilities in their community.[287] Disclosure furthers individual autonomy by creating awareness of the risks involved in specific choices and allowing individuals to decide whether or not to encounter these risks.

Businesses should be generally supportive of an auditing requirement, since it is a practice that many have voluntarily embraced. Auditing, unlike substantive environmental regulation, does not intrude on management prerogatives or dictate how a firm must satisfy regulatory requirements. It is a process for identifying whether a firm is meeting environmental requirements and can help a company avoid far more intrusive enforcement actions. Still, mandating audits, and in particular the public disclosure of audits, is certain to generate business opposition.

---

[283] As discussed above, however, there are important limitations on the ability of the marketplace to promote compliance with environmental laws. ...

[284] ... Michael M. Sthal, Enforcement in Transition, Envtl. F., Nov.-Dec. 1995, at 19,22.

[285] Steven A. Herman, *It Takes a Partnership*, 14 Envtl. F., May-June 1997, at 26, 30. ... *See* [Sanford Lewis, Feel-Good Notions, Corporate Power and the "Reinvention" of Environmental Law (Good Neighbor Project for Sustainable Industries, Working Paper, March 17, 1997) http://www.envirolink.org/orgs/gnp/fgnful.htm]. ...

[286] ... *See* [Malcolm K. Sparrow, Imposing Duties Government's Changing Approach to Compliance (1994) ...] at 96. ...

[287] Not all environmental audits will necessarily reveal this information, but many likely will.

One reason for opposition is the costs of audits.[288] Publicly traded corporations, however, should be able to absorb this expense without great hardship. Moreover, audits usually save firms money by identifying more efficient production processes and ways to reduce waste generation, as well as by reducing their exposure to enforcement actions and liability suits.[289] For smaller businesses that cannot afford auditing programs, however, the EPA and states should provide financial assistance for third-party auditors or offer auditing services for free, perhaps creating a cadre of trained governmental auditors. A good model is suggested by EPA's Region I, which recently began providing free compliance and pollution prevention audits to small and medium-sized companies.[290]

Firms will object strongly to forced public disclosure of audit results, and in particular to the unfairness of the use of audit information as the basis for government enforcement actions or third-party liability suits. However, regulated entities already are required to monitor, record, and in many cases, report extensive aspects of their compliance with environmental laws to government agencies.[291] ... Permitted hazardous waste facilities also have extensive monitoring and reporting obligations.[294] Thus, a requirement that audit reports be disclosed is in many ways a logical extension of existing law.[295] The fear of third-party toxic tort lawsuits is more imagined than real because these cases are enormously difficult to prosecute and win.[296] But the more fundamental

---

[288] ... *See* [Price Waterhouse LLP, The Voluntary Environmental Audit Survey of U.S. Business 1, 5 (Mar. 1995)], at 6. ... *See also* Don Sayre, *Inside ISO 14001 The Competitive Advantage of Environmental Management* 140 (1996) ...

[289] *See* [Ian Ayres & John Braithwaite, Responsive Regulation: Transcending the Deregulation Debate 22 (1992) ...], and *infra* notes 301-05 ... .

[290] ... *See* George S. Hawkins, *Compliance and Enforcement Changes in Congress and EPA*, Nat. *Resources & Env't*, Spring 1997, at 45.

[291] *See* [Lucia Ann Silecchia, *Ounces of Prevention and Pounds of Cure: Developing Sound Policies for Environmental Compliance Programs*, 7 Fordham Envtl. L.J. 583, 625-26 & n. 134 (1996)]. ... *See* Michael, *supra* note [279], at 589.

[294] For example, they must keep records of their training of personnel, internal facility inspections and repairs of facility equipment, waste analyses, operating logs, and other matters, all of which are available for review by agencies during facility inspections. These entities must also submit to regulators reports regarding releases, fires, and explosions at their facilities, and reports about facility compliance with schedules set forth in the permit; they must conduct extensive on-site environmental monitoring and report the results to regulators. *See* [Clifford Rechtschaffen, *Enforcement of Hazardous Waste Management Requirements, in California Land Use and Environmental Practice* 54-40 to -43 (Kenneth Manaster & Daniel Selmi eds., 1995)] at 54-26 to -27.

[295] Moreover, government agencies report that they have rarely, if ever, used audit data as the basis for enforcement actions. *See infra* note 304.

[296] *See* [Daniel Farber, *Toxic Causation*, 71 Minn. L. Rev. 1219, 1227-1229 (1987); *Developments in the Law - Toxic Waste Litigation*, 99 Harv. L. Rev. 1458, 1617-30 (1986)...; *supra* notes 61-62 ... .]

rejoinder to these arguments is that the information in audits is largely of a public character, reflecting whether a firm is in compliance with publicly enacted requirements designed to protect the public.[297] As previously explained, depriving the public of access to this material denies them knowledge fundamental to their ability to make fully-informed and well-considered political and economic decisions a cost too high to protect firms from the possibility of lawsuits.

c.   The disadvantages of audit privilege and immunity laws to enforcement:

A mandatory audit requirement just for publicly traded companies, notwithstanding its many benefits, is unlikely to be adopted any time soon. In the meantime, a key policy question is the appropriateness of an evidentiary privilege for audits or immunity from prosecution for violations. ...

Advocates of privilege and immunity provisions argue that these laws create a critically important incentive for firms to conduct audits. Without these legal protections, many firms would forego audits because of fear that the information discovered will be used against them in enforcement actions or third-party lawsuits. In fact, the audit reports would provide a road map of violations for enforcement agencies. Moreover, the argument goes, self-audits uncover and correct many violations that the government would never discover on its own.[302] Thus, absent protection from future enforcement, firms would expose themselves to greater risk by conducting audits.[303] A 1995 Price Waterhouse survey found that two-thirds of the firms with auditing programs in place would conduct more audits if penalties were waived for violations voluntarily discovered and disclosed.[304]

The opposing camp contends that audit privileges or immunities are not necessary to stimulate auditing for a number of reasons. First, many businesses will voluntarily conduct audits to reduce their liability and

---

[297] To the extent that audits discuss trade secrets or confidential business information, this information should be withheld.

[302] *See, e.g.,* [James M. Weaver, Robert J. Martineau, Jr. & Michael K. Stagg, *State Environmental Audit Laws Advance Goal of a Cleaner Environment,* 11 Nat. Resources & Env't, Spring 1997], at 7...

[303] *See* [Kirk F. Marty, Note, *Moving Beyond the Body Count and Toward Compliance: Legislative Options for Encouraging Environmental Self-Analysis,* 20 Vt. L. Rev. 495, 544-45 (1995)]...

[304] *See* Voluntary Environmental Audit, *supra* note [288], at 6. ...

for other sound business reasons.[305] Many will audit to comply with voluntary environmental management codes.[306] Additionally, firms already realize important enforcement benefits from conducting audits, under the EPA's voluntary disclosure policy, the Department of Justice's guidelines for criminal prosecution of environmental violations, and the EPA's policy on criminal environmental investigations.[307] Even in the absence of such formal policies, state and local agencies inevitably consider a firm's auditing practices when calculating penalties or making other enforcement decisions.[308]

The EPA contends its policy is effective by pointing to the more than 225 companies that had disclosed and corrected violations at more than 700 facilities as of October 1997.[309] Privilege proponents reply that privilege laws have resulted in a greater number of regulated entities reporting and correcting violations than under the EPA's policy.[310] In fact, the initial evidence does not support these latter claims; there apparently has been relatively little additional auditing and disclosure stimulated by the state statutes.[311] But this lack of activity may not be determinative either, since, as audit advocates are quick to point out, companies may be chilled from taking advantage of state laws by the prospect of direct federal actions or federal overfiling against them.[312] At the very least, while the evidence

---

[305] *See* [Michael R. Harris, *Promoting Corporate Self-Compliance: An Examination of the Debate Over Legal Protection for Environmental Audits*, 23 Ecology L.Q. 663, 679-83 (1996)]...

[306] *See* [Jennifer Nash & John Ehrenfeld, *Code Green: Business Adopts Voluntary Environmental Standards*, 38 Env't, Jan.-Feb. 1996]...

[307] *See supra* Part V.C.1.a. [in original version] ... *See* Weaver, et al., *supra* note [302], at 7. *See also* Jim Moore & Nancy Newkirk, *Not Quite a Giant Step*, Envtl. F., May-June 1995, at 16, 19.

[308] *See, e.g.*, Krista McIntyre, *Voluntary Disclosure - Gotcha!*, Nat. Resources & Env't 52, 53 (Spring 1997)...

[309] *See* [The Review of Activities by the Federal Government Concerining Individuals or Organizations Voluntarily Submitting to Environmental Audits: Hearings Before the Senate Comm. on Env't and Pub. Works, 105th Cong., 1st Sess. 51 (1997)], at 51 (statement of Steven Herman).

[310] *See* Weaver, et al., *supra* note [302], at 12-13... *See also* Environmental Audit Privileges, [*supra* note 309], at 85-86 ... .

[311] *See* Environmental Audits: State Immunity, Privilege Laws Examined for Conflicts Affecting Delegated Programs, Daily Env't Rep. (BNA) No. 181, at AA-1, 1 (Sept. 18, 1996) ...

[312] The Colorado Attorney General Office has complained that "it is impossible to measure the success of audit programs if companies are discouraged from participating in them ... by EPA's threats of overfiling. EPA's response [to State privilege and immunity laws], in practice, nullifies State laws." Hearings on the Relationship Between Federal and State Governments, [The Relationship Between Federal and State Governments in the Enforcement of Environmental Laws: Hearings Before the Senate Comm. on Env't and Pub. Works, 105th Cong. 190 (1997)], at 200 ... .

is not conclusive, it suggests that most businesses (especially larger firms) will likely audit for business reasons even in the absence of privilege/ immunity protections.[313]

Opponents of audit privilege and immunity measures also contend, with considerable justification, that privilege laws would complicate and increase the costs of enforcement. These provisions would invite litigation over what material is or is not privileged, a problem compounded by the lack of clear guidelines in many state statutes over the scope of the privilege.[314]

Beyond these concerns, there are two overriding flaws of privilege/ immunity measures. First, they seriously undermine the incentives for facilities to take preventative steps to achieve compliance. To varying degrees, they permit firms to sit back and wait until an audit is conducted before coming into compliance. Then, so long as a firm corrects and discloses the violations, its sanctionable behavior will be excused. Privilege laws achieve this effect indirectly by making it more difficult and in some cases impossible for enforcement agencies to obtain evidence about violations contained in an audit report. Immunity statutes achieve this effect directly. The broader versions of these latter measures immunize intentional criminal conduct and serious violations that pose significant threats to the environment. This runs counter to the assumptions of most enforcement activity; as one prosecutor succinctly puts it, "you wouldn't expect that the act of confessing to a crime should bring with it an entitlement of immunity."[315]

Privilege/immunity laws also allow firms to retain the economic benefit they obtain from noncompliance, removing an important incentive for timely compliance. As the EPA argues in opposition to state measures that do not recoup economic benefit if violations are disclosed and corrected, "taxpayers expect to pay interest or a penalty fee if their tax payments are late; the same principle should apply to corporations that have delayed their investment in compliance."[316]

---

[313] *See* Silecchia, *supra* note [291], at 628.
[314] *See* [*Incentives for Self-Policing: Discovery, Disclosure, Correction and Prevention of Violations*, FRL-5400-1, 60 Fed. Reg. 66,706, 66,707 (1995) at 66,710; [Edwin F. Lowry, Environmental Audit Privilege Legislation: Necessary for Business or a Nightmare for Prosecutors?, 17 Prosecutor's Brief 5 (1995)], at 19.
[315] *See* Lowry, [*id.* at 5]. ...
[316] Incentives for Self-Policing, *supra* note [314], at 66, 707.

Second, privacy laws are highly objectionable because, as described above, they keep a category of public environmental information pertaining to the facility's compliance with environmental requirements secret and out of the public's reach.[317] As one commentator summarizes, these measures "[regard] third parties as almost unnecessary to administration of the regulatory system."[318]

The EPA's voluntary disclosure policy and similar state initiatives strike a better, albeit not perfect, balance between promoting self-policing and retaining a meaningful deterrent component of enforcement. The policies provide strong encouragement to audit by waiving all gravity-based penalties and generally not recommending criminal enforcement when violations are voluntarily disclosed and corrected, but they do not grant any privileges to audit documents. The policies contain insufficient incentive, however, for firms to take steps to prevent violations before the audits are conducted.[319] The only sanction facing a firm that does not act proactively to achieve compliance is potential action by the EPA or states to recover the economic benefit gained from noncompliance. However, this merely puts a firm back in the position it would have been had it originally complied; it does not alter the firm's basic cost-benefit calculation as a way to deter violations in the first place. A better approach would be not to waive all penalties, but to allow enforcement agencies to consider the voluntary disclosure and correction of the violations when determining enforcement responses and the size of penalties to impose.[320] Audits should also be the basis for agencies to provide firms with other enforcement and permit benefits, such as less frequent inspections or inspections reduced in scope, accelerated permit

---

[317] The EPA's position is that "in the final analysis, an audit privilege invites secrecy and breeds distrust." Herman, *supra* note 285, at 30.

[318] [Keith Welks, *Voluntary Compliance Measures in the United States* 26 (Oct. 1996) (unpublished report for the Commission of Environmental Cooperation, on file with author)] at 46.

[319] There is an important qualification to this point, however. The EPA policy also provides enforcement benefits to firms that voluntarily disclose and correct violations detected through "a documented, systematic procedure or practice which reflects the regulated entity's due diligence in preventing, detecting, and correcting violations." Incentives for Self-Policing, *supra* note [314], at 66,708. ...

[320] It also is desirable for enforcement officials to retain some discretion in choosing enforcement responses rather than being bound by fixed policies. There is extensive evidence demonstrating that, contrary to popular misconception, agency officials act flexibly and pragmatically in meting out penalties. There may be some instances where, despite the voluntary disclosure and correction of a violation, a small penalty would be appropriate; the EPA approach would preclude this.

reviews, and eligibility to participate in other flexible regulatory initiatives.[321]

2. Environmental Management Systems

Environmental management systems are more comprehensive than environmental audits. Audits are intended to measure, at a fixed point in time, a facility's compliance with a specific set of regulatory requirements or other criteria. Management systems, by contrast, seek to evaluate and typically improve the environmental impacts of all activities of a firm.[322] Moreover, the systems are process-oriented; the underlying notion is that having better systems in place will lead to better environmental performance and less pollution. Many environmental management systems, therefore, do not focus on a facility's actual performance in complying with regulatory standards.[323] Like environmental audits, management systems have grown over the past decade in response to growing liability concerns and enforcement actions.[324]

a. The key environmental management systems:

The three most important environmental management systems for U.S. companies are the standard contained in the ISO 14000 series, a recently published set of environmental standards issued by the International Organization for Standardization (ISO);[325] the Eco-Management and Audit Scheme (EMAS), a voluntary management system adopted by the European Union;[326] and the EPA's Environmental Leadership Project (ELP).

---

[321] *[S]ee* Silecchia, *supra* note [291], at 615-24. ...

[322] *See* Kerry E. Rodgers, *The ISO Environmental Standards Initiative*, 5 N.Y.U. Envtl. L.J. 181, 184 (1996).

[323] *See* [Richard Welford, *Environmental Strategy And Sustainable Development - The Corporate Challenge For The Twenty-First Century* 56 (1994)], at 75.

[324] Their growth has also been fueled by the desire of some corporations to import total quality management principles into the environmental area, and the desire of some firms to adopt sustainable environmental practices.

[325] ISO is an international standards-setting organization whose purpose is to promote international standards to facilitate international trade. It consists of the standards-setting organizations of 100 member nations. ISO standards are documented agreements of technical specifications that companies use as guidelines to ensure that materials and products fit their purpose. For example, the format of automatic teller machine cards is based on an ISO standard.

[326] ... *See* Welford, *supra* note [323], at 72.

ISO's standards have been highly influential in the past,[327] and the ISO 14000 environmental standards are likewise predicted to become the most widely accepted global environmental standards and a condition of doing business with a number of countries and corporations.[328] The management standard of the ISO 14000[329] consists of several key components. The first element is planning: Top management must establish an environmental policy for their organizations;[330] firms must identify the "environmental aspects" of their activities, products and services, and applicable legal requirements;[331] and they must establish environmental objectives and targets, and a program documenting how and when these will be achieved.[332] The second element is implementation: Firms must put in place a number of internal processes to carry out their policies and objectives, including designation of responsible managers, training programs, communication systems and documented operating procedures.[333] The final element is monitoring and review: Firms must regularly measure the key characteristics of their activities that have a significant environmental impact, and must periodically conduct management system audits to verify compliance with the ISO standard.[334]

Under the EMAS, companies are required to establish an environmental policy based on eleven basic principles of good management practice. For each participating site, companies must develop an environmental program that describes the company's environmental protection objectives and an environmental management system.[335] As with the ISO 14001 standard, companies must implement their policies and programs through a variety of internal systems, including maintaining a registry

---

[327] ... Michael Prince, *ISO Now Offering Voluntary Standards, Bus. Ins.*, Nov. 11, 1996, at 21.

[328] *See* Marc E. Gold, *ISO 14000: A New Global Business Benchmark*, 12 Envtl. Compliance & Litig. Strategy 1 (May 1995).

[329] ... For a comprehensive list of sources discussing the ISO 14001 management system, *see* [Donald A. Carr & William L. Thomas, *Devising a Compliance Strategy Under the ISO 14000 International Environmental Management Standards*, 15 Pace Envtl. L. Rev. 85, 152 & n.160 (1997)].

[330] *See* International Standards Organization 14001, Environmental Management Systems General Guidelines on Principles, Systems and Supporting Techniques, 4.0-4.1 (1996) [hereinafter ISO 14001].

[331] *See id.* 4.2.1-4.2.2.

[332] *See id.* 4.2.3-4.2.4.

[333] *See id.* 4.3.1-4.3.7.

[334] *See id.* 4.4.1-4.4.4.

[335] *See Allowing Voluntary Participation by Companies in the Industrial Sector in a Community Eco-Management and Audit Scheme*, Council Regulation 1836/93, Annex I, C (1993), available in WESTLAW, ENFLEX-EU database ...

of "significant" environmental effects at each site.[336] Each facility must also engage in periodic environmental auditing at least once every three years that reviews both compliance issues and the facility's management system.[337] Unlike the ISO standard, facilities also must prepare and publicly disseminate statements that summarize in nontechnical form the findings of internal audits. The statements must include an assessment of "all the significant environmental issues of relevance," and a summary of information about emissions, waste generation, consumption of resources, and other factors regarding environmental performance. These public statements are verified by "accredited environmental verifiers" who check to ensure that the company is in compliance with all aspects of the EMAS regulation.[338] Once the statements are verified, they are disclosed to the public.[339]

The EPA's vehicle for encouraging environmental management systems, ELP, began as a pilot project in 1995 with ten private and two governmental facilities, and has expanded to include any eligible facility.[340] To participate, firms must have a "mature" environmental management system that expands on the ISO 14001 management requirements.[341] The environmental management system must specifically include systems for achieving continual compliance with all legal requirements, continually improving the organization's environmental performance, implementing pollution prevention practices to stop the generation of pollution at its source, and communicating with community stakeholders about the organization's environmental management system.[342] The facility also must have an auditing program that periodically evaluates compliance with regulatory standards and with EMS requirements.[343] Finally, the firm must prepare an annual report, available to the public, that discusses the facility's environmental performance and success in meeting its management

---

[336] *See* Council Regulation, *supra* note 335, Annex I, A-C. ...

[337] *See id.* Annex II, C. ...

[338] *See id.* art. 6.1-.7. ...

[339] *See* Council Regulation, *supra* note 335, art. 4.7. ...

[340] ... *See* Proposal for Using Voluntary Environmental Management Systems in State Water Programs, FRL-5678-7, 62 Fed. Reg. 3036 (Jan. 21, 1997). ...

[341] *See* U.S. Envtl. Protection Agency, Draft ELP Proposed Framework (visited Feb. 1997) <http:www.envirosense.com/elp/om5frm.html> [hereinafter ELP Proposed Framework]. ...

[342] *See id.* The definition of pollution prevention is broader than that used in the ISO 14001 standard.

[343] *See id.* Audits must be conducted, at a minimum, in the second and fifth years of a six-year cycle.

objectives, and the results of environmental audits and any agency inspections conducted during the year.[344] Firms that participate in ELP will receive a number of enforcement benefits.

b.   Environmental management systems as the basis for enforcement benefits:

Environmental management systems are likely to improve compliance and better the environmental performance of regulated entities.[345] Therefore, firms with environmental management systems in place should be granted enforcement benefits, provided that several conditions are met. First, the system should require compliance with environmental requirements and prophylactic measures to prevent violations in advance of any self-audits. Second, adherence to the system should be verified by outside parties to ensure the system's integrity to agencies, the public, and other private parties, including companies and consumers doing business with the firm. Third, the environmental management system should provide the public with access to environmental information. The EPA's ELP and the EMAS standard meet all of the above criteria; the ISO 14001 standard does not.

The orientation of the ISO 14001 standard, for example, fails to assure that a firm will realize any specific compliance benefits. ISO 14001 does not prescribe specific operational practices or set numeric or other kinds of performance standards. It also does not require emissions and discharge reductions. By its own terms, ISO 14001 does not necessarily expect immediate, tangible environmental improvements from the management systems.[346] Moreover, the standard cannot be counted on to ensure compliance with environmental regulations. While firms must include in their environmental policies a commitment to comply with relevant environmental legislation and regulation, outside auditors certifying a firm's conformance to ISO 14001 are not expected to audit the company's actual compliance.[347] By contrast, both the EMAS standard

---

[344] *See id*.

[345] ... Welford, *supra* note [323], at 51. ... Christopher L. Bell, *Bench Test*, 14 Envtl. F., Nov.-Dec. 1997, at 24, 25 ...

[346] As described in the standard's guidance: "Although some improvement in environmental performance can be expected due to the adoption of a systematic approach, it should be understood that the environmental management system is a tool which enables the organization to achieve and systematically control the level of environmental performance that it sets itself. ... " Council Regulation, *supra* note 335, Annex A, A.4. ...

[347] *See* ISO 14001, *supra* note 330, 4.1, 4.4.1. ...

and ELP require participating firms to assure compliance with all environmental requirements.

Likewise, the ISO 14001 standard does not mandate that independent, third parties verify adherence to the ISO requirements.[348] Under EMAS, a company's environmental policy, program, management system and audit findings must be validated by independent, accredited environmental verifiers. ELP also requires outside verification; facilities may use internal auditors to check compliance with a firm's management system, but their work must be monitored by third-party observers.[349]

The ISO 14001 standard also fails to provide for meaningful public disclosure of a facility's environmental performance.[350] It does not require disclosure of a facility's environmental audits, releases, or other pertinent information about the environmental impacts of its activities and products. The only information that must be disclosed is a company's environmental policy.[351] Both EMAS and ELP have much stronger disclosure elements requiring release of annual environmental reports. As Eric Orts argues, disclosure of these reports will increase public trust that environmental business practices are sincere, as well as increase the general level of information available concerning important environmental issues.[352] EMAS' required public statements are broader than those required by ELP; they must include information about emissions, waste generation, consumption of resources, and the like, although firms may keep the data underlying the statements confidential. ELP's public outreach component the Community Outreach/Employee Involvement Program that every firm is required to have is also disappointingly vague. It requires facilities to "have a written policy to demonstrate its commitment to open communication with its employees and with the community for the purpose of understanding and

---

[348] ... *See* Nash & Ehrenfeld, *supra* note [306].

[349] *See* ELP Proposed Framework, *supra* note 341.

[350] *See* [Benchmark Environmental Consulting, ISO 14001: An Uncommon Perspective 6-10, 15-17 (rev. 1996)], at 19-21.

[351] These very limited disclosure requirements resulted from pressure by the United States during drafting of the ISO standard. *See* [Naomi Roht-Arriaza, *Shifting the Point of Regulation: The International Organization for Standardization and Global Lawmaking on Trade and the Environment*, 22 Ecology L.Q. 479, 504 (1995)]. They run counter to the trend toward greater disclosure of environmental information in international environmental agreements and voluntary industry codes. See Benchmark Consulting, *supra* note [350], at 19.

[352] *See* [Eric W. Orts, *Reflexive Environmental Law*, 89 Nw. U. L. Rev. 1227, 1323 (1995)]. *See also* Benchmark Consulting, *supra* note [350], at 20 ...

responding to environmental issues," as well as a "strategy for identifying and interacting with affected communities, identifying community needs and a plan of action for addressing those community needs."[353] The most concrete specification is that the facility must educate the community on any environmental impact the facility may have. These hortatory guidelines do relatively little to ensure that affected communities will become meaningful partners in corporate environmental decisions or have any greater access to environmental information than they enjoy under existing laws. If, as the EPA envisions, the ELP program is designed to publicly recognize facilities that "demonstrate outstanding environmental management practices,"[354] firms should be required to do considerably more, such as committing to allow citizen auditors direct access to the facility to monitor compliance with a firm's environmental management objectives.[355]

Despite these limitations, the EPA's ELP contains sufficient safeguards to ensure improvements in compliance, and the EPA has appropriately proposed to provide firms participating in ELP with enforcement benefits.[356] Specifically, the EPA will reduce facility inspections for participating firms and also waive gravity-based civil penalties for the violations, provided that the firms promptly correct any detected instances of noncompliance with essentially the same exceptions that apply to disclosures by firms that voluntarily conduct audits.[357] Unlike the case with audits, the ELP prompts far less concern that waiving gravity-based penalties will undermine an important element needed to deter violations in the first place.[358] This is because the ELP includes systems designed to achieve ongoing compliance, effectively requiring

[353] The substantive requirements of the Community Outreach/Employee Involvement Program are that it (1) "should be designed to impart an environmental message or contribution;" (2) "should respond to a community need or desire [and] provide...a means of obtaining feedback from the community regarding facility environmental issues;" and (3) "should involve employees and recognize that employees are one of the best resources of the facility [and] provide training or information for employees to ensure that the employees know about the facility's position on environmental and health issues, and environmental policies and plans." U.S. Envtl. Protection Agency, Draft - Community Outreach/Employee Involvement (visited Mar. 5, 1998) <http://es.epa.gov/elp/pf4.html> (emphasis added).

[354] Environmental Leadership Program: Request for Pilot Project Proposals, FRL-5001-5, 59 Fed. Reg. 32,062, 32,062 (June 21, 1994) [hereinafter Pilot Project Proposals].

[355] ... *See also* Susan Casey-Lefkowitz, The Evolving Role of Citizens in Conference Proceedings, Fourth International Conference on Environmental Compliance Enforcement 221, 227-28 (1996). ...

[356] Firms that implement the EMAS should also be entitled to similar benefits from enforcement agencies.

[357] *See* discussion [notes 274-77 and accompanying text in original version.]

firms to take preventive measures before violations are detected. This more confident view is particularly true if independent parties certify the integrity of the environmental management system program. The EPA should follow through on other benefits it has suggested for participating firms, including expedited permit approval and a streamlined process for modifying permits.[359] ...

---

[358] This is not to say that some deterrence value is not lost by waiving penalties. One could certainly argue that firms will carry out preventative measures less diligently knowing that they will not be sanctioned for any violations that nonetheless occur if the violations are voluntarily discovered and remedied.

[359] *See Enforcement: EPA Preparing for 1997 Launch of Environmental Leadership Program*, Daily Env't Rep (BNA) No. 200, at AA-1 (Oct. 16, 1996). Participating firms also receive public recognition and a logo that can be used for limited advertising purposes (in facility advertisements but not on product advertising). Although the EPA should be commended for insisting that the ELP surpass the ISO 14001 standard in several key areas, the ELP is nonetheless insufficiently ambitious. Most notably, the ELP does not require a substantive commitment to any specific set of environmental goals, such as requiring all facilities to endorse a Code of Environmental Management Principles (as the EPA initially considered). *See* Environmental Leadership Program, FRL-4552-6, 58 Fed. Reg. 4,802 (Jan. 15, 1993) (outlining possible elements of Corporate Statement of Environmental Principles); Pilot Project Proposals, *supra* note 354 (announcing that the EPA would not develop its own principles but would work with organizations that have developed their own corporate or industry codes). ...

Talking with the Donkey: Cooperative Approaches to Environmental Protection

Kathryn Harrison

2(3) JOURNAL OF INDUSTRIAL ECOLOGY 51 (1998)

Introduction

In the past decade, governments throughout the world have expressed growing interest in more flexible cooperative approaches to environmental protection. In the United States, this trend can be viewed as a reaction against the uniquely conflictual American approach to environmental regulation. ... Interestingly, there is also renewed interest in cooperative policy instruments in countries such as the Netherlands, Canada, Australia, the United Kingdom, and Japan, where environmental regulation has traditionally been relatively cooperative (Harrison and Hoberg 1994; Brickman et al. 1985). ...

Defining Cooperation

It is important to clarify at the outset just what is meant by "cooperation," because the term is likely to have different meaning from different perspectives. The Oxford Concise Dictionary defines cooperation as "working together to the same end" (Allen 1990). Several aspects of this definition warrant closer examination. First is the implicit question of just who is "working together." Many cooperative approaches that have emerged in recent years focus on partnerships between business and government, to the exclusion of other parties. Such approaches may enhance government cooperation with one group at the expense of conflict with others, such as environmentalists, who may resent exclusion or have substantive objections to agreements reached between government and business. ...

A second element of the definition of cooperation concerns commonality of objectives. Cooperation is predicated on some measure of agreement or consent. However, when one is considering agreements between government and nongovernmental interests, the nature of that consent requires closer examination. This is because government, unlike private actors, has legitimate authority to coerce others (subject of course to constitutional limitations) (Stanbury 1993, 53). This raises the question of whether business–government agreement with respect to environmental policy constitutes genuine cooperation, in the same way as one might question whether handing over one's wallet to an armed assailant constitutes cooperation. ...

The third element of the definition of cooperation is "working together." Government and business may collaborate in devising or implementing policies, or both. It is questionable, however, whether a government's choice not to intervene at all can be considered a form of business–government cooperation. ...

A. Typology of Cooperative Approaches

One of the most straightforward typologies of policy instruments is that offered by Doern and Phidd (1992) who argue that governments choose among five broad classes of policy tools:

- Regulation (legal requirements backed by government sanctions);

- Government enterprise (direct provision of goods and services by either government agencies or government-owned enterprises);

- Expenditure;

- Exhortation;

- Inaction

In terms of the familiar analogy of how to get a donkey to pull a cart, these policy instruments correspond to using a stick to coerce the donkey (regulation), the driver pulling the cart herself (government enterprise), inducing the donkey to move with carrots (expenditure), encouraging the donkey through ear stroking and persuasion (exhortation), and leaving it up to whomever want the goods in the cart to work out their own arrangements with the donkey (government inaction).

These categories are, of course, not as simple as they seem. There is a broad range of tools within each category. Moreover, as noted above, there can also be a fine line between informal persuasion and formal regulation, because a donkey that has felt the stick in the past may respond to ear stroking less out of good will than fear. However, this typology nonetheless offers a useful starting point to distinguish among the variety of cooperative approaches to environmental protection that have emerged in recent years.

The vast majority of cooperative reforms fall into the three categories of regulation, exhortation, and government inaction. Assuming comparable policy objectives, these three classes of policy instruments can be placed along a continuum of coerciveness from regulation to exhortation to government inaction (Doern and Phidd 1992), although with considerable variation within each category.[3] ...

Exhortation: Talking with the Donkey

Governments can seek to persuade individuals or firms to change their behavior in a variety of ways. Although such approaches are nominally voluntary, in that no formal legal requirement is applied, they vary in degree of coerciveness. Closest to regulation along the spectrum of coercion are "voluntary agreements" between business and industry and government-sponsored codes of conduct. Voluntary agreements, such as the Dutch covenants discussed below, are characterized by strong expectations on the part of government that industry will comply. Such agreements are typically accompanied by an explicit or implied threat of regulation or other mandatory instruments should voluntary measures fail. Voluntary agreements or codes are usually negotiated by government and the private sector. Although many agreements take the form of nonbinding "gentlemen's agreements," others are legally binding contracts. Such contracts can still be considered voluntary, however, in

---

[3] This is not the case if policy goals differ in stringency, because one can imagine a weak regulation being less coercive than a hortatory policy backed by the threat of strong regulation.

the sense that the parties consent to assume certain obligations, in contrast to laws and regulations, which apply equally to all regardless of consent.

In contrast to voluntary agreements, governmental efforts to persuade target groups to change their behavior via "voluntary challenges" involve little or no arm-twisting in the form of threats of regulation or penalties for nonparticipation. Requirements of participation tend to be very flexible. Examples of these less coercive voluntary challenge programs include the U.S. Environmental Protection Agency's (EPA's) 33/50 program and Environment Canada's Accelerated Reduction/Elimination of Toxics program (ARET), discussed below. ...

Reducing Environmental Impacts

One oft-cited advantage of negotiated voluntary agreements is that they take advantage of business expertise and thus can incorporate better solutions to environmental problems. ... Critics of voluntary approaches view government's partnership with industry with skepticism, however. Many have argued that government limits itself unnecessarily by pursuing only measures to which industry consents, particularly because such measures may not be sufficient to achieve societal environmental objectives (Hajer 1994). As Ayres and Braithwaite (1992, 55) note, "The very conditions that foster the evolution of cooperation are also the conditions that promote the evolution of capture and indeed corruption." Similarly, Rennings and colleagues (1997, 253) argues that "once the government commits itself to a corporatist style of environmental policy, the other negotiating partner is granted a potential to delay and water down goals that should not be underestimated."

A second way that voluntary programs might advance environmental objectives is through development of networks that provide opportunities for technology transfer and sharing of environmental expertise within the business community (Georg 1994). Voluntary networks can be used to forge links not only within sectors but across the product chain. The flexibility and emphasis on collaborative networks of voluntary agreements may render them particularly well suited to approaches that cross media and span the life cycle (EEA 1997).

The risk, however, is that sectoral or crosssectoral business networks will use the opportunity to participate in policymaking to collectively resist environmental change, as they often have with respect to ecolabeling (Salzman 1997; Udo de Haes 1997). The voluntary nature of participation in business networks also raises the specter of "free ridership." Free riding occurs when firms either decline to participate in a voluntary program or participate but fail to adhere to their voluntary commitments. ...

Some have argued that the flexibility and collaboration offered by voluntary approaches can foster innovation, which many in the industrial ecology community have posited to be critical to long-term environmental improvement (Graedel and Allenby 1995, 8). Others, however, assert that voluntary agreements present a weaker stimulus for innovation than performance-based regulation, which mandates compliance from all sources (Friends of the Earth 1995; Clark 1995).

Koppen (1994) among others has argued that implementation will be smoother and rates of compliance higher, thus yielding environmental benefits, because firms "buy in" to voluntary agreements. Various arguments also have been made about "soft effects" of voluntary approaches (EEA 1997). For instance, many authors have stressed that voluntary agreements improve relations between business and government. ...

Democratic Accountability and Participation

Although proponents of voluntary approaches applaud government's inclusion of business as a partner in policymaking, critics have raised a number of concerns about democratic accountability. Environmentalists argue that the purported ease with which voluntary approaches can be negotiated and implemented owes much to their operation beyond the procedural safeguards of administrative law, thus reducing opportunities for participation by third parties. Concerns have also been raised that there are insufficient opportunities for involvement by democratically elected legislatures when the executive relies on informal agreements and contracts rather than statutory authority to achieve its environmental objectives (Bastmeijer 1997; Baggott 1986). ...

Voluntary Challenges

This section considers evidence concerning the costs and benefits of two voluntary challenge programs, the U.S. EPA's 33/50 program and Canada's ARET program, and of various European negotiated voluntary agreements.

The U.S. 33/50 Program

In 1991, the U.S. EPA challenged the business community to voluntarily reduce its releases and transfers of 17 high priority chemicals by 33% by the end of 1992 and 50% by the end of 1995, dubbing its challenge program "33/50." In terms of the typology presented above, the 33/50 program is an example of a voluntary challenge program. The goals were simple and uniform across all sectors. Indeed, the simplicity of the program was one of its attractions. To participate, a firm needed only to write to the EPA pledging some reductions of the 33/50 chemicals. In turn, the EPA would provide a certificate of appreciation and recognize 33/50 participants in its annual report on the Toxic Release Inventory (TRI). Incentives to participate thus were exclusively positive; there were no penalties for nonparticipation or for failure to achieve commitments.

The relationship of the 33/50 program with the TRI was significant. TRI is a regulatory program that mandates public reporting of waste re-leases and transfers, although it does not mandate reductions of those releases or transfers. To the extent that it encourages voluntary reductions of discharges, it is through the negative mechanism of community pressure and bad public relations. The EPA consciously sought to complement this negative incentive with a positive inducement of recognition through the 33/50 program.

Only 16% of firms contacted by EPA agreed to participate, although a higher rate of participation was achieved among larger companies with greater discharges (Davies and Mazurek 1996). Despite this, evaluation of the program relative to the reference year is encouraging. The goal of 33% reduction was achieved one year early, by the end of 1991, and the 50% reduction goal was also achieved early, by the end of 1994. However, when one applies a stricter standard of evaluation, whether reductions were achieved relative to a "business as usual" baseline, the benefits of the 33/50 program are not as clear.

The first concern is that the reported reductions in discharges and transfers include those made by firms that chose not to participate in the program. ... [T]hese reductions constitute one quarter of all reductions of 33/50 chemicals between 1988 and 1994. It seems highly unlikely that reductions by nonparticipants were motivated by the program. A second problem lies in the fact that when the program was launched in early 1991, EPA chose 1988 as the reference year, because it was the most recent year for which TRI data were available. That made it possible for firms to claim reductions under the 33/50 program made before its inception. An evaluation of the program by the environmental nonprofit organization, INFORM (1995, 498–9) concluded that one-third of participating firms in fact pledged only what they had already done. The data ... indicate that one-third or more of the 51% reductions achieved between 1988 and 1994 occurred before the program's inception in 1991.[5] Clearly, such reductions cannot be attributed to the 33/50 challenge.

Moreover, the factors that caused firms to reduce their releases before 1991 may have continued to influence their behavior after the 33/50 program was launched. In particular, it is difficult to separate the negative publicity associated with the TRI program from the positive reinforcement offered by 33/50.

The INFORM study also expressed concern that reductions were achieved primarily through recycling, end-of-pipe measures, and energy recovery rather than source reduction (INFORM 1995, 499). This is noteworthy in light of the claim that the 33/50 program is a success story of pollution prevention (Anderson 1994) and the more general argument that voluntary programs are particularly well suited to pollution prevention.

There is, however, circumstantial evidence that 33/50 encouraged firms to make reductions over and above what they would have made otherwise. As the data ... indicate, releases and transfers of the 17 33/50 chemicals fell by 42% from 1990 (the year before the program was launched) to 1994, compared with a 22% reduction of non-33/50 chemicals in the TRI inventory over the same period (Davies and Mazurek 1996, 15). (However, the fact that releases and transfers of non-33/50 chemicals fell by a greater percent than those for 33/50 chemicals before 1991 suggests a possible "water balloon" effect [Arora and Cason 1995], with the 33/50 program merely redirecting firms' efforts from one set of chemicals to another.) Moreover, the data ... indicate that firms participating in the 33/50 program reduced their discharges of the 33/50 chemicals by more than nonparticipating firms did, 49% from 1990 to 1994 as compared with 30% for nonparticipating firms. This 19%

---

[5] The analysis here treats TRI data as if it represents an annual rate of discharges at the end of each reporting year. Thus, reductions from TRI years 1988 to 1990 are considered to have occurred before the 33/50 program was announced in early 1991, constituting roughly one-third of reductions from 1988 to 1994 (i.e., (1494-1262)/ (1494-737)). However, uncertainty is introduced by the fact that the TRI data are in fact total annual discharges rather than point estimates at the end of the year. Thus, an unknown fraction of the reductions from 1990 to 1991 TRI reports also would have occurred before the introduction of the program.

difference in reductions by participating firms constitutes an 11% reduction relative to the *total* releases and transfers of 33/50 chemicals in the 1990 reference year.[6]

One can question even this remaining 11% reduction. The potential for self-selection is problematic in evaluating any voluntary program. Firms already inclined to make reductions of 33/50 chemicals, whether in response to TRI publicity, market forces, or other factors, simply may have been the ones to sign on for credit. This is supported by Arora and Cason's (1996) finding that the larger a firm's releases and transfers, the more likely it was to participate in 33/50, because these are the firms that would be expected to respond most aggressively to release of TRI data in the absence of the 33/50 program. Thus, the fact that 33/50 participants made greater reductions than nonparticipants does not necessarily indicate that those reductions were in fact prompted by the 33/50 program. It is problematic that none of the analyses discussed above controlled for the effects of concurrent regulations. Arora and Cason (1996) note that two of the 33/50 chemicals were being phased out by regulations concerning ozone-depleting substances. The 1990 Clean Air Act Amendments also mandated further regulation of discharges of volatile organic compounds (to achieve ground level ozone objectives) and hazardous air pollutants, both of which could be expected to cover all 17 33/50 chemicals.[7] This potential influence of regulation is also supported by O'Toole and colleagues' (1997) finding that state level discharges of 33/50 chemicals were strongly correlated with the stringency of state toxics regulation. Thus, it is not known to what degree the apparent success of the voluntary 33/50 program is in fact owed to regulation.

The Canadian ARET Program

The Canadian ARET Challenge, launched in 1994, is similar in many respects to the 33/50 program, although more ambitious. Industry is challenged to reduce discharges of 30 chemicals considered to be toxic, persistent, and bioaccumulative by 90% by the year 2000 and of 87 others by 50% by the same year. Characteristic of a voluntary challenge program,

---

[6] The calculation is 19% of the 1990 transfers and releases of 33/50 chemicals by participants divided by the total 1990 transfers and releases of 33/50 chemicals or 0.19(751)/1262 (data in table 1). Although Davies and Mazurek (1996,18) attribute the full 19% reduction relative to the 1990 reference year to the 33/50 challenge, that figure is relative to releases and transfers only from participating firms, not total 1991 releases and transfers.

[7] I am indebted to Mark Atlas for this point.

there is no threat of penalties for failure to achieve those goals. Indeed, as in 33/50, firms that choose to participate are not required to commit to the full 90% and 50% reductions. However, in contrast to 33/50, the ARET challenge emerged from extensive negotiations with stakeholders.

In 1991, Environment Canada established a multipartite committee to recommend policies to reduce use and discharges of toxic substances. The committee comprised 29 members from industry, government, labor, environmental groups, Aboriginal peoples, and others (Leiss and Associates 1996). Although the group reached consensus on which substances to target, participants could not agree on two issues: the degree to which pollution prevention rather than discharge reductions should be emphasized and whether regulatory or voluntary approaches should be favored. As a result, environmentalists, labor, and Aboriginal representatives withdrew in protest. The remaining industry and government participants carried on and achieved consensus in early 1994. The resulting ARET Challenge is voluntary and focuses on reducing discharges, the two features to which environmental groups objected.

Only preliminary assessments of the impact of ARET can be made at this time, because only two years of data are available. By the end of 1995, action plans had been received from 278 facilities in eight industrial sectors, comprising 40% of all Canadian industrial production (ARET 1997). Discharges of ARET substances had already been reduced 49% relative to base year levels, including a 60% reduction of the 30 highest priority substances. Participating facilities have promised an additional 20% overall reduction relative to base year levels by the year 2000. This will surpass the program objective of 50%, although reductions promised by company action plans received to date do not yet meet the 90% reduction target for the subset of highest priority chemicals.

As with 33/50, the degree to which these reductions are attributable to the ARET program is unclear. Similar concerns arise with respect to base year, overlapping regulations, self-selection by industry leaders, and free riding, whereas others are unique to ARET. The base year problem is exacerbated in the ARET case, because each participating facility can pick its own base year anytime after 1987 (Gallon 1998). This allows firms to claim credit toward the ARET program for discharge reductions they made as much as six years before the program's inception, and to strategically choose a year with particularly high discharges to maximize apparent reductions. To address this problem, the ARET secretariat has attempted to track reductions since a common base year of 1993 and reports that releases of ARET chemicals were reduced by 19% between 1993and the end of 1995.[8]

This contradicts the program's own claim that "For the most part . . . [the full 49%] reductions are directly attributable to the commitment of ARET participants to this voluntary initiative"(ARET 1997, 1).

As with 33/50, there are also questions about whether the reductions attributed to ARET are in fact voluntary, and if so, whether they are attributable to the program. A survey of participating firms indicated that less than half (47%) believed that participation in ARET had helped them "identify opportunities to significantly reduce toxic emissions" (Roewade 1996, 23), suggesting that many firms are simply doing what they would have done anyway. No analysis has been done of the extent of regulatory overlap at the federal or provincial level, although anecdotal evidence provides cause for concern that at least some of the reported voluntary reductions are attributable to mandatory measures.[9]

In other cases, as with 33/50 and TRI, voluntary reductions may have been driven less by the positive publicity associated with the ARET challenge than the negative publicity associated with mandatory reporting of discharges to Canada's National Pollutant Release Inventory (NPRI). Because only half of the ARET chemicals are included in the NPRI list, there is an as yet unrealized opportunity for research to compare reductions under ARET of NPRI and non-NPRI chemicals. However, the fact that the ARET list of chemicals does not correspond completely with mandatory reporting under NPRI poses difficulties for the verification of participants' discharge reports. Indeed, the absence of any provisions for third party verification of firms' own claims of discharge reductions has been called the "Achilles heel" of the ARET program (Leiss and Associates 1996).

Free ridership is less problematic than in the 33/50 program, with an average participation rate of 68% across eight sectors, although this falls short of the rate of participation that one might expect from rigorously enforced regulation or discharge fees. Participation is uneven, ranging

---

[8] As with reliance on TRI data to evaluate the 33/50 program, this is a relatively generous interpretation because some fraction of the reductions made between the 1993 and 1994 NPRI reporting years for the National Pollutant Release Inventory (NPRI) would have been made before the ARET program was announced.

[9] Gallon (1998) notes that the 90% reduction in sulfur dioxide emissions claimed by the International Nickel Company (INCO's) Sudbury smelter under the ARET program were in fact legally mandated.

from 97% in the chemical sector (where participation in the Responsible Care program is a requirement for membership in the Canadian Chemical Producers' Association) to 46% in the oil and gas sector (Roewade 1996, 6). The low rate of participation has even led some firms to call for "field leveling regulations" to mandate similar levels of effort from all firms within a sector (Van Nijnatten 1998; Gallon 1998). Participants account for 83% of all emissions of the NPRI chemicals covered by the ARET program, suggesting, as with 33/50, that nonparticipants tend to be smaller producers (ARET 1995, 2).

Finally, criticisms have been made about the process from which the ARET Challenge emerged. The fact that the terms of the ARET Challenge resulted from extensive government–industry negotiations does seem to have resulted in higher rates of participation than for the 33/50 program. However, it is noteworthy that industry–government consensus was achieved at the expense of environmentalist, labor, and Aboriginal support, which many believe has undermined the program's credibility (Van Nijnatten 1998).

Voluntary Agreements

Negotiated voluntary agreements are variously referred to as environmental agreements, codes of conduct, and cooperative management regimes. The interchangeable use of these terms can mask important distinctions within this class of policy instruments. Voluntary agreements differ along several dimensions (Storey 1996; European Commission 1997):

- Who participates in development and implementation. Negotiations typically involve government and industry but may also include environmental groups, labor, or others.

- The nature of the commitment. Although most are nonbinding "gentlemen's agreements," some take the form of legally binding contracts, which are enforceable under civil law.

- The relationship to other policy instruments, including subsidies, taxes, and regulations.

- Whether it is the objectives or the means of achieving them that are being negotiated.

Negotiated voluntary agreements have grown dramatically in popularity in Europe since the mid-1980s (EEA 1997). An inventory of environmental agreements conducted by the European Commission in 1996 found 305 such agreements among the member countries, although roughly two thirds of those were equally divided between the Netherlands and Germany (European Commission 1997).

The Netherlands Experience

The Dutch "covenants" are arguably the bestknown example of negotiated voluntary agreements. Reliance on negotiated covenants increased in the Netherlands after the first National Environmental Policy Plan in 1989 called for a more cooperative approach to environmental protection in recognition of the shared responsibilities of government and industry. The government negotiates with "target groups" to identify the measures necessary to achieve the objectives set in the national plan. Typically, covenants are negotiated with trade associations, with individual firms subsequently signing on via letters of declaration. To date, far-reaching agreements have been negotiated with 18 sectors responsible for the vast majority of industrial pollution in the Netherlands, although there are dozens of other covenants concerning energy efficiency and other environmental issues (Ministry of Housing 1997; Beardsley et al. 1997).

Evaluation of the Dutch approach is complicated by considerable variation among covenants within the Netherlands (Bastmeijer 1997). To some degree, this variation reflects evolution of the approach. The early covenants were criticized for exclusion of third parties and the elected legislature, unclear objectives, and inattention to monitoring. A 1995 study of 154 covenants, including 85 in the environmental field, by the Dutch Auditor General concluded that most lacked sufficient safeguards to ensure effective implementation (Algemene Rekenkamer 1995). In two-thirds of the substantive (as opposed to procedure-oriented) covenants examined, the parties agreed only to strive to achieve their obligations, not to actually achieve them. Deadlines were unclear in half of the cases studied. The Auditor General was also critical of the unclear legal status of many covenants and inadequate justifications provided for the use of covenants as opposed to other policy instruments.

In response, more recent covenants place greater emphasis on clarity of commitments, monitoring requirements, and legal formality (Bastmeijer 1997; Van Zijst 1993). There are also greater opportunities for third-party involvement, although bipartite negotiation is still the norm and concerns remain about public access to the details of agreements and reports on performance (Biekart 1995; Van Zijst 1993). Despite the considerable variation among covenants, two unique features of the Netherlands's approach warrant emphasis, particularly because they distinguish the approach from that used in many other countries and thus may limit the applicability of lessons learned from the Dutch covenants to other voluntary programs.

First, it is significant that negotiations take place within the context of national performance objectives. The government sets nonnegotiable goals—percentage reductions in discharges, packaging waste, energy use, and so on—and then negotiates the means to achieve those goals with the target groups. The issue is thus "how," not "what." Glachant (1994) offers a compelling theoretical analysis of the importance of this distinction. When collective performance objectives are previously established, government and industry have compatible objectives for negotiations: to find the most cost-effective means to achieve those goals (though Glachant notes that this might be achieved more efficiently through a system of marketable permits than via negotiations). However, when the goals themselves are negotiable, strategic behavior and "capture" by industry are serious threats.

A second distinctive feature, at least of more recent covenants, is that they are legally binding. Recent covenants tend to take the form of legally binding private contracts, with commitments in many cases subsequently being incorporated in statute-based permits (Bastmeijer 1997; OECD 1997). It is noteworthy, though, that the effort to recognize negotiated commitments in formal permits seems to have been motivated not only to strengthen enforcement of covenants, but to protect negotiated agreements from legal challenges by third parties after the courts failed to uphold some early covenants (Van Zijst 1993, 16; Biekart 1995, 144). Koppen (1994) argues that the effort to integrate negotiated agreements within the existing framework of environmental laws and to achieve binding commitments is the greatest strength of the Dutch approach, in that it offers the potential to combine the advantages of informal negotiation with those of legal formality.

A 1997 review of progress by the Netherlands government concluded that good progress was being made with respect to most national objectives for the year 2000, with a few notable exceptions, including oxides of nitrogen (NOx) and carbon dioxide emissions (Ministry of

Housing 1997). Government and industry officials both cite greater cooperation and trust as benefits of the approach, and industry officials claim greater cost effectiveness (Beardsley et al. 1997). The Dutch Ministry of the Environment believes that "Long range covenants (5–10 years) which permit some flexibility over the nature and timing of implementation actions are proving more efficient and effective than direct regulation in many cases" (Ministry of Housing 1997, 18). It is, however, difficult to assess to what extent the impressive strides toward sustainability being made in the Netherlands are attributable to the covenants approach, as opposed to other concurrent policy reforms, including extension of the permit system to cover virtually all sources, introduction of environmental taxes, and enhanced enforcement.[10]

Reviews of individual covenants are mixed. Hajer (1994) is critical of the effectiveness of a negotiated agreement to reduce acid rain because reductions in discharges per unit of production have been more than offset by growth in production volume. However, Hajer does not attempt analysis of performance relative to a business as usual baseline or alternative policy instruments. Storey (1996) is more sanguine about the Long Term Agreements to promote energy efficiency, although he estimates that about half of the resulting improvements in energy efficiency would have been achieved under a "business-as-usual" scenario. He also notes that the remaining achievements may be due in large part to supporting regulatory measures to prevent free riding. Biekart (1995, 146) offers a critical appraisal of the covenant with the base metals industry, reporting that companies failed to meet 1995 targets and were expected to fall short of their year 2000 targets as well.

Agreement on a packaging covenant was reached in 1991 by the Dutch government and the Foundation on Packaging and the Environment, an association representing some 250 firms in the packaging chain (OECD 1997). However, consensus was achieved only after environmentalists withdrew from the process in protest (Koppen 1994). OECD (1997) reports that signatories met their targets for 1994 and are on track to achieve targets for the year 2000. No analysis is provided of performance relative to a business-as-usual baseline or counterfactual regulatory or market incentives scenarios. Government and business participants agree that the negotiations were an important learning exercise (OECD 1997, 28). The OECD (1997) also concluded that participation by firms across

---

[10] The number of enforcement staff and prosecutions both rose by roughly one-third from 1991 to 1992 alone (Ministry of Housing 1997).

the product chain facilitated a combination of both upstream solutions, such as redesign of packaging, and downstream solutions, such as recycling. Environmentalists, however, are critical that the negotiated measures are insufficiently ambitious and that compliance information is inaccessible (Biekart 1995). The OECD also notes an unresolved free rider problem.

Other European Experience

Negotiated voluntary agreements are also popular in Germany but take a different form. Although industry and government typically negotiate agreements, because of legal constraints on government participation in private contracts, agreements are written in the form of industry-only codes of conduct (EEA 1997; European Commission 1996). Threats of regulation, or market-based instruments, or litigation are cited as important motivating factors for negotiations (EEA 1997; Rehnbinder 1994).

Despite this, several authors who have written on the German agreements are quite critical of their effectiveness. Rennings and colleagues (1997) conclude that agreements concerning climate change and chlorofluorocarbons (CFCs) yielded only no-regrets measures, which firms would have had incentives to take in the absence of negotiated agreements. The European Environmental Agency (EEA 1997) was also skeptical of the benefits of the declaration on climate change, which involved 19 industrial sectors, concluding that it "runs the risk of achieving little more than an increase in the dissemination of information by the industry associations" (see also European Commission 1997, Annex 5, 22). Storey (1996, 28) concluded that the agreement was actually *less* ambitious than the business-as-usual scenario.

Rennings and colleagues also conclude that an agreement involving 15 industrial sectors concerning end-of-life vehicles was comparable with the regulatory proposal that launched negotiations four years earlier. A study conducted for the European Commission (1997, Annex 5, 26–7) is even less positive concerning that agreement, stressing that exceptions negotiated by the industry are likely to limit its effectiveness and that the agreement will likely need to be renegotiated as a result. Concern was also expressed that pressure for vertical integration from large automobile manufacturers will undermine the "functioning, highly innovative" disposal and recycling industry.

The European Commission study (1997, Annex 5, 21–8) also reports that German-negotiated agreements have had mixed success in achieving their environmental objectives, although no data on environmental benefits relative to reference year, baseline scenario, or alternative policy instruments are offered. Although agreements to phase out some products, including CFCs, have succeeded, in other cases they have not achieved their goals because consumers have been reluctant to accept the reformulated products. Agreements concerning product-related waste have been less successful; in some cases regulations were eventually adopted in response to noncompliance. Agreements that call for reduction of industrial emissions have also met with mixed success.

A recent study by the European Environmental Agency (1997) is one of the most ambitious evaluations of voluntary agreements to date. The Agency conducted rigorous case studies of six negotiated agreements in order to assess performance relative to the reference year, business- as-usual baseline, and alternative policy instruments. Despite an impressive conceptual and research effort, what is most striking about the EEA study is how little the authors were able to conclude. They were able to confirm environmental improvements relative to the reference year in only two of six cases and relative to the business-as-usual baseline only with respect to some aspects of one case.[11] ...

Environmental Protection

As noted above, there is limited evidence of environmental effectiveness. Although the two challenge programs considered, 33/50 and ARET, appear promising at first glance, it is not clear what proportion, if any, of the reductions achieved relative to base years are in fact attributable to these programs. ...

There is even less evidence with which to evaluate the environmental effectiveness of voluntary agreements. With respect to the anticipated

---

[11] The EEA report analyzed "environmental agreements," which were more broadly defined than voluntary agreements are here. Thus, the case studies included two statute or regulation-driven programs, a Swedish packaging program and enforcement of Portuguese pulp mill regulations, which would not qualify as voluntary according to the typology presented here. In addition to the German global warming declaration, discussed above, EEA (1997) reported that the Netherlands covenant with the chemical industry had yielded significant reductions relative to the 1992 reference year and relative to the historical baseline, although the potential impact of concurrent regulatory reforms was not considered. No data were available to evaluate a Danish agreement concerning recycling of transport packaging or a French agreement on end-of-life vehicles.

benefits, little can be said about the speed of implementation and higher rates of compliance anticipated relative to regulation. The European Environmental Agency (1997) also concluded that it was impossible to draw general conclusions about the benefits of voluntary agreements in stimulating innovation, a key consideration in industrial ecology. ...

The characteristics of the agreements themselves provide considerable cause for concern regarding their environmental effectiveness. Most voluntary agreements in Europe are nonbinding (86 of 137 studied by the European Commission) and few provide for verification and public reporting. The vast majority (110 of 137) contain no provisions concerning free riders, yet there is evidence of less than full participation in virtually all programs reviewed here. Indeed, the low rate of participation, particularly by small- to medium-sized enterprises, has led some industry sectors in Europe to call for field-leveling regulation (EEA 1997). Concerns about free ridership have prompted some authors to emphasize that voluntary agreements or codes are more likely to be effective if there is a relatively small number of partners or stable well-organized trade associations and if compliance costs are manageable and evenly distributed across the sector (EEA 1997; Office of Consumer Affairs 1998).

It is extremely difficult to assess whether government cooptation by business resulted in weaker standards in voluntary agreements. However, Rennings and colleagues (1997, 247) conclude based on their analysis of German agreements that "For the government side the price for an agreement often consists in reducing the announced level of environmental protection. ... [A]s the case studies in connection with this study bear out, a 'decrease in the stringency of regulations' is always observable." The fact that voluntary agreements often lack clear targets, reporting requirements, and deadlines (EEA 1997) lends support to this conclusion. ...

Implicit in this discussion is the question of what motivates business to participate in voluntary environmental programs. Storey (1996) has argued that nonbinding approaches are more likely to be effective when the actions being promoted are already in firms' economic self-interest. However, a strong threat of regulation and binding agreements are critical if that is not the case. In other words, if the donkey has its own reasons to pull the cart, ear stroking and gentle persuasion should not be problematic (although they may not add much). However, if it is not the ear stroking so much as the implied threat of the stick that is motivating

247

the donkey, maintaining a credible threat of the stick is essential (Glachant 1994).

... A survey by the European Commission found that the potential to forgo or postpone regulation was cited as the most important benefit of voluntary environmental agreements by roughly two-thirds of industry respondents (European Commission 1997). In Canada, KPMG (1994) reported that 95% of firms cited "compliance with regulations" as one of the top five factors motivating their environmental improvements. The next most frequently cited factor at 69% was directors' liability, whereas factors such as cost savings, customer requirements, and public pressure were all cited by less than half of respondents. This suggests that government coercion, rather than market forces, remains the most important factor driving firms to improve their environmental performance. In this regard, there is much to be said for the Dutch approach of negotiating implementation rather than policy objectives, because the clearer and firmer government is with respect to its policy objectives at the outset, the more credible the threat of the stick.[12]

A government committed to a cooperative approach thus must strike a delicate balance between demonstrating a commitment to negotiations and maintaining a credible threat of withdrawal and regulation. Ironically, the very fact of a government embracing voluntary approaches may undermine their effectiveness. As Rennings and colleagues (1997, 253) note, "A binding commitment giving priority to cooperative solutions can deprive the instrument of voluntary agreements of the basis for effective environmental policy improvements." They conclude that the German government's promise not to impose additional taxes on disposal of old cars undermined its bargaining position with the automobile industry. Similarly, Chang and colleagues (1998) attribute the failure of Ontario's voluntary agreement to promote municipal recycling programs through industry subsidies to relaxation of the threat of regulation after election of a government openly committed to deregulation. ...

---

[12] The distinction between negotiating goals and means in practice is blurred, however, because policy objectives can be set with varying degrees of specificity, from ambient environmental quality objectives, to total environmental burden, to discharges from different sectors, to discharges limits or even control practices for individual sources. The more specific government is with respect to its objectives, the stronger its position in negotiations with industry. However, as critics of command and control regulation have noted, excessive specificity can sacrifice opportunities to capture efficiency gains from negotiations.

Combining Policy Instruments

The importance of binding commitments and legal threats is supported by the widespread conclusion that voluntary programs work best in combination with other policy instruments, such as regulation and market-based instruments, which encourage participation and reduce the threat of free ridership (Beardsley 1996; European Commission 1996, 1997; Davies and Mazurek 1996; Rennings et al. 1997). The European Environmental Agency (1997) concluded that "Wherever environmental improvement was noted, the Environmental Agreement was accompanied by other measures or incentives." ...

Conclusion

It is impossible to draw overarching conclusions about the effectiveness of cooperative approaches to environmental protection because the form and context of those approaches differ so greatly. Even among voluntary approaches, there are significant differences between a program like the flexible 33/50 challenge and the Dutch approach of negotiated legally binding implementation agreements. ... An empirically grounded understanding of what works and what does not can only emerge from a self-conscious research agenda. Recent efforts by the U.S. EPA to develop methods to measure policy effectiveness, the dependent variable, are thus commendable. The forgoing discussion suggests a number of independent variables that warrant greater attention, including whether a program is regulatory or voluntary (and if the latter whether voluntary commitments are legally binding), its relationship to other policies such as regulations and market based instruments, who participates, whether goals or means to achieve them are the issue, economic characteristics of the industrial sector in question, and sociopolitical context.

REFERENCES

Arora, S. and T. N. Cason. 1995. An experiment in voluntary environmental regulation: Participation in EPA's 33/50 Program. *Journal of Environmental Economics and Management* 28(3): 271–286.

1996. Why do firms volunteer to exceed environmental regulations? Understanding participation in EPA's 33/50 program. *Land Economics* 72(4): 413–432.

Arrandale, T. 1996. Reinventing the pollution police. *Governing* 9(4): 32–35.

1997. Can polluters police themselves. *Governing* 10: 36–39.

Ashford, N. A. 1997. *The influence of information-based initiatives and negotiated environmental agreements on technological change.* Fondazione Eni Enrico Mattei, Nota Di Lavoro working paper 16.97.

Ayres, I. and J. Braithwaite. 1992. *Responsive regulation: Transcending the deregulation debate.* New York: Oxford University Press.

Baggott, R. 1986. By voluntary agreement: The politics of instrument selection. *Public Administration* 64: 51–67.

Bardach, E. and R. A. Kagan. 1982. *Going by the book: The problem of regulatory unreasonableness.* Philadelphia: Temple University Press.

Bastmeijer, K. 1997. The covenant as an instrument of environmental policy: A case study from the Netherlands. In OECD 1997. *Cooperative approaches to regulation.* OECD Public Management Occasional Papers No. 18.

Beardsley, D. 1996. *Incentives for environmental improvement: An assessment of selected innovative programs in the states and Europe.* Prepared for the Global Environmental Management Initiative, Washington, DC.

Beardsley, D., T. Davies, and R. Hersh. 1997. Improving environmental management. *Environment* 39(7): 6–9, 28–35.

Biekart, J. W. 1995. Environmental covenants between government and industry: A Dutch NGO's experience. *Review of European Community and International Environmental Law* 4(2): 141–149.

Brickman, R., S. Jasanoff, and T. Ilgen. 1985. *Controlling chemicals: The politics of regulation in Europe and the United States.* Ithaca, NY: Cornell University Press.

Burby, R. J. and R. G. Paterson. 1993. Improving compliance with state environmental regulations. *Journal of Policy Analysis and Management* 12(4): 753–772.

Chang, E., D. MacDonald, and J. Wolfson. 1998. Who killed CIPSI? Alternatives 24(2): 21–25.

Clark, K. 1995. *The use of voluntary pollution prevention agreements in Canada: An analysis and commentary*. Toronto: Canadian Institute for Environmental Law and Policy.

Clinton, B. and A. Gore. 1995. *Reinventing environmental regulation*. Washington, DC: Council on Environmental Quality. March 16.

Coglianese, C. 1997. Assessing consensus: The promise and performance of negotiated rulemaking. *Duke Law Journal* 46(6): 1255–1349.

Davies, J. C. and J. Mazurek. 1996. *Industry incentives for environmental improvement: Evaluation of US federal initiatives*. Prepared for the Global Environmental Initiative, Washington, DC.

Doern, G. B. and R. W. Phidd. 1992. *Canadian public policy: Ideas, structure, process*. 2nd ed. Scarborough, ON: Nelson Canada.

European Commission. 1996. *Communication from the commission to the Council and the European Parliament on environmenta lagreements . COM ...* (96) 561.

European Commission Directorate General III.01 — Industry. 1997. *Study on voluntary agreements concluded between industry and public authorities in the field of the environment*. Final Report, Brussels, January.

EEA (European Environment Agency). 1997. *Environmental agreements: Environmental effectiveness*. Copenhagen: EEA.

Friends of the Earth. 1995. *A superficial attraction: The voluntary approach and sustainable development*. London: Friends of the Earth Trust.

Gallon, G. 1998. Accuracy is optional in reporting voluntary success. Alternatives 24: 12.

Georg, S. 1994. Regulating the environment: Changing from constraint to gentle coercion. *Business Strategy and the Environment* 3(2): 11–20.

Glachant, M. 1994. The setting of voluntary agreements between industry and government: Bargaining and efficiency. *Business Strategy and the Environment* 3 (2): 43–49.

Graedel, T. and B. Allenby. 1995. *Industrial ecology*. Englewood Cliffs, NJ: Prentice Hall.

Hajer, M. A. 1994. Verinnerlijking: the limits to a positive management approach. In *Environmental law and ecological responsibility*, edited by G. Teubner, L. Farmer, and D. Murphy. New York: John Wiley and Sons.

Harrison, K. 1995. Is cooperation the answer? Canadian environmental enforcement in comparative context. Journal of Policy Analysis and Management 14: 221–244.

Harrison, K. and G. Hoberg. 1994. *Risk, science, and politics: Regulating toxic substances in Canada and the United States.* Montreal: McGill-Queen's University Press.

Harter, P. J. 1982. Negotiating regulations: A cure for the malaise. *Georgetown Law Journal* 71: 1–118.

Hoberg, G. 1993. Environmental policy: alternative styles. *In Governing Canada: State institutions and public policy,* edited by M. Atkinson. Toronto: Harcourt Brace Jovanovich.

Hoberg, G. and K. Harrison. 1994. It's not easy being green: The politics of Canada's Green Plan. *Canadian Public Policy 20*: 119–137.

INFORM. 1995. Toxics watch 1995. New York: INFORM.

Koppen, I. 1994. Ecological covenants: Regulatory informality in Dutch waste reduction policy. In *Environmental law and ecological responsibility*, edited by G. Teubner, L. Farmer, and D. Murphy. New York: John Wiley and Sons.

KPMG. 1994. *Canadian environmental management survey*. Toronto: KPMG.

Leiss, W., and Associates, Ltd. 1996. Lessons learned from ARET: A qualitative survey of perceptions of stakeholders, Final Report. Working Paper Series 96-4, Environmental Policy Unit, School of Policy Studies. Queen's University. June.

Ministry of Housing, Spatial Planning and the Environment, The Netherlands. 1997. *Towards a sustainable Netherlands*. The Hague: Ministry of Housing, Spatial Planning and the Environment.

Nash, J. and J. Ehrenfeld. 1997. Codes of environmental management practice: Assessing their potential as a tool for change. *Annual Review of Energy and Environment* 22: 487–535.

NRC (National Research Council). 1997. *Fostering industry-initiated environmental protection efforts*. Report of the Committee on Industrial Competitiveness and Environmental Protection. Washington, DC: National Academy Press.

OECD (Organization for Economic Cooperation and Development) 1997. *Extended producer responsibility: Case study on the Dutch packaging covenant.* OECD Headquarters. November 5–6.

OECD. 1996. *Regulatory reform: A country study of Australia*. Paris.

Office of Consumer Affairs and Regulatory Affairs Division, Treasury Board Secretariat, Canada. 1998. *Voluntary Codes: A guide for their development and use.*

O'Toole Jr., L. J., C. Yu, J. Cooley, G. Cowie, S. Crow, T. DeMeo, and S. Herbert, 1997. Reducing toxic chemical releases and transfers: Explaining outcomes for a voluntary program. *Policy Studies Journal* 25 (1): 11–26.

Powers, C. W. and M. R. Chertow. 1997. Industrial ecology: Overcoming policy fragmentation. In *Thinking ecologically: The next generation of environmental policy*, edited by M. R. Chertow and D. C. Esty. New Haven: Yale University Press.

Rehnbinder, E. 1994. Ecological contracts: Agreements between polluters and local communities. In *Environmental law and ecological responsibility*, edited by G. Teubner, L. Farmer, and D. Murphy. New York: John Wiley and Sons.

Rennings, K., K. L. Brockmann, and H. Bergmann. 1997. Voluntary agreements in environmental protection: Experiences in Germany and future perspectives. *Business Strategy and the Environment*. 6: 245–263.

Roewade, D. 1996. *Voluntary environmental action: A participant's view of ARET*. Prepared for Industry Canada.

Salzman, J. 1997. Informing the green consumer: The debate over the use and abuse of environmental labels. *Journal of Industrial Ecology* 1(2): 11–21.

Scholz, J. T. 1991. Cooperative regulatory enforcement and the politics of administrative effectiveness. *American Political Science Review* 85: 115–136.

Socolow, R. 1994. Six perspectives from industrial ecology. *In Industrial ecology and global change,* edited by R. Socolow, C. Andrews, F. Berkhout, and V. Thomas. Cambridge: Cambridge University Press.

Stanbury,W.T.1993.*Business-governmentrelationsin Canada*. Scarborough, ON: Nelson Canada.

Storey, M. 1996. Demand side efficiency: Voluntary agreements with industry. Annex I. Expert Group on the UN FCCC, supported by the OECD and IEA, December.

Udo De Haes, H. 1997. Slow progress in ecolabelling: Technical or institutional impediments. *Journal of Industrial Ecology* 1(1): 4–6.

U.S. GAO (General Accounting Office). 1997. *Environmental protection: Challenges facing EPA's efforts to reinvent environmental regulation*. GAO/RCED-97-155. July.

Van Nijnatten, D. L. 1998. The day the NGOS walked out. *Alternatives* 24(2): 10–15.

Van Zijst, H. 1993. A change in the culture. *Environmental Forum* (May/June): 12–17.

Vogel, D. 1986. *National styles of regulation*. Ithaca, NY: Cornell University Press.

Environmental Compliance and Enforcement in the NIS: A Survey of Current Practices of Environmental Inspectorates and Options for Improvements

ORGANIZATION FOR ECONOMIC COOPERATION AND DEVELOPMENT (OECD), Task Force for the Implementation of the Environmental Action Programmes for Central and Eastern Europe (EAP), Twelfth Meeting of the EAP Task Force, 18-19 October 2000, Almaty[*]

...

Context in the NIS

2.   After the political changes of early 1990's, all New Independent States (NIS) of the former Soviet Union developed new environmental policies and National Environmental Action Programmes (NEAPs). The main goal of these new programmes was to establish the overall policy framework for environmental protection adapted to the process of political, economic and social changes which they were undergoing. The new programmes were comprehensive and served a variety of purposes: establishing an information base, elaborating principles of new policies, and redesigning policy instruments and institutions.

3.   In many cases, however, the implementation of these programmes has been slower than expected. The new policy and legal frameworks developed by NIS governments, in many cases, followed the old patterns of planning with ambitious, often unrealistic goals and prohibitive standards and lack of effective implementation methods. In particular, enforcement has not received sufficient attention and violations of environmental laws have been widespread. At the same time, compliance by enterprises

---

[*] *Available at* http://www.oecd.org/dataoecd/32/51/1904683.pdf.

was constrained. The slow pace of economic reform, complicated legal frameworks and the poor economic situation, as well as cultural and social development factors, were major factors of non-compliance. In some countries the economic downturn and cuts in production helped enterprises to comply with the existing environmental regulations in the short term. ...

Institutional Framework for Enforcement

5.   The environmental enforcement agencies in the NIS possess wide responsibilities for controlling compliance by enterprises and enforcing them but their current institutional set-up hinders the achievements of these goals. Their position in the governmental structure is weak and their relations with policy-making bodies, i.e. Environmental Ministries and Committees, are blurred. These features limit inspectorates' impacts on other governmental agencies and industry. Limited financial and human resources of enforcement agencies is also a major cause of low effectiveness of their efforts. Resources are spread too thinly among many functions which include permitting, compliance control, environmental monitoring, reporting and compliance promotional functions. ...

[Compliance Assistance in the NIS]

107.   Compliance promotion is any activity that encourages voluntary compliance with environmental requirements. Most compliance promotion strategies involve both activities to promote and enforce requirements. Policy makers need to determine the most effective mix of compliance promotion and enforcement response. Experience has shown that promotion alone is often not effective. Enforcement is important to create a climate in which members of the regulated community will have clear incentives to make use of the opportunities and resources provided by promotion. By the same token, enforcement alone is not as effective as enforcement combined with promotion. This is particularly true for example when:

- The size of the regulated community far exceeds the programme's resources for enforcement, e.g., when the regulated community consists of numerous small sources, such as individual gasoline stations.

- The regulated community is generally willing to comply voluntarily.
- There is a cultural resistance to enforcement.

108. Thus, promotion is an important element of most enforcement programs. There are various approaches to compliance promotion. They include:

- **Providing education and technical assistance to the regulated community**. Education and technical assistance lay the groundwork for voluntary compliance. They are essential to overcome barriers of ignorance or inability that otherwise would prevent compliance. Education and technical assistance make it easier and more possible for the regulated community to comply by providing information about the requirements and how to meet them, and by providing assistance to help regulated facilities take the necessary steps for compliance. Education and technical assistance are particularly important in the early stages of a new requirement-based enforcement programme, and whenever the programme requirements change.

- **Building public support.** The public can be a powerful ally in promoting compliance. Public support can help create a social ethic of compliance. The public can also serve as watchdogs that alert officials to non-compliance. If the laws provide the appropriate authority, members of the public or non-government organisations representing the public can bring a citizen suit against non-complying facilities. Public support can also help ensure that enforcement programmes continue to receive the necessary funding and political support to be effective. Building public support may be particularly important groundwork in societies where personal economic concerns compete with concern for environmental quality, or where there is a general lack of awareness about or concern for environmental problems. The public can be educated about causes and effects of pollution, its short-and long-term threats to human health and natural resources, and the costs to society. The extent of environmental damage may be surprising new information to the public. Enforcement programmes can build public support by developing and distributing information about environmental problems, the importance of compliance, enforcement activities and successes, and ways the public can support enforcement. Enforcement officials can also work with non-government organisations that represent the public to develop and distribute information and promote public involvement. NGOs can independently help promote compliance by publicising information to increase public awareness of environmental problems and to build support and pressure for compliance.

- **Publicising success stories.** Enforcement officials can provide an incentive for the regulated community to comply by publicising information about facilities that have been particularly successful in achieving compliance. In societies where the public does support environmental protection, positive publicity about a firm's compliance can enhance its reputation and public image. Such publicity helps create a positive social climate that encourages compliance.

- **Creative financing arrangements.** One barrier to compliance is cost. Facility managers may want to comply but may not be able to afford the cost of fulfilling the requirements. Creative financing arrangements that can help solve this problem may include: offsetrequirements (i.e. investors interested in building a new facility are required to pay for modifications - e.g. installation of new process technology or control on existing technology - that will reduce or "offset" pollution at existing facility), peer-matching (investors interested in building a new facility are asked to "adopt" an existing facility and help it to reduce pollution), sales of shares (the facility can raise money by selling shares in the facility to investors where a state-owned facility is being privatised), loans (institutions loaning money for new investment require that a certain portion of the loan be applied to restoration or protection of environment), environmental bonds (owners of a facility subject to environmental requirements can issue bonds to raise money to finance the changes needed to meet the requirements).

- **Providing economic incentives.** Environmental programmes can encourage compliance by providing economic incentives for compliance. This may be an effective approach in public agencies, which are less likely to be deterred by monetary penalties, since they are funded by the government. The benefit from compliance can be applied to the facility generally, or to an individual based on his or her performance. Incentives include: environmental charges, tax incentives, subsidies for complying facilities, facility or operator bonuses or promotion points for senior managers in state-owned facilities achieving compliance.

- **Building environmental management capability within the regulated community.** Enforcement officials can also promote the concept of environmental auditing (or cleaner production, waste minimisation, environmental management systems) as an integral part of good business practice. Ideas for promoting environmental management in enterprises, include: pilot projects to introduce the concept of auditing to small- and medium-sized environmental, environmental advisors that assist firms in setting up simple internal auditing systems; regional auditing or cleaner production centres run by industry or independent associations that can provide auditing and advisory services to industry upon request. international workshops to bring the concept of environmental auditing to countries that would like to encourage this practice among their regulated facilities; hiring university staff or other management specialists to develop programmes to train auditors; required disclosure of environmental liabilities (environmental impacts and violations) in the written statements made when a company is issuing stocks or bonds. ...

[Examples in the NIS:] Interaction between inspectorates and industry

Kazakhstan. In July 1999 the Ministry of Natural Resources and Environment initiated a framework for voluntary agreements between the Ministry, business and regional authorities (akimat). The agreement states that companies signing up to it will benefit from simplified inspection procedures, but in exchange they have to ensure full compliance with environment requirements, improve internal monitoring and report regularly on emissions to the akimat. Currently companies are subject to a large number of inspections from different organisations, which can result in significant bureaucratic burdens. However, under the agreement much of these would be combined within a single comprehensive inspection, producing a single statement of environmental control. Voluntary agreements consist of a standard part and a work programme. The standard part contains a commitment to simplified inspections (providing compliance is maintained) and a commitment by the company to finance environmental improvements (relating mainly to environmental monitoring). By the end of February 2000, 147 agreements had been signed. Although it is too early to assess the success of these arrangements it is thought that, given problems of effectiveness of traditional enforcement procedures, the use of voluntary agreements is likely to be positive. Potential benefits include:

- A reduction in the potential for corruption, given that inspectors work as a team in the comprehensive inspection;
- Improved dialogue between the inspectors and the company;
- Reducing inspection activity may enable enforcement institutions to focus on other priorities;
- Bringing together different enforcement authorities will enhance cross-disciplinary environmental management;
- Providing a stimulus to review existing procedures and challenge traditional practices.

There are also potential problems. Initial results show that companies most interested are foreign companies and domestic companies undergoing significant restructuring – there is less interest from existing domestic companies; there may be problems of consensus between the authorities involved.

Ukraine. Interaction with industry is carried out through lectures delivered by experts of the Ministry of the Environment at training courses organised both by the research institute of the MOE and by the industrial associations. Participation in the certification commissions of enterprises and associations and working groups which examine various projects and programmes is also helpful in promoting compliance. ... Waste oils have been traditionally collected and disposed by industry. However, the Inspectorate is now supporting the efforts by companies to re-use the waste as fuel. Similar trends are also occurring with timber waste. ... Some industrial associations and enterprises in certain regions of Ukraine have nature reserve territories and sites in their care. Experts of the State Environmental Inspectorate, while performing their functions of compliance control in these nature reserve territories and sites, provide consultations to enterprise officials in charge of protecting them, on such issues as management of reserves, administrative practices, application of laws and regulations, and in keeping records. ...

[Voluntary Compliance in the NIS]

243.   The survey of practices in the NIS uncovered only very limited number of compliance promotion activities, which are undertaken with varying frequency and effectiveness. They are usually carried out outside environmental inspectorates. Principally, these activities can be categorised as follows: [information provision and promotion of Environmental Management Systems.]

6.2   Information Provision

244.   Although information provision and exchange between regulating and regulated community is believed to be the key to successful compliance promotion only few examples of such approaches have been found in the NIS. The most common information provision is the publication of state of environment reports. Virtually all countries produce environmental reports which contain information about the state of environment, including information on quality of air, water and land as well as emissions from industrial sectors and individual enterprises. The reports, in some cases, present statistics on enforcement activities (e.g. number of inspections, their results) and other policy responses. In addition, other reporting activities take place, as in Moldova for example, where the emission register is maintained. The register contains information on emissions from individual enterprises which is accessible to the authorities and to the public.

245.   In many cases failure to comply with environmental regulations can be due to ignorance, or unawareness, of what is required, or procedures to be followed. Only few examples of the provision of such information to enterprises have been found. For example, the Baku City Committee on the Environment in Azerbaijan, the Ministries in Kyrgyzstan and Moldova and both local and central agencies of the State Environmental Inspectorate in Ukraine reported the publication of information related to the

environmental requirements, non-compliance cases and compliance responses in the mass media. Some countries reported meetings and seminars which were organised for industrial managers and inspectorate staff on which requirements, enforcement procedures and problems were discussed and solutions to problems sought.

246. Taking into account a very limited cases of information provision efforts there should be more attempts to provide industrial managers with information on environmental requirements and to involve them into discussion on enforcement and compliance problems. Such dialogues should also include highlighting best practice and successful examples of co-operation between stakeholders. The Inspectorates should consider using the following means of information provision:

- Publications, such as information flyers/brochures, guidance, manuals, etc.
- Workshop, conferences on specific topics, e.g. for specific industrial sectors.
- "Help lines" for industry to consult with the inspectorate.
- Media announcements.

247. Successful examples of applying these promotion tools should be presented within the NIS network of inspectors. In addition, supporting documents with the descriptions of selected tools used in OECD countries and elsewhere could be prepared for the NIS inspectors. ...

6.4 Promoting Environmental Management in Enterprises

251. The promotion of environmental management systems within industry can help to incorporate a culture of responsibility towards the environment, rather than an occasional consideration of rules imposed by a regulatory institution. In many cases the "win-win" opportunities exist, i.e. environmental performance can be increased by introducing certain management changes and they can stimulate economic benefits at the same time. Promotion of environmental management systems should include advice from the inspectorate, but it will necessitate other forms of support, such as environmental audits, introduction of cleaner production and training provided by others.

252. The success of environmental management systems within industrial and other enterprises in the NIS is variable, both between and within individual countries (Box 20). In some countries, e.g. Armenia and Georgia, environmental management systems are still being developed. In others, e.g. Kazakhstan, Kyrgyzstan, Moldova, the Russian Federation and Turkmenistan problems related to the economic slow down mean that the number of enterprises implementing such systems is limited, even though the practice may be promoted by enforcement institutions. However, in the Russian Federation, for example, some joint stock companies have become willing to adopt environmental management systems, complying with international standards, in order to compete on foreign markets.

[Examples in the NIS:] Promotion of environmental management systems and cleaner production

Azerbaijan: As a general rule, major enterprises have their own environmental manager or environmental department. These managers or departments develop environmental action plans for their enterprises. The plans are drawn up at the beginning of the year and are co-ordinated with the local committee of the environment. If necessary, the plans are adjusted and amended. When an enterprise is inspected, the fulfilment of the approved action plan is checked. Some of the enterprises, such as the Novo-Baku Oil Refinery, show a concrete approach to environmental management. The refinery has set up the joint venture Azinteroil to remove the oil sludge that accumulates in the treatment facilities. The company is thriving. The Baku City COE has been encouraging this joint venture and trying to spread its experience. However, attempts to establish it in another similar company have been unsuccessful so far.

Ukraine: Encouragement by the government of enterprises using good environmental management systems is provided for by the current legislation in the Ukraine. In particular, article 29 of the Water Code provides for tax, credit and other benefits to be extended to the water users if they introduce low-waste, no-waste, energy and resource saving technologies or implement other measures reducing adverse effects on water bodies. Concrete environmental programmes are launched at enterprises and in ministries. For instance, the Ministry of Coal Industry has developed, and is implementing an "Integrated programme of resolving environmental problems in the coal-mining industry of Ukraine".

Uzbekistan: A UNIDO project "Presenting Cleaner Production in Uzbekistan" involving the State Committee of Environmental Protection was implemented in 1997-98.The objective of the project was to assist industries in carrying out a cost-effective and environmentally acceptable restructuring of production processes, including reduction of harmful emissions and minimisation of waste and consumption of energy and other resources. The immediate recipients of this kind of assistance were oil and gas industries, machine-building enterprises, chemical and food industries. Training and a series of demonstration projects in the optimisation of industrial processes allowed savings over 4 million soum per year to be achieved. The cost efficiency of the project was 5 dollars on each dollar invested. ...

255.   The use of voluntary approaches by industry is an interesting option to promoting environmental management systems which occurred recently in some NIS... .Such agreements usually commit industry to meeting environmental targets, but leave the means of achieving these up to the industries concerned. This enables them to consider a wider range of options than might be addressed within ordinary regulatory environments and enable the development of more imaginative and cost-effective solutions. The by-product, however, is that management will spend considerably more time addressing environmental performance than with a simple permit application. The use of voluntary approaches has been encouraged by enforcement institutions throughout the NIS, however, poor economic conditions in these countries make the use of such approaches very limited. Rather than sector-wide approaches, voluntary responses which have been stimulated by Inspectorates' pressure, occurred in larger and export oriented enterprises. Examples include:

- *Georgia*: general environmental action plans drawn up voluntarily by the oil company Gruzneft;
- *Moldova*: voluntary adoption of paint recycling by industry manufacturing washing machines;
- *Turkmenistan*: the purchase of special oil-collecting vessels in the Caspian Sea;
- *Turkmenistan*: enterprises in Turkmenistan have been encouraged to prepare general strategies for pollution abatement. As a result the government cotton company Turkmenpakhta plan a reconstruction of dust collectors and dust-settling chambers and construction of sewage and waste water treatment facilities to neutralise hydrogen sulphide effluents in the Maryi velayat.

- Uzbekistan: following the change of ownership from the state to the foreign investor the Samarkand Refrigerator Factory phased out CFC use;

[Conclusions]

256. In general, the promotion of environmental compliance is a relatively new area of activity for enforcement institutions in the NIS. In encouraging processes to improve environmental management several NIS consider the following activities which would focus on enterprises:

- Development of a formal *environmental compliance policy*, including provision for a broader application of Cleaner Production measures and promotion of Environmental Management Systems, economic incentives and targeted financial support;
- Developing *specific goals for* enterprises *and processes*, through for example compliance schedules, between inspectors and industry;
- *Seminars and training programmes* for staff and enterprise managers on compliance promotion to establish the contacts between the two stakeholders and to lay the ground for voluntary compliance;
- *Organising information and dissemination seminars* and workshop with the participation of policy makers, inspectors and industry to discuss the environmental requirements and problems with, and opportunities for, compliance;
- Developing *communication lines*, using seminars, information documentation, and other tools, between the inspectorates and the citizen's groups to build the public support for enforcement efforts and promoting compliance.

257. These activities may be promoted by exchange of information in the network and by individual inspectorates (or groups of inspectorates) undertaking the following:

- Assistance in pilot projects.
- Provision of environmental advisors to assist process operators.

- Development of regional environmental management, Cleaner Production and audit centres.
- Facilitation of workshops on environmental management.

258. In considering further activities for promoting compliance the NIS should strive to implement a Policy Statement on Environmental Management in Enterprises was adopted by Environment Ministers in 1998. The Policy Statement was intended to focus attention on environmental management in enterprises and generationg of the commitments required to promote cleaner industrial production in Central and Eastern Europe and the NIS. The Policy Statement recognised that there were potentially large benefits, both environmentally and economically, to be achieved from introducing cleaner production methods. The Statement called the governments to deveop a policy framework which would provide appropriate incentives for enterprises to adopt good environmental management practices in enterprises. Effective enforcement was also mentioned as crucial to provide an incentive to enterprises. ...

CHAPTER TEN

REGULATORS' CHOICE OF STRATEGIES

INTRODUCTION

This chapter introduces a selection of the best literature on the choices that face compliance officials in diagnosing problems and designing appropriate compliance and enforcement tools to solve a wide array of environmental problems. The analysis here complements and builds on earlier discussions about competing domestic theories of compliance, the various approaches available to regulators – including deterrence and detection, sanctions, liability and information measures – as well as the potential roles of different actors and institutions, including non-governmental organizations, courts and tribunals.

A major challenge facing officials is selecting the right tools for the job and designing the strategies to effectively implement them. Compliance officials, for instance, must choose the right mix of enforcement and compliance assistance mechanisms, which may vary by the industry sector and size.[1] Within enforcement, officials must choose how much to invest in detection strategies such as inspection, monitoring, and confirming self-reporting; sanctioning, including whether to pursue an administrative, civil, or criminal prosecution; and a communication

---

[1] For example, sectors with only a few players generally will be easier to regulate than a sector with hundreds, or thousands of players; and small and medium-sized industries generally need more assistance than larger firms, as they have fewer resources, less time and less technical capability. See, e.g., Chapter Nine: Compliace Assistance & " Beyond Complinace", Introduction n.9 (describing SMEnvironment 2003 Survey in UK). For a discussion on numerous policy tools that decision-makers use to regulate the dry cleaning industry, *see* Timothy Malloy & Peter Sinsheimer, *Pollution Prevention as a Regulatory Tool in California: Breaking Barriers and Building Bridges* (2001), *available at* http://www1.law.ucla.edu/~erg/pubs/MalloyBuildingBridgesReport.pdf. These tools include education about alternative cleaner technology, technical assistance and training, increased enforcement efforts (in the form of increased fines, for example), taxes or fees on certain solvents, financial incentives (in the form of direct or tax subsidies) for alternative technology, and complete bans on the use of certain solvents. *Id.* at 13-21.

strategy to alert the broader community and encourage deterrence.[2] Within compliance assistance, officials must choose among another set of strategies, such as providing information, technical support, training, or incentives.[3]

Given limited and fixed budgets, most enforcement and compliance agencies need to find the most cost effective means to ensure compliance.[4] Agencies generally consider what is feasible, what is most important, and what presents the greatest risk, and then focus on the problems that cause the most severe environmental or public health damages.[5] The Dutch environmental agency, for example, looks at the risk and the compliance rate in setting its priorities, utilizing the following 2 x 2 matrix.[6]

Risk ↑	**Priority 2** Need some attention	**Priority 1** Need immediate attention
	Priority 3 Not urgent	**Priority 2** Need some attention

→ non-compliance rate

---

[2] For a discussion on detection strategies, sanctions, court systems, and information regulation, *see* Chapter Four: Domestic Enforcement Strategies; Chapter Five: Courts, Tribunals, & Liability; and Chapter Seven: Information Regulation.

[3] For more information on compliance assistance, *see* Chapter Nine: Compliance Assistance & "Beyond Compliance".

[4] *See* INTERNATIONAL NETWORK FOR ENVIRONMENTAL COMPLIANCE AND ENFORCEMENT, PRINCIPLES OF ENVIRONMENTAL ENFORCEMENT, Chapter 10, at 6-7, *available at* http://inece.org/enforcementprinciples.html (hereinafter"INECE Principles"); *see also* ORAN YOUNG, COMPLIANCE & PUBLIC AUTHORITY, 112 (1979) (suggesting that it is useful to recognize that public officials generally will approach compliance issues as an investment problem, choosing how to invest their resources in various compliance mechanisms to obtain the best returns); Sandra Rousseau & Stef Proost, *The Cost Effectiveness of Environmental Policy Instruments in the Presence of Imperfect Compliance*, working paper series # 2002-04 (2002), *available at* http://www.econ.kuleuven.ac.be/ew/academic/energmil/downloads/ete-wp02-04.pdf (studying the impacts of various costs on the choice of environmental policy instruments and analyzing the administrative, implementation, enforcement and monitoring costs of different combinations of regulatory instruments (such as taxes and standards) and enforcement instruments (such as criminal and administrative fines)).

[5] *See* MALCOLM SPARROW, IMPOSING DUTIES: GOVERNMENT'S CHANGING APPROACH TO COMPLIANCE, xxv (1994); *see also* MALCOLM SPARROW, THE REGULATORY CRAFT, Chapter 14 (2000) (discussing different stages that regulatory agencies go through in choosing risk control strategies).

[6] Figure adapted from Van Der Schraaf & A. A., *The Compliance Strategy in the Netherlands*, 7th INECE Conference Proceedings (forthcoming 2005).

Where the risk is high and the non-compliance rate is high, policy makers target their compliance and enforcement resources. On the other hand, where risk is low or non-compliance rate is relatively low, the policy makers invest fewer resources.

Similarly, the U.S. Environmental Protection Agency (EPA) has adopted an "effective targeting" approach to reduce the cost of compliance measures. "Effective compliance and enforcement is dependent on effective targeting of the most significant public health and environmental risks. Because of this and a recognition that government resources are finite, EPA has worked … to improve [its] ability to target [its] efforts to the areas of greatest need."[7] By selectively targeting enforcement efforts, EPA seeks to achieve greater compliance with environmental regulations with the maximum benefit to human health and the environment at a reduced cost.[8]

In many agencies around the world, early enforcement efforts focused on particular industries that were high polluters, such as the power and steel industries, so that enforcement officials could regulate these key pollution sources and ensure that basic pollution controls were in place.[9] In recent years, agencies have begun setting priorities not only to address pressing environmental and health problems but also to maximize deterrence.[10] Moreover, newer programs are often more tailored and responsive to local priorities and needs.[11]

In designing appropriate compliance mechanisms, agencies study the regulated industries' sophistication, ability, motivation, and willingness to comply so that they can choose the optimal compliance strategies.[12] Information that may help agencies in this endeavor includes: the firms' geographic location, the type of business or operation, the types and quantities of regulated materials or emissions that the businesses produce, and any risks associated with such releases.[13]

---

[7] U.S. Environmental Protection Agency, Protecting Your Health and the Environment Through Innovative Approaches to Compliance: Highlights From the Past 5 Years, EPA/300-K-99-001 (1999).

[8] *See* Lana Friesen, *Targeting Enforcement to Improve Compliance with Environmental Regulations*, 46 J. Envtl Econ. & Mgmt 72 (2003).

[9] *See* INECE Principles, *supra* note 4, at 6.

[10] *Id.* at 6-7.

[11] *Id.* at 7.

[12] *Id.*, Chapter 4, at 2.

[13] *Id.*

It is worth noting that NGOs, media, competitors, and private certifiers, among others, have significantly helped the budget-constrained agencies by providing the necessary resources to augment incentives for firms to reduce pollution.[14] For instance, in the context of information regulation, the regulators can focus their limited resources on enforcing the disclosure requirement and providing third parties with good-quality information about actual emissions. This disclosed information can, in turn, be used by these third parties to exert direct pressures on firms through the market or citizen suits.[15] Moreover, these stakeholders have also helped identify new priorities not previously considered by enforcement agencies.[16]

In addition to cost-benefit analysis,[17] policy makers may also consider the following factors in selecting regulatory and non-regulatory instruments: fairness; demands on government; effectiveness; environmental equity and justice issues; flexibility; incentives for technology innovation and diffusion; and protection and restoration of environmental quality and public health.[18]

In making these instrument choices, policy makers must be aware that instruments that are successful in developed nations—where resources for enforcement and compliance assistance generally are more readily available—are not necessarily appropriate in some developing countries or countries with economies in transition. For instance, more flexible instruments such as the tradable permit system may help reduce emission levels more cost effectively in some developed nations.[19] However, such

---

[14] Agencies are learning how best to empower a broader set of actors who have their own resources to help them with various aspects of compliance. For more discussion, *see* Chapter Six: NGO Compliance Strategies; Chapter Seven: Information Regulation; and Chapter Nine: Compliance Assistance & "Beyond Compliance".

[15] *See* Annette Killmer, *Fostering Effective Civil Society Involvement in the Enforcement of Pollution Prevention Policies*, 7, 7th INECE Conference Proceedings (forthcoming 2005); *see also* Neil Gunningham, Martin Phillipson & Peter Grabosky, *Harnessing Third Parties as Surrogate Regulators: Achieving Environmental Outcomes by Alternative Means*, 8 Bus. Strategy & Env't 211 (1999).

[16] *See* Sparrow, Imposing Duties, *supra* note 5, at 110.

[17] There is significant uncertainty surrounding benefits and costs of implementation tools, however, and this uncertainty can hamper the policy makers from making an accurate cost-benefit analysis. *See* Robert Stavins, *Correlated Uncertainty and Policy Instrument Choice*, 30 J. Envtl Econ. & Mgmt, 218 (1996).

[18] U.S. Congress, Office of Technology Assessment, Environmental Policy Tools: A User's Guide, OTA-ENV-634 (1995); *see also* INECE Principles, *supra* note 4, Chapter 4, at 3.

[19] For more information on emissions trading programs, *see* Chapter Eight: Emissions Trading Compliance.

an instrument may not be appropriate in a country that lacks a strong foundation for the rule of law that can ensure the proper functioning of the permit system. Rather, in such a country, instruments that are more "command and control" oriented may work better since they are relatively easier to monitor and implement.[20]

This chapter reviews various scholarly works that have studied how public agencies make the challenging decisions on appropriate environmental instruments. It begins with Robert M. Friedman, Donna Downing, and Elizabeth M. Gunn's piece that essentially is a "user's guide" that may help decision makers narrow the choice of environmental instruments for addressing a particular problem.[21] The article first describes twelve policy tools, and then rates the effectiveness of these instruments.

The next article analyzes the factors that affect an agency's policy choice. Jeremy Firestone looks at how agencies behave when making environmental enforcement venue choices between administrative, civil, and criminal prosecutions.[22] Specifically, the study analyzes numerous factors that appear relevant to U.S. EPA's decision-making, among them: the enhanced procedural protections afforded criminal defendants; the possibility that a judge will impose non-monetary sanctions on a criminal defendant; the collateral consequences that may result from a criminal conviction; and the control that can be exercised in the administrative realm.[23]

---

[20] For a discussion of effectiveness of command-and-control regulations, *see e.g.*, S. Dasgupta, B. Laplante, & N. Mamingi, *Pollution and capital markets in developing countries*, 42 J. ENVTL ECON. & MGMT, 310 (2001); J. Foulon, P. Lanoie, & B. Laplante, *Incentives for pollution control: Regulation or information?*, 44 J. ENVTL ECON. & MGMT, 169 (2002); Gunningham, Philipson & Grabosky, *supra* note 15; W. Harrington, *Enforcement leverage when penalties are restricted*, 37 J. PUB. ECON., 29 (1988); E. Hentschel & A. Randall, *An integrated strategy to reduce monitoring and enforcement costs*, 15 ENVTL & RES. ECON., 57 (2000); A.G. Heyes, *Implementing environmental regulation: Enforcement and compliance*, 17(2) J. REGULATORY ECON., 107 (2000); B. Laplante & P. Rilstone, *Environmental inspections and emissions of the pulp and paper industry in Quebec*, 31 J. ENVTL ECON. & MGMT, 19 (1996); World Bank, *GREENING INDUSTRY: NEW ROLES FOR COMMUNITIES, MARKETS, AND GOVERNMENTS* (2000).
[21] Robert M. Friedman, Donna Downing & Elizabeth M. Gunn, *Environmental Policy Instrument Choice: The Challenge of Competing Goals*, 10 DUKE ENVTL. L. & POL'Y F 327 (2000).
[22] Jeremy Firestone, *Enforcement of Pollution Laws and Regulations: An Analysis of Forum Choice*, 27(1) HARVARD ENVTL L. REV. 105 (2003).
[23] For a full discussion on environmental criminal enforcement, *see* Kathleen Brickey, *Environmental Crime at the Crossroads: The Intersection of Environmental and Criminal Law Theory*, 71 TUL. L. REV. 487 (1996).

Peter Krahn's article provides case studies of numerous industries in British Columbia, and compares the varying impacts of different mandatory and voluntary enforcement measures in inducing compliance.[24] Generally, he found that mandatory measures are much more effective than voluntary programs.

The chapter concludes with Ruth Greenspan Bell's piece, which reminds us that environmental instruments in developed countries may not necessarily be appropriate or applicable in some developing countries and countries with economies in transition.[25] The author points out that some of these countries lack necessary institutions, infrastructure, and human capital to implement, monitor, and enforce the sophisticated environmental instruments that the developed nations promote.

---

[24] Peter Krahn, *Enforcement versus Voluntary Compliance: An Examination of the Strategic Enforcement Initiatives Implemented by the Pacific and Yukon Regional Office of Environment Canada 1983 to 1998*, 5th INECE Conference Proceedings, Vol. 1 (1998), *available at* http://www.inece.org.

[25] Ruth Greenspan Bell, *Choosing Environmental Policy Instruments in the Real World*, Presented at OECD Global Forum on Sustainable Development: Emissions Trading, Concerted Action on Tradeable Emissions Permits Country Forum, March 17-18, 2003.

Environmental Policy Instrument Choice: The Challenge of Competing Goals

Robert M. Friedman, Donna Downing & Elizabeth M. Gunn

10 Duke Environmental Law & Policy Forum 327 (2000)

I.   Introduction

The search for "smarter" ways to prevent and control pollution has generated heated debate on almost every topic related to setting goals, improving institutional arrangements, and choosing the most effective means for achieving those goals. Given the need to balance other competing concerns, choosing the means or policy instruments to meet environmental goals can be a surprisingly complex task for decision-makers. Unfortunately, today's environmental policy toolbox contains numerous and varied instruments yet lacks a clear set of instructions for their use. ...

The "user's guide" that we developed presents a pragmatic set of instructions to help decision-makers narrow the choice of instruments for addressing a particular problem. First, the Report describes twelve policy tools and how and where they are currently being used. Then, we rated the relative effectiveness of these tools in achieving each of seven criteria often considered when evaluating and creating environmental policy. The ratings were based on state, federal and international experiences, as well as on scholarly literature. Third, because the strengths and weaknesses of a policy tool depend greatly on the environmental problem being addressed,[6] we provided a series of key questions to be considered along with our judgments about "typical" instrument performance. Given a decision-maker's preferences for certain criteria,

---

[6] *See* Giandomenico Majone, Choice Among Policy Instruments for Pollution Control, 2 Policy Analysis 589 (1976).

this framework draws attention to those instruments which might be particularly effective - or warrant some caution - in addressing a particular problem. ...

III. The Toolbox

Environmental policy tools could be categorized in any number of ways, depending on which attributes one wishes to emphasize. One useful approach is to group twelve policy instruments into two major categories depending on whether or not they impose fixed pollution reduction targets. These two categories help focus attention on a common concern in environmental policy - namely, the extent to which particular behavior is mandated by regulation. Table 1 provides a brief description of each of the twelve policy tools. Figure 1 shows how frequently each instrument is used in the approximately thirty major pollution control programs under the CAA, CWA and RCRA.

TABLE 1: THE ENVIRONMENTAL POLICY TOOLBOX

Tools *With* Fixed Pollution Reduction Targets

Focus on single sources or products	
Harm-based Standards	A harm-based standard prescribes the end result, not the means, of regulatory compliance. Regulated entities are responsible for meeting some regulatory target, but are largely free to choose or invent the easiest or cheapest methods to comply. Sometimes referred to as health-based standards or performance standards, harm-based standards are widely used, primarily in combination with design standards.
Design Standards	A design standard is a requirement expressed in terms of the state of the art of pollution abatement at some point in time, for example, "best available"[27] or "best practicable"[28] technology. In a permit, design standard requirements are typically, but not always, stated as the level of emissions control the model approach is capable of achieving. Design

standards written as emissions limits allow individual sources the freedom to achieve the required emissions control by using the model approach or equivalent means. Design standards are very widely used, most often as part of a technology-based strategy.

Technology Specifications   A technology specification is a requirement expressed in terms of specific equipment or techniques. The standard is to be met by all entities; facilities are not free to choose their means of pollution abatement or prevention. Explicit technology specifications in statutes or regulations are very rare. However, some design standards can be considered *de facto* technology specifications when it is extremely difficult to prove to the regulatory agency that an alternative is equivalent to the model technology.

Product Bans and Limitations   This regulatory approach bans or restricts production, processing, distribution, use, or disposal of substances that present unacceptable risks to health or the environment. It focuses on the commodity itself, rather than polluting byproducts. As a result, the instrument is used most heavily under the Federal Insecticide, Fungicide, and Rodenticide Act (FIFRA)[29] and other statutes where the hazard is the commodity.

---

[27] See, e.g., Clean Water Act, 33 U.S.C. 1311(b)(2)(A).
[28] See CWA, 33 U.S.C. 1311(b)(1)(A).
[29] 7 U.S.C. 136-136y (1994).

Focus on multiple sources or products:

Tradable Emissions   Emissions trading is achieved through government-issued permits that allow the owner to emit a specific quantity of pollutants over a specified period of time, and which can be bought from and sold to others. The government typically caps aggregate emissions from sources within a geographic region by issuing only the number of permits consistent with environmental goals. A relatively new approach to tradable emissions is an "open market" approach where unregulated sources may voluntarily opt into the program. Emissions trading has been used most widely under the Clean Air Act,[30] and to a more limited degree to address water quality issues.[31]

Integrated Permitting   Integrated permits contain facility-wide emission limits, either for a single pollutant across multiple individual sources or media, or for several pollutants emitted to a single medium. An integrated permit might use one or several other environmental policy instruments. "Bubble" permits are used under the Clean Air Act, and to a very limited extent under the Clean Water Act.[32] Other types of integrated permits are still uncommon but are being studied as part of several state pilot projects.

Challenge Regulation   Challenge regulations ask target groups to change their behavior and work toward a specific environmental goal, with mandatory requirements imposed if the goal is not reached. The government identifies a goal and gives the groups time to select and implement an effective means of achieving it. As a result, challenge regulations have the potential to be a less-intrusive way to achieve environmental goals. The concept of challenge regulation is attracting interest, but is still uncommon as a stand-alone regulatory tool.

---

[30] *See, e.g.,* 42 U.S.C. 7651-7651.
[31] *See, e.g.,* U.S. Environmental Protection Agency, EPA-800-R-96-001, Draft Framework for Watershed-Based Trading (May 1996) [hereinafter Watershed-Based Trading] <http://www.epa.gov/owow/watershed/framework.html>.

Pollution Charges	With pollution charges, a regulated entity must pay a fixed dollar amount for each unit of pollution emitted or disposed. Pollution charges do not set a limit on emissions or production. Instead, the government must calculate what charge will change the behavior of regulated entities enough to achieve environmental objectives. Sources are free to choose whether to emit pollution and pay the charge, or to pay for the installation of controls to reduce emissions. This report considers only those charges set high enough to significantly alter environmentally harmful behavior, not charges used primarily for raising revenues. In the United States, pollution charges have been used for solid waste control,[33] but rarely for control of other types of pollution.
Liability	Liability provisions require entities that cause environmental harm to pay those who are harmed to the extent of the damage. Liability can provide a significant motivation for behavioral change because the dollar amounts involved can be huge. This report focuses on statutory liability, not common law theories of liability or enforcement penalties. Several environmental statutes impose statutory liability, including the Comprehensive Environmental Response, Compensation, and Liability Act (CERCLA) and the Oil Pollution Act.[34]

[32] *See* Emissions Trading Policy Statement: General Principles for Creation, Banking, and Use of Emission Reduction Credits, 51 Fed.Reg. 43814 (December 4, 1986) [hereinafter Policy Statement](describing the bubble policy under the CAA); Standards of Performance for New Stationary Sources, 40 C.F.R. pt. 60 (1987) (allowing an air bubble method as an alternative means of compliance); Iron and Steel Manufacturing Point Source Category Effluent Limitations Guidelines, Pretreatment Standards, and New Source Performance Standards, 40 C.F.R. pt. 420 (1982)(creating the iron and steel water bubble).

[33] See, e.g., Don Fullerton & Thomas Kinnaman, Household Demand for Garbage and Recycling Collection with the Start of a Price per Bag (National Bureau of Economic Research Working Paper No. 4670, 1994); Summary of Project 88/Round II Workshop Proceedings: Incentive-Based Policies for Municipal Solid Waste Management (Kennedy School of Government, CSIA Discussion Paper 91-7, 1991).

[34] See 42 U.S.C. 9607 (1994); 33 U.S.C. 2702 (1994).

Information Reporting	Information reporting requires targeted entities to provide specified types of information to a government agency or to the public directly. Required information typically involves activities affecting environmental quality, such as emissions, product characteristics, or whether risk to the public exceeds a threshold.
Subsidies	Subsidies are financial assistance given to entities as an incentive to change their behavior, or to help defray costs of mandatory standards. Subsidies might be provided by the government or by other parties, who thus bear part of the cost of environmentally beneficial controls or behavior. Historically, government subsidies have been widely used, particularly in wastewater treatment. [35] Subsidies from other parties are becoming more common as government budgets shrink.
Technical Assistance	The government offers technical assistance to help targeted entities prevent or reduce pollution. These programs educate sources that might not be fully aware of the environmental consequences of their actions, or of techniques or equipment to reduce those consequences. Technical assistance may take many forms, including manuals and guidance, training programs, and information clearinghouses. Some types of technical assistance, such as facility evaluations, are conditioned on facilities agreeing to respond with environmentally beneficial behavior. Technical assistance is very common, particularly in combination with other tools.

---

[35] *See, e.g.*, Clean Water Act , 33 U.S.C. 1281-1299, 1381-1387.

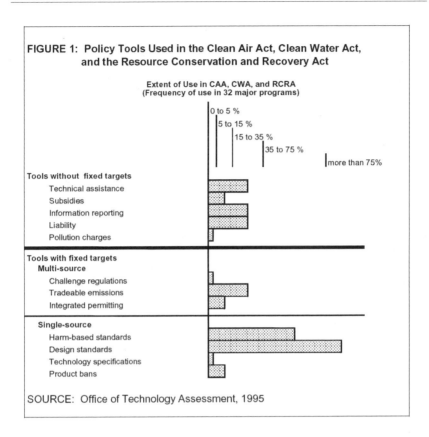

FIGURE 1: Policy Tools Used in the Clean Air Act, Clean Water Act, and the Resource Conservation and Recovery Act

SOURCE: Office of Technology Assessment, 1995

A.   Tools with Fixed Pollution Reduction Targets

...

1.   Single-Source Tools

...

Single-source tools seem to be effective choices where environmental results are of primary concern, and where there is less of a focus on costs. Although the tools provide varying levels of flexibility when telling sources "what to do," they all establish explicit emission targets for each source, and therefore, provide a relatively straightforward basis for verifying compliance. As a result, single-source tools are the most effective of the dozen tools that we consider in this article for providing assurance that environmental goals will be met. However, they are not as effective for addressing concerns about minimizing compliance costs because they are relatively less flexible than other instruments, and thus reduce opportunities for achieving goals in a cost-effective manner. In addition, they can impose substantial administrative burdens on regulatory agencies and regulated entities.

2. Multi-Source Tools

...

Multi-source tools are an effective choice when resource demands are of particular concern, and environmental results a close second. The tools allow facilities to seek the most cost-effective approach to achieving a particular level of aggregate emissions, whether through negotiation of emissions control responsibilities with other facilities or through use of an integrated permit with flexible source emission limits at a particular facility. Multi-source tools still require a particular level of pollution abatement, and thus provide a significant degree of assurance that environmental goals will be met, although perhaps less assurance than with the straightforward, single-source tools. The actual degree of assurance depends on the capability to monitor regulated pollutants.

B. Tools Without Fixed Pollution Reduction Targets

...

Behavior-modifying tools that do not set fixed pollution control targets, are particularly appropriate if the decision-maker desires an environmental program that can readily adapt to changing science and control capabilities. Because these tools do not mandate any particular behavior, they should be used with caution where assurance of meeting environmental goals is a primary criterion. ...

VI. Choosing Instruments

Whether Congress prefers to specify the choice of policy tools itself or delegate the choice to EPA, states, localities, or even the private sector, someone is faced with the difficult problem of matching tools to problems. Table 3 summarizes the OTA Report's judgments about how well each instrument addresses each of the seven criteria.[125]

Table 3: Comparison of the Effectiveness of Policy Instruments Tools *With* Fixed Targets

		Single-source				Multi-source		
		Product bans	Technology specifications	Design standards	Harm-based standards	Integrated permitting	Tradeable emissions	Challenge regulations
Environmental Results	Assurance of meeting goals	●	●	●	●	●	○	.
	action forcing	●	●	●	●	●	●	○
	monitoring capability	●	●	○	.	○	▽	▽
	familiarity with use	.	▽	●	●	.	.	▽
	Pollution prevention	●	○	○	.	.	.	.
	gives prevention an advantage	●	○	○	.	○	.	.
	focuses on learning	.	▽	▽	▽	.	.	○
	Environmental equity and justice	.	.	.	.	.	▽	▽
	distributional outcomes	.	.	.	●	.	▽	▽
	effective participation	.	.	.	.	.	▽	▽
	remediation	.	.	.	.	.	.	.
Costs and Burdens	Cost effectiveness and fairness	▽	▽	.	.	○	●	○
	cost effective for society	▽	▽	.	.	.	●	○
	cost effective for sources	▽	▽	.	.	○	●	○
	fairness to sources	▽	▽	.	.	.	●	●
	administrative burden to sources	.	.	.	.	▽	▽	▽
	Demands on government	.	.	.	▽	.	.	○
	costs	.	.	.	▽	.	.	○
	ease of analysis	▽	.	.	▽	▽	○	○
Change	Adaptability	▽	▽	▽	.	.	.	○
	ease of program modification	▽	▽	▽	▽	▽	▽	.
	ease of change for sources	▽	▽	▽	.	○	●	●
	Technology innovation and diffusion	●	.	.	.	.	○	○
	innovation in regulated industry	●	▽	▽	.	.	○	○
	innovation in EG&S industry	.	▽	●	.	.	○	○
	diffusion of technologies	.	●	●	.	.	.	.

●= Effective, ○= It Depends, ▽= Use With Caution, . = Average

[125] See [Office of Tech. Assessment, U.S. Congress, Rep. No. OTA-ENV-634, Environmental Policy Tools - A User's Guide (1995), <http://www.wws.princeton.edu/<diff>ota/>] at 143-200...

Table 3 *(continued)*: Comparison of the Effectiveness of Policy Instruments Tools *Without* Fixed Targets

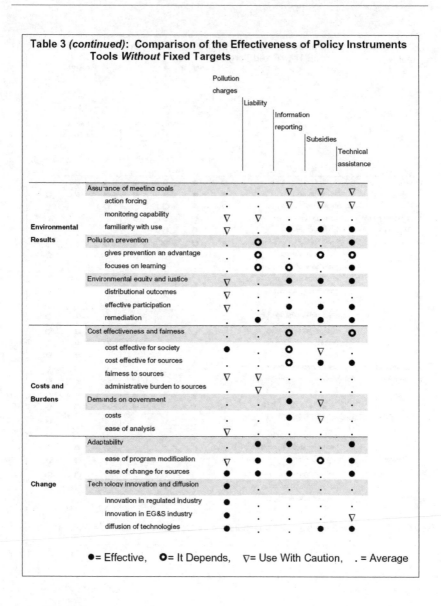

		Pollution charges	Liability	Information reporting	Subsidies	Technical assistance
Environmental Results	Assurance of meeting goals	.	.	∇	∇	∇
	action forcing	.	.	∇	∇	∇
	monitoring capability	∇	∇	.	.	.
	familiarity with use	∇	.	●	●	●
	Pollution prevention	.	○	.	.	●
	gives prevention an advantage	.	○	.	○	○
	focuses on learning	.	○	○	.	●
	Environmental equity and justice	∇	.	●	●	●
	distributional outcomes	∇	.	.	.	.
	effective participation	∇	.	●	●	●
	remediation	.	●	.	●	●
Costs and Burdens	Cost effectiveness and fairness	.	.	○	.	○
	cost effective for society	●	.	○	∇	.
	cost effective for sources	.	.	○	●	●
	fairness to sources	∇	∇	.	.	.
	administrative burden to sources	.	∇	.	.	.
	Demands on government	.	.	●	∇	.
	costs	.	.	●	∇	.
	ease of analysis	∇	.	.	.	.
Change	Adaptability	.	●	●	.	●
	ease of program modification	∇	●	●	○	●
	ease of change for sources	●	●	●	.	●
	Technology innovation and diffusion	●	.	.	.	.
	innovation in regulated industry	●	.	.	.	.
	innovation in EG&S industry	●	.	.	.	∇
	diffusion of technologies	●	.	.	●	●

●= Effective,　○= It Depends,　∇= Use With Caution,　. = Average

The OTA Report presented a two-part framework to help policy-makers first narrow down the choice of instruments based on how they perform on each of the seven criteria presented previously, and then, if needed, to help them buttress weaknesses of any single tool by using more than one instrument. A series of key questions about the particular problem can provide answers that may point - in combination with the evaluations presented in Table 3 - to one set of instruments rather than another. These are summarized in Box 3 (below).

A decision-maker is likely to first ask, "Is there a reason to specify a fixed environmental target for this pollutant?" Do the quantities and location of a pollutant, or the characteristics of its sources, provide a reason to prefer a fixed control target? To answer this, one needs to know how harmful or risky the pollutant is in the quantities that are being released. Again, the more serious the problem, the more heavily one weights "assurance of meeting goals." The first rows in Table 3 display OTA's judgments of the assurance provided by each of the instruments.

BOX 3: KEY QUESTIONS FOR MATCHING POLICY TOOLS TO PROBLEMS

Given the pollutant and the quantities and location of release, is there a reason to specify a fixed environmental target? If so, do these targets need to be source specific?

1.) How harmful or risky is the pollutant in the quantities that are being released?
2.) Is this problem typically quite localized or regional in nature?
3.) Does the technology exist to monitor the pollutant at a reasonable cost?

Given the pollutant and its sources, are we likely to be particularly concerned about costs and burdens to industry, individuals, or government?

1.) Are the sources of the pollutant reasonably similar or do they vary considerably from source to source even within industrial categories?
2.) Are there large differences in control costs among sources?
3.) Are there either very many sources or very few?
4.) Do we just not know very much about how to control the problem, the costs of control, or how to set environmental targets?

> **Given the pollutant and its sources, do we anticipate or hope that tomorrow's understanding of this problem or its solution will be significantly different than today's?**
>
> 1.) Is our uncertainty about the nature of the risk relatively high? Are the environmental goals very much in flux or are they likely to remain fixed for a reasonable period of time?
> 2.) Is technology changing rapidly--either the technology to prevent or control pollution or within the industry or sector itself?
> 3.) Can we achieve congressional environmental goals with today's technology at an acceptable cost?

Not at all surprising, those tools without fixed targets are marked with a caution. One cannot say that goals will not be met - there are certainly instances when these instruments have been quite effective in the past. However, there is decreased certainty that environmental goals will be met if tools without fixed targets are used alone.

If one prefers a fixed environmental target, the next question to ask is, "Does this target need to be source-specific?" Some environmental problems are regional in nature - for example, urban ozone and acid rain - and thus, can be successfully addressed by regulatory programs that incorporate marketable emissions or another multisource tool. For those problems that are local in nature, such as exposures to some toxic air pollutants, many will judge multi-source instruments to be inappropriate. Similarly, the more difficult it is to monitor sources, the harder it is to use multi-source tools.

The desire to allow sources to retain as much autonomy as possible leads one to prefer instruments with no fixed target - those on the second page of Table 3. The desire for greater assurance pushes one further towards instruments placing direct limits on pollution. However, many other concerns complicate the decision. Foremost among these issues is, "Will costs and burdens to industry and government be acceptable?"

Increased autonomy to sources often can improve the cost-effectiveness and fairness of pollution prevention or control. However, government burdens might increase along with source flexibility if increased oversight appears necessary to keep the same level of assurance that goals will be met. We highlight several questions that help assess the overall costs and burdens in the context of a specific pollution problem. Some questions focus on the nature of targeted sources, including question such as: "Are there large differences in control costs among sources?" "Are there very many sources, or very few?" Other questions consider our knowledge basis by asking: "Do we know how to set environmental targets, how to control the problem, or what it would cost to control?"

Government burdens are affected greatly by available knowledge and the complexity of required analytical tasks. For example, a potentially risky pollutant that one might otherwise wish to control with a harm-based standard may be so poorly understood that a different choice might be necessary. Identifying available methods of control under a design standard poses fewer analytical difficulties than determining acceptable pollutant concentrations under a harm-based standard, though a design standard might require a less-than-ideal level of pollution control. Such tradeoffs are not theoretical; Congress changed the harm-based approach to air toxics to a design standard in the 1990 Clean Air Act Amendments because the harm-based approach had proven virtually impossible to implement. ...

There is one more related concern that may alter one's choice of instrument: given the pollutant and its sources, do we anticipate or hope that tomorrow's understanding of this problem or its solution will be significantly different than today's?

If the uncertainty about the nature of the risk is relatively high or if technology is changing rapidly, one might be drawn to those instruments that are most adaptable to change. Technical assistance programs, information reporting, and liability usually push sources to make changes without government approval and can be relatively easily modified by government when the need arises.

If, for a particular problem, Congress' environmental goals just cannot be achieved with today's technology at an acceptable cost, one might choose those instruments that spur technology innovation. Pollution charges can be effective because of the continuing pressure they exert. Product bans also spur innovation, but they are typically avoided unless the risks from the pollutant are quite high. Multisource instruments, such as tradeable emissions or challenge regulations, offer sources additional flexibility for using new technologies and thus may also help. ...

VII. Using More than One Instrument

As one can readily glean from our Table 3 … it is indeed rare that one instrument alone will satisfy all of the desires that policy-makers may have when attempting to solve an environmental problem. Thus, one finds historically a reliance on the use of multiple instruments when addressing a problem. The single most common combination is the use of design standards in conjunction with harm-based standards. About half of the 30 major pollution control programs under the CAA, the CWA, and RCRA follow this approach. Control of conventional water pollutants, such as biological oxygen demanding materials (BOD) and suspended solids, is typical of this combination. For water bodies that meet the desired level of water quality set by each state, sources that discharge directly into lakes and streams are required to control discharges to a level defined by a design standard specific to each source category and pollutant.[128] Municipal sewage treatment plants are required to control to a level equivalent to "secondary treatment," and industrial dischargers must control equivalent to "best available technology economically achievable."

However, if the water body does not meet the desired level of water quality, sources are subject to a harm-based standard; that is, sources are required to clean up their effluent to a level that allows the lake or stream to maintain the specified water quality. The simpler design standard becomes a "floor" or minimum level of control. However, if the desired water quality is not achieved, the more analytically complex harm-based standard then applies. This mix of instruments is a compromise allowing the relative speed, simplicity, and lower administrative burden of design standards in cleaner areas and the potential for more efficient controls using a harm-based approach in areas where more stringent and expensive controls are needed.

Our Table 3 rates both design standards and harm-based standard about the same for cost-effectiveness and fairness of control, but design standards have an edge when it comes to demands on government. The key difference is the ease of analysis. For example, the difficulty of setting harm-based standards was probably the primary reason for the slow pace of regulating air toxic emissions since the 1970s, which led Congress to change strategy in the 1990 CAA amendments. As discussed earlier, Congress abandoned a strategy based primarily on the use of harm-based

---

[128] *See, e.g.,* Clean Water Act, 33 U.S.C. 1311.

standards and adopted an approach that directs EPA to first issue a design standard (emissions equivalent to those achieved by using "maximum achievable control technology") and then to analyze whether "residual-risk" goals are exceeded, and if so, to require additional controls. Thus, by using a multi-source approach, Congress attempted to buttress the weaknesses of harm-based standards with the simpler approach of design standards.

However, both the "single-source" design and harm-based standards are merely average with respect to efficiency and fairness of control, though harm-based standards are probably the better of the two. Hence, the reason for the great attention being given to multi-source instruments, which have the potential for improved cost effectiveness. As can be seen in Table 3, we rate "multi-source" instruments such as tradeable emissions and integrated permitting (which, in our definition, includes facility-wide "bubbles" or emission caps) as potentially more cost effective. Several problems addressed by the CAA currently combine tradeable emissions with more traditional single source approaches. To date, these have primarily been limited to emissions of pollutants such as sulfur dioxide and nitrogen oxides - pollutants whose effects are regional as opposed to the more localized impacts of toxic air pollutants. For example, trading has been extensively used to allow new sources to locate in nonattainment areas - areas that do not meet ambient air quality standards. New sources can locate in nonattainment areas if they "offset" their emissions with reductions from existing sources. Another area where trading has been used is compliance with exhaust emission standards for heavy-duty diesel engines.

The topic of instrument choice is important precisely because it is so rare for one instrument alone to satisfy all of the desires that policy-makers may have when attempting to solve an environmental problem. Moreover, it is even difficult to choose a mix of instruments that achieves high marks on all seven of the criteria considered in this study. As societal values and priorities change, and as new problems emerge to challenge our existing taxonomies and frameworks, we agree with Richards that, far from being an academic exercise, the issue of instrument choice is in fact worth our collective efforts to help move the nation's environmental performance in the right direction.

Enforcement of Pollution Laws and Regulations: An Analysis of Forum Choice

Jeremy Firestone

27 HARVARD ENVIRONMENTAL LAW REVIEW 105 (2003)

I. Introduction

Regulatory agencies are imbued with substantial discretion as a result of vague delegations of authority from Congress. Thus, it is more than mere academic curiosity to pose the question: Why does a regulatory agency behave in the manner that it does and with what effect? Indeed, this core question goes to the heart of regulatory policy. As a starting point to answer this question, one might surmise that in addition to the legal framework imposed by the Constitution and by Congress, a given regulatory agency's organizational mission, culture and structure play a role. It also is conceivable that the private actors whom an agency regulates and the political milieu in which an agency operates influence its behavior as well. These factors likely shape not only the development of substantive regulations and agency implementation of the same, but also an area where agencies have even more discretion — the enforcement of laws and regulations. Although enforcement plays a leading role in the modern regulatory state and, more specifically, in the area of pollution control, little empirical work has been conducted on environmental enforcement. Hence, policymakers may not fully appreciate the interplay among administrative, civil judicial, and criminal sanctions — that is, venue choice. ...

[T]his Article reports on findings from a random sample of 325 Clean Air Act ("CAA"), Federal Water Pollution Control Act ("Clean Water Act" or "CWA"), and Solid Waste Disposal Act ("Resource Conservation and Recovery Act" or "RCRA") penalty enforcement actions commenced

289

during fiscal years 1990–1997 and examines the choice of the U.S. Environmental Protection Agency ("EPA" or "Agency")[2] among administrative, civil judicial, and criminal enforcement venues to seek sanctions against firms and governments[3]. ...

After first placing EPA's choice among enforcement proceedings in context, this Article constructs models of how agencies behave when making environmental enforcement venue choices and reviews the literature on environmental targeting and sanctions. In light of that institutional and theoretical backdrop, a data set of violators from whom EPA sought penalties and pursued administratively, civil judicially, and criminally under the CAA, CWA, and RCRA, is constructed and empirically analyzed. A cross-media, cross-firm size, and cross-industry methodology is employed. ...

II.   The Context in Which EPA Chooses Among Administrative, Civil Judicial, and Criminal Remedies

Criminal sanctions impose different costs than civil sanctions on society and on violators, and serve a different function as well. Consequently, it is important to place the empirical analysis of the choice among enforcement venues in context. In this Part, the discussion focuses on the normative characteristics that distinguish criminal from civil law, procedural and substantive distinctions among the fora, and EPA's efforts to guide its discretion in choosing among enforcement fora as well as its institutional preferences.

A.   Norms and Normative Distinctions

... Although the primary goal of civil enforcement is to secure compliance, criminal sanctions function on a broader plane; society can use criminal sanctions to change beliefs, attitudes, values, and goals, and to effectuate policies by influencing what individuals think they ought or want to do in a particular situation.[13] Given societal norms and normative effects of criminal prosecutions, the extent to which a violator's conduct deviates

---

[2] Although referred to as EPA's choice in this Article, the U.S. Department of Justice or the local U.S. Attorney participate respectively in the decision to file a civil or criminal matter in court.

[3] As such, the study population is conditional on EPA commencing a penalty action

[13] [Harry V. Ball & Lawrence M. Friedman, *The Use of Criminal Sanctions in the Enforcement of Economic Legislation: A Sociological View*, 17 Stan L. Rev., at 220 (1965)]; John C. Coffee, Jr., *Does "Unlawful" Mean "Criminal"?: Reflections on the Disappearing Tort/Crime Distinction in American Law*, 71 B.U. L. Rev. 193, 223–38 (1991).

from societal norms, as well as the benefits to society from expressing to the maximum extent possible its moral outrage at the conduct, likely influence enforcement personnel decision-making.

B.   *Procedural and Substantive Distinctions*

In addition to considering normative distinctions and the normative goals of enforcement when choosing among enforcement fora, a regulator/ prosecutor also must be attuned to the numerous procedural and substantive characteristics that differentiate criminal from civil law. Indeed, procedural and substantive differences likely carry great weight with EPA enforcement decision-makers.

Many procedural differences are common knowledge, including the requirement that the government prove its case beyond a reasonable doubt to a unanimous jury, the double jeopardy bar, and the right to "take" the Fifth Amendment and refuse to testify against oneself in a criminal matter. The criminal system also contains more powerful information-gathering tools than the civil system with which to build a case. ...

If EPA decides to pursue a penalty case civilly, it has two options: it may seek fines in federal court or handle the matter internally, using its administrative authorities. Administrative and civil judicial enforcement share many attributes. The primary distinguishing characteristic is that with administrative enforcement, EPA typically functions as both the enforcer of the statutory command and the adjudicator, although the two functions within the Agency technically remain separate. A judge or EPA, as appropriate, may impose a civil sanction in an environmental matter whenever a person has violated or is violating a law or permit condition.[16] Regardless of whether the forum is a judicial or administrative one, a civil sanction may be imposed if the government proves the existence of a violation without regard to a violator's level of care, diligence, or good faith. In other words, liability is strict.[17]

---

[16] *See*, e.g., 42 U.S.C. § 7413(a)(3) (2000) (authorizing the EPA administrator to issue penalties on compliance orders and to institute civil actions to remedy violations.)

[17] There are a few minor exceptions to the strict liability nature of civil environmental violations. For example, under 33 U.S.C. § 311(7)(D), EPA may seek enhanced penalties for the grossly negligent or willful discharge of oil into waters of the United States in addition to, or instead of, strict liability penalties for oil discharge violations. 33 U.S.C. § 311(7)(D) (2002).

A court possesses the authority to impose a relatively large environmental civil sanction on a liable defendant.[18] Although EPA also has authority to impose administrative penalties of up to $25,000 per day, that authority is generally subject to certain limitations. For example, Section 113(d) of the CAA[19] limits the total amount of civil penalty sought to $200,000 and requires that the action be commenced within twelve months of the first alleged date of violation.

In the 1990 CAA amendments, Congress provided EPA with another administrative tool—field citation authority—that is akin to issuing a traffic ticket, albeit an expensive one. Under Section 113 of the CAA, EPA can issue field citations not to exceed $5,000 per day for minor violations.[20] Although a person issued a field citation has a reasonable opportunity to be heard and present evidence, that person is not entitled to the full complement of processes otherwise mandated by the Administrative Procedure Act.[21]

Finally, Congress has expanded the civil net by encouraging citizens to assist the government's enforcement effort. Citizen suit provisions authorize citizens (often nonprofit organizations) to file civil suits against alleged violators after providing the government with sixty to ninety days notice, depending on the nature of the violation.[22] A notice of citizen suit may provoke EPA to file an administrative or civil judicial action or spur the notified party to enter into a settlement with EPA or the relevant state agency.[23]

In 1970, Congress initiated the modern era of criminalizing environmental violations with the adoption of a provision that sought to punish negligent CAA violations as misdemeanors. Throughout the 1970s, Congress added criminal misdemeanor provisions to the other environmental laws.

---

[18] *See, e.g.,* 42 U.S.C. § 7413(b) (authorizing civil judicial fines of up to $25,000 per day for each violation).

[19] *Id.* § 7413(d)(1).

[20] *Id.* § 7413(d)(3).

[21] *Compare id. with* 5 U.S.C. §§ 554, 556 (2000).

[22] *See, e.g.,* 42 U.S.C. § 6972.

[23] Federal or state court action commenced prior to the expiration of the relevant notice period denies the citizen jurisdiction to pursue his or her statutory claim. *See, e.g.,* Jones v. City of Lakeland, 224 F.3d 518, 522 (6th Cir. 2000) (en banc) (CWA suit barred if state or EPA is diligently prosecuting an action in court; administrative enforcement not material under the statute). In any event, a citizen would remain free to pursue other remedies such as a state law damage claim.

Although the criminal program commenced for all practical purposes in 1970, the federal government prosecuted only twenty-five environmental criminal cases during the 1970s. It was not until the early 1980s that the use of criminal proceedings became standard practice. This resulted after Congress created environmental felonies, beginning with the adoption of the 1980 RCRA amendments, and EPA and the U.S. Department of Justice ("DOJ") formed units dedicated solely to the investigation and prosecution of environmental crimes.[24] With the additional enforcement resources provided by the Pollution Prosecution Act of 1990,[25] the criminal program grew dramatically both in absolute terms and in its relationship to the federal government's civil environmental enforcement program.[26] Indeed, in 1995, the number of matters that EPA referred to the DOJ for criminal prosecution exceeded the number of matters EPA referred for civil judicial enforcement for the first time.[27]

The major environmental laws that regulate waste disposal—the CAA, CWA, and RCRA—now generally provide a three-tier system of criminal sanctions: misdemeanor penalties for "negligent" violations, felony penalties for "knowing" violations, and enhanced penalties for knowingly placing an individual in "imminent danger of death or serious bodily injury."[28] Knowing violations typically provide for terms of imprisonment not to exceed three (or in some instances, five) years and fines of up to $50,000 per day of violation.[29] Crimes of knowing endangerment carry terms of imprisonment of up to fifteen years for individuals and organizational fines of up to $1,000,000.[30] Many environmental laws also call for a doubling of the penalty in the event of a subsequent conviction.[31] ...

---

[24] Dick Thornburgh, *Criminal Enforcement Priorities for the 1990s*, 59 Geo. Wash. L. Rev. 775, 777–78 (1991).

[25] 42 U.S.C. §§ 4321–4370(d) (2000).

[26] James M. Strock, *Environmental Criminal Enforcement Priorities for the 1990s*, 59 Geo. Wash. L. Rev. 916 (1991); Thornburgh, *supra* note 24, at 778–80.

[27] Yet even during the period examined for this study, October 1989 through September 1997, administrative penalty cases represent almost seventy-five percent of all environmental enforcement cases in which EPA seeks to sanction violators. Jeremy M. Firestone, Environmental Enforcement Choice: Trading Off Equity for Environmental Benefits 84 (2000) (unpublished Ph.D. dissertation, University of North Carolina at Chapel Hill) (on file with the Harvard Environmental Law Review).

[28] The requirement that the government establish negligence in misdemeanor environmental criminal cases, and more generally, mens rea as an element of proof in a criminal matter, be it a misdemeanor or a felony, is the "rule, rather than exception to, the principles of Anglo-American jurisprudence." United States v. United States Gypsum Co., 438 U.S. 422, 436 (1978) (quoting Dennis v. United States, 341 U.S. 494, 500 (1951)).

[29] *See, e.g.*, 33 U.S.C. § 1319(c)(2) (2000).

The primary substantive distinction between sanctions in the criminal and civil systems is the availability of criminal nonmonetary sanctions, such as the incarceration of individuals and the intrusion into firm management through conditions on probation. It is primarily through the imposition of nonmonetary sanctions that the criminal system prevents individuals and firms from passing on environmental violations as a cost of doing business.

When a firm is convicted of a felony, a judge may place it on probation for up to five years;[34] order it to develop and implement a program to prevent and detect further violations; require its knowledgeable employees to submit to interrogation; and conduct unannounced examinations of its records.[35] In those situations where the government believes that continued judicial supervision of a firm is warranted, perhaps because of past waste handling practices or expected future behavior, the ability to place that firm on supervised probation offers the government an indispensable tool that it lacks in a civil forum.[36] Indeed, although the incarceration of corporate officials likely will cause a firm to install other persons within the corporate hierarchy, absent court supervision of the firm, the new officers may respond to the organizational environment in a manner similar to their predecessors.[37]

In light of the potential for harm associated with poor (let alone criminal) waste handling practices, supervised probation also provides the government with a tool that is analogous to the incarceration of an individual: in a sense, it disables[38] the corporate environmental criminal.[39] Through the use of supervised probation, the government can significantly reduce the likelihood that a firm will commit further crimes during the probationary period. Moreover, when a court intervenes into

---

[30] *See, e.g., id.* § 1319(c)(3).

[31] *See, e.g.,* 42 U.S.C. § 6928(d)(7) (2000).

[34] 18 U.S.C. § 3561(c)(1) (2000).

[35] *See, e.g.,* United States v. Palm Beach Cruises S.A., 204 B.R. 634 (S.D. Fla. 1996).

[36] Stephen A. Saltzburg, *The Control of Criminal Conduct in Organizations,* 71 B.U.L. Rev. 421, 429 (1991).

[37] *See* Michael B. Metzger, *Organizations and the Law,* 25 Am. Bus. L.J. 407, 419 (1987).

[38] By disabling the corporate environmental criminal, supervised probation serves at least two purposes of sentencing: deterrence and protection of the public from further crimes of the defendant. *See* 18 U.S.C. § 3553(a)(2)(B)–(C) (2000).

[39] *See* Fred L. Rush, Jr., *Corporate Probation: Invasive Techniques for Restructuring Institutional Behavior,* 21 Suffolk U. L. Rev. 33 (1986); Saltzburg, *supra* note 36, at 429; Metzger, *supra* note 37, at 438–39.

a firm's business practices, the loss of corporate autonomy serves as a powerful deterrent to other potential violators.[40]

A criminal conviction also may give rise to a number of direct or collateral consequences that may be of equal or greater significance than the immediate consequences of conviction.[41] First, in addition to the costs of incarceration or probation, the criminal justice system may impose stigma costs on a defendant. Moreover, when a firm is convicted criminally, rather than being found civilly liable, there may be "reputational rub-off" on upper management.[42]

Second, evidence of a conviction can be used against a defendant in subsequent civil matters that are factually unrelated to the matter for which the defendant was convicted. Evidence of a prior crime can be admitted to prove motive, opportunity, intent, preparation, plan, knowledge, identity, or absence of a mistake or accident.[43] Further, counsel may use evidence of a prior felony conviction to impeach the credibility of a witness.[44]

Third, criminal fines are not dischargeable in bankruptcy. The bankruptcy code provides that debt is not dischargeable to the extent a debt is for a "fine, penalty, or forfeiture payable to and for the benefit of a governmental unit."[45] ...

Fourth, an order requiring a defendant to pay for the costs of remediating environmental pollution in a criminal context may have different tax implications than if a similar order had been issued in a civil proceeding. Criminal restitution obligations fall within a gray area between criminal and civil fines, which are not deductible as necessary business expenses,

---

[40] *See* Michael J. Woods, *Environmental Compliance Programs as a Condition of Organizational Probation,* 8 Fed. Sentencing Rep. 209 (1996).

[41] Two sources on the collateral consequences of an environmental conviction are particularly illuminating. *See* John F. Cooney et al., *Criminal Enforcement of Environmental Laws: Part III — From Investigation to Sentencing and Beyond,* 25 Envtl. L. Rep. (Envtl. L. Inst.) 10,600–622 (1995); David T. Buente Jr., et al., *The "Civil" Implications of Environmental Crimes,* 23 Envtl. L. Rep. (Envtl. L. Inst.) 10,589, 10,598–600 (1993); *see also* Mark A. Cohen, *Environmental Crime and Punishment: Legal/Economic Theory and Empirical Evidence of Enforcement of Federal Environmental Statutes,* 82 J. Crim. L. & Criminology 1054 (1992).

[42] For a discussion of reputational rub-off in the criminal context, [see V.S> Khanna, *Corporate Criminal Liability: What Purpose Does it Serve?,* 109 Harv. L. Rev., at 1510 (1996)].

[43] Fed. R. Evid. 404(b).

[44] Fed. R. Evid. 609.

[45] 11 U.S.C.A. § 523(a)(7) (West Supp. 2002).

and civil restitution obligations, which are deductible.[47] Whether a criminal restitution obligation is tax-deductible depends on whether the obligation is primarily characterized as punitive or compensatory.[48]

Finally, a criminal conviction may have significant consequences for a firm's present and future dealings with its shareholders and federal and state governments. For example, when a publicly traded firm has been convicted of a crime, it must disclose that information in its Security and Exchange Commission ("SEC") filings and thus may open itself up to shareholder derivative suits, securities fraud, or SEC enforcement. Moreover, as soon as an indictment is issued, the government has the authority to suspend contracts and grants,[49] and, upon criminal conviction, can disqualify a contractor for a period of time. Further, federal agencies are prohibited from entering into procurement contracts with persons convicted under the CWA and the CAA.[50] These last sanctions apply government-wide and can apply to all of a company's activities. In a similar vein, many states also have provisions that allow regulatory agencies to consider a permit applicant's criminal and compliance record when deciding whether to issue a permit. For example, New Jersey allows consideration of these factors when it weighs the merits of an application for a solid waste license.[51]

Therefore, to the extent an agency has discretion to choose among enforcement fora, there are a number of factors that appear relevant to that consideration: the enhanced procedural protections afforded criminal defendants; the possibility that a judge will impose nonmonetary sanctions on a criminal defendant; the collateral consequences that may result from a criminal conviction; and the control that can be exercised in the administrative realm.

---

[47] 26 U.S.C. § 162(f) (2000).

[48] *Compare* Kraft v. United States, 991 F.2d 292 (6th Cir. 1993) (restitution not deductible even where defendant also received jail time and was ordered to pay a fine because it arose out of criminal proceedings) *with* Stephens v. Comm'r, 905 F.2d 667, 674 (2d Cir. 1990) (restitution obligation is deductible when it is ordered "in addition to" punishment and paid directly to a victim).

[49] 40 C.F.R. § 32.405(b) (2002). Although civil fraud can likewise give rise to debarment and suspension, the federal government rarely asserts a claim of fraud in an environmental civil penalty case.

[50] *See* 33 U.S.C. § 1368(a) (2000); 42 U.S.C. § 7606(a) (2000). These prohibitions are generally restricted to the offending facility.

[51] N.J. Stat. Ann. § 13:1E-133.1(a) (West 2002).

C.   EPA Discretion To Choose Among Venues

…

EPA has provided less insight into the factors that it considers germane to the decision of whether to proceed with a matter in an administrative or judicial forum. In that regard, EPA has stated that "if the bottom line requires higher penalties than can be achieved in an administrative proceeding," civil judicial enforcement is the appropriate course of action.[79] In addition, EPA has indicated that novel legal issues present particularly delicate considerations. On one hand, a favorable decision on the merits in federal court will set a strong precedent. However, if the case would have to be filed in a judicial district or circuit that has been hostile to EPA enforcement in the past, administrative action may be preferable. …

When EPA regional offices exercise discretion, they likely do so with a preference to resolve violations civilly rather than criminally. Even with the relaxed scienter requirement in environmental felony matters, it remains easier for EPA to meet the civil burden of proof. Moreover, in a criminal matter, the government is required to prove its case with greater certainty. Perhaps as important, EPA may prefer civil rather than criminal cases because it is far easier to build on existing precedents and make new law in civil than in criminal court.[85]

When it undertakes its role as gatekeeper, EPA also likely has a general preference for administrative actions, despite the greater public drama and publicity that attaches to a judicial proceeding.[86] EPA's preference arises for a number of reasons. First, administrative proceedings require EPA to dedicate fewer personnel and financial resources. Second, they also evoke a less defensive response from the alleged violator, thus increasing the chances of settlement and providing less procedural due process. Third, making a referral to DOJ delays resolution of a matter.[87]

---

[79] EPA, Civil Penalty Policy for Section 311(b)(3) and Section 311(j) of the Clean Water Act 4 (1998) (on file with the Harvard Environmental Law Review); *see also* EPA, Clean Air Act Stationary Source Civil Penalty Policy (1991) (on file with the Harvard Environmental Law Review). As noted previously, one of the primary distinguishing characteristics between administrative and civil judicial enforcement is that in the former, the total penalty amount may be limited.

[85] [Although civil judicial and administrative sanctions also may censure and stigmatize conduct, when society imposes criminal sanctions, there is a "deliberate intent to inflict punishment in a manner that maximizes" stigma. John C. Coffee, Jr., *Paradigms Lost: The Blurring of the Criminal and Civil Law Models — And What Can Be Done About It*, 101 Yale L.J., at 1891 (1992).]

[86] *Id* at 1888.

[87] [*See* Kenneth Mann, *Punitive Civil Sanctions: The Middleground Between Criminal and Civil Law*, 101 Yale L. J., at 1869-70 (1992)]; Coffee, *supra* note [85] at 1887.

In fact, differing views over what constitutes appropriate factual development on which to base a civil suit may result not only in delay, but also a decision by DOJ not to proceed.[88]

Fourth, EPA regional personnel also have much greater control over an ongoing administrative matter than a civil judicial or criminal action. With an administrative action, there is usually little or no EPA Headquarters involvement, and regional personnel do not have to take a backseat to or be upstaged by DOJ staff lawyers or Assistant U.S. Attorneys on case or courtroom strategy and decisions.[89] Conversely, with a criminal prosecution in particular, despite its public nature, EPA may get little credit for the successful resolution of the matter.[90]

Fifth, it might be more than a matter of not wanting to share decision-making power with another branch of government. Rather, EPA may not wish to share, and to an extent cede, decision-making authority to a branch of government that is quite differently organized. While EPA tends to vest its staff lawyers with a degree of authority, DOJ tends to be hierarchical. These different cultures may give rise to conflict that EPA desires to avoid. Indeed, enforcement can be problematic when it requires coordination with government agencies such as DOJ whose organizational objectives likely differ from those of EPA.[91]

Sixth, EPA may prefer administrative as opposed to judicial resolution of a matter because, when proceeding administratively, EPA does not lose control over the timing or the manner of proceeding, concede sanctioning authority to a judge, or have to rely on the whims of a jury. Thus, the basic appeal of administrative proceedings may well be the larger power EPA enjoys in such cases rather than in quanta of proof or questions of procedure.[92]

Hence, normative, procedural, and substantive distinctions are relevant to EPA's choice among enforcement venues because, even in the face of documents informing the public of how it intends to exercise its

---

[88] *See* Joseph F. DiMento, *Criminal Enforcement of Environmental Law*, 525 Annals Am. Acad. Pol. & Soc. Sci. 134 (1993); Peter C. Yeager, The Limits Of Law: The Public Regulation of Private Pollution (1991).

[89] *See* Joel A. Mintz, Enforcement at the EPA: High Stakes and Hard Choices (1995); Rosemary O'Leary, Environmental Change: Federal Courts and the EPA (1993).

[90] *See* Yeager, *supra* note 88.

[91] Dimento, *supra* note 88; Yeager, *supra* note 88.

[92] *See* Franklin E. Zimring, *The Multiple Middlegrounds Between Civil and Criminal Law*, 101 Yale L.J. 1901 (1992); Coffee, *supra* note [85]; MINTZ, *supra* note 89.

discretion, EPA retains substantial discretion to choose among administrative, civil judicial, and criminal venues. However, as noted above, the power EPA is able to exercise in each forum is as likely as procedural and substantive distinctions to guide that discretion. ...

V.   Empirical Evidence of EPA Enforcement Choice

A.   *Description of the Sample and Population of Violators*

... For this study, I analyzed the choices available to EPA to penalize violators under the CAA, CWA, and RCRA. ...

Turning first to the issue of enforcement targets, EPA pursued almost 15% of all violators criminally, yet handled only 9% of all cases criminally. This suggests that, on average, a criminal matter is more likely than a civil matter to have multiple violators. Firms were the most prevalent targets of EPA enforcement in the sample; however, individuals dominated the criminal forum. Indeed, while firms comprised approximately 67% of the overall number of enforcement targets, when one considers only the criminal forum, individuals comprised approximately 67% of the defendants. Government-entity violators represented slightly more than 11% of the total violators, and EPA targeted most of them administratively. In contrast, although small firms make up approximately 40% of the organizational violator targets, they make up a disproportionate share (more than 60%) of the organizational violator criminal targets.

[T]he means and standard errors of per capita income ("PCI") are remarkably consistent across enforcement fora. This suggests that as far as enforcement choice is concerned, EPA's actions do not present "economically based" environmental justice concerns. Turning to county unemployment rates, there is a great disparity between the mean in the administrative venue (13.4%) and the means in the civil judicial and criminal venues. At first glance, this suggests that EPA may have forgone the use of more potent enforcement tools in economically depressed areas. However, because of the large standard error associated with the administrative venue (6.5), the disparity might not be statistically significant when complex modeling is undertaken. EPA appears to have used toxicity to distinguish among fora, having reserved civil judicial enforcement for the most toxic substances and administrative enforcement for the least. Finally, the data indicate that on average civil judicial matters took at least 50% longer to resolve than either administrative or criminal matters.

If one assumes that violation severity increases as one moves from a "level 0" to a "level 7" violation, the results indicate that, as a general matter, EPA was more likely to pursue cases in court and in the criminal forum as violations became more serious. Using the zero to seven scale, the "average" violation per enforcement forum is 3.50 for administrative, 4.37 for civil judicial, and 5.93 for criminal enforcement. However, even in those instances when a case involved the spilling or other uncontrolled release of pollutants into the environment (Violation 7), EPA chose administrative enforcement more than 50% of the time.

B.   General Models of EPA Enforcement Choice

With the descriptive statistics as a backdrop, we now turn to complex modeling.[243] I first consider a series of models that compare the likelihood of criminal versus civil enforcement (a "logit" model). Because there may be differences among civil judicial and administrative enforcement, I then examine a series of models that make pairwise comparisons among administrative, civil judicial, and criminal enforcement.

1.   Criminal to Civil Judicial Comparison

...Focusing first on the constrained model, EPA was less likely to criminally charge the largest firms ("500") and government bodies than small firms (the excluded violator category).[248] Indeed, the odds of EPA charging an organization criminally decreased by 90% when the organization was a government entity rather than a small firm, holding all other variables constant, while the odds decreased by 68% for the largest firms.[249] EPA also was less likely to criminally charge medium-

---

[243] Complex modeling that involves multiple independent variables—in the present context, those variables such as pollutant toxicity that may help to explain EPA's venue choice—allows one to examine the effect of any given independent variable on the variable of interest, holding all other independent variables constant.

[248] When there are multiple categories that are exclusive (i.e., an organizational entity can be a 500 firm, medium firm, small firm, or government entity, but cannot fall within more than one of those categories), the model requires that one of the categories in the comparison group be excluded. For firm/size type, the excluded category is small firms; for environmental media, CAA; and for the violation severity, VIOLMAJ (major violations). ... These figures can be interpreted by converting the logit (the log of the odds) to the odds. *See infra* note 249.

[249] The logit is the log of the odds of criminal prosecution compared to civil enforcement. The exponential of a coefficient is simply the odds. *See* J. Scott Long, Regression Models for Categorical and Limited Dependent Variables 79–82 (1997). Thus, $e^{-1.146} = .318$. $1 - .318 = .682$ or 68%.

sized firms than small firms...As mentioned previously, the mere fact that small and large firms are treated differently does not necessarily mean that EPA is motivated by political considerations. ...

Next, I combined all firms together into one variable, FIRM, and rerun the model. With this model, EPA remained significantly less likely to pursue government entities than firms criminally. Exactly why EPA treats governments differently than firms is unclear because of the very small number (two) of governments subject to criminal sanctions in the sample. The small number of governments prosecuted criminally suggests that a positive bias in favor of governments may exist or, more realistically, that EPA treats governments differently than firms because they are in fact different (e.g., in the CWA context they are both a regulator and regulatee).

2.   *Criminal to Civil Judicial to Administrative Comparison*

In order to gain additional insight into EPA's behavior, the civil forum was divided into administrative and civil judicial venues and then the choice among the three enforcement fora estimated simultaneously.[252] ...

---

[252] This model, which is comprised of a series of pairwise comparisons (*e.g.*, criminal to civil judicial enforcement), is known as a multinomial logit model. With multinomial models there is a concern that choice between any two categories may not be independent of the other choices. In other words, using the present research as an example, it is important that the comparison between administrative and civil judicial fora remained invariant whether or not the criminal choice existed. I employed the Hausman test of the independence of irrelevant alternatives ("IIA") to test this proposition. Low x^2 values suggest that the multinomial model is appropriate. Although negative x^2 values are possible, the Hausman test does not work with negative values. Using another test method in those instances when x^2 values were negative, Jerry Hausman and Daniel McFadden, *Specification Tests for the Multinomial Logit Model*, 52 Econometrica 1219 (1984), found that in each instance IIA was not violated. In general, the multinomial models performed quite well, the one exception being the constrained model comparison between criminal and civil judicial enforcement.

I also attempted to construct a nested logit model. In the present context, one might assume, for example, that EPA first makes a choice between civil and criminal enforcement and then, assuming it chooses the civil option, makes a choice between administrative and civil judicial enforcement. In other words, one might assume that the choice is nested. Although it is theoretically possible to run a nested logit model when one focuses on individual characteristics (*e.g.*, pollutant discharged) rather than attributes of the choice (*e.g.*, cost of bringing a case in a particular forum), nested logit capability is primarily geared toward the latter. As a result, those models would not converge, and I was left with the multinomial option. However, as mentioned above, the Hausman specification test suggests that the multinomial models performed well. *See id.*

Considering first the constrained model, EPA differentiated little between violator types when deciding whether to enforce administratively or civil judicially. This implies that violator characteristics play little role in EPA's decision to shed the comfort and control of the administrative forum for the more public drama of the judicial forum. On the other hand, consistent with the results from the earlier comparison between criminal and civil enforcement, EPA was significantly less likely to target large- and medium-sized firms and government entities than small firms for criminal as compared to civil judicial enforcement. ...

Environmental Medium-Specific Effects

[I]t is apparent that firms pursued under RCRA or CWA are significantly more likely than those pursued under the CAA to face criminal charges. We can gain additional insight into EPA program-specific enforcement if we disaggregate the data by statute and consider environmental medium-specific effects.

Turning first to descriptive statistical data, a number of environmental medium-specific trends are apparent. First, EPA invoked only one statute in most cases and did not pursue multimedia enforcement in the administrative venue. This does not necessarily mean that the existence of violations across environmental media "caused" EPA to file a matter in a judicial forum. Rather, once EPA decided to proceed in a judicial forum, it may have sought to charge violators with any and all violations.

Second, EPA conducted more than half of its enforcement actions administratively, regardless of environmental medium or violator type/ size. Given that EPA pursued almost all RCRA enforcement actions against organizations administratively (87%) or criminally (8%), with the substantial portion of those cases being administrative, overall RCRA enforcement appears consistent with a violation minimization strategy. In contrast, overall CWA enforcement is relatively balanced while CAA enforcement is substantially skewed toward civil enforcement.

Third, given local government's leading role in the treatment of water pollutants through the ownership and operation of POTWs, not surprisingly, EPA directed a substantial percentage (25%) of its total CWA organizational violator penalty actions against government entities. In contrast, EPA brought less than 2% of similar CAA penalty violations against governments.

Fourth, although small firms were EPA's most prevalent targets under the CAA and CWA, medium firms assumed that role in RCRA enforcement. Fifth, EPA commenced approximately 70% of all CAA and RCRA criminal actions against small firms compared to just less than 60% of all CWA criminal actions. Finally, in the sample selected, EPA did not initiate a single CAA criminal action against a government entity or one of the largest firms. ...

VI. Conclusions

Overall, the evidence presented here is encouraging. In its choice of enforcement venue under the CAA, CWA, and RCRA, EPA appears to be motivated by a desire to minimize environmental harm and maximize social welfare. Conversely, there is little evidence that EPA is motivated by a desire to maximize political benefits. Importantly, EPA's enforcement choice does not implicate socioeconomic-based environmental justice concerns as evidenced by the lack of significance of community per capita income.

To the extent a cautionary note can be sounded with regard to EPA enforcement, that note implicates fairness. The evidence indicates that federal regulators target small firms for criminal prosecution because the detected violations of small firms are more harmful or potentially more harmful than those committed by large firms. However, even after accounting for the harm of the violation, small firms remain more likely than large firms to face criminal sanctions. Indeed, after taking into account the harm of the violation, the probability of a small firm facing a criminal sanction is still twice as great as that of a large firm. This finding suggests that factors other than the desire to minimize environmental harm influence EPA's allocation of resources. ...

Indeed, practical considerations likely play a role in creating this disparity. Such considerations include the greater difficulty of proving a knowing violation against a large firm given the embedded nature of large firm violations as well as the technical and legal resources employed by large firms that in many instances allow large firms to avoid the most patently notorious violations and to stave off indictment when those prophylactic efforts fail.

Enforcement versus Voluntary Compliance: An
Examination of the Strategic Enforcement Initiatives
Implemented by the Pacific and Yukon Regional Office of
Environment Canada, 1983 to 1998

Peter K. Krahn

5TH INECE CONFERENCE PROCEEDINGS, Vol. 1 (1998)

...

2   CASE STUDY #1: THE ANTISAPSTAIN WOOD PRESERVATION INDUSTRY COMPLIANCE PROMOTION AND ENFORCEMENT PROGRAM

British Columbia supplies an estimated 39% of the world's soft wood lumber supply and annual sales often exceeded CDN$4,000,000,000 providing major employment and tax revenues. Prior to 1983, water borne solutions of pentachlorophenol (PCP) and tetrachlorophenol (TTCP) were the primary chemicals used to protect freshly cut lumber from moulds and fungi which attacked the spruce, pine and fir (SPF) species. There were no regulations or codes of practice which defined how the chemicals were to be applied and how the treated lumber was to be stored.

Prior to 1986, approximately 108 mills in British Columbia used to treat wood in this manner. The basic process involved dipping or spraying water borne solutions of up to 1% PCP/TTCP onto green, rough cut lumber. The treated lumber was then moved to exterior storage yards with gravel or paved surfaces which may be up to 80 acres in size. British Columbia coastal rainfall can exceed 1.9 meters annually and it was estimated that over 250 million cubic meters of acutely lethal effluent discharged annually from these facilities into fresh water and marine environments that supported valuable salmon and other fish/shellfish stocks. ...

The Fraser River has a flow rate which ranges from 3,340 to 3,360 cubic meters per second (m³/s). During the winter rainy season, pentachlorophenol could be detected in water samples throughout the lower Fraser River estuary downstream of the Port Mann Bridge Crossing. A scientific assessment confirmed that this was due to a very large discharge of chlorophenols from the Antisapstain Wood Preservation Industry.

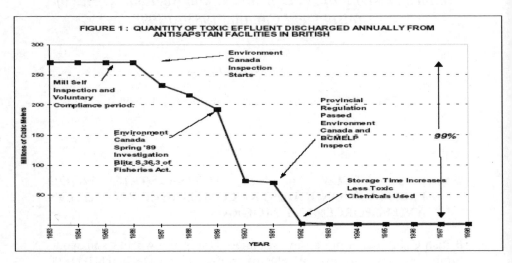

FIGURE 1 : QUANTITY OF TOXIC EFFLUENT DISCHARGED ANNUALLY FROM ANTISAPSTAIN FACILITIES IN BRITISH

From 1983 to 1986, voluntary implementation of code of practice recommendations was the only tool used and mills were permitted to self inspect. During this period there was negligible improvement in operations which reduced toxic discharges.[3,4,5]

From 1986 to 1989, Environment Canada formalized the inspection protocol using specific checklists and onsite visits from inspectors combined with compliance promotion seminars. Training courses were provided to British Columbia Ministry of Environment, Lands and Parks Inspectors and the mills were divided into primarily provincial responsibility and federal responsibility for inspection purposes. The progressive mills implemented proper chemical handling and treatment procedures or constructed facilities necessary to control or prevent releases, however, a significant proportion of the mills did not implement corrective measures. Legal charges were not laid for improper practices during this period.

In the spring of 1989, Environment Canada's enforcement staff embarked on a strategic enforcement initiative and targeted five of the worst known mills for investigation and ultimate prosecution. A significant number of mills improved their operating procedures but there were specific issues which were argued to be too costly. ...

In 1991, Environment Canada, the British Columbia Ministry of Environment, Lands and Parks and the Department of Fisheries and Oceans cooperated to draft a regulation which was enacted by the provincial government to make certain operating practices mandatory. This was followed by a comprehensive inspection and sampling program by Federal and Provincial Inspectors which resulted in the rapid development and use of new antisapstain chemicals which were significantly lower in toxicity. The mills constructed improved lumber treatment facilities including increased covered storage which prevented wash off of chemicals immediately after treatment. The number of mills using these chemicals decreased from 108 to 51. This was achieved by using alternate methods to protect the wood and develop new markets which did not require preservation. By 1993 it was estimated that a 99% reduction in the discharge of acutely toxic effluent was achieved.

This industry group is now undergoing a reevaluation to determine if the practices and preservatives currently in use may be causing significant sub-lethal effects in the receiving environment. If this were determined to occur then a new baseline would be established and regulatory and compliance enforcement initiatives would have to be developed and a new phase 1 program implemented.

3   CASE STUDY #2, THE BRITISH COLUMBIA PULP AND PAPER MILLS, CANADIAN ENVIRONMENTAL PROTECTION ACT, DIOXIN AND FURAN REGULATIONS, COMPLIANCE PROMOTION AND ENFORCEMENT PROGRAM

In 1998/99 there was significant international pressure to eliminate the use of chlorophenols as an anti-sapstain chemical especially by non governmental environmental organizations such as Green Peace. In British Columbia there were several protests at suppliers and sawmills and wood preservation companies which used these products.

Chlorophenols and their associated dioxin and furan contaminants were entering the pulp and paper products as a result of shipment of chlorophenate treated wood shavings and mill ends which were chipped and sent from sawmills to pulp mills as supplemental feed stock.

Pulp mills also formed chlorinated dioxins and furans from petroleum based defoamer products which combined with chlorine added during the pulp bleaching process. As soon as the chlorophenols were on the verge of elimination from the sawmill industry, Green Peace representatives collected samples of sediment and crab from the receiving waters near the Harmac Pulp mill on Vancouver Island which were found to contain chlorinated dioxins and furans. Environment Canada and the Department of Fisheries and Oceans collected numerous samples in areas near sawmills and pulp mills which confirmed the presence of the same chemicals. The contamination resulted in the closure of 1,200 square km of crab and shellfish harvesting areas.[3,14]

The development of the Pulp and Paper Mill Effluent Chlorinated Dioxins and Furans Regulations[15] and the Pulp and Paper Mill Defoamer and Wood Chip Regulations[16] under the Canadian Environmental Protection Act[18] began in 1989 in consultation with stake holders (e.g., environmental groups, the local public, native bands, chemical or equipment suppliers, etc.) and the pulp and paper industry. In this case there was no industrial code of practice development phase as the issue was deemed a significant national priority that required direct regulatory action. An inspection program was developed immediately.

Draft regulations were developed which required an immediate ban on the purchase and use of wood products contaminated with chlorophenols and defoamers contaminated with dioxin and furan precursors. The mills implemented these bans in anticipation of the regulations resulting in an immediate decline in the discharges of the two regulated chemicals, 2,3,7,8 - tetrachloro-dibenzo-para-dioxin (2,3,7,8-TCDD) and 2,3,7,8-tetrachlorodibenzofuran (2,3,7,8-TCDF) as shown in Figure 2.

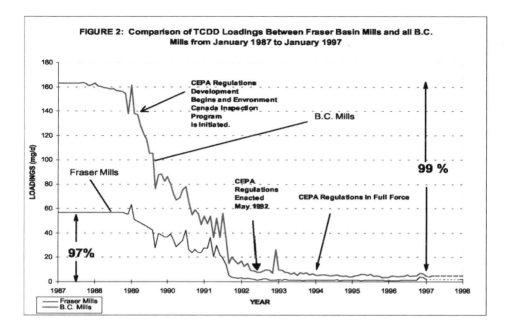

FIGURE 2: Comparison of TCDD Loadings Between Fraser Basin Mills and all B.C. Mills from January 1987 to January 1997

Any mill which was constructed before June 1, 1990 was permitted to apply for an extension to comply with the regulations by January 1, 1994. All British Columbia mills were constructed prior to this date and applied for the extension. Figure 2 shows that all mills were essentially in compliance by the January 1994 deadline. Several excursions over the regulated limits occurred due to technical factors such as re-suspension of previously contaminated sludges in treatment lagoons and hog fuel (tree bark fed to power boilers) which was contaminated by saltwater during transport to mills via log booms.

The frequency of federal Inspections during the pre and post regulation phase averaged a minimum of twice per year or more for mills which were considered high risk. The federal inspection program required a significant diversion of resources away from the antisapstain industry to concentrate on the new pulp and paper program. The inspections were sometimes coordinated with provincial inspectors or conducted as random, unannounced inspections.

These inspections included sampling and testing for biochemical oxygen demand, total suspended solids and acute toxicity which were required under the Fisheries Act, Pulp and Paper Effluents Regulations.[18,19] The same pattern of decline was observed in these three parameters but are not depicted in Figure 2.[3]

4   CASE STUDY #3, DISCHARGES OF ACUTELY LETHAL EFFLUENT FROM HEAVY DUTY WOOD PRESERVATION MILLS IN BRITISH COLUMBIA

In 1983, the production of pressure or thermal treated lumber and poles resulted in similar contamination of storm water runoff as was observed in the anti-sapstain industry. There were an average of 19 to 21 operating mills in British Columbia compared to the 108 in the antisapstain group which used preservatives such as oil borne pentachlorophenol, creosote and water based mixtures of copper, chromium, arsenic and ammonia.

In cooperation with stakeholders and industry associations, Environment Canada developed 5 codes of practice which were not legally binding on the industry. (6,7,8,9,10) In 1987, Environment Canada informed the industry of the results of studies concerning contamination of soils and in particular, storm water runoff. The volume of acutely toxic storm water effluent discharged from six facilities in the Greater Vancouver Area was calculated to exceed 600,000 cubic meters per year[3] (Figure 3).

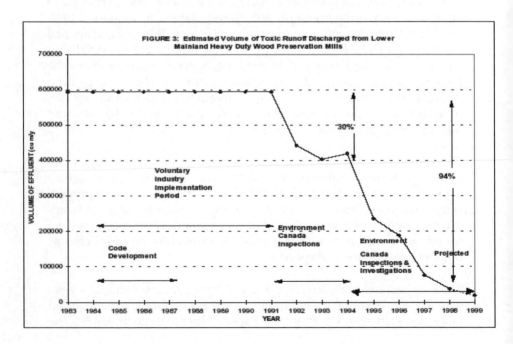

From 1983 to 1991 the industry operated under a voluntary program to implement code of practice recommendations as the enforcement resources of Environment Canada were primarily directed towards the anti-sapstain and subsequently the pulp and paper industry. As these two industries moved towards compliance Environment Canada diverted inspection resources from them and implemented an inspection protocol which resulted in some improvement during the 1991 through 1993 period. In 1991 Environment Canada conducted further scientific research which confirmed that these mills were still discharging significant quantities of acutely toxic effluent and informed each mill by providing copies of the report which identified each facility.[11] Significant operational changes did not occur after the release of this information to the mills.

Under the federal Fraser River Action Plan (FRAP) Environment Canada's Inspection and Investigation divisions initiated an intensive inspection and investigation program which targeted all six Greater Vancouver mills. The program was initiated in February 1994 and continued into 1998. In Figure 3, the points on the curve indicate the reduction in the discharge of acutely lethal effluent which resulted as successive mills implemented physical and operational changes to reach near zero effluent discharges.

The enforcement program was conducted in cooperation with the British Columbia Ministry of Environment, Lands and Parks where Environment Canada conducted all the essential sampling and physical plant inspections. Four of the six mills were issued provincial pollution abatement orders under provincial legislation based on the data collected by Environment Canada. One mill (which was located on land under sole federal jurisdiction) was investigated however the mill managers initiated structural changes and soil cleanup programs in such a rapid manner that charges were not laid.

The surface assets of the sixth mill were sold to an operating company while the original owner retained the contaminated land. Operational practices conducted before and after the sale resulted in charges under the federal Fisheries Act being laid against both companies at the same site. At this site the Fisheries Act is the primary legislative enforcement tool for contaminated surface runoff and contaminated groundwater which may discharge into surface waters. The provincial legislation is used as the primary enforcement tool to control the movement of liquid contaminants and contaminated groundwater across property boundaries and cleanup of surface soils.

A 34% to 85% reduction in the quantities of environmentally harmful substances in Fraser River sediments adjacent to the five mills where investigations were initiated has recently been verified by follow up inspections.

5 EVALUATION OF THE THREE CASE STUDIES

The data from Figures 1, 2 and 3 were normalized by calculating the ratio of the quantity of pollutant discharged at any time divided by the quantity prior to the enforcement initiatives and converting to a percentage value. The three curves were then replotted in figure 4.

Figure 4: Normalized Graphs of Three British Columbia Forest Sector Industries Response to Environmental Law Enforcement Programs

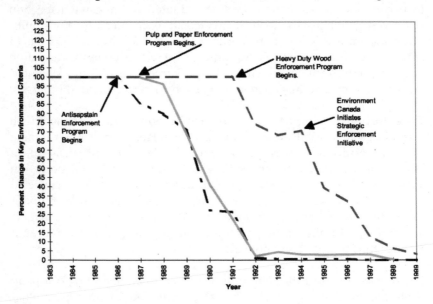

Figure 4 shows that the period of voluntary compliance resulted in negligible or unsatisfactory changes in the quantity of pollutants discharged in the Antisapstain Industry until the stronger inspection and investigation initiatives were implemented. This is followed by the decline in discharges from the pulp and paper industry as enforcement resources were diverted to deal with the dioxin, furan, BOD, TSS and toxicity issues.

As long as stronger enforcement resources were diverted to the anti-sapstain and pulp and paper industries the voluntary compliance and limited inspection activity in the Heavy Duty Wood Preservation industry resulted in negligible changes in the discharge of acutely toxic effluent. In 1991 inspection resources were diverted to the Heavy Duty Wood Preservation sector and minor improvements were observed but reached a plateau in 1992. In 1994, as soon as the strategic enforcement initiative was implemented and the mills were served with federal charges or provincial pollution abatement orders the discharge of pollutants declined dramatically.

These observations support the data reported in the 1996 Canadian Environmental Management Survey conducted independently by the KPMG Environmental Risk Management Practice (A division of KPMG Chartered Accountants).[12] The KPMG study surveyed 1000 of the largest companies in Canada as ranked by the Financial Post, and 400 companies from the Canadian Corporate Disclosure data base (sales under $28,000,000), as well as hospitals, municipalities, universities and school boards across Canada.

The 27% response rate was tabulated and determined that the overall ranking of top factors influencing organizations to take action on environmental issues remained unchanged in 1995.

The most influential factors for organizations to take action on environmental issues were:
- Compliance with regulations   > 90%
- Board of Director Liability   >70%
- Employees   >60%

The Least influential factors were:
- Voluntary programs   15% to 20%
- Interest groups   10% to 12%
- Trade considerations   <10%

This explains the rapid change in the British Columbia industries performance when corporate directors were faced with warning letters, pollution abatement orders and federal prosecutions. ...

References

1. British Columbia, Council of Forest Industries Report, Part 3 - Mitigative Options Report by Industry. (1988)

2. December 1996 report, "Subcommittee on Antisapstain Chemical Waste Control Regulation Amendments of the British Columbia Stakeholder Forum on Sapstain Control.

3. Environment Canada, Pacific and Yukon Region, " 1996 Annual Compliance Status Reports, Green Lane Internet Site, http://www.pwc.bc.doe.ca/ep/program/eppy/ enforce/index.html

4. Krahn, Peter K. , Glue, Richard D "An Assessment (1987) of Wood Protection (Anti-Sapstain) Facilities in the British Columbia Lower Mainland Area.", Environment Canada Regional Program Report 87-20.

5. Krahn, Peter K. "Assessment of Storm Water Related Chlorophenol Releases From Wood Protection Facilities in British Columbia, Environment Canada Regional Program Report 87-14.

6. Creosote Wood Preservation Facilities, Recommendations for Design and Operation, Report EPS 2/WP/1, April 1988.

7. Pentachlorophenol (PCP) Wood Preservation Facilities, Recommendations for Design and Operation, Report EPS 2/WP/2, April 1988.

9. Ammoniacal Copper Arsenate (ACA) Wood Preservation Facilities, Recommendations for Design and Operation, Report EPS 2/WP/3, April 1988.

10. Chromated Copper Arsenate (CCA) Wood Preservation Facilities, Recommendations for Design and Operation, Report EPS 2/WP/4, April 1988.

11. Krahn, Peter K. "Assessment of Storm Water Related Chlorophenol Releases From Wood Protection Facilities in British Columbia, Environment Canada Regional Program Report 87-15

12. KPMG Chartered Accountants, "The 1996 KPMG Canadian Environmental Management Survey", KPMG Environmental Risk Management Practice.

13. Environment Canada, National Office of Pollution Prevention and Canadian Institute of Treated Wood, "Recommendations for the Design and Operation of Wood Preservation Facilities, June 1997

14. Dept. of Fisheries and Oceans, News Release.

15. Dept. of Environment, "Pulp and Paper Mill Effluent Chlorinated Dioxins and Furans Regulations", SOR/92-267, 7 May, 1992

16. Dept. of Environment, "Pulp and Paper Mill Defoamer and Wood Regulations", SOR/ 92-267, 7 May, 1992

17. Dept. of Fisheries and Oceans, "Pulp and Paper Mill Effluent Regulations, Fisheries Act," SOR/92-269M, 7 May, 1992

18. Department of Environment, "Canadian Environmental Protection Act", June 1988.

19. Department of Fisheries and Oceans, " Fisheries Act", R.S.C., 1985, C. F-14.

20. Department of Environment, "Migratory Birds Convention Act, 1994." 1994,c.22

Choosing Environmental Policy Instruments in the Real World

Ruth Greenspan Bell

Presented at OECD Global Forum on Sustainable Development:
Emissions Trading, Concerted Action on Tradeable Emissions Permits
Country Forum, March 17-18, 2003.

1.   INTRODUCTION

...

The choice of environmental policy instruments should value efficiency
as much as possible, but the policy choices must also be politically
acceptable to a wide range of stakeholders, and must be supportable by
existing institutions, notably the legal system, human capital and
infrastructure, and by the dominant culture, traditions and habits of each
country. Choices about the tools and goals must reflect domestic resolve,
will and readiness to perform, since environmental protection requires
so much of so many actors in society.[3] It is therefore understandably rare
in any of the developed economies that any one group of experts or
stakeholders would have such a predominant role as do the economists
in policy setting in the developing world.

As a consequence, the countries most in trouble are not getting a well-
rounded picture about what is achievable. What the Consensus does not
say is that the institutions, infrastructure, and human capital needed to
support the sophisticated environmental instruments the West promotes
are not present in much of the developing world. The other missing truth

---

[3] One obvious example is the effort to control non-point pollution. The very nature of
non-point is that it is generated, and therefore controlled at uncountable locations, and
requires widespread cooperation and willingness to act.

is that the experience with the most highly sophisticated instruments is not very extensive even in the mature environmental regimes – indeed, some instruments popular with advisors are still more theoretical than applied. This presents little reason to hope that they will be easy to apply in the more difficult contexts of the developing world and countries in transition. ...

This paper sets out a brief history of the development of market-based instruments and their dissemination. It then discusses some of the practical and institutional reasons why they are very difficult to genuinely apply – as opposed to plan – in the countries in economic and political transition. ...

4.   LESSONS FROM THE COUNTRIES IN TRANSITION

There was much effort through the 1990s in places like Kazakhstan, Poland, the Czech Republic, the Slovak Republic, and other transitional countries to jump directly to market-based instruments, especially emissions trading. These are often held up as examples of the success of market-based instruments (MBIs). In fact, these were largely planning efforts, or confined to models, demonstrations, or pilots. The Slovak Republic wrote a law, but it is not clear whether that law will meet the same fate as many of the environmental laws written in the 1990s throughout the countries in transition, that sit on the books unimplemented. In fact, none of these plans or pilots have gone beyond the experimental, because the prescriptions simply did not fit the conditions for which they were suggested. The intuition that these countries were stronger candidates than developing countries overlooked the fact that they lacked the important institutions and skills that serve as cornerstones of sophisticated market-based instruments for environmental control.

Perhaps the most important of these was motivation. Although it does not seem to have been articulated in the literature, there must have been two assumptions among the advisors: one, that enterprises were motivated to be efficient; and two, because of this motivation, that firms would be natural allies in support of the most efficient environmental tools. But industry in the U.S. did not become advocates for emissions trading on the basis of theory; if that had been the case, perhaps the laws would have included this tool at an earlier stage. They (or some) did so after they had been forced to grapple with actual environmental regulation and genuine enforcement (even now, some resist). Then, the price tag for meeting environmental requirements was made clear in a way that theory can never teach. Economic pain is a great motivator. Importantly, industry in the western economies was able to understand and analyse its economic pain because it was the beneficiary of a century of experience with cost accounting. ...

But even had there been genuine motivation, there are still other important issues to take into account. A key consideration is whether institutions exist to manage failure. People who trade emissions, exchange an exceedingly complex and intangible property right. They are selling rights to air, and not only that, often rights that extend into the future.[8] These are extremely sophisticated market concepts. Sellers default; buyers go into bankruptcy; participants fall victim to the temptation of false accounting, as did the U.S. firms Enron and WorldCom in a different context. When real money is at stake, some authority, administrative body, or court must be available to police trades and ensure their integrity.

Donor advice on emissions trading rarely mentions the possibility that transactions might fail. Indeed, the same advice was peddled in countries with working legal systems and those without such institutions. Some of the transitional countries recently have begun to restore a European legal system, free of "political and economic safety valves – the legal means of last resort by which Party and state authorities could avoid their own rules," in the words of Daniel Cole (Cole, 1998). To the east, in Russia and the other parts of the Former Soviet Union, there was no rule-of-law tradition to revive.

There must also be basic trust within society that trading regimes are administered in a fair manner and that allowances represent real commitments to reduce emissions. Particularly since air is such an ephemeral commodity, these are transactions that can easily be abused. The possibility of abuse becomes clearer when you consider that emission trading can result in very different environmental standards for similar industries. If the system works, plant A will pay plant B to reduce its emissions, instead of doing so itself. The potential bottom line is a series of varied requirements that hopefully refer back to the trading transaction. But what if Plant A is owned by the most influential politician in the country, in a culture accustomed to helping out privileged people. It is easy to obscure the fact that the grant of discretion to Plant A to pollute

---

[8] One interesting test of a country's capacity for environmental MBIs could be whether it is running successful financial markets; money is a familiar and relatively simple concept, compared with emissions permits.

less is not based on a legitimate trade, and the outcome benefits the owner of the plant, not the environment. Nordhaus has pointed this problem out in the context of global CO_2 emissions trading:

> An emissions-trading system creates a scarcity where none previously existed and in essence prints money for those in control of the permits. Such wealth creation is potentially dangerous because the value of the permits can be used for non-environmental purposes by the country's leadership rather than to reduce emissions. It would probably become common practice for dictators and corrupt administrators to sell parts of their permits, pocket the proceeds, and enjoy wine, partners and song along the Riviera. [To illustrate the perils,] [a] Russian scientist recently reported the people in Moscow were already considering how to profit from the 'privatization' of the Russian carbon emissions permits. Alternatively... [I]f Nigeria could sell its allowances... [they] could easily sell for between $0.2 and $2 billion each year of hard currency. This in a country whose non-oil exports in 1999 were around $600 million (Nordhaus, 2002).

...

The final area of serious weakness in the support structure for emissions trading in the former Soviet bloc is monitoring—knowing which pollutants, and in what amounts, are released into the environment by particular plants. Although one can argue about the degree of precision that is necessary, it is beyond dispute that regulators and the public must be assured that real, not imaginary, pollution reductions are being traded. Counting through monitoring can be costly. It requires good equipment, but also a level of integrity (it is as easy to turn off monitoring equipment at inconvenient times as it is to turn off pollution control equipment). It also requires that the monitoring be of plant-specific emissions, not of ambient conditions, as is common in many countries.

These are the factors that have prevented the experiments in market-based instruments from developing into full-fledged programs for controlling environmental pollution. Although there has been much trumpeting of the efforts, there has been far less written about actual outcomes, and a seeming reluctance to admit the importance of these issues, except to vaguely caution that market-based instruments are effective if implemented properly and under the right conditions. Most important, little of the literature acknowledges that those conditions are rare outside the Western democracies.

5.   WHAT ABOUT THE DEVELOPING WORLD?

If transparency, accurate monitoring, a working legal system, and realistic incentives to trade are scarce in transitioning economies, the problems run much deeper in the developing world. There are fewer people with the necessary skills and experience to implement these sophisticated programs, the available talent is generally concentrated in capitals rather than field posts, monitoring equipment is in short supply, even baseline data is unreliable, and informal and even institutionalised corruption is rampant.

Despite this, a few advisors have compounded the confusion by holding out the tantalising, but unsupported, hope that adoption of economic instruments might even eliminate the need for regulatory bodies and enforcement programs.[11] Another claim that is totally at odds with empirical evidence from the United States is that economic instruments as a group substitute for efforts to enforce compliance and "tend to have lower institutional and human resource requirements than command and control regulations" (Panayotou, 1994). Perhaps this is true in an ideal world or a model, but the assertion cannot be backed up with experience, particularly in the gritty conditions in the developing world and the countries in transition. ...

We have also pointed out how misleading the arguments are for using taxes or levies to achieve environmental protection goals. It is far from easy to collect this revenue in a reliable way. Efforts to collect sales and income taxes in most of the countries in which these ideas are proposed already encounter the difficulty of monitoring sales or wages, and corruption. Taxes on pollution raise the same collection concerns, and additional ones also, as they are highly dependent on good environmental monitoring. Pollution discharges generally must be measured by special equipment as they occur, and monitoring capability does not exist in much of the developing world.

---

[11] Theodore Panayotou of Harvard University has argued that economic instruments take full advantage of the selfinterest and superior information of producers and consumers without requiring the disclosure of such information or creating large and costly bureaucracies. *See, e.g.*, Panayotou (1994).

The more fundamental question is whether or not the governments of the developing world have the political will to impose and actually collect charges significant enough to force industry to seek new technology. After all, many of these governments have insulated certain firms from market pressures by the equivalent of soft budget constraints. In other places, firms are accustomed to benefiting from loans made on the basis of connections and favouritism, rather than sound business principles and sober assessment of credit. Using the market to spur technological change is only plausible if the many ways in which market forces are undermined can be ruled out.[12]

In the final analysis, market-based instruments do offer some highly desirable features when appropriate conditions exist. To make them work, however, requires data gathering, mathematical modelling, and monitoring or auditing of emissions, skills and understanding in both government and industry, and considerable political will —a tall order in the small, understaffed, and under-funded environmental ministries of much of the world. This hardly makes MBIs the free lunch they are made out to be.

5.1   The case of China

A number of donors and advisors have focused on China as a place to introduce emissions trading. Their logic echoes the arguments previously heard in both the countries in transition and the developing world. China is developing a market economy, and it presents all the dilemmas of the developing world that create a compelling rationale in favour of the maximum efficiency for environmental regulation. It is not a country that can afford wasted effort and it is confronted with significant environmental health problems. Human exposures to harmful pollutants are so severe and unrestrained in some cities that western governments

---

[12] Financial Times, New York Times and other newspapers have reported repeatedly on lax banking practices in China. *See, e.g.,* New York Times, February 1, 2002, "Bank of China's Mounting Problems," reported by Elisabeth Rosenthal: China's most prominent state bank, the Bank of China, was hit first by a report from China's National Audit Office, which found that $320 million of bank funds had been diverted from several branches of the bank through "unlawful loans, off-the-books business and the unlawful granting of letters of credit and issuing bank bills," and then by a lawsuit between the Bank and former clients in New York. American bank regulators said an investigation begun in 1999 had turned up the same kinds of irregularities at Bank of China's United States operations during the 1990s. Eventually this led to the dismissal of one of China's most influential bankers.

are conducting epidemiological studies in China that cannot be conducted elsewhere.

5.2 SO$_2$ emissions trading and conditions in Taiyuan

Typically, China pilots or tests new ideas for environmental control before they are adopted for nationwide use. China's environmental agency, SEPA, has made the development and piloting of SO$_2$ emissions trading programs a priority, building on on-going efforts of a number of prominent Chinese environmental experts. ...

5.3 Taiyuan conditions/Chinese standards

Taiyuan, with a population of 2.7 million, is a heavily polluted industrial city in the coal belt of northern China about 500 kilometres southwest of Beijing. With mountains on three sides, Taiyuan traps air pollutants much in the way that smog is contained in Los Angeles. Particulate matter (PM) and sulphur dioxide (SO$_2$) represent a serious public health threat. SO$_2$ concentrations averaged 200 ug/m3 in 2000 (a representative year), more than three times China's Class II annual standard (60 ug/m3). Some data indicates that SO$_2$ emissions have been relatively flat despite economic growth.

Current pollution policy sets standards for stack gas concentration of SO$_2$. As there is currently no reliable monitoring, pollutant concentrations are based on self-reported data from the enterprises and periodic stack testing by the local Environmental Protection Bureaus (EPBs). These estimated concentrations are combined with limited data on pollutant flows to calculate mass emissions from the enterprises, which form the basis of a small emissions levy ($25/ton), whose proceeds support the local EPB's activities with the balance returned to individual enterprises to finance their pollution control investments.

China has worked for a decade to develop a new, more sophisticated mass-based system –the so-called "Total Emissions Control" (TEC)– as a supplement to the existing stack-gas concentration standards, "but has only recently achieved the capacity to implement *pilot* mechanisms reflecting the concept" (Smith, 2003 - emphasis added). The TEC system is similar in many ways to individual facility-level caps on SO$_2$ emissions imposed under Title IV of the U.S. Clean Air Act (1990).

Consistent with the policy of "experiments," the Taiyuan city government began experimenting with emissions permits and earlier pilot versions of the TEC in the 1980s, including a 1985 local regulation. The city conducted experiments with emissions offsets and (administratively-determined) trading in the mid 1990s. In 1998, the Taiyuan city government issued "management rules" for TEC, including a provision for "permit exchange," a form of emissions permit trading. The Taiyuan EPB has issued about three dozen updated permits with TEC-based limits to large enterprises.

5.4   Institutional issues

Conceptually, market-based controls for environmental purposes are attractive to Chinese policymakers because the idea fits the general thrust of Chinese economic policy – the push toward a market economy "with Chinese characteristics." But there is still a disconnect between policy and on-the-ground conditions. Much of industry continues to be owned in whole or in part by some part of government, an inherent conflict of interest that bedevilled other socialist economies. In similar economies, the environmental regulators' lack of independence significantly impacted their ability to enforce environmental requirements, particularly when environmental requirements collided with other government goals such as production targets or full employment.

Other institutional challenges are also very similar to those found in the countries formerly dominated by the Soviet Union. Despite the interest expressed in Chinese environmental policy circles for using market-based instruments, there is still a considerable learning curve to be overcome by officials and also by industrial managers. Chinese officials do not appear to understand the connection between environmental enforcement and the prospects for a robust trading program. Indeed, most observers agree that, "despite China's rapidly evolving and complex network of environmental policies and laws, compliance with environmental regulations remains low" (Karasov, 2000).

There is little if any experience in the details of complex markets to trade intangible commodities. As noted above, trades to date in other parts of China have been administratively determined, which fits the comfort level of the Chinese. Many in Taiyuan wanted to do the same. In addition, Chinese officials sometimes appear to have the impression that trading is a costless way of achieving environment reductions; there has been less emphasis than I think warranted on the plain fact that in a trading system, someone, somewhere, must engage in concrete emission reduction practices, which are likely to be costly. In sum, the institutional factors would argue against the success in China of market-based instruments, and particularly of emissions trading. ...

5.6   What lessons can be learned from the Taiyuan experiment?

Genuine progress toward environmental reductions using any tools, including market-based instruments and emissions trading schemes, is in my view, hampered by the unrealistic way in which pollution reduction goals are set in China. This, and lack of serious efforts to pursue compliance and apply the pain of enforcement removes the incentive industry might have to participate in schemes to reduce the cost of environmental compliance and reduces the seriousness with which industry might consider supporting such plans. Finally, the specific regulation passed in Taiyuan to support emissions trading has serious deficiencies, in addition to questions that can be raised about what the meaning of laws is in China.

A)   Overly ambitious pollution reduction goals accompanied by a history of retreat would challenge the effectiveness of any environmental tool

The Tenth Five-Year Plan for Taiyuan calls for 2005 SO_2 emissions to be reduced by about 50 percent below 2000 levels, a goal widely seen as extremely ambitious....[15]

Unsurprisingly, even when goals are firm, experience indicates that industry needs adequate time to plan environmental investments. The extended period in which goals are set in the U.S. and then built into plant-specific permits is one way in which industry is put on notice of its ultimate responsibilities and has time to engage in the planning, financing, and specific activities (to identify, purchase and install technology, for example, or make in-plant process changes) necessary to come into compliance. These decisions and activities include whether to install technology, or make other adjustments to reduce emissions or to purchase allowances. Our experience indicates that even after industry is able to identify appropriate technology, for example, the identified

---

[15] It appears that previous goals were equally ambitious, for example calling on China to hold total pollutant emissions to the 1985 level by 2000, and bringing them even lower in the designated "key" pollution control areas. ...

technology isn't always immediately available. Similarly, financial analysis is necessary in order to determine whether to purchase allowances and at what price. It is certainly appropriate to make adjustments or to update allocations every five years, but sources need enough certainty to properly plan investments.

Moreover, experience in the United States suggests that if industry senses that goals will be eased, some will wait until the last minute to undertake their own responsibilities, on the chance that they won't have to make the environmental investment. Goals and targets that consistently overreach are likely destined to be modified as reality sets in or at the stage when industry does have some form of access to the decision process. This in turn encourages industry to wait out the goal setters (the situation may be even worse when the goal setters, the enforcers, and the owners of industry can all be traced back to the same source, the government; then, decisions are made in inner councils that sort out which value or demand will take precedence).

If China is interested in real emissions reductions, it could build explicit consultation with industry and environmental regulators, enforcers, and the public into the process during the time the goals and targets are being set, and make the entire process more transparent and publicly accessible. Emission reduction goals appropriately represent a combination of both political and technical targets. But the relatively closed process suggests China is weighted toward appearance, not reality, much like the "show laws" of the former Soviet Union. A more transparent process would increase the amount of knowledge and data available to the planners, and begin the process of setting targets that are ambitious but achievable. On the one hand, a more inclusive process might increase the planners understanding of what is truly feasible, what technology is available, what the costs might be of compliance, and other factors that affect the likelihood of achieving genuine reductions. On the other hand, the greater the isolation of the planner from critical information and data, the more likely it is that targets will be set that cannot be met.[16]

B) Poor history of environmental enforcement

...

Whatever tools are used, enterprises must receive a steady, reliable message that the environmental requirements are serious and require

---

[16] This reasoning assumes that China can and will work out the conflicts of interest between industrial and governmental goals.

continuous efforts on the part of all involved toward meeting the regulatory goals. If it is known that the environmental regulator has only weak tools (or motivation) for catching violators, the probability of getting caught appears to be low, reducing substantially the chances of the program being a success. But it would also help if enforcers were independent enough to enforce the rules without fearing that they might arouse powerful interests and endanger their own wages and social benefits.

Finally, as noted above, experience in the western democracies indicates that enforcement is more likely to succeed if sources know what their real and actual targets are. The impact of a process in which allocations are not known until the early part of the five year period, and might be modified during that period, may be to discourage enterprise compliance; enterprises may be more likely to take a "wait and see" attitude, than to invest for pollution control. Allocations can be updated every five years, but a process that appears to move both directions —setting goals but then moving away from them— sends the wrong signals. ...

In summary, my own view is that the Taiyuan project provides no evidence about the ultimate success of market-based instruments in China or any other developing world context. If anything, because there is no independent enforcement, the rules are so riddled with practical exceptions, monitoring is so weak and the basic incentives lacking, the Chinese situation is much more like the countries in transition before 1989, than after, in that China lacks basic institutional prerequisites and domestic motivation that might make effective emissions trading possible.

6.   HOW CAN GENUINE ENVIRONMENTAL PROGRESS BE STIMULATED IN THE DEVELOPING WORLD?

Being realistic about the challenges to be faced in the countries in transition and the developing world does not mean abandoning hope for environmental improvement. A concerted but realistic effort to support these countries as they tackle their environmental challenges is necessary, if for no other reason than the cliché that pollution respects no borders, but more to the point, because many face the health consequences of heavily polluted air and water.

I would start with the question: is it realistic to expect that countries only beginning the process of environmental protection can start with the most difficult environmental instruments? As I strongly believe the evidence shows the answer to this question to be "no," then the next question is, what can be done? Institutional inadequacies such as low functioning legal systems, historical experience (or inexperience) with markets, distorting and often institutionalised corruption, and public acceptance certainly can be fixed, and it is important to start to do so. But changing these fundamentals will take a long time. What can be done in the meantime?

Russell and I have suggested … that the donors and advisors start instead by thinking small, and considering alternative approaches. One way is to encourage, rather than disparage, incremental improvements and pragmatic goals, even if they are not the most efficient approaches. Countries might consider a transitional or tiered approach that will take into account existing capabilities and institutions, and explicitly acknowledge that a long learning curve lies ahead with inevitably uneven implementation and slippage from time to time.

A concrete way to think about this would be a tiered approach. Countries with a low level of institutional capability and environmental protection experience might start with simple discharge-control technology requirements, which are hard enough when experience and funding is lacking. Tools would be selected by asking what is achievable and relatively easy to monitor. Ideally, success will breed regulatory confidence and more success.

Countries with a bit of experience under their belts could move to technology-based discharge limitations similar to those found in the U.S. Clean Water Act. They might establish discharge standards, such as plume opacity, which can be easily monitored, or put in place deposit-refund systems, not only for beverage containers but also for car batteries, tires, and dry cleaning fluid. Only the highest functioning countries should attempt the most difficult of the economic instruments: making discharge permits tradable or charging per unit of pollution discharged.

Another approach would be to find examples of small, admittedly imperfect, efforts that seem to be working, find out why they are achieving some measure of environmental progress, and build on them. There are a number of interesting such examples. These could include China's apparent success with energy efficiency and the Kitakyushu,

Japan effort to control air pollution that started when housewives noticed that newly washed clothes on the Kitakyushu clotheslines were instantly turning black.

Air quality in Delhi, India, a city that was incurring an annual health cost of ambient air pollution on the order of about U.S.$200 million, is another example. RFF is about to undertake a study of this, to see what lessons might be more broadly applicable. A 1998 Indian Supreme Court order required Delhi's public vehicles (buses, taxis, and three-wheelers) to convert from diesel to compressed natural gas (CNG) fuel, and public vehicles more than eight years old to be retired. The public interest environmental organisations were happy with the Court's ruling, but the Court was demanding costly and inconvenient changes, particularly for some parts of Indian society without great resources. The Court's decision was opposed by bus, taxi, and three-wheeler operators and by numerous special interests, including diesel fuel dealers, companies that own and operate diesel busses, parts of the government such as the Ministry of Petroleum and Natural Gas and the Delhi Administration, and competing users of CNG. Lines of three-wheelers waiting for CNG fill-ups sometimes stretched for kilometres, forcing the drivers to spend hours away from their livelihood and families. Various attempts were made to systematically discredit CNG technology and others argued that the Court's solution was not cost effective. These dynamics explain why the apparent result, the current phase out of diesel and increasing reliance on CNG, was not necessarily predictable or expected. In view of this, how was it that the phase-out took place, and what might this experience teach future environmental regulators, both in India and elsewhere?

The most important thing the donors and advisors can do is to encourage the development of credible behavioural rules, mechanisms for verifying and encouraging compliance, and a culture in which compliance is the first choice of action rather than the last.

7.   CONCLUSION

Institutional capacity should not be an eternal barrier. Regulatory capacity and confidence can be developed in a number of ways. In my view, the effort to promote market-based instruments has been a distraction from the urgent task of developing appropriate actions with a likelihood of success, that would in turn, build the requisite institutional confidence.

The suggestion (connected with development assistance dollars) that market instruments should be the first goal, sets the standard for success too high and may have created a crisis of confidence. The developing countries are not environmental laboratories; they are real places with severe problems and limited resources. They are not the right places to insert theories that have only been tested in models and in the minds of the people who thought of them, where confounding facts and poor conditions can be assumed away.

Environmental protection is a gritty and difficult business. Theory has much to offer, but in the end, local traditions, culture, institutions, and infrastructure will determine the success of any policy. Policy selection should not be a function of fads or ideology. Like good doctors, the Environmental Consensus should examine the patient before, not after, it prescribes the cure.

If credibility and success are built incrementally, institutions, like people, have the opportunity to practice and to learn from both their successes and their mistakes. Environmental policy is a particularly good practice ground because clean air and clean water is something most societies want; in many places, it will be possible to find the requisite public support for undertaking reasonable steps.

Taking more measured steps does not have the same sense of adventure as a great environmental leap forward. But it will result in real, although initially small, environmental gains, and could be accomplished without losing sight of the ultimate goal, which is to reach the goals of environmental quality at least cost to society.

Introduction

This chapter introduces a selection of the best literature on environmental compliance and enforcement indicators. During the past decade, there has been a growing interest in measuring the results of environmental compliance and enforcement activities, both to help reduce illegal activities and to improve the ultimate state of the environment.[1] At the same time, policy makers and the general public increasingly are holding compliance program managers accountable for the efficient use of their resources. All of these players benefit from indicators.

Efforts to build better compliance systems must be based on a solid empirical foundation. Indicators are a method of displaying information about complex phenomena in a logical and concise manner that can be readily understood and communicated to decision-makers and other intended audiences. In the environmental context, indicators have been used to measure the status of air and water quality, waste management, and land use.[2] Indicators are an important part of a pragmatic, empirically-grounded approach to environmental management based on the collection of hard data on actual consequences of decisions that then can inform subsequent rounds of decision-making "in a continuous information feedback loop that enables dynamic readjustment of policy and practice."[3]

---

[1] Durwood Zaelke & Thomas Higdon, *Strengthening Environmental Enforcement and Compliance: The International Network for Environmental Compliance and Enforcement*, 6th INECE Conference Proceedings Vol. 1 (2002), *available at* http://www.inece.org. *See also* Malcolm K. Sparrow, Imposing Duties: Government's Changing Approach to Compliance, xv-xvi, 145-50 (1994).

[2] *See* OECD, *OECD Environmental Indicators: Development, Measurement, and Use* (2003), *available at* http://www.oecd.org/dataoecd/7/47/24993546.pdf. This paper describes OECD's approach and framework for developing, measuring, and using environmental indicators.

[3] Bradley C. Karkkainen, *Toward a Smarter NEPA: Monitoring and Managing Government's Environmental Performance*, 102 Colum. L. Rev. 903, 907-08 (2002) (citing John Dewey, Logic:

continued

Despite repeated calls from the international community for their development,[4] there is no comprehensive set of indicators of law and policy responses to environmental problems, and in particular those related to compliance and enforcement.

In response to this demand, INECE launched a project at the 2002 World Summit on Sustainable Development to create a framework for developing indicators to measure the effects of compliance and enforcement activities on the quality of the environment.[5] These indicators will help agencies, as well as parliaments and the public, understand which activities or combination of activities are most effective.

Through the INECE Environmental Compliance and Enforcement (ECE) Indicators Project, an expert team of practitioners from around the world is collaborating to develop a scalable framework to guide the development of ECE indicator programs at the country level.[6] Initial steps for the Project have included assessing how countries are using "input," "output," and "intermediate outcome" indicators to manage environmental enforcement programs.[7] The Expert Working Group plans to expand the scope of the Project to include additional indicators for compliance assistance activities as well.

THE THEORY OF INQUIRY 39-40 (1938) and John Dewey, *Logical Method and Law*, 10 CORNELL L.Q., 17 (1924)). *See also* Daniel C. Esty, *Environmental Protection in the Information Age*, 79 N.Y.U. L. REV., 115 (2004).

[4] *See* Agenda 21 Chapter 8 and 40. For example, Chapter 8.6 states that "[c]ountries could develop systems for monitoring and evaluation of progress towards achieving sustainable development by adopting indicators that measure changes across economic, social and environmental dimensions."

[5] *Measuring Enforcement to Promote Sustainable Development*, 6ᵀᴴ INECE NEWSLETTER (2002), *available at* http://www.inece.org/Newsletter6.pdf.

[6] *Performance Measurement Guidance for Compliance and Enforcement Practitioners*, 7ᵗʰ INECE Conference Proceedings (forthcoming 2005).

[7] "Input indicators" (e.g., number of inspectors) show the amount of resources used to carry out activities; "output indicators" (e.g., the number of inspections) show the extent of activities carried out; and "intermediate outcome indicators" (e.g., pounds of pollutant reduced) measure progress towards achieving final outcomes. "Final outcome indicators" (e.g., improvements in water quality), which measure the real impacts of compliance promotion and enforcement actions on the state of the environment, are difficult to implement because of the number of factors affecting environmental quality. *See* Kenneth. J. Markowitz *et al.*, *Improving Environmental Compliance and Enforcement Through Performance Measurement: The INECE Indicators Project*, 4(1) SUSTAINABLE DEV. LAW & POL'Y 17(2004).

Based on this framework, INECE is collaborating with several countries to develop indicator programs to monitor and report on their enforcement and compliance promotion activities.[8] Most of these programs are starting with output indicators, which measure government activities, work products, or actions, such as the number of enforcement cases settled per year.[9] In Costa Rica, for example, the Ministry of the Environment, in conjunction with INECE, has begun designing a pilot project to measure enforcement of laws protecting Costa Rica's forests. The indicators will aid the Ministry in determining the appropriate mix of information resources, personnel, and enforcement and compliance strategies to combat illegal logging in that country.

In more advanced ECE indicator programs, such as those of the United States, Canada, and the Netherlands, practitioners may also use an intermediate outcome indicator—for example, the actual pounds of pollutant reduced as a result of compliance and enforcement activities— to measure their progress towards achieving a change in behavior or knowledge. It is anticipated that most of these programs eventually will also develop the final outcome indicators that measure the results or impacts of compliance promotion and enforcement actions on the state of the environment; that is, they will measure improvement to water quality, or air quality, and so on.[10]

ECE indicators also can be used to demonstrate how environmental compliance brings countries closer to achieving the Millennium Development Goals and other sustainable development objectives.[11] To this end, INECE is collaborating with the United Nations Environment Programme (UNEP) and the Organisation for Economic Co-operation

---

[8] These countries include Argentina, Belarus, Brazil, Chile, Costa Rica, Czech Republic, Mexico, Russia, and Thailand. For case studies on the countries currently developing environmental enforcement indicators programs, *see* INECE and OECD, *Measuring What Matters: Proceedings from the INECE-OECD Workshop on Environmental Compliance and Enforcement Indicators* (2003), *available at* http://www.inece.org/indicators/workshop.html.

[9] INECE Expert Working Group on Environmental Compliance and Enforcement Indicators, *INECE-OECD Workshop on Environmental Compliance and Enforcement Indicators: Measuring What Matters*, October 22, 2003, *available at* http://www.inece.org/IndBackPaper.pdf.

[10] Frank Barrett & Dave Pascoe, *Environmental Compliance and Enforcement Indicators: Environment Canada Pilot Projects – Addressing Challenges*, INECE-OECD Workshop on Environmental Compliance and Enforcement Indicators: Measuring What Matters, November 3-4, 2003, *available at* http://www.inece.org/indicators/2-WhatMatters(Barrett).pdf.

and Development (OECD) to develop ECE indicators for the international context. INECE and UNEP are working together in select countries to use indicators to measure successful compliance strategies for multilateral environmental agreements (MEAs). They also will work with stakeholders within each country to coordinate successful implementation strategies for thematically-similar MEAs. INECE is working with OECD to develop a strategy to integrate ECE indicators into OECD's country performance reviews.

The articles in this chapter discuss the various uses of ECE indicators, provide sectoral and country-specific examples of their use, and describe INECE's framework for identifying, designing, and using indicators.

In the first article, Kenneth Markowitz, Krzysztof Michalak, and Meredith Reeves describe efforts to develop good practices and implementation tools for the INECE ECE indicators projects worldwide.[12] The article also provides a general introduction to the types and applications of ECE indicators, as well as an overview of several of the pilot projects being initiated around the world.

In the next article, Michael Stahl, the leading expert on ECE indicators, discusses the importance of using indicators to measure the results of environmental compliance and enforcement programs, including their specific benefits to environmental enforcement practitioners.[13] Stahl's article presents a three-stage model for developing ECE indicators programs: identification, design and implementation, and use. This model is further described in the (*Performance Measurement Guidance for Compliance and Enforcement Practitioners*).[14]

---

[11] The final conference statement from the 6th International Conference on Environmental Compliance and Enforcement called upon INECE to develop uniform minimum criteria and to pilot test INECE Environmental ECE Indicators, in cooperation with regional networks, with a view to improving performance, public policy decisions, and environmental governance globally, ultimately contributing to the improvement of the quality of the environment. Final Conference Statement, 6th International Conference on Environmental Compliance and Enforcement at 19f, *available at* http://www.inece.org/conf/proceedings2/2-ConfStatement.pdf.

[12] Kenneth J. Markowitz, Kraysztof Michalak, & Meredith Reeves, *Improving Environmental Compliance and Enforcement Through Performance Measurment: The INECE Indicators Project*, Updated from 4(1) Sustainable Dev.L. & Pol'y 17(2004).

[13] Michael Stahl, *Using Indicators to Lead Environmental Compliance and Enforcement Programs*, 7th INECE Conference Proceedings (forthcoming 2005).

[14] The guidance document is available through the INECE Indicators Web Forum at http://www.inece.org/forumsindicators.html.

In the final article, Nalin Kishor and Kenneth Rosenbaum present a World Bank case study on using indicators to monitor the effectiveness of law enforcement in the forestry sector.[15] The article describes characteristics of reliable indicators and concludes by describing the applicability of indicators to forest law enforcement and governance initiatives.

---

[15] Nalin Kishor & Kenneth Rosenbaum, *Indicators to Monitor Progress of Forest Law Enforcement and Governance Initiatives to Control Illegal Practices in the Forest Sector*, 5(3) INT'L FORESTRY REV., 211 (2003).

Improving Environmental Compliance and Enforcement Through Performance Measurement: The INECE Indicators Project

Kenneth J. Markowitz, Krzysztof Michalak, and Meredith Reeves

updated from 4(1) Sustainable Development Law & Policy 17 (2004)

1   INTRODUCTION

There is a significant body of knowledge and experience concerning environmental indicators, which may be defined as "parameters, or values derived from parameters, which point to, provide information about, or describe the state of a phenomenon/environment/area, with a significance extending beyond that directly associated with a parameter value."[1] Over the past decade, many countries have begun to adapt the concept of indicators for measuring the effectiveness and efficiency of environment enforcement programs.[2] Environmental compliance and enforcement indicators aid enforcement agencies and practitioners by:

- Assisting in monitoring enforcement operations and non-compliance responses, to help ensure that personnel and resources are being used effectively.

- Enhancing program accountability by providing information to the decision-makers and the public about the number, type, and impacts of enforcement operations.

- Helping to assess the performance of environmental compliance and enforcement programs. These indicators

---

[1] *INECE Expert Working Group on Envtl. Compliance and Enforcement Indicators*, INECE-OECD Workshop on Envtl. Compliance and Enforcement Indicators: Measuring What Matters (October 22, 2003), *available at* http://inece.org/IndBackPaper.pdf [hereinafter *Expert Working Group*].
[2] *See id.*

help program managers learn what is working and what is not working and determine what needs to be done differently to achieve desired results.[3]

Such indicators have been in use in some countries but their methodological base has not been well developed and their application not widespread. Several countries have expressed an interest to carry comprehensive analysis and enlarge the scope of using ECE indicators.[4]

The INECE project responds to this need by creating a framework for identifying, designing, and using indicators that respond to the implementation, enforcement, and compliance with environmental laws in developed, transition, and developing nations.[5]

The environmental compliance and enforcement indicators project builds on one of INECE's major publications, the internationally cited *Principles of Environmental Enforcement,*[6] which emphasizes the importance of evaluating program success and establishing accountability.

2   METHODOLOGICAL APPROACH

The development of ECE indicators will be guided by criteria selected based on the best practices around the world. These criteria include transparency in development and in use, informative value for range of users, comparability between developed and developing countries, relevance to current policies and country resource systems, credibility and flexibility measurements, compatibility with existing reporting requirements, technological sophistication, and measurability (cost-effectiveness).[7] This will facilitate the use of the ECE indicators in

---

[3] *Id.*

[4] *Summary Report of the INECE-OECD*, INECE-OECD WORKSHOP ON ENVTL. COMPLIANCE AND ENFORCEMENT INDICATORS: MEASURING WHAT MATTERS (March 31, 2004), *available at* http://www.inece.org/indicators/workshop_pro.html [hereinafter *Summary Report*].

[5] *Special Edition on Environmental Compliance and Enforcement Indicators*, INECE NEWSLETTER 6 (INECE), 2002, *available at* http://inece.org/Newsletter6.pdf.

[6] Components of a successful compliance and enforcement program adapted from USEPA, PUB. NO. 300F93001, PRINCIPLES OF ENVIRONMENTAL ENFORCEMENT (1992). The PRINCIPLES OF ENVIRONMENTAL ENFORCEMENT were developed by the USEPA in consultation with the Netherlands' Ministry of Housing, Spatial Planning and the Environment; the Polish Ministry of Environmental Protection, National Resources, and Forestry; and the Katowice Ecology Department in Poland. The full text of the PRINCIPLES is available on the INECE Web site at http://inece.org/enforcementprinciples.html.

[7] ZAELKE, DURWOOD ET AL., THE INECE ENFORCEMENT INDICATORS: EXECUTIVE SUMMARY AND ANNOTATED OUTLINE FOR A MULTIYEAR PROJECT (2002), *available at* http://www.inece.org/conf/indDZ08_30.htm.

conjunction with other existing environmental and sustainability indexes.[8]

Box 1: Key Principles Resulting from the INECE-OECD November Workshop

- Carefully consider and reflect on the needs of different user groups.
- Meet the challenges of decision-making and program management
- Link indicators to policy targets and ensure that indicators are responsive to evolving policy objectives
- Reflect and address factors that determine compliance
- Help track progress in solving priority problems
- Recognize that indicators must be interpreted correctly and meaningfully.
- Use different categories of indicators in conjunction to maximize their value

---

The ECE indicators will be designed for a wide range of applications, including: to serve as measures of compliance promotion, compliance monitoring, and non-compliance response within regional, national, and international enforcement programs. A secondary application for the ECE indicators will provide a more global view towards gauging steps taken to achieve specific sustainable development commitments, agreed by the governments in the Johannesburg Plan of Implementation.[9] Achieving the sustainable development goals requires good governance,

---

[8] One such index is the Pressure-State-Response (PSR) framework developed by OECD. OECD's PSR model classifies environmental indicators into indicators of environmental pressures, both direct and indirect; indicators of the state of the environmental; and indicators of societal responses. "Pressure" refers to human pressures on the environment. "State" refers to the state of environmental resources (air, water, soil, the biosphere). "Response" refers "to individual and collective actions and reactions, intended to i) mitigate, adapt to or prevent human-induced negative effects on the environment; ii) halt or reverse environmental damage already inflicted; iii) preserve and conserve nature and natural resources," including environmental enforcement actions. *See* OECD, OECD ENVIRONMENTAL INDICATORS: DEVELOPMENT, MEASUREMENT, AND USE (2003). *Available at* http://www.oecd.org/dataoecd/7/47/24993546.pdf.

[9] UNITED NATIONS, JOHANNESBURG PLAN OF IMPLEMENTATION (2002), *available at* http://www.un.org/esa/sustdev/documents/WSSD_POI_PD/English/POIToc.htm.

the rule of law, and effective, consistently applied, enforcement. Effective enforcement calls for measuring actions taken to achieve full compliance against a baseline and reporting them openly. ECE indicators are one method to meet this need.

Since INECE launched its indicators project in 2002, INECE participants have researched and surveyed existing environmental indicators programs worldwide, set up an Expert Working Group to guide the project, and presented the concept at conferences and workshops to solicit feedback and to identify partnerships.

In November 2003, INECE and the Organization for Economic Co-operation and Development (OECD) co-hosted an international workshop on the subject. The Workshop was attended by representatives from developed, transitional, and developing countries; international organizations; multilateral environmental agreement secretariats; and nongovernmental organizations. Participants outlined several guiding principles for the development of ECE indicators (see Box 1) and developed three major recommendations[10] for next steps in the ECE indicator development process:

- develop common definitions;

- reach agreement on a methodology model; and

- articulate and apply guiding principles for using indicators to assess performance, through in-country projects.[11]

3   WHAT ARE ECE INDICATORS AND WHAT DO THEY MEASURE?

Conventionally, environmental authorities measure enforcement capacities or activity levels using "input" and "output" indicators. Input-related indicators (e.g., the number of inspectors and the

---

[10] *Summary Report, supra* note 4.

[11] The outcomes of the Workshop are available through the INECE Web site at http://www.inece.org/indicators/workshop.html. The common definitions were developed in March 2004 and released on the INECE Web site at http://inece.org/forumsindicators.html. In the coming moths, INECE will work with its partners at OECD, the World Bank Institute, Environment Canada, the United States Environmental Protection Agency, and many other national governments to further implement this process of identifying, designing, and using indicators to assess the impact of compliance and enforcement activities at the national, regional, and international levels.

enforcement agency budgets) identify the allocation of financial and human resources, while output-related indicators (e.g., the numbers of inspections and the numbers of enforcement actions) show the extent of activities carried out. [12] However, as Michael Stahl of the USEPA discusses, although "these [traditional] indicators give some sense of enforcement presence, they do not provide all the types of feedback needed to effectively manage program performance, and they have several limitations." [13]

Countries are now developing "intermediate outcome" indicators and "outcome" indicators. Changes in behavior, knowledge, or conditions that result from enforcement program activities [14] are examples of "intermediate outcome" indicators. They should help to measure progress towards achieving final outcomes – the ultimate changes in the state of the environment as a result of the environmental policies and actions (see Table 1).

Table 1: Basic Types of ECE Indicators

Indicator	Measures	ECE Examples
Input Indicator	Resources (human, material, financial, etc.) used to carry out activities, produce outputs and/or accomplish results. [15]	- # of staff assigned to a task - $ spent per inspection - Ratio of # of staff to # of regulated facilities
Output Indicator	Government activities, work products, or actions. [16]	- # of enforcement cases settled per year - # of fines issued per year
Intermediate Outcome Indicator	Measure progress towards achieving final outcomes, such as changes in behavior, knowledge, or conditions that result from program activities. [17]	- pounds of pollutants reduced through enforcement actions
Outcome Indicator	The real impacts of compliance promotion and enforcement actions [18] and the ultimate change in the state of the environment	- improved water quality - improved air quality

[12] *Expert Working Group, supra* note 1.
[13] Michael Stahl, *Performance Indicators for Environmental Compliance and Enforcement Programs: the U.S. EPA Experience*, 6ᵀᴴ INT'L. ENVTL. CONF. ON COMPLIANCE AND ENFORCEMENT, (2002), *available at* http://inece.org/conf/proceedings2/27-Performan%20Indicators.pdf.
[14] *Expert Working Group, supra* note 1.
[15] Treasury Board of Canada, Results-Based Management Lexicon, *available at* http://www.tbs-sct.gc.ca/rma/dpr/00-01/guidance/lexicon-e.asp (last modified Apr. 9, 2004).
[16] *Expert Working Group, supra* note 4.

continued

4   ECE INDICATORS IN PRACTICE

At the INECE-OECD Workshop, country representatives described their efforts to develop more adequate performance indicators. European country representatives discussed the applicability of outcome indicators to their European Union reporting requirements. The Netherlands, for example, has developed a risk-compliance indicator matrix, which is used to assess enforcement goals and target inspections.[19] (Figure 1) The matrix allows the Dutch Inspectorate to focus resources on priority activities that fall within the upper right hand corner of the matrix, indicating both a high level of risk to public health, safety, and the environment and a high potential for non-compliance.

Other country representatives, including those from Canada[20] and Mexico,[21] described the development pilot projects in selected areas to measure outputs and outcomes of compliance promotion and enforcement activities. Representatives from transition and emerging economies, including those from Czech Republic,[22] Russia,[23] Belarus,[24] and Thailand,[25] described the quantitative "input" and "output" indicators used in their countries.

[17] *Id.*

[18] Frank Barrett & Dave Pascoe, *Environmental Compliance And Enforcement Indicators: Environment Canada Pilot Projects – Addressing Challenges,* INECE-OECD WORKSHOP ON ENVTL. COMPLIANCE AND ENFORCEMENT INDICATORS: MEASURING WHAT MATTERS (2004), *available at* http://www.inece.org/indicators/workshop_pro.html.

[19] Angelique A.A. van der Schraaf, & Jan van der Plas, *Environmental Compliance and Enforcement Indicators in The Netherlands,* INECE-OECD WORKSHOP ON ENVTL. COMPLIANCE AND ENFORCEMENT INDICATORS: MEASURING WHAT MATTERS (2004), *available at* http://www.inece.org/indicators/workshop_pro.html.

[20] Barrett & Pascoe, *supra* note 18.

[21] Alejandra Goyenechea, *PROFEPA's Strategic Information System,* INECE-OECD WORKSHOP ON ENVTL. COMPLIANCE AND ENFORCEMENT INDICATORS: MEASURING WHAT MATTERS (2004), *available at* http://www.inece.org/indicators/workshop_pro.html.

[22] Jirí Fencl et al., *Used and Proposed Indicators At Czech Environmental Inspectorate,* INECE-OECD WORKSHOP ON ENVTL. COMPLIANCE AND ENFORCEMENT INDICATORS: MEASURING WHAT MATTERS (2004), *available at* http://www.inece.org/indicators/workshop_pro.html.

[23] Vladimir Schwartz, *Analysis of System of Environmental Enforcement and Compliance Indicators in the Russian Federation,* INECE-OECD WORKSHOP ON ENVTL. COMPLIANCE AND ENFORCEMENT INDICATORS: MEASURING WHAT MATTERS (2004), *available at* http://www.inece.org/indicators/workshop_pro.html.

[24] A.A Kovaltchiuk, *Analysis of System of Indicators for Inspection Activities in the Republic of Belarus,* INECE-OECD WORKSHOP ON ENVTL. COMPLIANCE AND ENFORCEMENT INDICATORS: MEASURING WHAT MATTERS (2004), *available at* http://www.inece.org/indicators/workshop_pro.html.

[25] Thasanee Chantadisai, *Country Report on Environmental Indicators in Thailand. Published in INECE,* INECE-OECD WORKSHOP ON ENVTL. COMPLIANCE AND ENFORCEMENT INDICATORS: MEASURING WHAT MATTERS (2004), *available at* http://www.inece.org/indicators/workshop_pro.html.

Figure 1: The Netherlands Environmental Inspectorate Risk-Compliance Matrix[26]

risk

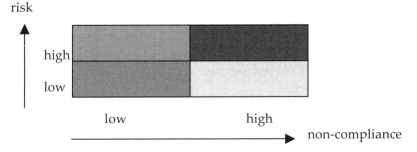

                                                    non-compliance

Environment Canada has been a leading contributor to the development of ECE indicators, launching pilot projects on performance measures for compliance promotion activities on six program areas including environmental emergency regulations, mining, agriculture activities, and volatile organic compounds. Recently, Environment Canada held a workshop to discuss results and lessons from these pilot projects. Workshop participants recognized the need to engage stakeholders including risk managers and compliance promotion and enforcement officers and to ensure that results are analyzed, interpreted, and used to make decisions and trigger changes along the compliance continuum.[27]

Country representatives also described the ways in which indicators are being used to assess performance on a facility-by-facility basis. In Poland, a list of "worst polluters" has been used for monitoring compliance and assessing performance of inspectors.[28] The U.S. Environmental Protection Agency uses the Toxic Release Inventory as a resource to target inspections.[29] In the Netherlands, the Pollutant Release and Transfer Registry system is used for the same purpose.[30]

However, there are many impediments to the establishment of ECE indicator projects in transition and developing countries. María Eugenia di Paola, presenting on the relevance of ECE indicators to Argentina,

---

[26] Van der Schraaf & van der Plas, *supra* note 19.
[27] Press Release, Drolet, Rene, Environment Canada's Workshop on Performance Measures for Compliance and Enforcement (2004) *available at* http://inece.org/news/canadaindicators.pdf.
[28] *Summary Report, supra* note 4.
[29] *Id.*
[30] *Id.*

identified legal and institutional development processes that need to occur prior to the creation of an ECE indicator program, including:

- clear differentiation of responsibilities between levels of government;

- development of environmental strategic plans and systematized environmental compliance and enforcement programs;

- prioritization of environmental issues in the public budget;

- full implementation of the right to get access to environmental information, public participation in the decision-making process, and access to justice regarding environmental issues; and

- creation of an environmental information system, which the authorities must organize and implement to provide information.[31]

5   FUTURE STEPS

The INECE ECE Indicators Working Group, in cooperation with its partners, has achieved several significant advances in developing a framework to support the implementation of ECE indicators in national, regional, and global enforcement contexts. One of the most important accomplishments of the INECE ECE Indicators Working Group was the launch of a pilot ECE indicators project in Costa Rica. INECE is working with Costa Rica's Ministry of the Environment to design and implement an indicators project to measure enforcement responses to illegal logging in Costa Rica's forestry sector. The indicators will aid the Ministry in determining appropriate personnel and resource allocations to combat illegal logging in Costa Rica.

---

[31] María Eugenia di Paola, *Environmental Compliance and Enforcement Indicators in Argentina: Primary Concerns*, INECE-OECD WORKSHOP ON ENVTL. COMPLIANCE AND ENFORCEMENT INDICATORS: MEASURING WHAT MATTERS (2004), *available at* http://www.inece.org/indicators/workshop_pro.html.

Other significant achievements include:

- publishing 20 case studies, along with workshop outcomes, from the INECE-OECD Indicators Workshop in English and Russian and distributing the Proceedings to practitioners around the world;

- hosting global e-dialogues on ECE indicators;

- developing a Web-based, searchable "common definitions" glossary for ECE indicators terminology;

- partnering with the United Nations Environment Programme to develop indicators that identify synergies between the implementation of and compliance with multilateral environmental agreements;

- raising awareness to the importance of ECE indicators to audiences in Chile, the United States, Costa Rica, Thailand, Canada, and other locations; and

- holding an expert panel and numerous workshops on the implementation and use of ECE indicators at the 7th INECE Conference in April 2005.

Using Indicators To Lead Environmental Compliance And Enforcement Programs

Michael M. Stahl

7TH INECE CONFERENCE PROCEEDINGS (forthcoming 2005)

Many environmental compliance and enforcement (ECE) programs around the world are making good progress in identifying and implementing performance indicators. But at present, very few countries have moved into the next stage of actually using performance indicators to: 1) monitor and manage operations; 2) improve program effectiveness; and 3) enhance accountability to political overseers and the public. This article explains why ECE programs need to develop and use performance indicators, describes patterns emerging from the progress being made by many countries toward identifying and implementing ECE indicators, discusses how indicators can be used to manage and improve ECE programs, and suggests ways to ensure continued progress for ECE indicators and programs.

1   Why Do ECE Programs Need Performance Indicators

For many years, international organizations, environmental protection agencies of national and provincial governments, and various non-governmental organizations (NGOs) interested in environmental matters have used indicators to characterize environmental conditions. These indicators provide a sense of the current condition of the air, land, and water and help identify whether their quality is improving or deteriorating.[1]

Many forces contribute to the state of environmental conditions. In the "pressure/state/response" model used by the Organization for Economic

---

[1] A relatively recent example of indicators pertaining to environmental conditions can be found in, EPA, "Draft Report on the Environment 2003,"EPA-260-R-02-006, June 2003, also available at *http://www.epa.gov/indicators/*.

347

Cooperation and Development (OECD), various human activities (often involving energy, transport, industry, agriculture, and others) put direct and indirect pressure on the air, water, land, and other living resources, and these pressures are mitigated by various societal responses, including economic forces and actions by government agencies and programs.[2]

Among the responses of government are programs designed specifically to protect the environment by setting standards and regulating behavior and industrial practices that have an adverse impact on the environment. A fundamental element of environmental protection programs at the local, provincial, national, and international level is to ensure compliance with environmental laws and regulations.

1.1   The Special Mission and Obligation of ECE Programs

A premise of this article is that programs to ensure compliance with environmental laws deserve and need their own distinct effort to develop and use performance indicators. There are three arguments in support of this premise. The first argument is that environmental protection systems cannot be effective in improving environmental conditions if the laws and regulations designed to protect the environment are not known, respected, and obeyed. ECE programs play a crucial role in ensuring compliance with environmental laws, it is their primary mission to bring about such compliance. Second, the absence of a credible environmental compliance program will mean that a major incentive for voluntary efforts to go beyond compliance will also be absent if no one is even bothering to comply, why even consider going beyond compliance? Thus, programs designed to ensure compliance are not just a building block in an environmental protection system, they provide the foundation on which the system is built. The third and less recognized argument is that ECE programs often use tools (e.g., enforcement actions) that impose penalties and/or obligations. These programs are, in turn, obligated to use these authorities fairly and wisely. Performance indicators, especially when shared with the public, can help determine whether authorities and resources are being used appropriately.

For all of the above reasons, it is crucial for environmental ministers, staff and managers of ECE programs, regulated industries and facilities, legislative overseers, and the public to know if environmental compliance

---

[2] Linster, Myriam, "OECD Work on Environmental Indicators," in *Measuring What Matters*, Proceedings from the INECE-OECD Workshop on Environmental Compliance and Enforcement Indicators, November 3 - 4, 2003, pg. 168.

efforts are succeeding, and if they are not, how they can be improved. ECE indicators can help provide this knowledge.

A well-designed set or system of performance indicators can be a powerful tool to direct ECE programs toward the most important results. Indicators can be used to:

1. Monitor and manage day-to-day operations of ECE programs;

2. Identify and correct performance issues and problems in ECE programs;

3. Adjust strategies and resource allocation to improve the effectiveness of ECE programs;

4. Provide an account of program performance to political overseers and the public.

Each of these uses will be described further in this article under Section 3, "Using Indicators to Manage and Improve ECE Programs."

2   Progress Toward Identifying and Implementing ECE Indicators

Under the auspices of organizations such as the International Network for Environmental Compliance and Enforcement (INECE), the World Bank Institute, and the OECD, good progress is being made by many countries in developing performance indicators for their ECE programs. While one uniform set of indicators is not emerging from these efforts, some of these countries are being guided by a three-stage framework which suggests: 1) identifying indicators; 2) designing and implementing indicators; and 3) using indicators as three steps on a path to follow for developing ECE indicators.[3] For each of these three stages a set of best practices has begun to emerge to help countries manage their ECE indicators projects. Figure 1 lists the best practices for each of the three stages of the indicators framework[4]

---

[3] Stahl, Michael, "Performance Indicators for Environmental Compliance and Enforcement Programs: The U.S. EPA Experience," in *Measuring What Matters*, Proceedings from the INECE-OECD Workshop on Environmental Compliance and Enforcement Indicators, November 3 - 4, 2003, pg. 150 - 157.

[4] These best practices are described in an upcoming INECE publication entitled, "Performance Measurement Guidance for Compliance and Enforcement Practitioners," written by Michael Stahl in consultation with the INECE Indicators Expert Working Group.

Figure 1. Three-Stage Model for Developing and Using Indicators

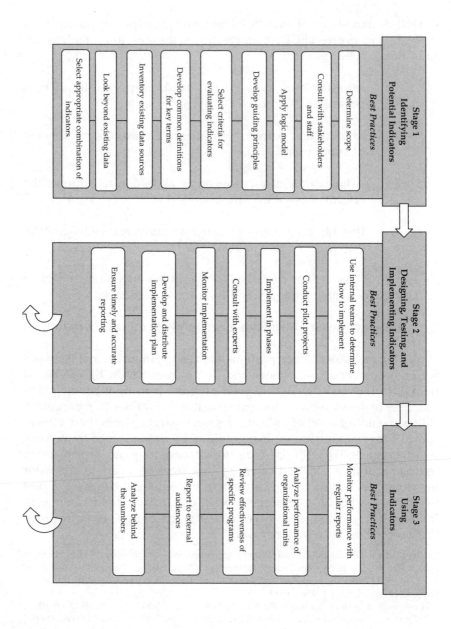

2.1   Emerging Patterns

As more countries make progress along the path of developing ECE indicators, there are some patterns that can now be identified.

1.   <u>Most Participating Countries in Identification and Implementation Stages</u>. In addition to providing a path for countries to follow, the framework also serves as a set of basic milestones for assessing the progress of countries currently developing ECE indicators. Many countries are now on this path and have progressed to the first milestone (i.e., they are identifying indicators) or even to the second (i.e., they are designing and implementing indicators). Projects in Brazil, Mexico, Argentina, and Costa Rica, among others, are currently involved in identifying and implementing indicators. Only a few countries have taken the path all the way to the point of using indicators to manage their programs, and these countries are only in the early stages of using indicators as a management tool. Projects in the United States and Canada are beginning to use indicators to manage all or part of their ECE programs.[5]

2.   <u>Indicators Tailored to Unique Circumstances</u>. Most countries in the identification and implementation stage are developing indicators that are tailored for their unique circumstances. While many ECE programs are learning from examples used by other countries, indicators are being selected for implementation based on institutional needs and conditions of individual agencies or programs. This means that there is not one universal set of ECE indicators being adopted, but varying sets with some common indicators or characteristics.

3.   <u>Four Types of Indicators Projects</u>. The ECE indicators projects going on around the world fit into one of four categories, depending on whether they are comprehensive or focused with respect to the laws and requirements they include, and whether they are national or sub-national in terms of the jurisdiction they cover. The four categories are:

---

[5] Descriptions of many of these projects can be found at the INECE web site, *http://www.inece.org/forumsindicators.html*.

a)   Comprehensive national indicators - These are used to assess effectiveness of national ECE programs' efforts to ensure compliance with all national statutes and regulations. Developing a set of comprehensive national indicators is very complex, since it involves many persons, multiple agencies, collection of data from many sources, and may necessitate development of a national data system.

b)   Comprehensive sub-national indicators - These are used to assess effectiveness of an ECE program of a regional or district office of a national agency, a state/provincial environmental agency, or a local or municipal agency. This type of effort has the advantage of being a more manageable size than a comprehensive national effort, and can often provide a means of testing a system of indicators that can later be applied to the national program.

c)   Focused national indicators - These are used when a national environmental agency wants to assess the effectiveness of a focused national initiative to address a specific noncompliance pattern or environmental risk. For example, focused national indicators might be developed for an inspection and enforcement initiative to improve compliance among the petroleum refining industry, a targeted enforcement initiative to improve compliance with all air pollution requirements, or a strategy that integrates incentives and enforcement to reduce emissions of a specific pollutant into water bodies.

d)   Focused sub-national indicators - These are used when a regional, provincial/state, or local/municipal agency wants to assess the effectiveness of a focused initiative to address a specific non-compliance pattern or environmental risk. For example, this type of indicator system might be developed for a regional or state effort to use inspections and enforcement to control deforestation, or a municipal initiative to combine assistance followed by enforcement actions to limit illegal dumping of waste on the land.

4.   Common Set of Barriers. Another pattern that can be identified from the indicators projects going on around the

world is a set of barriers that many ECE programs confront as they try to develop indicators. Those barriers are:

a) Compliance culture in formative stages - In some countries, the obligation to comply with environmental (and other) laws is not yet ingrained deeply and the rule of law is not yet embraced fully by citizens, businesses and institutions of government.

b) Environmental laws not fully implemented - Environmental laws may be relatively new, they may have been changed significantly, and there may be impediments to implementation of specific sections of a law.

c) Environmental agencies not mature - The operation of environmental agencies may not be very sophisticated, they may possess limited capabilities, or they may have resource shortages.

d) Systematic data collection lacking - Some countries may lack data systems or may be only beginning to develop them.

e) Duration of implementation - Identifying and implementing a useful set of performance indicators takes a significant amount of time and commitment of personnel, and the effort required may sometimes seem disproportionate to the value to be gained from developing and using performance indicators.

f) Lack of analytical skills - Agencies often lack the ability to interpret the meaning of indicators, i.e., to determine what's behind the numbers, as this requires a sophisticated understanding of program operations and a skill for diagnosing problems.

g) Misuse by external audiences - The prospect of performance indicators being inadvertently or knowingly misused by advocacy groups or legislative overseers sometimes discourages program managers from developing and using indicators.

3   Using Indicators to Manage and Improve ECE Programs

Public management literature suggests that performance indicators can be used for a wide range of purposes in public sector programs and organizations. In his article entitled, "Why Measure Performance? Different Purposes Require Different Measures," Robert Behn of Harvard University[6] identifies eight specific managerial purposes that can be served by performance indicators. According to Behn, the eight purposes are to evaluate, control, budget, motivate, promote, celebrate, learn, and improve. Behn asserts that no single indicator is appropriate for all eight purposes, and that each purpose addresses a different management question and requires specific input, output, or outcome indicators. A very similar list of uses of performance indicators was previously offered by Harry Hatry of the Urban Institute.[7]

3.1   Four Uses of ECE Indicators

These purposes are relevant (in varying degrees) to any public program or organization, not just ECE programs. Building on these eight broad purposes, it would be useful to adapt them to describe the specific uses that ECE practitioners are making of performance indicators. For ECE practitioners, four distinct but related uses seem appropriate.

The first use of performance indicators for ECE practitioners is to monitor and manage program operations. Monthly or quarterly reports to program managers and staff about key outputs and outcomes can be a very useful management tool to ensure that resources are being used appropriately to produce specific activities or results. Such reports can be organized to break out data for a program as a whole (e.g., the national enforcement program), for specific program components (e.g., the enforcement of air pollution laws), and for particular organizational units (e.g., a regional or provincial office of a national program).

The second use of performance indicators for ECE practitioners is to identify and correct performance issues and problems. Data from input, output, and outcome indicators can be organized to compare the current year to the previous year, illustrate a trend over a longer period of years,

---

[6] Behn, Robert D., "Why Measure Performance? Different Purposes Require Different Measures," *Public Administration Review,* Vol. 63, No.5., September/October 2003, pg. 586 - 606.

[7] Hatry, Harry, *Performance Measurement: Getting Results,* The Urban Institute Press, Washington, D.C., 1999, p.158

compare the performance of one program component or organizational unit to another during the same period, and to assess performance in achieving a particular goal or target. Indicators can highlight deficiencies and anomalies, allowing staff and managers to further analyze the cause of performance which deviates from past trends or current targets.

A third use of indicators by ECE practitioners is to evaluate and adjust program strategies and resource allocation to improve effectiveness. By analyzing patterns between inputs, outputs, and outcomes, ECE practitioners can learn more about what combination of activities produces the most important results. Such analysis can build a chain that improves the effectiveness of the ECE program B resources are shifted to produce more of the right combination of activities, which increases the contribution of the ECE program to important outcomes that protect the environment.

A fourth use of indicators by ECE practitioners is to report to political overseers and the public about program performance. ECE programs can be well-served by providing to external audiences an annual (or more frequent) account of activities performed and results achieved. Reports that emphasize results and outcomes achieved through activities and outputs of the program can enhance support for the compliance and enforcement mission. By describing accomplishments in terms that emphasize results - pounds of pollution reduced through enforcement actions, improved environmental management practices at facilities from compliance assistance, improved rates of compliance in an industry sector - an account of performance is provided that is meaningful to multiple audiences.

3.2   Lessons that Inform Use of ECE Indicators

As ECE practitioners use performance indicators for these purposes, they should be informed by two lessons from the experience of countries that have begun using indicators to manage their ECE programs. The first lesson is that the limitations of indicators need to be understood. Indicators that show the amount of an output or outcome produced do not tell program personnel all they need to know about that output or outcome. For example, an indicator can tell ECE program managers that the number of inspections conducted in 2004 is fifteen percent lower than the number conducted in 2003, but it cannot explain why the number is lower. To learn that, more analysis is needed of program operations, sometimes using qualitative information to understand the reasons for the reduction in inspections. Thus, indicators provide a kind of warning light that signals a need for deeper analysis or further investigation of the forces and influences that shape program performance.

A second lesson learned from the use of ECE indicators is that intermediate outcomes provide very valuable management information. Efforts to develop indicators often attempt to leap from measuring basic outputs (e.g., the number of enforcement actions taken) to measuring complex end outcomes (e.g., improvements in ambient air quality), ignoring many valuable results that are produced between activities and ultimate outcomes. Hatry defines intermediate outcomes as events, occurrences, or changes in conditions, behavior, or attitudes "expected to lead to the ends desired but are not the ends themselves."[8] Thus, in the context of ECE programs, examples of intermediate outcomes might be investment in pollution control equipment or implementation of improved environmental management practices resulting from enforcement actions taken at facilities. These outcomes will contribute to the end outcome (e.g., an improvement in ambient air quality) but they are not the ends themselves.

Hatry points out two advantages of intermediate outcomes that are relevant and important for ECE practitioners and programs.[9] Intermediate outcomes, by definition, occur before B and are expected to help lead to B the end outcomes. As a result, intermediate outcomes usually provide more timely information than end outcomes. A second advantage is that programs almost always have more influence over intermediate outcomes than they do over end outcomes. Stated another way, there is often a direct causal link between a program activity (e.g., an enforcement action) and an intermediate outcome (e.g., an investment in pollution control equipment required as a condition of the enforcement settlement). This direct causal link allows ECE programs to make a clear and credible claim that they have produced outcomes that would not have occurred in the absence of the program.

3.3   Benefits of Using ECE indicators

When used appropriately, indicators have been able to provide a variety of benefits to ECE practitioners.

---

[8] Hatry, Harry, IBID, p.16.
[9] Hatry, Harry, IBID, p.19.

1. <u>Improved Control of Program Operations</u>. Even a very basic set of outcome indicators will increase understanding about what is being accomplished, and when combined with data about inputs, judgments can be made about whether resources are being used efficiently. At a minimum, basic output indicators can help determine whether program staff are performing fundamental program activities.

2. <u>Improved Goal-setting and Strategy Development</u>. By using indicators as a management tool, goals can be set regarding the amount of activities or results that should be produced over a period of time. Indicators can also be used to identify needed adjustments in the mix of activities or results the program is producing.

3. <u>Improved Resource Allocation Decisions</u>. Output and outcome indicators can be analyzed to determine whether resources need to be increased, shifted, or altered in some way to meet goals and achieve desired results. Indicators provide an understanding of the relationship between outputs and outcomes, thereby enhancing the ability of program managers to increase resource investments in preferred outcomes.

4. <u>Improved Identification and Correction of Performance Problems</u>. Indicators that can be organized by type of output or outcome, by organizational unit, and by program area increase program managers'ability to identify performance problems and investigate them further to design solutions.

5. <u>Improved Ability to Motivate Employees</u>. There is much truth to the oft-repeated statement, "What gets measured gets done." Performance indicators send a clear signal to program personnel about what needs to be accomplished. Setting a goal to achieve a certain amount of a specific output tends to organize and focus some portion of resources on achieving the goal.

6. <u>Improved Ability to Communicate with the Public</u>. Performance indicators help external audiences understand and support program activities. Output indicators can

> convey to the public that funds are producing some amount of inspections, enforcement actions, or other activities. Outcome indicators can convey that these activities are resulting in important outcomes such as reduced pollution, increased compliance, and improved environmental management at facilities.

Although the challenges and barriers associated with identifying and implementing ECE indicators are formidable, the benefits derived from using the indicators to manage and improve programs are significant. Countries that have made it to the third milestone on the path - i.e., using indicators - have recognized that the benefits of using indicators outweigh the costs of implementing.

4   Ensuring Further Progress for ECE Indicators and Programs

ECE practitioners using indicators as a management tool need to form a community of practice to learn from each others' experience and to show the way for other practitioners who are on the path of identifying, implementing, and using indicators. Such a community is necessary if ECE programs want to receive the maximum benefit from performance indicators.

4.1   The Need for a Community of Practice

While the creation of sets or systems of indicators is an important step toward making ECE programs more effective, systems of indicators by themselves cannot bring about improved performance in ECE programs. Setting up a system of indicators can be seen as acquiring a tool, but the tool needs to be used continuously by program managers and staff. Over time, program personnel gain more experience and skill in using the tool, they hone and sharpen the tool to make it more useful, and ultimately the program to which they apply the tool becomes more effective.

There is not much accumulated experience in using ECE indicators for program management and improvement, since most countries are still in the identification and implementation stages of their ECE indicators projects. But a community of practice for ECE indicators could make a significant contribution to creating a cadre of experienced, thoughtful program leaders who document their knowledge, report it to interested colleagues around the world, and advance the collective learning of ECE practitioners. This community of practice should encourage its members to report periodically to a central repository about the progress or challenges associated with their indicators projects. Members should also be encouraged to post "indicator bulletins" to provide examples of how indicators are being used to manage and improve ECE programs, and e-dialogues about specific topics can be used to promote more frequent communication among members about ideas and developments in performance measurement.[10]

4.2 Toward Performance-Based Management for ECE Programs

Ultimately, if ECE programs are to make their maximum contribution to environmental protection, they will need to join other government programs in moving toward performance-based management. This movement toward performance-based management is global, as described in various books and articles about global trends in public management reform.[11] In his article entitled "Performance-Based Management: Responding to the Challenges," Joseph Wholey defines performance-based management as "the purposeful use of resources and information to achieve and demonstrate measurable progress toward agency and program goals."[12] The United States Government Accountability Office (GAO) describes three key steps in performance-based management: (a) developing a reasonable level of agreement on mission, goals, and strategies for achieving the goals; (b) implementing performance measurement systems of sufficient quality to document performance and support decision making; and (c) using performance information as a basis for decision making at various organizational levels.[13] Wholey suggests that in coming years there will be a premium on managers and staff with the knowledge, skills, and abilities to apply performance-based management to their programs. This will require training on how to use performance information: in agency and program management systems; to provide accountability to key stakeholders and

---

[10] The INECE web site currently provides many useful features for practitioners interested in ECE indicators, and could easily be adapted to provide a visible forum for "indicators bulletins." INECE has also conducted e-dialogues on indicators topics on their web site.
[11] See, for example, Kettl, Donald F., *The Global Public Management Revolution*, Brookings Institution Press, Washington, D.C., 2000, pg. 2. Kettl describes "accountability for results," and a "focus on outputs and outcomes instead of processes and structures "as a core characteristic of the global movement toward reform of public management.
[12] Wholey, Joseph S., "Performance-Based Management: Responding to the Challenges," *Public Productivity and Management Review*, Vol. 22, No. 3., pg. 288.
[13] Wholey, Joseph S., IBID, pg. 289.

the public; to demonstrate effective or improved performance; and to support resource allocation and other policy decision making.[14]

ECE practitioners, through their work on indicators, have established a steady pace of progress toward "implementing performance measurement systems of sufficient quality" and applying performance-based management to their programs. Managers and staff of ECE programs can determine whether they have succeeded in becoming performance-based programs by watching for specific changes. (Perhaps these are best viewed as five indicators of program improvement.) ECE programs have reached the threshold for high performance when they are: addressing significant environmental, public health, and compliance problems; using data to make strategic decisions for better utilization of resources; using the most appropriate tool to achieve the best outcome; assessing the effectiveness of program activities to ensure desired program performance; and effectively communicating the environmental, public health and compliance outcomes to the public. When this threshold is reached, the hard work of identifying, implementing, and using performance indicators will have paid off and the effectiveness of ECE programs can be fully realized.

---

[14] Wholey, Joseph S., IBID, pg. 303.

Indicators to monitor progress of forest law enforcement and governance initiatives to control illegal practices in the forest sector

N.M. Kishor and K.L. Rosenbaum

5(3) INTERNATIONAL FORESTRY REVIEW 211 (2003)

INTRODUCTION

This paper offers a preliminary and conceptual look at the use of indicators to evaluate forest sector law enforcement and governance. Corrupt and illegal practices are widespread in the forest sector, they pose a major threat to the sustainable management of forest resources, and hamper economic growth, equitable income distribution, and efforts at poverty reduction. More specifically illegal practices may:

1. Put at risk the livelihoods of the poor and forest dependent populations who rely heavily on timber and non-timber forest products.

2. Distort markets for timber and pose an obstacle to responsible forest operators attempting to practice SFM.

3. Lead to a leakage of resources (tax revenues in particular) that legitimately belong in the government treasury for possible use in protecting and improving the quality of the resource and other development activities[1].

---

[1] A low-end estimate of the royalties, reforestation fund and export tax payments that are not being paid to the Government of Indonesia on stolen timber amount to US$600 million per annum. This amount is more than twice what the government spent on subsidised food programmes for the poor in 2001.

4.   Make a significant addition to the illegal or unofficial economy and therefore jeopardise national monetary and exchange rate policies, and encourage other illegal activities.

5.   Directly threaten ecosystems, biodiversity and environmental services in protected areas and parks.

6.   Reduce the intended beneficial impacts of forest sector projects and contribute to their failure.

Improving forest law enforcement and governance reduces illegalities and establishes a better environment for sustainable forest management. To be successful, it requires a reasonably good understanding of the illegal practices in the sector. It also requires the establishment of a baseline, which can capture the extent of the problem and a set of indicators to monitor progress of the recommended actions.

ILLEGAL PRACTICES IN THE FOREST SECTOR

Recent papers have identified a broad range of illegal practices in the forest sector:

- 'There are many types of illegal forest practices.... Public servants may approve illegal contracts with private enterprises. Private commercial corporations may harvest trees of species that are protected by law from timber exploitation. Individuals and communities may enter public forests and illegally take products that are public property. Illegal activities do not stop at the forest. They travel down the line to operations in transportation, processing and trade of forest products. Individuals or corporations may smuggle forest products across international borders or process raw forest materials without a licence. Corporations with strong international links may artificially inflate the price of imported inputs or deflate the volume and prices of their exports to reduce their tax liability and to facilitate the illegal transfer of capital abroad' (FAO 2001).

- 'Illegal acts include ... unauthorised occupation of public and private forestlands, logging in protected or environmentally sensitive areas, harvesting protected species of trees, woodland arson, wildlife poaching,

> unlawful transport of wood and other forest products, smuggling, transfer pricing and other fraudulent accounting practices, unauthorised processing of forest products, violation of environmental regulations, and bribing government officials' (Contreras-Hermosilla 2002a).

- 'Examples of the types of illegal practices that have been detected in the forest industry largely fall into three categories: illegal logging of various forms; movement of wood products (which may or may not have been harvested legally) without proper authorisation or in contravention of controls; and activities directly aimed at avoidance of payment of taxes or forestry charges' (Callister 1999).

- ''Illegal logging' has no single definition. It is not a legal term derived from treaties, statutes, or court opinions. Neither is it a technical term that professionals use in a consistent way. In a general sense, 'illegal logging takes place when timber is harvested, transported, bought or sold in violation of national laws' (Brack and Hayman 2001). This broad definition includes almost any illegal act that may occur between the growing of the tree and the arrival of the forest-based product in the hands of the consumer' (Rosenbaum 2003).

Consistent with the above definitions, Box 1 presents examples of some of the most prevalent illegal acts in the forest sector.

BOX 1 *Examples of illegal practices in the forest sector*

Illegal occupation of forestlands

- Invasion of public forested lands by either rural families, communities or private corporations to convert them to agriculture or cattle ranching

- Practice of slash and burn agriculture on invaded lands

- Induce landless peasants to illegally occupy forested areas to force governments to grant land ownership rights to them and then buying these lands from peasants.

Woodlands arson

- Setting woodlands on fire to convert them to commercial uses

Illegal logging

- Logging protected species

- Counterfeit duplication of felling licenses

- Girdling or ring-barking to kill trees so that they can be legally logged

- Contracting with local entrepreneurs to buy logs from protected areas

- Logging in protected areas

- Logging outside concession boundaries

- Logging in prohibited areas such as steep slopes, riverbanks and water catchments

- Removing under/oversized trees from public forests

- Extracting more timber than authorised

- Passing off volumes extracted from non-authorised areas outside the concession boundaries as those legally harvested

- Logging without authorisation

- Obtaining logging concessions through bribes

Illegal timber transport, trade and timber smuggling

- Transporting logs without authorisation

- Transporting illegally harvested timber

- Smuggling timber

- Falsifying and/or reusing timber transportation documents

- Exporting and importing tree species banned under international law, such as CITES.

- Exporting and importing timber in contravention of national bans

Transfer pricing and other illegal accounting practices

- Declaring lower values and volumes than have exported

- Declaring higher purchase prices above the prevailing market prices for inputs such as equipment or services from related companies

- Manipulating debt cash flows to transfer money to subsidiary or parent company, for example by inflating debt repayment to avoid taxes on profits

- Colluding in submitting bids/tenders to obtain timber concessions cheaply

- Avoiding royalties and duties through under-grading, under-valuing, under-measuring and misclassification of species exported or for the local market

- Non-payment of license fees, royalties, fines and other government charges

Illegal forest processing

- Operating without a processing license

- Ignoring environmental, social and labour laws and regulations

- Using illegally obtained wood
  Based on Callister 1999 and Contreras-Hermosilla 2002b.

INDICATORS TO MONITOR PROGRESS: GENERAL CONSIDERATIONS

Indicators are necessary to pick up early warning signs of forest crime, to identify problem areas, to track the progress of interventions, and to allow for appropriate modifications and timely correction of intervention strategies. That is why indicators are often considered synonymous with instruments for monitoring and evaluation.

Indicators can be harbingers of 'good-news' as well as 'bad-news'. For example, an indicator of scholastic achievement that all of us have grown up with, and have viewed with pride at some time but with dread at other, is our school report card! However, 'good news' should not lull us into complacency, but should encourage us to look closely for opportunities for improvement. By the same token, 'bad-news' should not be seen as a failure per se but as an opportunity to learn from mistakes and to minimise the scope of future errors.

Indicators come in a variety of forms, with varying qualities:

1. *Indicators can be Booleans, scalars, or arrays.* Mostly we think of indicators as scalars: that is, single numbers indicating the magnitude of a phenomenon. Examples include the amount of revenue from timber taxes or the rate of deforestation in an area. It is also possible to have valid replicable Boolean indicators, which reflect the presence or absence of a phenomenon. Examples include whether a government awards concessions through public auction or whether concession accounts face annual outside audits. Indicators can also be arrays of linked numbers, such as the pay scale of civil servants (which may shed light on their vulnerability to bribes).

2. *Indicators can be continuous or discrete.* We mostly think of scalar indicators as being continuous, but there are also indicators that take on discrete values. These include ordinal indicators, reflecting rank amongst a set of peers (such as an indicator ranking a country's deforestation rate compared to other countries in the region of similar geography, or of similar GDP). They also include indicators that measure phenomena on arbitrary scales of, say, 1–5 or 1–10, or ask people to assign situations to a limited set of ordered

categories (e.g. 'Are concession terms violated almost always, often, sometimes, seldom, or never?').

3. *Indicators can vary in precision.* An indicator of economic activity may report a figure to the nearest dollar or to the nearest million dollars. An indicator of deforestation may report in hectares or thousands of hectares. Ideally, an indicator's precision should reflect its presumed accuracy, or the reported figures should include some notion of the uncertainty attached.

4. *Indicators can vary in accuracy.* The distinction between accuracy and precision is worth remembering. An indicator can report a figure to the nearest dollar and be off by a factor of ten, or it could report to the nearest million and be exactly right. The first is precise but not accurate. The second is accurate but not precise.

5. *Indicators can be largely objective or can contain subjective elements.* An indicator that reports on the area of timber harvested or price paid for stumpage is largely objective. An indicator that relies on professional judgment (percentage of forest officers adequately trained in law enforcement) is somewhat less so. An indicator that relies on general opinion (the reputation of forest officers for honesty) has an even larger subjective component. However, even subjective indicators can be measured in replicable ways.

To identify useful indicators decision-makers need to screen indicators against a set of desirable characteristics. These are as follows:

1. *Appropriate in the context of project objectives*[2]: The selected indicator (or indicators) must be directly relevant to the project objectives and the problems that the project seeks to address. This is a key requirement for a good indicator. This also implies that the project objectives must be defined very clearly. Otherwise, it would be difficult to identify clear-cut indicators. Fuzzy objectives will lead to fuzzy indicators and a generally poor prognosis for a successful project.

---

[2] In this paper, 'project' will be used for all proposed interventions whether they are policy reforms or actual investment projects.

2. *Appropriate to the scale of the project:* Indicators can track illegalities globally (e.g. the World Bank's estimate of revenues lost to governments from illegal activities in the sector), locally (e.g. an estimate of illegal harvest volume associated with a particular concession), or at any scale in between. The scale of the indicator should reflect the scope of the project being monitored.

3. *Sensitive to the objectives and quick to change:* In part this is a matter of precision, and in part appropriateness. An indicator must be sensitive to project interventions and it should respond to changes quickly and with as small a lag as possible. Further, indicators should be insensitive to "outside" factors, or the effect of outside factors should be well understood. Therefore, if lumber price is a project indicator, the monitor should understand that a gradual rise in prices in the legal market could reflect a clampdown on the illegal markets or it could reflect general economic conditions.

4. *Reasonably accurate, and therefore replicable:* Even highly subjective indicators can be defensible if they are unbiased and replicable. Even highly objective indicators are of little use if attempts to verify them prove them to have little accuracy.

5. *Free of hidden bias:* Every indicator embodies some notion of what is good. Sometimes that is apparent from the nature of the indicator itself. Sometimes it is hidden in the way the indicator is measured. Sometimes the notion is widely held or reflects accepted project objectives, sometimes not. Since biases cannot be eliminated they should be left out in the open, to be analysed and critiqued. If a project monitor chooses an indicator with an unpopular bias, the monitor should be prepared to defend it.

6. *Easy and inexpensive to measure:* Indicators should be easy to measure and should not be prohibitively expensive to construct. The reality of the situation is that indicators which entail high cost of collection are rarely chosen, even though they may be perceived as the most useful.

7.   *Politically palatable:* Here we leave the realm of measurement for the realm of diplomacy. Projects will want to promote a climate of constructive debate and increased willingness to undertake reforms. Strong indicators of poor performance can lead those in power to attack the monitor or the objectives of the project rather than the problem. At the same time, failing to point out poor performance will hamper reform. In a search for a middle way, some studies have pointed to the benefits of shaping indicators to avoid recriminations and rancor (WB-WWF-IIED, 2002, 2003; Thomas *et al.* 2000).

From a practical perspective, the monitor will have to face up to the challenge of 'trading-off' amongst the desirable qualities of indicators. For example, an indicator may be both easy and cheap to measure, but it may be relatively insensitive to the project objectives. Political palatability is likely to be a frequently contentious issue, and often the monitor may have to compromise by trading-off cardinal rankings against broader ordinal categories. In addition, in all likelihood several indicators will be necessary to monitor project progress in a reliable and comprehensive way. Finding the compromises amongst the desirable qualities, and determining the most relevant set of indicators is not an easy task. It is best opened up to a broad-based consultation process involving the stakeholders responsible for the execution, and affected by the outcomes of the project. This will likely result in objective selection of indicators, identification of the responsibilities for their timely collection and dissemination, and consensus on how to use them in positive ways.

Examples of indicators to monitor the progress of FLEG initiatives

What indicators can monitors use to measure the progress of FLEG initiatives? Table 1 contains an extended though preliminary list of illegalities and associated indicators. For each class of illegality the table identifies some ideal indicators, which are probably unavailable but which identify the desired focus of monitoring. It also identifies some more practical indicators that might cast some light on progress.

As an example, consider the indicators that might track the extent of illegality in awarding concessions. The ideal indicators would report the relative number of awards influenced by unlawful activities. If the monitor knew the following with confidence, it would have an excellent way to track the progress of efforts to ensure that concession awards were lawful:

- The percent of concession awards influenced by bribery, cronyism, patronage, or the like.

- The percent of concession awards involving fraudulent applications.

- The percent of concession awards affected by extortion.

- The percent of concession awards affected by unintentional but unlawful acts, such as failure to follow legal mandated award processes.

These ideal indicators are almost certainly unavailable. Indeed, if unlawful concessions could be so readily identified, honest governments could easily prevent or suppress the unlawful acts.

The obtainable quantitative data is likely to provide a much less direct measurement of illegal activity. Depending on the transparency of the concession system, the available indicators might include these:

- The percent of major concession awards drawing multiple competitive bids.

- The percent of awards granted to the highest bidder.

- The percent of awards (determined by number, area, or volume) that on their face comply with law regarding location, size, and number of concessions.

- The records of concessions voided after discovery of illegality.

These indicators all have some correlation to illegal activity, but each is flawed. Auctions can draw multiple bids and still be fixed. High bids can come from irresponsible operators whom the government legitimately avoids. Concessions that appear lawful can still involve corruption. In addition, many illegal concessions are never exposed as such.

The above indicators are scalar; some Boolean (i.e. true or false) indicators also could be useful. These include the following:

- Whether public notice and opportunity to bid is given before the award of a major concession.

- Whether bids are made public after the concession is awarded.

- Whether the rules for awarding concessions are publicly available.

- Whether there is a process for unsuccessful bidders and other interested parties to challenge concession awards.

- Whether there is an independent internal government watchdog that polices the concession process.

- Whether there is a requirement for government forest officials to disclose financial interests in the forest sector, or for concession holders to disclose familial connections to the government.

These are all statements about the process rather than the outcome. They are neither necessary nor sufficient to guarantee that all concessions are lawful. However, they all reflect aspects of the process that tend to prevent or suppress illegality. Taken singly none is a strong indicator of legality, but a large group of Boolean indicators like these taken together can provide a replicable and comparable snapshot of the prevalence of deterrence mechanisms.

With some investment of effort, a monitor might be able to collect new data and generate new indicators. For example, even if the government itself kept few records, the monitor could select a sample of recent concessions and investigate how they were awarded. Alternatively, the monitor could conduct an opinion survey measuring the reputation of the concession process for honesty.

CONCLUSIONS

Corrupt and illegal practices in the forest sector can be a strong constraint to achieving sustainable forest management and there is an urgent need to control such practices through initiatives to improve forest law enforcement and governance. In this context, developing appropriate indicators to measure the performance of FLEG initiatives is a key requirement, and this paper makes a preliminary contribution to this need. It also provides a point of departure for policy makers to go about identifying a set of indicators for a specific FLEG initiative in the context of its own special circumstances such as the country situation, etc. It is envisaged that the selection of indicators takes place through a consultative process involving all major stakeholders who stand to be affected by the FLEG initiative. It is also anticipated that the consultative process will identify the agency/ies responsible for collecting information on the indicators and how the associated costs will be met. In overall terms, consultations will likely ensure that the monitoring information is used effectively to bring about improvements in the FLEG initiative.

Furthermore, the information in Table 1 can be helpful in alerting policy makers to the opportunity of 'piggy-backing' on to reforms in other sectors to control illegal practices in the forest sector. As an example, making a provision that the financing of new processing capacity be financed only by banks and agencies subscribing to the Equator principles into a programme of general banking system reforms would clearly have favourable impacts on controlling illegal logging. Thus, the forestry community should be on the lookout to capitalise on such opportunities.

Finally, it must be emphasised that documenting the lessons learned from field-testing of indicators and their widespread dissemination will be an important means to make progress in this area. The international community of practice should be prepared to take up this challenge.

REFERENCES

BRACK, D. and HAYMAN, G. 2001. Intergovernmental Actions On Illegal Logging: Options for intergovernmental action to help combat illegal logging and illegal trade in timber and forest products. (available at: http://www.riia.org/pdf/research/sdp/Intergovernmental%20Actions%20on%20Illegal%20Logging%20March%2001.pdf).

CALLISTER, D. J. 1999. Corrupt and Illegal Activities in the Forestry Sector: Current understandings, and implications for World Bank Forest Policy (draft for discussion, prepared for the World Bank Group, Forest Policy Implementation Review and Strategy

Development: Analytical Studies). Available at: http:// wbln0018.worldbank. org/essd/forestpol-e.nsf/ HiddenDocView/ BCE9D2A90FADBA73852568A 3006493E0?OpenDocument

CONTRERAS-HERMOSILLA, A. 2002a. Policy Alternatives to Improve Law Compliance in the Forest Sector (background paper prepared for FAO meeting of experts, Rome, January 2002).

CONTRERAS-HERMOSILLA, A. 2002b. Law Compliance in the Forestry Sector: An Overview. WBI Working Papers. World Bank Institute, The World Bank 2002. Also available at: http:// lnweb18.worldbank.org/eap/eap.nsf/ 2500ec5f1a2d9bad852568a3006f557d/c19065b26241f 0b247256ac30010e5ff?OpenDocument

FAO 2001. The State of the World's Forests 2001. (FAO, Rome.) (available through the web at ftp site: ftp://ftp.fao.org/docrep/ fao/003/y0900e/).

ROSENBAUM, K. L. 2003. Defining Illegal Logging: What is it, and what is being done about it? (A background paper for the 44th meeting of the FAO Advisory Committee on Paper and Wood Products, May 2003).

THOMAS, V., DAILAMI, M., DHARESHWAR, A., KAUFMANN, D., KISHOR, N., LOPEZ, R. and WANG, Y. 2000. *The Quality of Growth.* Oxford University Press, New York, USA, September 2000.

WB-W WF-IIED 2002: The Pyramid: A Diagnostic and Planning Tool for Good Forest Governance. Prepared by James Mayers, Stephen Bass, and Duncan Macqueen for the World Bank W WF Alliance for Forest Conservation and Sustainable Use.

Other literature consulted

CIFOR, 1999. The CIFOR Criteria and Indicators Generic Template. The Criteria and Indicators Toolbox Series#2. CIFOR, Bogor, 1999.

DANISH CENTRE FOR FOREST, LANDSCAPE AND PLANNING, 2000. For Whom and for What? Principles, Criteria, and Indicators for Sustainable Forest Resources Management in Thailand. Danish Centre for Forests, Landscape and Planning, proceedings #6-2000.

A World Bank supported Expert Consultation at the Forest Management Unit Level.

DFID-WB, 2002. Second Generation Governance Indicators. Report prepared by Steve Knack, Mark Kugler and Nick Manning. Draft.

SEGNESTAM, L. 2002. Indicators of Environment and Sustainable Development: Theories and Practical Experience. Paper #89, Environmental Economics Series. The World Bank.

Table 1 Examples of indicators to measure the progress of FLEG initiatives

Problem area	Ideal indicators	Existing or obtainable scalar data	Boolean data (true/false)	Possible extensions
Illegalities in awarding concessions	Percent of concession awards influenced by bribery, cronyism, nepotism, patronage, or the like Percent of concession awards involving fraudulent applications Percent of concession awards affected by extortion Percent of concession awards affected by unintentional but unlawful acts (clerical errors, failure to follow mandated process, etc.)	Percent of concession awards drawing multiple competitive bids Percent of concession awards granted to highest bidder Percent of awards (determined by number, area, or volume) that on their face comply with laws regarding location, size, and nature of concessions Records of concessions voided after discovery of illegality	The public has notice and opportunity to bid before awards Bids are made public after awards Award rules are publicly available Unsuccessful bidders and other interested parties may challenge awards An independent internal government watchdog polices the process Forest officials must disclose financial interests in the forest sector, and concession holders must disclose familial connections to government	Detailed investigation of a random sample of awards Opinion survey of the reputation of the concession system for honesty and fairness

Illegal acts related to valid concessions	Ratio of authorised to actual harvest, by species Ratio of expected to actual concession revenues Ratio of expected to actual successful completion rate of non-harvest operations (planting, stand improvement etc.) Rate of compliance with management practice requirements (maintenance of buffers, disposal of slash, protection of sensitive soils, limits on skidding and yarding of logs, etc.) Amount or number of bribes to concession system enforcement officials	Pre-harvest and post-harvest inventory estimates of concession Reported revenue payments Site inspection reports indicating evidence of management practices GIS information on logging activity within a concession GIS information on access roads and skid trails within concession GIS information on unauthorised logging in nearby areas that might be "laundered" through concessions	Concession contracts inventories, and plans are publicly available Rules regarding forest practices are publicly available Citizens may bring lawsuits or file administrative complaints to enforce concession requirements	Detailed independent investigation of conditions at a random sample of concessions sites
Theft or other illegal harvest of trees from private lands	Volume or value of stolen or illegally harvested timber, perhaps broken down by species, perhaps as a percentage of legal harvest Bribes paid to obtain permission to harvest or to avoid taxation	Periodic inventory-based estimates of volume on private lands, as a means of estimating harvest volumes Official reports of trees harvested or marked for harvest on private land, as collected for tax or regulatory purposes Taxes paid on timber harvested from private lands, as a means of determining reported harvest Police reports of timber theft Records of prosecution for bribery	Special timber trespass laws allow recovery of damages above market value of trees stolen Branding or marking laws allow log branding unique to ownership	Surveys of private owners regarding the prevalence of theft, unauthorised harvest, and tax evasion

Theft of non-timber forest illegally, or ratio of illegal to of illegal to products, including wildlife	Amount of product harvested timber forest illegally, or ratio of illegal to total harvest	Periodic inventory-based estimates of resource Availability/price of products in marketplace Records of police reports, arrests, or prosecutions for product theft	Laws restrict sale or possession of protected species	
Illegal occupation of forest land	Percentage of forest land with clear title Area of forest lands used for illegal private, non-forest uses	Unauthorised agricultural or residential use of government forest lands, as determined by remote sensing Numbers of court suits filed concerning evictions from or ownership of forest lands	Workable survey system allows boundaries of properties to be reliably determined in field Government maintains reliable records of property ownership	Field survey/census of forest area residents cross-checked against property records
Arson and vandalism	Area/volume/ecosystem services affected by arson-caused fires Volume or ecosystem services lost to vandalism	Total area or volume lost to fires, perhaps divided into natural and human-caused fires Expenditures to replace or repair public forest property subject to vandalism Police reports, arrests, or prosecutions for forest-related arson or vandalism		

Timber trespass due to traditional versus modern tenure conflicts	Area or volume harvested under traditional rights not recognised under modern law Area otherwise used (grazed, cleared for agriculture etc.) under traditional rights not recognised under modern law Area harvested under modern rights in conflict with traditional uses Area subject to conflicts between traditional and modern claims of right (whether used or not)	Geographical distribution of peoples potentially claiming traditional rights to forest Number of complaints, arrests, or prosecutions of people tied to exercise of traditional rights	Forest laws recognise specified traditional rights	Survey of traditional identify conflicts communities to identify objects
Violations of police power laws (laws to promote health, safety, or harvest forest management welfare) governing	Percentage of forest harvests conforming to required plans Percentage of harvest operations in compliance with particular forest practice standards (fire prevention measures, measures to protect sensitive soils, water quality, wildlife etc.) Percentage of harvest operations in compliance with business, labour, and safety laws. Percentage of forest roads built to standards Percentage of harvest areas where regeneration requirements were met Rate of compliance with laws governing forest pesticide use Bribes paid to avoid enforcement of above requirements	Percentage of forests covered by required management and operational plans Percentage of forest covered under required inventories Numbers of licenses or permits secured for forest operations Complaints, arrests, or prosecutions for violations of forest management laws Complaints, arrests, or prosecutions for other forestrelated violations of health, safety, or welfare laws Percentage of lands managed under certification of code of conduct that requires compliance with local regulations	Law requires management and operational plans for public forests	Random sampling of operational sites to determine rate of compliance, including sites subject to certification

Violations of timber transport laws	Number of trips or volume hauled in violation of timber transport laws. Percentage of illegal transport associated with illegal harvest. Bribes paid or solicited to issue transport licenses	Number of permits or licenses granted for timber transport and associated volume covered by issued permits (to be compared with estimates of volumes harvested or sold). Arrests or prosecutions for violation of transport laws	Sampling of transporters arriving at mill gate or market to determine compliance rates
Illegalities in sales of forest products	Sales volumes and values traded in grey and black markets. Sales subject to misrepresentation of species, grade, volume, certification status, or place of origin. Bribes paid to evade sale taxes or restrictions. Collusion among bidders at auctions for timber and other forest products	Sales taxes collected on legal sales. Required reports of legal sales including sales of government products or sales to government buyers. Volume data in government-monitored markets.	Investigation of origins of forest products available in sample of public markets

Illegalities in processing of forest products	Volume of protected species processed Percentage of processing facilities without proper licenses Extent (in monetary value) of processing taxes evaded Extent of violation of pollution control, labour, or other health, safety, or welfare laws in processing Payment of bribes to avoid enforcement of above laws	Taxes paid by processing facilities Volumes reported (if required) by processing facilities Complaints, arrests, or prosecutions for violations of laws at processing facilities Estimates of actual production in an area compared to records of licensed prod	Law requires licensing or registration of commercial processing facilities Government performs regular inspections of processors	Percentage of processing subject to certification or code of conduct requiring compliance with regulations Percentage of new processing capacity financed by banks or agencies subscribing to codes of environmental practice (e.g. the Equator principles)
Illegalities in the export or import of forest products	Percentage of forest product exports conducted outside the legal requirements Percentage of forest product imports involving legally harvested and traded goods Extent of under-invoicing of exports Extent of over-invoicing of imports Bribes paid to custom	Total tax and tariff revenue from trade in forest products (as an indicator of legal trade) Volume of forest products legally exported Volume of forest products legally imported Records of trade subject to CITES control (as an indicator of lawful trade)	Customs officials trained to recognise restricted species	Estimates of exports based on estimates of production and internal consumption Estimates of exports based on records of imports from trading partners

Concealing revenues from illegal forest activities	Total amount of money not reported Amount of money laundered through legitimate businesses Money invested in illegitimate activities such as land speculation, drug trafficking, financing armed conflicts and political campaigns	Overall estimated size of the illegal economy Estimates of taxes evaded on forest activities Disclosure of sources of campaign finances by candidates/political parties	Banking system facilitates tracking of income	Percentage of lenders or loans subject to antimoney-laundering codes (e.g. Wolfsberg principles)
Civil service, social, and institutional factors that permit illegal activity	Ability of forest law enforcement officials to prepare prosecutable cases for forest offences Freedom of public access to information Level of discretionary powers subject to abuse available to field staff Level of honesty Vulnerability to bribes	Annual expenditures on training programmes to upgrade enforcement skills of forestry officials Annual expenditures and staffing on forest-related law enforcement Annual expenditures on training of officials regarding ethics and professionalism Civil servi	Forestry officials regularly trained to upgrade law enforcement skills Judges and prosecutors trained in forest sector issues Forest law sets clear limits for use of discretionary powers Civil service has code-of conduct and law has reporting requirement regarding conflict of interest Civil service laws discourage cronyism and patronage Whistleblowers protected by law Forest agency is subject to independent audits Ombudsman or other independent mechanisms responds to public complaints	Success rate of forest-related prosecutions, in terms of conviction rate and size of penalties Survey of reputation of forest officers for corruption

Chapter Twelve

Transgovernmental Networks

Introduction

This chapter presents a selection of the best literature on transgovernmental networks, an increasingly important part of modern global governance, and one that plays an important role in making law work for sustainable development. What are "transgovernmental networks" and how can they play a role in strengthening enforcement and compliance for sustainable development?

The lack of meaningful enforcement and compliance has often been seen as one of the greatest weaknesses of international law, and international environmental law in particular, but new models of cooperation present great promise for effective international action. The common conception of international governance, and global environmental governance in particular, is one of multilateral treaties and organizations negotiated by diplomats representing sovereign States. These treaties and organizations, described in the previous chapters, are often criticized by some as a threat to national sovereignty, secretive, and remote. Others criticize them as being ineffective at mitigating the environmental problems they were designed to address.

A different view of global governance has emerged amid these criticisms. Global governance, under this view, is not, or at least not solely, to be found in these treaties and organizations, but rather in complex global webs of "transgovernmental networks."

"Network" is a broad term that can be applied to many forms of cooperation. For example, the United Nations could be viewed as a network of governments across the globe. But in the context of global governance and the articles in this chapter, a "network" is a form of cooperation involving governments or government officials (and under some conceptions, NGOs and the business community as well) that operates without a formal treaty or international institution. In particular, this chapter focuses on what are often referred to as "transgovernmental networks," which involve the component institutions of states — such as legislators, regulators, and enforcement and compliance officials — interacting directly with their peers around the world.

Networks arise with different origins and purposes. Networks range from informal bilateral and multilateral networks to more institutionalized organizations such as the Basel Committee on banking. They are located within existing international organizations, are created by agreements, or spontaneously arise through regular contact. They can also involve somewhat surprising participants. For instance, judges are starting to network more, whether by means of information-sharing and mutual citation, or actively by means of forming organizations and cooperating on transnational litigation. As a recent example of this growing community of courts, UNEP and INECE, among others, organized a Global Judges Symposium at the UN Conference on Sustainable Development at Johannesburg in 2002, bringing together judges from around the world to review their role and the rule of law in the context of sustainable development.[1]

Networks can be more flexible, and thus potentially more effective, than the large formal institutions of international governance when it comes to certain functions. By working directly peer-to-peer, transgovernmental networks can quickly disseminate and distill information, enhance enforcement cooperation, harmonize laws and regulations, and address common problems from a shared perspective shaped by experience and expertise.

Enforcement networks in particular offer the potential to fill the compliance gap that many view as having hobbled international environmental law. Enforcement networks exist to enhance cooperation among national regulators to enforce national laws. These networks occur most intensively but not exclusively within the law enforcement community (e.g., police, customs agents, drug agents). Interpol, the international police network, facilitates information exchange and provides assistance to local police efforts.[2] Interpol has also created an

---

[1] *See* ANNE-MARIE SLAUGHTER, A NEW WORLD ORDER 14, 66 (2004). See also *Johannesburg Principles on the Role of Law and Sustainable Development*, adopted at the Global Judges Symposium held in Johannesburg, South Africa, on 18-20 August 2002, *available at* http://www.inece.org/wssd_principles.html.

[2] SLAUGHTER, *Supra* note 1, at 55-56.

environmental crime network, called Ecomessage, to facilitate information-sharing and enhanced coordination of enforcement efforts.[3] Another important environmental enforcement network is the European Union Network for the Implementation and Enforcement of Environmental Law (IMPEL), an informal network of the environmental authorities of the EU Member States, acceding and candidate countries of the EU, and Norway.[4]

Capacity building is a critical function of enforcement networks. A new Green Customs network, intended to build the capacity of customs officials, has been created and is supported by Interpol, the World Customs Organization, the Convention on International Trade in Endangered Species, the Basel Convention, and UNEP.[5] The U.S. Environmental Protection Agency offers courses to train regulators and environmental officials in other countries because building regulatory capacity in nations with weak or poorly developed legal systems allows cooperative enforcement efforts to occur. Their efforts stem "from the recognition that a global regulatory system based on transgovernmental networks is only as strong as its weakest link."[6]

This chapter presents a series of articles that explain the growth of networks, the types of networks that exist, the role that networks do and can play, and the implications of networks for global governance, national sovereignty, and the existing infrastructure of international organizations and treaties.

The chapter starts with an excerpt from Anne-Marie Slaughter's book, *A New World Order*,[7] which argues that transgovernmental networks — including INECE — are all around us but are underappreciated and underused to address the global problems facing the world today. She argues that the state is not being made obsolete, but rather is disaggregating into its component parts, and that the networking of these disaggregated government parts can be seen as retaining "sovereignty" and can resolve the global governance "tri-lemma" of needing global rules without centralized power but with political accountability.

---

[3] "Ecomessage: Reporting System for Environmental Crime" packet. Interpol & IFAW.
[4] *See* IMPEL Homepage *at* http://europa.eu.int/comm/environment/impel.
[5] *See* Green Customs Homepage *at* http://www.uneptie.org/ozonaction/customs/home.htm.
[6] SLAUGHTER, *supra* note 1, at 57.
[7] *Id.*, Introduction.

Kal Raustiala's article examines transgovernmental networks and their impact on the existing international infrastructure of "liberal internationalism."[8] Raustiala asserts that rather than replacing the existing array of treaties and organizations, transgovernmental networks will operate synergistically with the existing governance structure by making the treaties and organizations work better, by filling gaps where treaties are politically or economically precluded, and by smoothing the path for future negotiations. Raustiala also explores the implications of transgovernmental networks for the theories of international compliance discussed earlier in Chapter Two: Compliance Theories.

Peter Haas's article on "epistemic communities," a concept that could include some transgovernmental networks, highlights the implications of such communities for international policy coordination, particularly their ability in the face of ever-present uncertainty to provide expert opinions, narrow down policy choices, and help define state self-interests.[9]

Lastly, Donald Kaniaru's article examines more closely the role of institutions and networks in environmental enforcement, focusing on examples such as INECE and the role played by the UNEP Guidelines on MEAs.[10]

---

[8] Kal Raustiala, *The Architecture of International Cooperation: Transgovernmental Networks and the Future of International Law*, 43 VA. J. INT'L L. 1 (2002).

[9] Peter M. Haas, *Introduction: Epistemic Communities and International Policy Coordination*, 46(1) INT'L ORG. 1(1992).

[10] Donald Kinaru, *The Role of Institutions and Networks in Environmental Enforcement*, 6th INECE Conference Proceedings, Vol. 2 (2002), *available at* http://www.inece.org.

A NEW WORLD ORDER

Anne-Marie Slaughter

Introduction

(2004)

Terrorists, arms dealers, money launderers, drug dealers, traffickers in women and children, and the modern pirates of intellectual property all operate through global networks.[2] So, increasingly, do governments. Networks of government officials, police investigators, financial regulators, even judges and legislators increasingly exchange information and coordinate activity to combat global crime and address common problems on a global scale. These government networks are a key feature of world order in the twenty-first century, but they are underappreciated, undersupported, and underused to address the central problems of global governance.

Consider the examples just in the wake of September 11. The Bush administration immediately set about assembling an ad hoc coalition of states to aid in the war on terrorism. Public attention focused on military cooperation, but the networks of financial regulators working to identify and freeze terrorist assets, of law enforcement officials sharing vital information on terrorist suspects, and of intelligence operatives working to preempt the next attack have been equally important. ...

Turning to the global economy, networks of finance ministers and central bankers have been critical players in responding to national and regional financial crises. The G-8 is as much a network of finance ministers as of heads of state; it is the finance ministers who make key decisions on how to respond to calls for debt relief for the most highly indebted countries. ... The G-20, a network specifically created to help prevent future crises, is led by the Indian finance minister and is composed of the finance ministers of twenty developed and developing countries. More broadly, the International Organization of Securities Commissioners (IOSCO) emerged in 1984. It was followed in the 1990s by the creation of the International Association of Insurance Supervisors and a network of all three of these organizations and other national and international officials responsible for financial stability around the world called the Financial Stability Forum.[6]

Beyond national security and the global economy, networks of national officials are working to improve environmental policy across borders. Within the North American Free Trade Agreement (NAFTA), U.S., Mexican, and Canadian environmental agencies have created an environmental enforcement network, which has enhanced the effectiveness of environmental regulation in all three states, particularly in Mexico. Globally, the Environmental Protection Agency (EPA) and its Dutch equivalent have founded the International Network for Environmental Compliance and Enforcement (INECE), which offers technical assistance to environmental agencies around the world, holds global conferences at which environmental regulators learn and exchange information, and sponsors a website with training videos and other information.

Nor are regulators the only ones networking. National judges are exchanging decisions with one another through conferences, judicial organizations, and the Internet. Constitutional judges increasingly cite one another's decisions on issues from free speech to privacy rights. Indeed, Justice Anthony Kennedy of the U.S. Supreme Court cited a decision by the European Court of Justice (ECJ) in an important 2003 opinion overturning a Texas antisodomy law. Bankruptcy judges in different countries negotiate minitreaties to resolve complicated international cases; judges in transnational commercial disputes have begun to see themselves as part of a global judicial system. National judges are also interacting directly with their supranational counterparts on trade and human rights issues.

Finally, even legislators, the most naturally parochial government officials due to their direct ties to territorially rooted constituents, are reaching across borders. International parliamentary organizations have been traditionally well meaning though ineffective, but today national parliamentarians are meeting to adopt and publicize common positions on the death penalty, human rights, and environmental issues. They support one another in legislative initiatives and offer training programs and technical assistance.[7]

Each of these networks has specific aims and activities, depending on its subject area, membership, and history, but taken together, they also perform certain common functions. They expand regulatory reach, allowing national government officials to keep up with corporations, civic organizations, and criminals. They build trust and establish relationships among their participants that then create incentives to establish a good reputation and avoid a bad one. These are the conditions essential for long-term cooperation. They exchange regular information about their own activities and develop databases of best practices, or, in the judicial case, different approaches to common legal issues. They offer technical assistance and professional socialization to members from less developed nations, whether regulators, judges, or legislators.

In a world of global markets, global travel, and global information networks, of weapons of mass destruction and looming environmental disasters of global magnitude, governments must have global reach. In a world in which their ability to use their hard power is often limited, governments must be able to exploit the uses of soft power: the power of persuasion and information.[8] Similarly, in a world in which a major set of obstacles to effective global regulation is a simple inability on the part of many developing countries to translate paper rules into changes in actual behavior, governments must be able not only to negotiate treaties but also to create the capacity to comply with them. Understood as a form of global governance, government networks meet these needs. As commercial and civic organizations have already discovered, their networked form is ideal for providing the speed and flexibility necessary to function effectively in an information age. But unlike amorphous "global policy networks" championed by UN Secretary General Kofi Annan, in which it is never clear who is exercising power on behalf of whom, these are networks composed of national government officials, either appointed by elected officials or directly elected themselves. Best of all, they can perform many of the functions of a world government – legislation, administration, and adjudication – without the form. ...

Yet to see these networks as they exist, much less to imagine what they could become, requires a deeper conceptual shift. Stop imagining the international system as a system of states – unitary entities like billiard balls or black boxes – subject to rules created by international institutions that are apart from, "above" these states. Start thinking about a world of governments, with all the different institutions that perform the basic functions of governments – legislation, adjudication, implementation – interacting both with each other domestically and also with their foreign and supranational counterparts. States still exist in this world; indeed, they are crucial actors. But they are "disaggregated." They relate to each other not only through the Foreign Office, but also through regulatory, judicial, and legislative channels.

This conceptual shift lies at the heart of this book. Seeing the world through the lenses of disaggregated rather than unitary states allows leaders, policymakers, analysts, or simply concerned citizens to see features of the global political system that were previously hidden. Government networks suddenly pop up everywhere, from the Financial Action Task Force (FATF), a network of finance ministers and other financial regulators taking charge of pursuing money launderers and financers of terrorism, to the Free Trade Commission, a network of trade ministers charged with interpreting NAFTA, to a network of ministers in charge of border controls working to create a new regime of safe borders in the wake of September 11. At the same time, it is possible to disaggregate international organizations as well, to see "vertical networks" between national regulators and judges and their supranational counterparts. Examples include relations between national European courts and the ECJ or between national U.S., Mexican, and Canadian courts and NAFTA arbitral tribunals.

Equally important, these different lenses make it possible to imagine a genuinely new set of possibilities for a future world order. The building blocks of this order would not be states but parts of states: courts, regulatory agencies, ministries, legislatures. The government officials within these various institutions would participate in many different types of networks, creating links across national borders and between national and supranational institutions. The result could be a world ... crisscrossed by an increasingly dense web of networks.

This world would still include traditional international organizations, such as the United Nations and the World Trade Organization (WTO), although many of these organizations would be likely to become hosts for and sources of government networks. It would still feature states interacting as unitary states on important issues, particularly in security matters. And it would certainly still be a world in which military and economic power mattered; government networks are not likely to substitute for either armies or treasuries.

At the same time, however, a world of government networks would be a more effective and potentially more just world order than either what we have today or a world government in which a set of global institutions perched above nation-states enforced global rules. In a networked world order, primary political authority would remain at the national level except in those cases in which national governments had explicitly delegated their authority to supranational institutions. National government officials would be increasingly enmeshed in networks of personal and institutional relations. They would each be operating both in the domestic and the international arenas, exercising their national authority to implement their transgovernmental and international obligations and representing the interests of their country while working with their foreign and supranational counterparts to disseminate and distill information, cooperate in enforcing national and international laws, harmonizing national laws and regulations, and addressing common problems.

1.   THE GLOBALIZATION PARADOX: NEEDING MORE GOVERNMENT AND FEARING IT

Peoples and their governments around the world need global institutions to solve collective problems that can only be addressed on a global scale. They must be able to make and enforce global rules on a variety of subjects and through a variety of means. Further, it has become commonplace to claim that the international institutions created in the late 1940s, after a very different war and facing a host of different threats from those we face today, are outdated and inadequate to meet contemporary challenges. They must be reformed or even reinvented; new ones must be created.

Yet world government is both infeasible and undesirable. The size and scope of such a government presents an unavoidable and dangerous threat to individual liberty. Further, the diversity of the peoples to be governed makes it almost impossible to conceive of a global demos. No form of democracy within the current global repertoire seems capable of overcoming these obstacles.

This is the globalization paradox. We need more government on a global and a regional scale, but we don't want the centralization of decision-making power and coercive authority so far from the people actually to be governed. It is the paradox identified in the European Union by Renaud Dehousse and by Robert Keohane in his millennial presidential address to the American Political Science Association. The European Union has pioneered "regulation by networks," which Dehousse describes as the response to a basic dilemma in EU governance: "On the one hand, increased uniformity is certainly needed; on the other hand, greater centralization is politically inconceivable, and probably undesirable." [10] The EU alternative is the "transnational option" – the use of an organized network of national officials to ensure "that the actors in charge of the implementation of Community policies behave in a similar manner."[11] ...

Addressing the paradox at the global level is further complicated by the additional concern of accountability. In the 1990s the conventional reaction to the problem of "world government" was instead to champion "global governance", a much looser and less threatening concept of collective organization and regulation without coercion. A major element of global governance, in turn, has been the rise of global policy networks, celebrated for their ability to bring together all public and private actors on issues critical to the global public interest. [16] ...

Conservative critics have been most sensitive to th[e] problem [of ensuring that private actors uphold the public trust]. Assistant Secretary of State John Bolton, while still in the private sector, argued that "it is precisely the detachment from governments that makes international civil society so troubling, at least for democracies." ... Martin Shapiro argues that the shift from government to governance ... result[s] [in] advantag[ing] "experts and enthusiasts," the two groups outside government that have the greatest incentive and desire to participate in governance processes;[19] however, "while the ticket to participation in governance is knowledge and/or passion, both knowledge and passion generate perspectives that are not those of the rest of us. Few of us would actually enjoy living in a Frank Lloyd Wright house."[20] ...

The governance dilemma thus becomes a tri-lemma: we need global rules without centralized power but with government actors who can be held to account through a variety of political mechanisms. These government actors can and should interact with a wide range of nongovernmental organizations (NGOs), but their role in governance bears distinct and different responsibilities. They must represent all their different constituencies, at least in a democracy. ...

Government networks can help address the governance dilemma, offering a flexible and relatively fast way to conduct the business of global governance, coordinating and even harmonizing national government action while initiating and monitoring different solutions to global problems. Yet they are decentralized and dispersed, incapable of exercising centralized coercive authority. Further, they are government actors. They can interact with a wide range of NGOs, civic and corporate, but their responsibilities and constituencies are far broader. These constituencies should be able to devise ways to hold them accountable, at least to the same extent that they are accountable for their purely domestic activity.

2.   THE DISAGGREGATED STATE

...

The disaggregated state ... is simply the rising need for and capacity of different domestic government institutions to engage in activities beyond their borders, often with their foreign counterparts. ...

The significance of the concept of the disaggregated state only becomes fully apparent in contrast to the unitary state, a concept that has long dominated international legal and political analysis. International lawyers and international relations theorists have always known that the entities they describe and analyze as "states" interacting with one another are in fact much more complex entities, but the fiction of a unitary will and capacity for action has worked well enough for purposes of description and prediction of outcomes in the international system. ...

Looking at the international system through the lens of unitary states leads us to focus on traditional international organizations and institutions created by and composed of formal state delegations. Conversely, however, thinking about states the way we think about domestic governments – as aggregations of distinct institutions with separate roles and capacities – provides a lens that allows us to see a new international landscape. Government networks pop up everywhere.

Horizontal government networks — links between counterpart national officials across borders — are easiest to spot. Far less frequent, but potentially very important, are vertical government networks, those between national government officials and their supranational counterparts. The prerequisite for a vertical government network is the relatively rare decision by states to delegate their sovereignty to an institution above them with real power – a court or a regulatory commission. That institution can then be the genuine counterpart existence of a national government institution. ...

The concept of a "network" has many different definitions; I use a very broad one. The point is to capture all the different ways that individual government institutions are interacting with their counterparts either abroad or above them, alongside more traditional state-to-state interactions. For present purposes, then, a network is a pattern of regular and purposive relations among like government units working across the borders that divide countries from one another and that demarcate the "domestic" from the "international" sphere.[25] ...

3.   A NEW WORLD ORDER

...

A disaggregated world order would be a world latticed by countless government networks. These would include horizontal networks and vertical networks; networks for collecting and sharing information of all kinds, for policy coordination, for enforcement cooperation, for technical assistance and training, perhaps ultimately for rule making. They would be bilateral, plurilateral, regional, or global. Taken together, they would provide the skeleton or infrastructure for global governance. ...

Premises

There can, of course, be no one blueprint for world order. The proposal advanced here is part of an active and ongoing debate. In the spirit of such debate, it is important to acknowledge that the model of world order I put forward rests on a combination of descriptive and predictive empirical claims, which can be summarized in basic terms:

- The state is not the only actor in the international system, but it is still the most important actor.

- The state is not disappearing, but it is disaggregating into its component institutions, which are increasingly interacting principally with their foreign counterparts across borders.

- These institutions still represent distinct national or state interests, even as they also recognize common professional identities and substantive experience as judges, regulators, ministers, and legislators.

- Different states have evolved and will continue to evolve mechanisms for reaggregating the interests of their distinct institutions when necessary. In many circumstances, therefore, states will still interact with one another as unitary actors in more traditional ways.

- Government networks exist alongside and sometimes within more traditional international organizations. ...

HORIZONTAL NETWORKS

The structural core of a disaggregated world order is a set of horizontal networks among national government officials in their respective issue areas....

Horizontal information networks, as the name suggests, bring together regulators, judges, or legislators to exchange information and to collect and distill best practices. This information exchange can also take place through technical assistance and training programs provided by one country's officials to another. ...

Enforcement networks typically spring up due to the inability of government officials in one country to enforce that country's laws, either by means of a regulatory agency or through a court. But enforcement cooperation must also inevitably involve a great deal of information exchange and can also involve assistance programs of various types. Legislators can also collaborate on how to draft complementary legislation so as to avoid enforcement loopholes.

Finally, harmonization networks, which are typically authorized by treaty or executive agreement, bring regulators together to ensure that their rules in a particular substantive area conform to a common regulatory standard. Judges can also engage in the equivalent activity, but in a much more ad hoc manner. Harmonization is often politically very controversial, with critics charging that the "technical" process of achieving convergence ignores the many winners and losers in domestic publics, most of whom do not have any input into the process.

VERTICAL NETWORKS

In a disaggregated world order, horizontal government networks would be more numerous than vertical networks, but vertical networks would have a crucial role to play. Although a core principle of such an order is the importance of keeping global governance functions primarily in the hands of domestic government officials, in some circumstances states do come together the way citizens might and choose to delegate their individual governing authority to a "higher" organization – a "supranational" organization that does exist, at least conceptually, above the state. The officials of these organizations do in fact replicate the governing functions that states exercise regarding their citizens. Thus, for instance, states can truly decide that the only way to reduce tariffs or subsidies is to adopt a body of rules prohibiting them and allow an independent court or tribunal to enforce those rules. Alternatively, states can come together and give an international court the power to try war criminals – the same function that national courts perform – in circumstances in which national courts are unwilling or unable to do so.

These supranational organizations can be far more effective in performing the functions states charge them to perform if they can link up directly with national government institutions. Absent a world government, it is impossible to grant supranational officials genuine coercive power: judges on supranational tribunals cannot call in the global equivalent of federal marshals if their judgments are not obeyed; global regulators cannot impose fines and enforce them through global courts. Their only hope of being able to marshal such authority is to harness the cooperation of their domestic counterparts – to effectively "borrow" the coercive power of domestic government officials to implement supranational rules and decisions...

These vertical networks are enforcement networks. But they can also operate as harmonization networks, in the sense that they will bring national rules and supranational rules closer together. Still other vertical networks are principally information networks. The environmental ministers of NAFTA countries, for instance, benefit by working with the Commission on Environmental Cooperation (CEC), a NAFTA supranational institution charged with gathering information on environmental enforcement policies and compiling a record of complaints of nonenforcement by private actors. This is an attempt to enhance enforcement through the provision of information. ...

DISAGGREGATED INTERNATIONAL ORGANIZATIONS

...

In a world of disaggregated states that nevertheless still act as unitary actors under some circumstances, it is important to be able to distinguish between different types of international organizations in terms both of the relevant government officials who represent their states within them and the degree and type of autonomous power they can exercise. Where international organizations have become sufficiently specialized to develop the equivalent of an executive, judicial, and even legislative branch, vertical government networks become possible. Where they are specialized in a specific issue area but exercise little or no autonomous power, they can be hosts for horizontal government networks. But when they are regional or global organizations charged with assuring peace and security, or similar very general functions, they represent an older and much more formal model of international cooperation, conducted by diplomats more than domestic government officials. ...

Global Impact

[There are] three ways in which government networks currently contribute to world order: (1) by creating convergence and informed divergence; (2) by improving compliance with international rules; and (3) by increasing the scope, nature, and quality of international cooperation. Kal Raustiala, a young legal scholar and political scientist, has demonstrated ways in which government networks lead to "regulatory export" of rules and practices from one country to another. The result can be sufficient policy convergence to make it possible over the longer term to conclude a more formal international agreement setting forth a common regulatory regime.[30] Soft law codes of conduct issued by transgovernmental regulatory organizations, as well as the simple dissemination of credible and authoritative information, also promote convergence. Promoting convergence, on the other hand, can also give rise to informed divergence, where a national governmental institution or the government as a whole acknowledges a prevailing standard or trend and deliberately chooses to diverge from it for reasons of national history, culture, or politics.

Government networks also improve compliance with international treaties and customary law. Vertical enforcement networks do this explicitly and directly by providing a supranational court or regulatory authority with a direct link to a national government institution that can exercise actual coercive authority on its behalf. Equally important, however, are the ways in which technical assistance flowing through horizontal networks can build regulatory or judicial capacity in states where there may be a willingness to enforce international legal obligations but the infrastructure is weak.

Finally, government networks enhance existing international cooperation by providing the mechanisms for transferring regulatory approaches that are proving increasingly successful domestically to the international arena. ... Government networks create regional and even global transmission belts for information that can readily expand to include as many nations as can usefully participate. ...

[Let's examine] what could be if policymakers and opinion leaders around the world began looking through the lens of the disaggregated state and decided to recognize government networks as prime mechanisms of global governance, using existing networks and creating new ones to address specific problems. First, they could harness the capacity of government networks for self-regulation, drawing on the examples of private commercial networks that succeed in enforcing "network norms" against cheating or other undesirable behavior. ... But they could also bolster their members by enhancing the prestige of membership in a particular government network enough to give government officials who want to adhere to high professional standards ammunition against countervailing domestic forces. Just as international organizations from the European Union to the Community of Democracies have done, government networks could condition admission on meeting specified criteria designed to reinforce network norms.[31] ...

Note that government networks, both as they exist now and as they could exist, exercise different types of power to accomplish results. They have access to traditional "hard," or coercive, power. The central role of national government officials in government networks means that when the participants make a decision that requires implementation, the power to implement already exists at the national level. The power to induce behavior through selective admission requirements is also a form of hard power. At the same time, much of the work of many horizontal government networks depends on "soft" power – the power of information, socialization, persuasion, and discussion. An effective world order needs to harness every kind of power available.

4. A JUST NEW WORLD ORDER

...

Some observers see government networks as promoting global technocracy – secret governance by unelected regulators and judges. Others fear that the informality and flexibility of networks is a deliberate device to make an end run around the formal constraints – representation rules, voting rules, and elaborate negotiating procedures – imposed on global governance by traditional international organizations. Absent these constraints, critics charge, powerful nations run roughshod over weaker ones. Still others, however, worry more that weak nations will be excluded from powerful government networks altogether. At the domestic level, critics charge harmonization networks with distorting domestic political processes and judicial networks through the introduction of polluting or diluting national legal traditions. Still others picture government networks as vehicles for special interests – shadowy decision-making forums to which those who are "connected" or "in the know" have access.

In response to these criticisms, I propose a set of potential solutions:

- A conceptual move to recognize all government officials as performing both a domestic and an international function. Such recognition would mean that national constituents would automatically hold them accountable for their activities both within and across borders.

- An effort to make government networks as visible as possible. Creating a common website and linking the individual websites of participants in a government network will have the paradoxical effect of making a government network real by making it virtual.

- Increasing the number and activities of legislative networks, both to monitor the activity of regulatory networks and to launch initiatives of their own.

- Using government networks as the spine of broader policy networks, including international organizations, NGOs, corporations, and other interested actors, thereby guaranteeing wider participation in government network activities but also retaining an accountable core of government officials.

- A grab-bag of domestic political measures designed to enhance the accountability of government networks, depending on the extent to which a particular polity perceives a problem and what it decides to do about it.

None of these measures addresses the question of how members of government networks should treat each other, however, as fellow participants in, and constituents of, a world order. ... But the officials responsible should be guided by general constitutional norms in their relations with one another. In this context, I propose five basic principles designed to ensure an inclusive, tolerant, respectful, and decentralized world order. ...

Global Deliberative Equality. ... Global deliberative equality, building on ideas developed by Michael Ignatieff, is a principle of maximum inclusion, to the extent feasible, by all relevant and affected parties in processes of transgovernmental deliberation.

Legitimate Difference. The principle of "legitimate difference" is a principle of pluralism. ... [A] disaggregated world order begins from the premise of multiple ways of organizing societies and polities at the national level. ... Each must be prepared to recognize the validity of each other's approach, as long as all accept a core of common fundamental principles.

Positive Comity. ... [P]ositive comity is a principle of affirmative cooperation. As a principle of governance for transnational regulatory cooperation, it requires regulatory agencies, courts, and even legislators to substitute consultation and active assistance for unilateral action and noninterference.

Checks and Balances. All participating government institutions, national and supranational, must interact with each other in accordance with a global concept of checks and balances, whereby the distribution of power is always fluid on both the horizontal and particularly the vertical axes. ...

Subsidiarity. ... [T]he principle of subsidiarity ... is a principle of locating governance at the lowest possible level that closest to the individuals and groups affected by the rules and decisions adopted and enforced. ...

The choice and formulation of any such principles is inevitably personal and partial. The point here is that some set of constitutional principles must operate at a metalevel across all types of government networks, specifying basic ground rules for how the members of these networks treat each other and what the basic division of labor is between them. ...

5.   CONCLUSION: PUSHING THE PARADIGM

The mantra of this book is that the state is not disappearing; it is disaggregating. Its component institutions – regulators, judges, and even legislators – are all reaching out beyond national borders in various ways, finding that their once "domestic" jobs have a growing international dimension. ...

Global governance through government networks would mean harnessing national government officials to address international problems. It would be global governance through national governments, except in circumstances in which those governments concluded that a genuine supranational institution was necessary to exercise genuine global authority. In those circumstances, which would be the exception rather than the rule, the supranational institutions would be more effective than ever before through the operation of vertical government networks. ...

But this is only the beginning. Push the paradigm a few steps further and imagine the possibilities. ...

Suppose sovereignty itself could be disaggregated, that it attached to specific government institutions such as courts, regulatory agencies, and legislators or legislative committees. But as exercised by these institutions, the core characteristic of sovereignty would shift from autonomy from outside interference to the capacity to participate in transgovernmental networks of all types.[33] This concept of sovereignty as participation, or status, means that disaggregated sovereignty would empower government institutions around the world to engage with each other in networks that would strengthen them and improve their ability to perform their designated government tasks individually and collectively. ...

2. Naim, "Five Wars of Globalization," 29.

6. The Financial Stability Forum was initiated by the finance ministers and central bank governors of the Group of Seven (G-7) industrial countries in February 1999, following a report on international cooperation and coordination in the area of financial market supervision and surveillance by the president of the Deutsche Bundesbank. In addition to representatives from the Basel Committee, IOSCO, and the International Association of Insurance Supervisors (IAIS), its members include senior representatives from national authorities responsible for financial stability in significant international financial centers; international financial institutions such as the Bank for International Settlements (BIS), the IMF, the Organization of Economic Cooperation and Development (OECD), and the World Bank; and committees of central bank experts. "A Guide to Committees, Groups and Clubs," on the International Monetary Fund homepage (cited 7 July 2003); available from *http://imf.org/external/np/exr/facts/groups.htm#FSF.*

7. American readers may be skeptical of these reports due to the widespread and completely false statistic about how few members of Congress have a passport. In fact, 93 percent of all members hold passports and average two trips abroad a year. Indeed, 20 percent claim to speak a foreign language. Eric Schmitt and Elizabeth Becker, "Insular Congress Appears to be Myth," *New York Times*, 4 November 2000, sect. A, 9. What is true is that some members fear that their constituents will identify trips to meet their counterparts abroad with "junkets," but that is a matter of public education.

8. Nye, *Paradox of American Power* 9.

10. Dehousse, "Regulation by Networks in the European Community," 259.

11. Ibid., 254

16. Annan, We *the Peoples,* 70; see also Reinicke and Deng, *Critical Choices* and Reinicke, "The Other World Wide Web."

19. Ibid., 376.

20. Ibid., 374.

25. For a highly theoretical but comprehensive overview of the development of the idea of "policy networks" in U.S. and British political science, a concept that includes but is broader than my concept of government networks, see R.A.W. Rhodes, *Understanding Governance,* 32 45.

30. See Raustiala, "The Architecture of International Cooperation: Transgovernmental Networks and The Future of International Law," 1.

31. In Council for a Community of Democracies homepage (cited 7 July 2003); available from *http://www.ccd21.org/*

33. Chayes and Chayes, *The New Sovereignty*, 107.

The Architecture of International Cooperation: Transgovernmental Networks and the Future of International Law

Kal Raustiala

43 VIRGINIA JOURNAL INTERNATIONAL LAW 1 (2002)

...

This article assesses the future of international cooperation by examining transgovernmental networks and evaluating their relationship to liberal internationalism. My central claim is that transgovernmental cooperation is a significant development in international law, but it is likely to bolster liberal internationalism as much – or more – than it will undermine or displace it. Thus, rather than competitive architectures of cooperation, the two are often synergistic. (For simplicity I often refer to the two as networks and treaties). Under some conditions networks should make treaties work better. Under other conditions networks perform a gap-filling role: where treaties are politically or economically precluded, networks provide an alternative mode of cooperation. In still other situations networks may smooth the negotiation of treaties[17]. Liberal internationalism, in turn, can provide a focal point and setting for transgovernmental cooperation[18]. The relationship is complex, but the most plausible prediction is that transgovernmentalism will supplement, rather than supplant, the traditional tools of international law.

---

[17] For example, in competition policy. See, e.g., Andrew T. Guzman, Is International Antitrust Possible? 73 N.Y.U. L. Rev. 1501, 1504 (1998) ("The incentives facing individual countries make it extremely difficult perhaps impossible to negotiate substantive international antitrust agreements."). See also Beth A. Simmons, The International Politics of Harmonization: The Case of Capital Market Regulation, 55 Int'l Org. 589 (2001)

[18] Keohane & Nye, in TRANSATLANTIC GOVERNANCE IN THE GLOBAL ECONOMY (Mark A.Pollack & Gregory C. Shaffer eds., 2001)

My claim of synergy builds on several subsidiary arguments. First, an empirical examination of three networks – securities, competition (antitrust), and environmental regulation – demonstrates that networks are an active and growing part of contemporary cooperation. Second, I argue three chief factors are driving the evolution of regulatory networks: the expansion of domestic regulation, increased economic interdependence, and technological innovation. Third, while enforcement has been a key driver of transgovernmental cooperation, the cases suggest that networks promote what I term "regulatory export": the export of regulatory rules and practices from major powers to weaker states. While it is important not to overstate the case, this process promotes policy convergence among states[19]. I offer a theory of this process of convergence that builds upon the special qualities of networks and especially the role of what economists term "network effects."[20] Fourth, and most importantly, the cooperation that networks permit and the regulatory convergence that they facilitate, while significant in their own right, have important implications for liberal internationalism. In particular, by building bureaucratic capacity, networks can improve domestic regulation and thereby enhance treaty compliance and effectiveness. Put differently, there are good reasons to believe networks will, under some conditions, make treaties more effective by making governments more effective.

Together, these related claims lead me to predict that, far from a threat, transgovernmentalism will largely prove a positive force for liberal internationalism. In so arguing, I do not mean to imply that the rise of networks is normatively attractive on balance. That evaluation is one that requires extensive attention to factors that fall outside the scope of this article, such as the transparency and accountability of networks, the substantive law at issue, and even the value of international cooperation itself. Nonetheless, supporters of liberal internationalism – which are legion – should not reflexively reject transgovernmentalism as a dangerous and unwelcome development. The era of the international treaty is not ending; in fact, if the arguments in this article prove correct, treaties and international organizations may become more important – in the sense of more effective – than ever before. ...

---

[19] There is a significant debate about the degree of policy convergence generally in the global economy. See, e.g., Beth Simmons & Zachary Elkins, Globalization and Policy Diffusion: Explaining Three Decades of Liberalization (paper prepared for the Conference on Globalization and Governance, La Jolla, California, March 2001).
[20] Mark A. Lemley & David McGowan, *Legal Implications of Network Economic Effects*, 86 Cal. L. Rev. 479 (1998).

A.   The Rise of Networks

By all accounts transgovernmental cooperation has expanded enormously in recent years. ... The rise of the telephone, the jet, the fax and now email and the Internet has progressively made long-distance communication, and thus networks, far easier and (all else being equal) more prevalent[35] ... Technological innovation is thus one major factor behind the rise of networks. A second is the rise of the regulatory state itself. In the New Deal and immediate postwar eras, domestic regulatory law expanded markedly in the U.S. and across the globe.[37] ... The third factor, globalization (or economic interdependence), has now brought many of these substantive differences to the forefront of world politics.[39] ...

---

[35] Good data on the prevalence of networks is unavailable. But there is little evidence of networks in the pre-World War II era, and anecdotal data indicates that network activity has grown in the last decade.

[37] On the early development of the regulatory state in the U.S., see Stephen Skowronek, Building a New American State: The Expansion of National Administrative Capacities, 1877-1920 (1982); Robert L. Rabin, *Federal Regulation in Historical Perspective*, 38 Stan. L. Rev. 1189 (1986); *see also* Thomas K. McCraw, Prophets of Regulation 61 (1984). The history of U.S. regulation is presented via biography in McCraw, supra (presenting biographies of Adams, Brandeis, Landis, and Kahn).
The New Deal and World War II introduced a marked acceleration of the creation of the regulatory state. See Rabin, supra, at 1252-53 ("In historical perspective, the New Deal appears as a distinct break from the past...even the more traditional regulatory aspects of the New Deal conceived of government activity as a permanent bulwark against deep-rooted structural shortcomings in the market economy."). Charles Schultze describes the development of the regulatory state as follows:
> Even as late as the middle 1950s the federal government had a major regulatory responsibility in only four areas: antitrust, financial institutions, transportation, and communications. In 1976, eighty-three federal agencies were engaged in regulating some aspect of private activity. Thirty-four of those had been created since 1960 and all but eighteen since 1930.

Charles Schultze, The Public Use of Private Interest 8 (1977).
Another fertile period occurred beginning in the 1960s. ... These "rights revolution" era agencies – with the exception of the EPA – tend to be involved in transgovernmentalism to a far lesser degree than their New Deal era counterparts.
Internationally, the signal political achievement of the aftermath of World War II was what John Gerard Ruggie famously termed the "compromise of embedded liberalism." Modern western democracies sought international economic liberalism yet domestic economic stability achieved through the regulatory state. Liberalism was thus embedded in a structure of domestic interventionism and the welfare administration; regulation – both domestic and international – was central to the quest of avoiding the destructive unchecked nationalism of the 1930s. John Gerard Ruggie, *International Regimes, Transactions, and Change: Embedded Liberalism in the Postwar Economic Order*, in International Regimes (Stephen D. Krasner ed., 1983).

[39] Indeed, an earlier incarnation of transgovernmental theory was developed by Keohane and Nye, who also pioneered the study of interdependence in modern international relations theory. Keohane & Nye, Transgovernmental Relations and International Organizations, (Mark A. Pollack & Gregory C. Shaffer eds., 2001)

III.   Transgovernmental Regulatory Networks: Three Cases

...

Regulatory power is diffused in the environmental arena; largely duopolistic in the competition arena; and nearly monopolistic in securities law.

Despite these differences, networks are active in each case. However, the effects of networks vary in important ways. The concentration of regulatory power has two implications. First, it encourages harmonization because other jurisdictions typically have greater incentives to converge on the dominant actor's model.[110] When regulatory power is diffuse, harmonization is possible but less likely and less dramatic. Second, the significance, for international law, of regulatory convergence and especially of capacity building depends on the distribution of regulatory power. Where regulatory power is diffuse, multilateral treaties and organization are numerous. Consequently, convergence and capacity building can strengthen the operation of treaties, improving compliance and effectiveness. When regulatory power is concentrated, blunting incentives for liberal internationalist cooperation, the lack of treaties renders this process of synergy largely moot. ...

Unlike the first two cases, environmental regulation is an area with widely diffused regulatory power and, correspondingly, a myriad of international treaties. Multilateral environmental agreements were negotiated at a rapid pace in the 20th century.[204] While accords continue to be developed, implementing existing commitments has become a major focus.[205] This focus has drawn attention to the capacity – or lack thereof – for environmental regulation that many states possess. A contemporaneous and, as I will argue below, related development has been the rise of government networks.

---

[110] Though not always; see Simmons, International Politics of Harmonization, e.g., in competition policy. See, e.g. Andrew T. Guzman, Is International Antitrust Possible? 73 N.Y.U.L. Rev. 1501, 1504 (1998) ("The incentives facing individual countries make it extremely difficult, perhaps impossible, to negotiate substantive international antitrust agreements."). See also Beth A. Simmons, The International Politics of Harmonization: The Case of Capital Market Regulation, 55 Int'l Org. 589 (2001).

[204] See the partial list in the ENTRI database, at http://www.ciesin.org (last visited Oct. 5, 2002).

[205] International Environmental Commitments. See e.g., The Implementation and Effectiveness of International Environmental Commitments: Theory and Practice (David

continued

As with the securities law area where IOSCO is the primary forum for networking, the emerging environmental network has been solidified – though not controlled by – a forum organization: the International Network for Environmental Compliance and Enforcement (INECE). Here, however, networks play a different role than in securities regulation. Because treaties remain the core approach to environmental rulemaking, the network of environmental regulators is primary focused on enhancing the capacity of regulators to regulate. In other words, capacity building, rather than creating new agencies or embracing particular substantive rules, is the primary activity. ...

The combination of technical assistance, enforcement cooperation, and general peer-to-peer ties among environmental regulators appear to be forging some convergence in approaches. But because it is so closely tied to local conditions, and because regulatory power is so widely diffused, environmental regulation probably demonstrates the least convergence of the three cases in this article. ...

As in the competition and securities cases, the environmental network has served as a conduit for the export of regulation from the U.S., though not as dramatically as in the first two cases. And, as in the securities context, an organization of regulators (IOSCO, INECE) has developed to structure and promote the network. The NAFTA experience illustrates that the regulatory diffusion that networks promote can also be strongly influenced by existing liberal internationalist institutions. NAFTA provided additional incentives for regulatory cooperation and an institutional structure within which regulators' collaborative and capacity building activities are organized. ...

G. Victor, Kal Raustiala & Eugene B. Skolnikoff eds., 1998) [hereinafter International Environmental Commitments]. The relationship between compliance and implementation is not straightforward; see generally Kal Raustiala, Compliance and Effectiveness in International Regulatory Cooperation, 32 Case W. Res. J. J.Int'l L.387 (2000). But generally speaking implementation is a critical step toward compliance.

IV.   Transgovernmental Cooperation and Policy Convergence

...

A.   Networks and the Export of Regulation

A striking aspect of transgovernmental cooperation is that many jurisdictions appear eager to replicate U.S. and EU regulatory approaches as they increasingly interact with their counterparts in other nations. The result is the diffusion of regulatory rules and practices around the world. ... In networks, soft power is exercised by traditionally dominant states – no state has more soft power than the U.S. – and the dominant direction of diffusion is clearly from the U.S. (and EU) and toward less advanced economies.[239] ...

Regulatory convergence is important for two chief reasons: convergence can permit deeper cooperation over time and can decrease tensions in the trade arena. ... Rather than a formal, multilateral process of negotiation, convergence is fostered through a decentralized, incremental process of interaction and emulation.

... Networks provide a means for the transfer of regulatory ideas and policies. They socialize regulators from new jurisdictions. Most importantly, networks increase the gains for states to engage in capacity building efforts. ...

B.   Cooperative Choices and the Incentives for Diffusion and Convergence

1.   Why converge?

One clear lesson of the three cases in this article is that U.S. regulators often believe that regulatory convergence is useful and makes robust cooperation possible. For example, Douglas Melamed of the DOJ recently stated that "cooperation in specific cases ... can be successful only among

---

[239] There is certainly some small degree of cross-fertilization. The EPA, for example, has at least argued that "EPA staff benefit from working with partners outside of the International capacity building programs expose staff to alternative approaches to environmental management and, in turn, help inject creativity and innovation into our domestic programs." No firm examples are given. U.S. EPA, Best Practices for EPA's International Capacity Building Programs: Report of an EPA Task Force, at 8 (November 1999).

countries which have relatively similar legal systems [and] common economic experience and trust each other.'"[256] In Melamed's view, cooperation can in turn encourage the evolution of "common views and ... understandings" about substantive and procedural issues, which facilitates shared enforcement responsibility and leads to deeper, more effective cooperation.[257] Similarly, a top FTC official stated that "the constant contacts [with foreign regulators] enable us to understand each other's analysis, lead to convergence in our approaches toward competition matters—in some measure due to an increasingly common economic analysis—and benefit parties insofar as we are often able to arrive at complementary remedies." [258] Policy convergence and participation in networks are, in this view, mutually reinforcing. ...

2.   Convergence on What Model?

...

What incentives exist for weak jurisdictions to import the regulatory approaches of the advanced industrial democracies? In a complex, uncertain economic environment, the strategy of adopting successful

---

[256] A. Douglas Melamed, International Cooperation in Competition Law and Policy: What Can be Achieved at the Bilateral , Regional and Multilateral Levels, Address Before the WTO Symposium on Competition Policy and the Multilateral Trading System (Apr. 17, 1999), in 2 J. Int'l Econ. L. 423 (1999); Interview with Ed Hand, Antitrust Div., Dept. of Justice, In Washington D.C. (April 2000).

[257] Id. at 425. As the DevTech Report describes with regard to antitrust regulation: A Lithuanian staff professional described, for example, how the American advisors had "opened her eyes" to the difference between regulation or prevention of price "speculation," versus assuring that the prices advertised were not deceptive. This type of change in "mentality" or outlook, resulting from interaction with the American advisors, was described frequently by staff in respect to their understanding of key competition and consumer protection concepts, such as product and geographic market definition, barriers to entry, price collusion [etc.]. Its importance for sustainability lies first in the fact that these concepts underpin the fundamental re-orientation of the public sector institutions being assisted. Second, it was clearly the case that the persons who described their understanding of the concepts conveyed by the American advisors were quite capable of training other staff in these concepts. DevTech Report, I.d.; see also DevTech Systems, Inc., Final Evaluation of the Fed. Trade Comm'n And Dept. of Justice Component on the Project on Competition (1996) [Hereinafter DevTech Report].

[258] Debra Valentine, General Counsel of the FTC, Remarks at a 1998 American Bar Association panel, cited in Knight, supra note 174, at 30. As the DOJ ICPAC Report notes, "substantive and procedural differences between the U.S. and non-U.S. legal systems can also generate frictions between nations." ICPAC Report, Annex 1-C, supra note 83, at iii. See also Slaughter, Agencies on the Loose?, supra note 8, at 540 ("[MOUs] have led not only to greater cooperation between states, but also to more effective enforcement of the antitrust statutes of both parties.").

foreign models can markedly reduce regulatory costs.[271] Importing jurisdictions do not bear the (often considerable) expense of creating the regulatory institutions they adopt.[272] While these institutions "may not match domestic conditions precisely ... [they] are ready-made, pre-tested, and provide international compatibility."[273] Foreign regulatory rules and systems also may come "pre-interpreted" – with a body of case law and other decisions that have elaborated and improved the rules over time.[274] Finally, technical assistance programs further ease the transition and enable regulators to learn from experienced practitioners. ...

C.   A Network Economics Theory of Transgovernmentalism and Policy Convergence

...

Network effects exist when "the utility that a user derives from the consumption of a good increases with the number of agents consuming the good."[290] ... The telephone system is an actual network: one phone is worthless, only valuable when linked to others. The more phones, the more valuable each phone is. Virtual networks exist when increasing the number of members increases the utility of other members, even though a single item or member is not useless. ... Computer software exhibits virtual network effects: a program on its own is useful to the owner, but one shared by millions of others, such as Microsoft Word, is far more useful because users can easily trade files with one another. ... While transgovernmental networks are at the limit of what might be considered virtual networks, my claim is that the resemblance is sufficient to generate several arguments about networks and cooperation.

... Networks are characterized by extensive sharing of information, coordinating enforcement efforts, and joint policymaking activities. These activities plausibly exhibit network effects: the more regulatory agencies that participate in coordinating and reciprocating enforcement efforts,

---

[271] Giandomenico Majone, Cross-National Sources of Regulatory Policymaking in Europe and the United States, 11 J. Pub. Pol'y 79 (1991).

[272] Nancy Birdsall & Robert Z. Lawrence, Deep Integration and Trade Agreements Good for Developing Countries?, in Global Public Goods. For an extensive study of public gods see Global Public Goods: International Cooperation in the 21st Century (Inge Kaul et al. eds., 1999)

[273] Id.

[274] I thank Damien Gerardin for making this point.

for example, the better off are all the other agencies. The same logic applies to information-sharing: the more jurisdictions that share information about financial markets or international cartels, for instance, the better off any one jurisdiction is at enforcing its law and punishing (and deterring) corruption and collusion. If U.S. officials like Melamed are correct that "cooperation in specific cases can be successful only among countries which have relatively similar legal systems,"[293] then the greater the number of jurisdictions that resemble one another, the more valuable cooperation among them ought to be. ...

In a setting characterized by network externalities, returns to scale increase rather than decrease. The larger the number of individuals that have the same or compatible software, the more useful that software is. Networked markets, as a result, exhibit "lock-in" or "tipping" effects.[295] Once a standard emerges in a network, it can rapidly dominate that network. Once that occurs there is little incentive for actors to change standards, even if a more efficient alternative exists.[296] ...

[290] Katz & Shapiro, e.g. Michael L. Katz & Carl Shapiro, Network Externalities, Competition and Compatibility, 75 Am. Econ. Rev. 424 (1985); Lemley & Mc Gowan, Legal Implication of Network Economic Effects, supra note 20. A network effect exists when "the utility that a user derives from consumption of the good increases with the number of other agents consuming the good".

[293] A. Douglas Melamed, International Cooperation in Competition Law and Policy: What Can be Achieved at the Bilateral , Regional and Multilateral Levels, Address Before the WTO Symposium on Competition Policy and the Multilateral Trading System (Apr. 17, 1999), in 2 J. Int'l Econ. L. 423 (1999); Interview with Ed Hand, Antitrust Div., Dept. of Justice, in Washington D.C. (April 2000).

[295] Tipping can also occur outside of virtual networks. Malcolm Gladwell argues that tipping points frequently occur in social phenomena in a way that mimics the spread of epidemics. Gladwell acknowledges the link to network economics at times; in an afterword he describes network effects (in the context of the rising value of a fax machine as the virtual network expands) and argues that:

> epidemics create networks as well: a virus moves from one person to another, spreading through a community, and the more people a virus infects, the more "powerful" the epidemic is. But this is also why epidemics so often come to a crashing halt. Once you've had a particular strain of the flu, or the measles, you develop an immunity to it. ... Malcolm Gladwell, The Tipping Point: How Little Things Can Make a Big Difference 272-73 (2002). He goes on to argue something analogous in the context of virtual networks: while the expansion of a network demonstrates increasing returns to scale, as a network grows in size, however, it is also the case the time and nuisance costs borne by each member of the network grow as well. ...The phone network is so large and unwieldy that we are increasingly only interested in using it selectively. We are getting immune to the telephone.

Id. at 273.

[296] Lemley & McGowan, Mark A.Lemley &David McGowan, Legal Implications of Network Economic Effects, 86 Cal. L. Effects, 86 Cal. L. Rev. 479 (1998).

Given the existence of a government network, regulatory convergence increases the number of jurisdictions with which a state can usefully cooperate. Over time, network theory predicts that tipping occurs, leading to an equilibrium in which one (or more ...) regulatory standard dominates. Network effects thus aid policy standardization. Again, this is not to say that convergence is "caused" by network effects, but rather that network effects boost the existing incentives to standardize...

The interesting question is which "standard" dominates in a given situation and why. In regulatory networks, it is likely to be the standard of the most powerful actor, often the U.S.[300] ...

While this dynamic does not depend on the existence of networks to occur, network effects can strengthen this tendency toward convergence in asymmetric situations. When many agencies are regulating a field in a similar manner, and cooperating with one another through networks, network effects can push agencies to adopt the dominant regulatory standard, leading to or accelerating a tipping process...

Network effects thus create incentives for weak jurisdictions to import regulatory models in line with the emerging international "standards" in regulation, and for powerful jurisdictions to try to export their standards. For weak states the import of regulation can be thought of as "a price of admission" to the fullest range of benefits provided by the network. Particularly when regulatory bodies are new, that price may be negligible.[304] If so, it is likely to be outweighed by the benefits of rough harmonization with others in the network.

It is important to underscore that this network effects argument does not imply that multiple regulatory standards are impossible. In fact, the more a network is virtual rather than actual, the more likely there are to be multiple standards.[305] But network effects do imply that convergence on one or more standards is likely and this convergence is likely to be relatively sticky. Once actors in a network setting adopt a standard,

---

[300] In the economics literature there is much discussion of the first mover advantage. That is important here as well, as I note below. But in international politics not all states can be credibly vie to be first movers—for Botswana such an effort is hopeless; for the U.S., EU, and Japan, it is reasonable

[304] Or even negative, if the jurisdiction is introducing regulation for the first time.

[305] Mark Lemley & David McGowan, Legal Implications of Network Economic Effects, 86 Cal. L. Rev. 479 (1998). Moreover, they note that "Network effects are not always absolute; sometimes multiple products can each build a core of users with its own partial network effect." Id.

switching to a new standard requires extensive and costly, and hence rarely achieved, collective action. ...

V.   The Implications of Transgovernmentalism for International Law and Organization

...

A key underlying premise of my argument is that the incentives to create networks or to negotiate treaties vary across the spectrum of regulatory power. As a result, networks play different roles under different distributions of regulatory power, and in turn appear to interact with liberal internationalism differently. When regulatory power is highly asymmetric, as in securities law, liberal internationalism tends to be shunned and networks primarily fill gaps in cooperation. Conversely, when regulatory power is diffuse, and therefore treaties are an essential cooperative tool, the domestic capacity building that networks promote may increase compliance with, and the effectiveness of, treaty law. When regulatory power is moderately concentrated, networks may help smooth the path to a liberal internationalist solution by promoting convergence in regulatory approach.[326] In short, the distribution of regulatory power helps account for the presence of treaties and therefore helps explain when, and how, networks may interact with treaties. ...

There are many theories of compliance with treaties. An analysis of the influence of networks depends partly upon the particular theory of compliance one embraces. I will discuss the four leading theories of compliance and illustrate that three imply that transgovernmental networks should bolster treaty compliance.[336] Moreover, those theories supporting a claim of synergy between networks and treaties have the greatest empirical support. The same considerations that indicate improved

---

[326] Empirically, in the competition case the result could be multiple treaties on competition, each within a particular sphere—the European Union's or the United States'. I discuss this possibility further infra.

[336] A comprehensive overview of compliance theory can be found in Raustiala & Slaughter, Kal Raustila & Anne-Marie Slaughter, Compliance, International Law, and International Relations, in Handbook of International relations... Scholars of international law and of international relations increasingly focus on compliance as a central issue in international law. See e.g. John Norton Moore, Enhancing Compliance with International Law: A Neglected Remedy, 39 Va J. Int'l L. 881, 884 (1999) (" I believe that the greatest challenge for the future of the rule of law internationally is to enhance rates of compliance").

compliance imply that networks will also improve treaty effectiveness, a closely related but often much more important issue.[337] ...

The traditional realist (or economist) baseline is that states comply with treaties only when compliance is in their interest. ... [N]etworks may improve treaty compliance by improving domestic regulatory capacity; improved capacity should often lower the domestic costs of compliance...

Some scholars of compliance reject the enforcement approach and assert that states actually have a propensity to comply with their international commitments.[339] Managerialism, an approach to compliance most often associated with the work of Abram and Antonia Handler Chayes, argues that the primary drivers of non-compliance are actually rule ambiguity and, especially, lack of domestic regulatory capacity. ... If indeed, as managerialists argue, the most effective methods to improve treaty compliance are facilitative, interactive, and discursive, then networks should often improve treaty compliance – especially when they involve technical assistance that improves existing regulatory practices at the domestic level. ...

Other compliance theories emphasize the role of norms (though the role of norms is present in managerial theory as well). A prominent example is the theory of "transnational legal process," which stresses the interface

---

[337] Compliance generally refers to a state of conformity or identity between an actor's behavior and a specified rule. While most common-sense notions of effectiveness relate to "solving the underlying problem," the factors that may influence the solution of a complex international problem are myriad. In many cases disentangling them is impossible. Hence many analysts define and assess effectiveness in more modest terms: as observable, desired changes in behavior. Compliance is neither necessary nor sufficient for effectiveness. However, in general, and ceteris paribus, more compliance yields more effectiveness—particularly when high compliance is not the result of a change in the legal standard but rather results from actual behavioral change aimed at meeting that standard or that results in meeting that standard. For more on these distinctions, see generally Raustiala, Compliance and Effectiveness in International Regulatory Cooperation, The Implementation and Effectiveness of International Environment Commitments: Theory and Practice (David G. Victor. Kal Raustiala & Eugene B. Skolnikoff eds, 1998) [herinafter International Environmental Commitments]. The relationship between compliance and implementation is also straight forward; See generally Kal Raustiala, Compliance and Effectiveness in International Regulatory Cooperation, 32 Case W. Res. J. Int'l L. 387 (2000). But generally speaking implementation is a critical step toward compliance.

[339] See Abram Chayes & Antonia Handler Chayes, The New Sovereignty: Compliance with International Regulatory Agreements (1995); Abram Chayes & Antonia Handler Chayes, On Compliance, 47 Int'l Org. 175 (1993); Ronald Mitchell, Compliance Theory: An Overview, in Improving Compliance with International Environmental Law (James Cameron et al. eds., 1996).

between international norms and domestic legal processes.[348] Developed primarily by Harold Koh, the theory focuses on the incorporation of international norms in domestic legal systems.[349] Transnational legal process has three components: interaction, interpretation, and internalization...

The theory contends that treaty compliance is driven by the efficacy of domestic law and the degree to which international norms embed in this law. This argument too suggests a positive role for networks. Interaction is a central attribute of networks and a central part of Koh's theory. More, and more active, transgovernmental networks should provide increased opportunity for transnational legal processes to occur. Moreover, because a key part of transnational legal processes is socialization – the engagement of governmental actors, on a regular basis, in the articulation, interpretation, and promotion of norms and rules – it is plausible and even likely that networks will strengthen that process. ...

[L]egitimacy theory argues that states comply more with treaty rules that are legitimate and exhibit right process, less with rules that lack these qualities. While empirical support for legitimacy theory is slim, it has received extensive attention from international lawyers and thus I consider it here.

... Legitimacy theory focuses not on regulatory capacity but on the process by which the treaty rules in question were formed.[357] In general, the formal, procedural, and normative thrust of legitimacy theory is deeply in tension with the nature of cooperation embodied in transgovernmentalism. ...

---

[348] See, e.g., Harold H. Koh, *Bringing International Law Home*, 35 Hous. L. Rev. 623, 628 (1998); see also Harold H. Koh, *Why Do Nations Obey International Law?* 106 Yale J. Int'l L. 2599 (1997)

[349] While these rules and norms may be articulated in an international treaty, they need not be.

[357] Moreover, legitimacy theory casts doubt on the likelihood that MOUs, and transgovernmental cooperation in general, will exhibit high compliance. MOUs, because they are flexible and often vague, frequently lack the indicia of determinancy, coherence and so forth that legitimacy theory identifies as important. Because many of the "obligations" that exist in networks are avowedly non-legal, it may be a category mistake to apply legitimacy theory at all.

Introduction: Epistemic Communities and International Policy Coordination

Peter M. Haas

46(1) International Organization 1(1992)

...

In this volume of articles, we acknowledge that systemic conditions and domestic pressures impose constraints on state behavior, but we argue that there is still a wide degree of latitude for state action. How states identify their interests and recognize the latitude of actions deemed appropriate in specific issue-areas of policymaking are functions of the manner in which the problems are understood by the policymakers or are represented by those to whom they turn for advice under conditions of uncertainty. Recognizing that human agency lies at the interstices between systemic conditions, knowledge, and national actions, we offer an approach that examines the role that networks of knowledge-based experts [–] epistemic communities [–] play in articulating the cause-and-effect relationships of complex problems, helping states identify their interests, framing the issues for collective debate, proposing specific policies, and identifying salient points for negotiation. We argue that control over knowledge and information is an important dimension of power and that the diffusion of new ideas and information can lead to new patterns of behavior and prove to be an important determinant of international policy coordination.

An epistemic community is a network of professionals with recognized expertise and competence in a particular domain and an authoritative claim to policy-relevant knowledge within that domain or issue-area.[4]

---

[4] The term epistemic communities has been defined or used in a variety of ways, most

continued

Although an epistemic community may consist of professionals from a variety of disciplines and backgrounds, they have (1) a shared set of normative and principled beliefs, which provide a value-based rationale for the social action of community members; (2) shared causal beliefs, which are derived from their analysis of practices leading or contributing to a central set of problems in their domain and which then serve as the basis for elucidating the multiple linkages between possible policy actions and desired outcomes; (3) shared notions of validit that is, intersubjective, internally defined criteria for weighing and validating knowledge in the domain of their expertise; and (4) a common policy enterprise that is, a set of common practices associated with a set of problems to which their professional competence is directed, presumably out of the conviction that human welfare will be enhanced as a consequence.[5]

The causal logic of epistemic policy coordination is simple. The major dynamics are uncertainty, interpretation, and institutionalization. In international policy coordination, the forms of uncertainty that tend to

frequently to refer to scientific communities. In this volume, we stress that epistemic communities need not be made up of natural scientists or of professionals applying the same methodology that natural scientists do. Moreover, when referring to epistemic communities consisting primarily of natural scientists, we adopt a stricter definition than do, for example, Holzner and Marx, who use the term epistemic community in reference to a shared faith in the scientific method as a way of generating truth. This ignores that such faith can still bond together people with diverse interpretations of ambiguous data. By our definition, what bonds members of an epistemic community is their shared belief or faith in the verity and the applicability of particular forms of knowledge or specific truths. Our notion of epistemic community somewhat resembles Fleck's notion of a ["]thought collective[" —] a sociological group with a common style of thinking. It also somewhat resembles Kuhn's broader sociological definition of a paradigm, which is "an entire constellation of beliefs, values, techniques, and so on shared by members of a given community" and which governs "not a subject matter but a group of practitioners." See Burkhart Holzner and John H. Marx, *Knowledge Application: The Knowledge System in Society* (Boston: Allyn & Bacon, 1979), pp. 107 11; Ludwig Fleck, *Genesis and Development of a Scientific Fact* (Chicago: University of Chicago Press, 1979; translated from the 1935 edition printed in German); and Thomas S. Kuhn, *The Structure of Scientific Revolutions*, 2d ed. (Chicago: University of Chicago Press, 1970), pp. 174 210, with quotes drawn from pp. 175 and 180. Regarding scientific communities, see also Michael Polanyi, "The Republic of Science," *Minerva*, vol. 1, 1962, pp. 54-73.

[5] Other characteristics of epistemic communities that were mentioned or discussed during the preparation of this volume included the following: members of an epistemic community share intersubjective understandings; have a shared way of knowing; have shared patterns of reasoning; have a policy project drawing on shared values, shared causal beliefs, and the use of shared discursive practices; and have a shared commitment to the application and production of knowledge. These phrases were not incorporated in the formal definition listed here; they are simply provided to evoke additional notions that are associated with epistemic communities.

stimulate demands for information are those which arise from the strong dependence of states on each other's policy choices for success in obtaining goals and those which involve multiple and only partly estimable consequences of action...The information is thus neither guesses nor raw data; it is the product of human interpretations of social and physical phenomena.

Epistemic communities are one possible provider of this sort of information and advice. As demands for such information arise, networks or communities of specialists capable of producing and providing the information emerge and proliferate. The members of a prevailing community become strong actors at the national and transnational level as decision makers solicit their information and delegate responsibility to them. A community's advice, though, is informed by its own broader worldview. To the extent to which an epistemic community consolidates bureaucratic power within national administrations and international secretariats, it stands to institutionalize its influence and insinuate its views into broader international policies.

Members of transnational epistemic communities can influence state interests either by directly identifying them for decision makers or by illuminating the salient dimensions of an issue from which the decision makers may then deduce their interests. The decision makers in one state may, in turn, influence the interests and behavior of other states, thereby increasing the likelihood of convergent state behavior and international policy coordination, informed by the causal beliefs and policy preferences of the epistemic community. Similarly, epistemic communities may contribute to the creation and maintenance of social institutions that guide international behavior. As a consequence of the continued influence of these institutions, established patterns of cooperation in a given issue-area may persist even though systemic power concentrations may no longer be sufficient to compel countries to coordinate their behavior. ...

[W]hile the form of specific policy choices is influenced by transnational knowledge-based networks, the extent to which state behavior reflects the preferences of these networks remains strongly conditioned by the distribution of power internationally. Thus, the range of impact that we might expect of epistemic and epistemic-like communities remains conditioned and bounded by international and national structural realities. The extent of that conditioning the amount of flexibility in the international system available for reflection and understanding in the face of power and structure is the focus of this volume. ...

Under conditions of uncertainty, then, decision makers have a variety of incentives and reasons for consulting epistemic communities,[32] some of them more politically motivated than others. First, following a shock or crisis, epistemic communities can elucidate the cause-and-effect relationships and provide advice about the likely results of various courses of action. In some cases, they can help decision makers gain a sense of who the winners and losers would be as the result of a particular action or event, as was the case in considerations about banning chlorofluorocarbon use or facing a possible environmental disaster...

Second, epistemic communities can shed light on the nature of the complex interlinkages between issues and on the chain of events that might proceed either from failure to take action or from instituting a particular policy. Information is at a premium in the face of possible systematic volatility, when efforts to solve or curb a problem in one domain or issue-area may have unanticipated negative feedback effects on others.

Third, epistemic communities can help define the self-interests of a state or factions within it. The process of elucidating the cause-and-effect relationships of problems can in fact lead to the redefinition of preconceived interests or to the identification of new interests.

Fourth, epistemic communities can help formulate policies. Their role in this regard will depend on the reasons for which their advice is sought. In some cases, decision makers will seek advice to gain information which will justify or legitimate a policy that they wish to pursue for political ends. An epistemic community's efforts might thus be limited to working out the details of the policy, helping decision makers anticipate the conflicts of interest that would emerge with respect to particular points, and then building coalitions in support of the policy. If the policy is instituted and problems ensue, the decision makers have the option of pointing to the information given to them by experts and spreading the blame.[35] Again, however, it is important to stress that epistemic communities called in for political reasons may succeed in imposing their views and moving toward goals other than those initially envisioned by the decision makers.

[32] In *Markets and Hierarchies* (New York: Free Press, 1975), Oliver Williamson argues that under conditions of uncertainty, organizations are likely to develop internal methods to generate more and better information instead of turning to external sources.

[35] *See* Lauriston R. King and Philip H. Melanson, *Knowledge and Politics: Some Experiences from the 1960s, Public Policy* 20 (Winter 1972), p. 84. For similar observations, see Martin L. Perl, *The Scientific Advisory System: Some Observations, Science* 173 (September 1971), pp. 1211-15.

In less politically motivated cases, epistemic communities have a greater hand in the various stages of the policymaking process, including the introduction of policy alternatives, the selection of policies, and the building of national and international coalitions in support of the policies...By pointing out which alternatives are not viable on the basis of their causal understanding of the problems to be addressed, the community members can limit the range of alternatives under consideration. ...

[I]t is the combination of having a shared set of causal and principled (analytic and normative) beliefs, a consensual knowledge base, and a common policy enterprise (common interests) that distinguishes epistemic communities from various other groups.

The Role of Institutions and Networks in Environmental Enforcement

Donald Kaniaru

6TH INECE CONFERENCE PROCEEDINGS, Vol 2 (2002)

...

1   INTRODUCTION

Many formal institutions, intergovernmental at various levels exist today, and are prime movers in environmental policy development and implementation. Such institutions have mushroomed at the global and regional levels and have direct implications at the national level; the most important being ineffective implementation because of lack of human, financial, scientific and technical resources. Equally significant are increasing trends to evade laws and regulations put in place. Clearly, therefore, enhanced and streamlined institutions are needed as well as a network of informal networks, springing from national, regional to global level to enhance enforcement measures. Such is the challenge offered in this discussion.

2   INSTITUTIONAL FRAMEWORK

Legal and institutional arrangements for environmental management have gradually evolved and changed as scientific understanding of the dynamics of environmental processes and the impact of anthropogenic activities on such dynamics has increased. Trends indicate a move from sectoral approaches that isolate and exploit the environment, to a holistic eco-system approach that is concerned with sustainability and promotes an integrated and coordinated approach to environment and the economy. Institutional arrangements have also been influenced by participatory approaches to development and the devolution of power to sub-national levels, including the empowerment of grass-roots communities to decide and act on the political, economic and social issues that affect them.

Environmental laws and regulations are considered indispensable frameworks and basis for the effective implementation. They establish mandates for institutions as well as define roles and responsibilities for governments, civil society and individual citizens. These rights then have the backing of the law and, hence, are enforceable.

Thus, when one discusses the implementation of environmental laws and regulations one is also speaking about the implementation of the environmental management frameworks.

Since environment is an area that transcends all sectors, it is now accepted that its management requires the coordination of a multitude of stakeholders. In other words, its management requires inclusiveness. Effective management of the environment requires diverse national and international institutions and individuals with a wide range of skills to work in harmony.

National and international institutional arrangements for environmental management inevitably will compose all stakeholders in the formulation and implementation of environmental laws, including their enforcement. These will include: government institutions (coordinating bodies, line agencies, legislative/judicial branches, and the police); academic institutions; NGOs and CBOs; professional associations; and the private sector as well as international and regional networks.

3   AGENDA 21 CHAPTER 38

Agenda 21 recognizes in Chapter 38 the importance and the role played by international institutional arrangements in the integration of environment and development issues at national, sub-regional, regional and international levels. Chapter 38.21, for instance, emphasized the need for an enhanced and strengthened role of UNEP and its governing bodies. Agenda 21 also recognizes the specific roles played by other UN bodies including specialized agencies within their field of expertise, competence and comparative advantage including the need for these international bodies to cooperate and coordinate their relevant activities to avoid duplication in the implementation of Agenda 21. Consequently, UNEP has cooperated and will continue to cooperate with other relevant bodies to implement Agenda 21 in general and in particular in order to ensure coordinated action in implementation and enforcement of environmental law and policies.

4   THE ROLE OF INSTITUTIONS AND NETWORKS

The past decade or so, in particular, after the 1992 UNCED process, the international community has witnessed phenomenal growth, establishment and strengthening of institutions both at national, regional and global level dealing with different aspects on environment. With the growth in importance on the subject of environmental management came also the development of institutions to ensure and facilitate effective coordination and management of natural resources at all levels. Institutions at global and regional levels refocused their activities and environment became an important activity in a number of them. At national level, likewise, environmental management has been institutionalized with the establishment or designation of national institutions by law. Framework environmental laws of many countries today establish environmental management and/or interministerial bodies to oversee enforcement of environmental laws and regulations in a country...

Similar development is witnessed in the development of formal and informal environmental networks to support international, regional and national institutions in the enforcement of environmental laws and regulations. These networks both internationally, such as INECE, and regionally, such as Implementation and Enforcement of Environmental Law - EU Network (IMPEL) and Network for Environment and Sustainable Development in Africa (NESDA), to mention but a few, have become important mechanisms to reckon with. They support government efforts in their endeavor and activities on environmental enforcement of multilateral environmental agreements (MEA) and national laws. It is satisfying to see how networks have grown in recent years to ensure that no developments at national level pass unnoticed without the global chain of members being aware in virtually all countries. INECE and IUCN networks effectively use information technology facilities (email, internet and tele and video conferences) to reach their constituencies and instantly keep them abreast of developments in the field of environment, globally. These developments will inevitably continue to grow and offer opportunities for regional and international networks to work together to enhance environmental enforcement.

Environmental institutions, as mandated by Agenda 21 and re-emphasized by virtually all governing bodies, place focus on the need and importance to cooperate and collaborate with governments, relevant other bodies (networks and convention secretariats) in all related programmes and activities. Such collaboration and/or coordination of activities has an advantage of ensuring that limited and meager resources are used effectively to avoid waste and duplication. It creates synergy and harmonization of relevant policies and activities to effectively support and build upon existing activities by the partners or constituencies for the common goal. It is the need and importance of such collaboration that institutions like UNEP is a participatory member in the Executive Planning Committee (EPC) of INECE. This ensures that its environmental enforcement and compliance activities and policies are built in and/or complement those of INECE and create synergy and harmony taking into account its comparative advantage. Collaboration with relevant networks, INECE and others regionally and globally, provides a conduit for sharing and exchanging information, data, experiences and expertise which are vital for the effective implementation and enforcement of environmental laws. Focal points and/or persons have been established or designated in many institutions and networks to ensure smooth flow of data and information. Their importance continue to grow bearing in mind the fluid nature of national boundaries/frontiers and the sophisticated nature of criminal activities in violation of environmental laws and policies. All international, regional and national institutions have to work together with established networks to ensure the success of environmental enforcement and implementation of environmental framework laws.

5   INSTITUTIONAL FRAMEWORK UNDER UNEP GUIDELINES ON MEAs

Part D Chapter 2 of the UNEP Guidelines for [N]ational [E]nforcement and [I]nternational [C]ooperation in [C]ombating [V]iolations of [L]aws [I]mplementing MEAs urges states to consider institutional frameworks that promote effective enforcement of environmental laws and policies. The Guidelines urge states to designate agencies with responsibilities for enforcement of laws and regulations; monitoring and evaluation of implementation of laws and to raise awareness to the public, in particular, regulated community and the general public. The agencies will collect, report and analyze data as well as provide information about investigations. They will assist courts and tribunals, where appropriate, with relevant information and data for their work. Such institutional frameworks will endeavor to control import and export of substances and endangered species at border crossing ports and other areas of know or suspected illegal activities.

The Guidelines urge states to give clear authority to enforcement agencies involved in enforcement activities to enable them to obtain relevant information, have access to relevant facilities such as ports and border crossings and coordinate with other agencies. They require authority to monitor and verify compliance with national laws and regulations; be able to order action to prevent and remedy environmental law violations as well as impose sanctions including penalties for environmental law violations and non-compliance.

States are expected to promote policies and procedures that ensure fair and consistent enforcement and imposition of penalties based on established criteria and sentencing guidelines. There is also need to establish or strengthen national environmental crime units to complement civil and administrative enforcement programmes. Use of economic instruments has been identified as one of the measures institutions could use to promote compliance. Institutions should invariably promote access of the public and civil society to administrative and judicial procedures to challenge acts and omissions by public authorities and corporate persons that contravene national environmental laws including support for public access to justice. Participation of appropriate communities and NGOs in processes contributing to the protection of the environment ought to be guaranteed to ensure effective environmental enforcement. Use of media to publicize environmental law violations and enforcement actions as well as highlighting examples of positive environmental achievements should be encouraged. Periodic review of the adequacy of existing laws, regulations and policies for the fulfillment of environmental objectives needs to be put on the agenda of such institutions. Courts ought to be given authority to impose appropriate penalties for violations of environmental laws and regulations as well as other consequences.

The Guidelines thus provide a checklist of the functions, tools and mandates of a national institutional framework which states may wish to consider to put in place, if they do not yet exist or to strengthen the existing ones, so as to ensure and guarantee effective national environmental enforcement of laws and policies. If requested, UNEP would assist in such efforts and is in the process of preparing a manual that can be used by those in need.

However, for the institutional framework to work, coordination among relevant authorities and agencies becomes *sine quo non* for effective enforcement mechanism. Coordination is inevitable among various enforcement agencies, environmental authorities, tax, customs and other relevant officials at different levels of government. Linkage at the field level among cross agency task forces and points is equally crucial. Coordination by government agencies with NGOs and the private sector is required. Coordination among authorities responsible for promoting licensing systems to regulate and control the importation and exportation of illicit substances and hazardous materials cannot be avoided but should be encouraged.

Furthermore, consistent with relevant provisions in MEAs, national enforcement of laws and regulation implementing MEAs could be supported through international cooperation and coordination that can be facilitated by international institutions such as UNEP.

The Guidelines also encourage states to enhance international cooperation and coordination to contain or prevent environmental crimes with transboundary aspects. States are urged to consider strengthening institutional frameworks and programmes to facilitate international cooperation and coordination by designing and establishing channels of communication and information exchange. Such channels could be with MEAs Secretariats, World Customs Organization, NGOs, international law enforcement agencies such as International Criminal Police Organization (Interpol) and networks such as INECE and IMPEL.

Although the Guidelines are not binding but advisory in nature, they do provide a useful tool for states to use an instrument guiding their relations with other enforcement bodies or networks. The Guidelines have synthesized various expertise and experiences into a friendly useable document to guide states as appropriate.

Interpol, though not having actual enforcement function, has been active in coordinating and facilitating international cooperation between law enforcement agencies in the world during their investigations of international criminal cases. Interpol mostly pursues cases reported to it by its member countries through established national central bureaus. Hence, for Interpol, the necessity and effectiveness of the multi-agency approach has been recognized and extensively used in many countries is inevitable.

The World Customs Organization, on the other hand, promotes cooperation and communication among members and with other international organizations. It fosters human resource development, improvement in the management and working methods of customs administrations and share best practices. Members cooperation with each other and with international agencies in order to combat customs and other transborder offences.

UNEP, Interpol and World Customs Organization role in environmental enforcement are provided as examples for illustrative purpose. There are many institutions in the field of environment that deal with enforcement of laws. However, their work still depends on the established networks to further facilitate their work in terms of sharing relevant information, expertise and data. This should be encouraged and strengthened and more so in cooperative arrangement by neighboring countries, sub-regional and regional levels. In many regions there are many sub-regional arrangements dealing with environmental, social, economic and other matters. These constitute possible mechanisms for formal or informal networks that underscore the need for better use of resources in the enhancement of the implementation of MEAs.

CHAPTER THIRTEEN

COMPETITIVENESS & COMPLIANCE : THE PORTER HYPOTHESIS

INTRODUCTION

This chapter presents a selection of the best literature discussing compliance and competitiveness, including how firms can cut the cost of compliance—and even profit from it—and how regulators can design strategies to facilitate this.

The purpose of environmental regulation is to protect public health and to ensure that we use our natural resources—both "sources" and "sinks"—in a sustainable way. Environmental law does this by addressing externalities, including pollution, that firms impose on the public. Environmental law strives to make the polluter pay by using law to internalize the cost of pollution and other adverse social costs that are external to the market.

Historically, in the United States and most OECD countries, the polluters paid an aggregate cost of complying with environmental laws equal to 2 to 2.5% of GDP, with some highly polluting firms having to pay more to clean up their excess pollution, and other cleaner firms paying less.[1] The public benefits from making the polluter pay exceeds the cost paid by the polluter, in part, because environmental law does not yet require the polluter to pay for all of its pollution.[2]

---

[1] Paul Portney, *Counting the Cost: The Growing Role of Economics in Environmental Decisionmaking*, ENV'T MAGAZINE (1998) at 3, *available at*
http://www.weathervane.rff.org/refdocs/portney_enviro.pdf.
[2] OFFICE OF MANAGEMENT AND BUDGET, INFORMING REGULATORY DECISIONS: 2003 REPORT TO CONGRESS ON THE COSTS AND BENEFITS OF FEDERAL REGULATIONS AND UNFUNDED MANDATES ON STATE, LOCAL, AND TRIBAL ENTITIES (2003) at 7, *available at* http://www.whitehouse.gov/omb/ inforeg/2003_cost-ben_final_rpt.pdf. *See also* ECOTEC, THE BENEFITS OF COMPLIANCE WITH THE ENVIRONMENTAL ACQUIS FOR THE CANDIDATE COUNTRIES, DGENV CONTRACT: ENVIRONMENTAL POLICY IN THE APPLICANT COUNTRIES AND THEIR PREPARATIONS FOR ACCESSION, FINAL REPORT, iii-iv (2001), *available at* http://www.europa.eu.int/comm/environment/enlarg/pdf/ benefit_long.pdf (suggesting other benefits, including lower costs of production and maintenance due to availability of cleaner water that does not require pretreatment, and

continued

As environmental regulation progressed from the initial command-and-control model to embrace more flexible performance standards, firms and regulators began to appreciate that pollution not only imposed a cost on the public but also was a waste of the firms' resources. They also learned that pollution prevention and other improvements in environmental management could not only provide vital benefits to the public, but also actually save the firm itself money.[3] Waste was reduced at the source, before it became pollution, and the cost of compliance started to come down, and in some cases it actually provided a profit.

This is the holy grail of environmental regulation — win-win solutions — where firms might be forced to take strong medicine to clean up their pollution and protect the public, but where the medicine would save the firms money and make them, and the countries where they are located, healthier competitors in the long run. Professor Michael E. Porter and Class van der Linde developed the "Porter Hypothesis" to show how environmental compliance can achieve this.

Porter and van der Linde theorized that properly designed environmental regulations trigger innovations within the firm that partially or more than fully offset the costs of complying with those regulations. Such "innovation offsets" can not only improve product quality and value but also may lower the total cost by allowing companies to use a range of inputs more efficiently. Ultimately, according to Porter and van der Linde, this enhanced resource productivity makes companies—and countries—more competitive.

---

lower consumption of primary resources as a result of a more efficient use and higher levels of recycling). Estimates of the magnitude of public benefits from ecosystem services that environmental law protects are in the range of US $ 16 to 54 trillion per year, with an average of US $ 33 trillion per year. Ecosystem services include regulation of atmospheric chemical composition, global temperature, precipitation, and hydrological flows; storage and retention of water and nutrients; removal and decomposition of wastes; and provision of habit for various species. *See* R. Costanza, *et al.*, *The value of the World's Ecosystem Services and Natural Capital*, 387 NATURE, 253 (1997).

[3] An example is the case of distillers of coal tar in the United States. In 1991, many of these firms opposed the regulations requiring substantial reductions in benzene emissions because at the time, it was thought that the only means to achieve this goal was to cover the tar storage tanks with costly gas blankets. However, the regulations prompted Aristech Chemical Corporation to develop a method of removing benzene from tar in the first processing stage, eliminating the need for gas blankets and saving $ 3.3 million. *See* Michael Porter & Class van der Linde, *Green and Competitive: Ending the Stalemate*, HARVARD BUS. REVIEW (1995). *See also* STEPHEN O. ANDERSEN & DURWOOD ZAELKE, INDUSTRY GENIUS: PEOPLE AND INVENTIONS PROTECTING CLIMATE AND THE FRAGILE OZONE LAYER (2003).

There are two key design principles for the "Porter Hypothesis." First, it requires regulations that focus on outcomes, for example, by specifying performance standards, as opposed to regulations that impose technology standards or otherwise limit flexibility.[4] Second, it requires strict regulations that are complied with. Under these conditions, Porter and van der Linde show that firms re-examine their processes and technologies, and often find greater efficiencies and cleaner processes.

The first Porter design principle, flexibility, requires performance based regulations that set the goals the firms must meet, without specifying the means: firms are allowed to use whatever strategies they see fit to achieve the goals, providing incentive to innovate as they search for the most efficient and effective strategies.[5] An example of a successful flexible regulation is the Sulfur Dioxide regulation on electric generating facilities in the United States. The US government formerly regulated the emission at a cost of $ 7 billion a year by mandating specific technology—the installation of scrubbers on smoke stacks.[6] However, in 1990, the law was changed to a performance standard—an emission cap and trade system, allowing firms maximum flexibility, including the flexibility to innovate in their choice of technological solutions. As a consequence of this new flexible regulation and resulting innovation, the cost of compliance came down dramatically and about a fourth of firms were able to comply with the standard at a profit.[7]

The second element of the Porter hypothesis requires strict standards that are complied with.[8] Stringent regulations are necessary for

---

[4] For a discussion of reasons inflexible standards severely limit innovation, *see* ENVIRONMENTAL LAW INSTITUTE, INNOVATION, COST AND ENVIRONMENTAL REGULATION: PERSPECTIVES ON BUSINESS, POLICY AND LEGAL FACTORS AFFECTING THE COST OF COMPLIANCE (1999) (hereinafter "ELI").

[5] Some studies suggest that when an environmental manager in a firm is afforded a higher level of discretion, the firm interprets environmental issues as opportunities rather than threats, and achieves higher compliance and improved environmental performance. *See* Sanjay Sharma, *Managerial Interpretations and Organizational Context as Predictors of Corporate Choice of Environmental Strategy*, 43 ACAD. MGMT. J. 681, 691 (2000). For a fuller discussion of theories explaining such behaviors, *see* Chapter Two: Compliance Theories.

[6] ELI, *supra* note 4.

[7] *Id.*

[8] Without strict compliance with emission trading schemes, not only will firms not realize the Porter innovation off-sets, but the market itself will collapse. Traders need the confidence in the market before they participate, and only strict enforcement can provide this. The US Sulfur Dioxide regulation utilizes continuous real-time telemetry to ensure nearly 100% compliance. *See* EPA's Acid Rain Program 2003 Progress Report, *available at* http://www.epa.gov/airmarkets/cmprpt/arp03/summary.html, stating:

continued

innovation and innovation offsets because lax regulations can be dealt with incrementally and often with "end-of-pipe" or secondary treatment solutions, discouraging any innovation. Stringent regulations, on the other hand, focus greater company attention on discharges and emissions, and compliance with such regulations requires more fundamental solutions, like reconfiguring products and processes.

Porter and van der Linde have identified eleven design factors for innovation-friendly regulations: [9]

1. focus on outcomes, not technologies;

2. enact strict rather than lax regulation;

3. regulate as close to the end user as practical, while encouraging upstream solutions;

4. employ phase-in periods;

5. use market incentives;

6. harmonize or converge regulations in associated fields;

7. develop regulation in sync with other countries or slightly ahead of them;

8. make the regulatory process more stable and predictable;

9. require industry participation in setting standards from the beginning;

10. develop strong technical capabilities among regulators; and

11. minimize the time and resources consumed in the regulatory process itself.

The Porter design principles have been well received by many scholars, policy makers, and industry leaders, and an increasing body of empirical

---

As in years past, the electric power industry achieved nearly 100 percent compliance with Acid Rain Program requirements — only 1 unit had emissions exceeding the SO_2 allowances that it held and no units were out of compliance with the NO_x program. This exceptionally high level of compliance was, in part, achieved as a result of the Acid Rain Program's continued provision of accurate and complete SO_2 and NO_x emissions data. This process was augmented by a substantial auditing effort and accountability through rigorous, yet streamlined, reporting systems.

See also Stranlund, Chavez & Field, *Enforcing Emissions Trading Programs: Theory, Practice, and Performance*, 30 POLICY STUDIES J., 343 (2002) ("it is clear that the efficiency gains realized by emissions trading programs will depend on rates of compliance...").

[9] *See* Porter & van der Linde, *supra* note 3 at 124.

evidence confirms their success. For instance, in 2002, Daniel Esty and Michael Porter analyzed various countries' environmental regulations and their competitiveness and economic status in the world. In their study, they found that,

> there is no evidence that higher environmental quality compromises economic progress. Environmental performance is positively and highly correlated to GDP per capita. The...preliminary evidence suggest[s] that countries with stricter environmental regulations than would be expected at their level of GDP per capita enjoy faster economic growth.[10]

Indeed, Esty and Porter found that countries that have the most aggressive environmental policy regimes are the ones most competitive and economically successful.[11]

Moreover, Lawrence Pratt's 2000 study analyzed the relationship between environmental performance and competitiveness and concluded that,

> [s]uperior environmental performance will be rewarded in the long run in most industries and in national development.... Both theory and an emerging body of empirical evidence on the topic show that under most circumstances, improved environmental performance should improve a number of aspects of firm competitiveness, especially in developing countries.[12]

---

[10] Daniel C. Esty & Michael Porter, *Measuring National Environmental Regulation and Performance, in* THE GLOBAL COMPETITIVENESS REPORT 2001-2002 (M.E. Porter, J.K. Sachs, P.K. Cornelius, J.W. McArthur, & K. Schwab eds., 2002). *See also* Daniel C. Esty, *Environmental Protection in the Information Age*, 79 N.Y.U. L. REV. 115 (2004) (describing how information can translate into resource productivity).

[11] Daniel C. Esty & Michael Porter, *Ranking National Environmental Regulation and Performance: A Leading Indicator of Future Competitiveness?, in* THE GLOBAL COMPETITIVENESS REPORT 2001-2002 (M.E. Porter, J.K. Sachs, P.K. Cornelius, J.W. McArthur, & K. Schwab eds., 2002); *see also* P. Lanoie, M. Patry & R. Lajeunesse, *Environmental Regulation and Productivity: New Findings on the Porter Hypothesis*, CAHIER DE RECHERCHE (2001) (finding that environmental regulations do not have contemporaneous impacts on firm's productivity).

[12] Lawrence Pratt, *Rethinking the Private Sector-Environment Relationship in Latin America*, Background Paper for the Seminar on the "New Vision for Sustainability: Private Sector and the Environment" IDB/IIC Annual Meeting of the Board of Governors New Orleans, Louisiana, 3-4 (March 25, 2000), *available at* http://www.iadb.org/mif/v2/files/Pratt-eng.pdf.

continued

Even if a country has a well designed environmental regulation with both elements of the Porter design principles—flexibility and strictness—the country still must ensure compliance to enjoy the "innovation offsets" described by the Porter Hypothesis.

The Porter design principles apply of course to parliamentarians who need to consider them when drafting laws. They also apply to agencies that, under most environmental laws, still have considerable discretion when implementing the laws passed by parliaments. The design principles can be applied to the remedy stage of enforcement proceedings as well, at least in common law countries where judges have considerable discretion to impose a "Porter Remedy" that forces violators to re-evaluate their technologies and processes.

This chapter begins with Porter and van der Linde's seminal article setting out the foundation for their hypothesis, explaining how innovation offsets occur, describing how to design environmental regulations to encourage innovation, and addressing criticisms that their hypothesis has received.[13] The chapter also includes an empirical study testing the Porter Hypothesis in India. M.N. Murty and S. Kumar studied the relationship between environmental water pollution regulation and manufacturing industry's efficiency in India, and found that the technical efficiency of firms increases with the firms' degree of compliance with the environmental regulations.[14]

The chapter concludes with two articles that discuss the implications for developing countries. Lawrence Pratt and Carolina Mauri emphasize the need for sound enforcement and compliance initiatives to better equip developing countries as the world continues to discover the strong and

---

Pratt suggests that "[s]uccessful incorporation of environmental factors into [Latin America's] competitive fabric will align its productive sectors with more valuable market opportunities, make its business climate more attractive to foreign investors, offer new and exciting commercial potential and protect the resources the region needs to survive in the future." *Id.* at 3.

[13] Michael E. Porter & Class van der Linde, *Toward a New Conception of the Environment-competitiveness Relationship*, 9(4) J. ECON. PERSPECTIVES, (1995). For other criticism, *see* A.B. Jaffe, S.R. Peterson, P.R. Portney, & R.N. Stavins, *Environmental Regulation and International Competitiveness: What Does the Evidence Tell Us?*, 93 J. ECON. LITERATURE, 12,658-12,663 (1996); *see also* Michael Porter & Class van der Linde, *supra* note 3.

[14] M. Murty & S. Kumar, *Win-Win Opportunities and Environmental Regulation: Testing of Porter Hypothesis for Indian Manufacturing Industries*, 67 J. ENVTL MGMT 139 (2003).

positive relationship between good environmental performance and countries' competitiveness.[15] A final article by Glen Dowell, Stuart Hart, and Bernard Yeung analyzes multinational enterprises' behaviors and finds that adopting a single stringent corporate environmental standard enhances firm value more than defaulting to the less stringent or poorly enforced standards of some developing countries.[16] The study also concludes that developing countries may attract foreign investment in the short-run by lowering environmental standards, but that the type of companies they attract by doing so will be weaker, more pollution-intensive, and unable to invest in state-of-the-art plants and equipment.

---

[15] Lawrence Pratt & Carolina Mauri, *Environmental Enforcement and Compliance and Its Role in Enhancing Competitiveness in Developing Countries*, 7 th INECE International Conference Proceedings (Forthcoming 2005).
[16] Glen Dowell, Stuart Hart, Bernard Yeung, *Do Corporate Global Environmental Standards Create or Destroy Market Value?* 46 (8) MGMT SCI. 1059 (2000).

Toward a New Conception of the Environment-Competitiveness Relationship

Michael E. Porter & Claas van der Linde

9(4) JOURNAL OF ECONOMIC PERSPECTIVES 97 (1995)

...

The Link from Regulation to Promoting Innovation

It is sometimes argued that companies must, by the very notion of profit seeking, be pursuing all profitable innovations. In the metaphor economists often cite, $10 bills will never be found on the ground because someone would have already picked them up. In this view, if complying with environmental regulation can be profitable, in the sense that a company can more than offset the cost of compliance, then why is such regulation necessary?

The possibility that regulation might act as a spur to innovation arises because the world does not fit the Panglossian belief that firms always make optimal choices. This will hold true only in a static optimization framework where information is perfect and profitable opportunities for innovation have already been discovered, so that profit-seeking firms need only choose their approach. Of course, this does not describe reality. Instead, the actual process of dynamic competition is characterized by changing technological opportunities coupled with highly incomplete information, organizational inertia and control problems reflecting the difficulty of aligning individual, group and corporate incentives. Companies have numerous avenues for technological improvement, and limited attention.

...

441

We are currently in a transitional phase of industrial history where companies are still inexperienced in dealing creatively with environmental issues. The environment has not been a principal area of corporate or technological emphasis, and knowledge about environmental impacts is still rudimentary in many firms and industries, elevating uncertainty about innovation benefits. Customers are also unaware of the costs of resource inefficiency in the packaging they discard, the scrap value they forego and the disposal costs they bear. Rather than attempting to innovate in every direction at once, firms in fact make choices based on how they perceive their competitive situation and the world around them. In such a world, regulation can be an important influence on the direction of innovation, either for better or for worse. Properly crafted environmental regulation can serve at least six purposes.

First, regulation signals companies about likely resource inefficiencies and potential technological improvements. Companies are still inexperienced in measuring their discharges, understanding the full costs of incomplete utilization of resources and toxicity, and conceiving new approaches to minimize discharges or eliminate hazardous substances. Regulation rivets attention on this area of potential innovation.[1]

Second, regulation focused on information gathering can achieve major benefits by raising corporate awareness. For example, Toxics Release Inventories, which are published annually as part of the 1986 Superfund reauthorization, require more than 20,000 manufacturing plants to report their releases of some 320 toxic chemicals. Such information gathering often leads to environmental improvement without mandating pollution reductions, sometimes even at lower costs.

Third, regulation reduces the uncertainty that investments to address the environment will be valuable. Greater certainty encourages investment in any area.

Fourth, regulation creates pressure that motivates innovation and progress. Our broader research on competitiveness highlights the important role of outside pressure in the innovation process, to overcome organizational inertia, foster creative thinking and mitigate agency problems. Economists are used to the argument that pressure for innovation can come from strong competitors, demanding customers or

---

[1] Regulation also raises the likelihood that product and process in general will incorporate environmental improvements.

rising prices of raw materials; we are arguing that properly crafted regulation can also provide such pressure.

Fifth, regulation levels the transitional playing field. During the transition period to innovation-based solutions, regulation ensures that one company cannot opportunistically gain position by avoiding environmental investments. Regulations provide a buffer until new technologies become proven and learning effects reduce their costs.

Sixth, regulation is needed in the case of incomplete offsets. We readily admit that innovation cannot always completely offset the cost of compliance, especially in the short term before learning can reduce the cost of innovation-based solutions. In such cases, regulation will be necessary to improve environmental quality.

Stringent regulation can actually produce greater innovation and innovation offsets than lax regulation. Relatively lax regulation can be dealt with incrementally and without innovation, and often with "end-of-pipe" or secondary treatment solutions. More stringent regulation, however, focuses greater company attention on discharges and emissions, and compliance requires more fundamental solutions, like reconfiguring products and processes. While the cost of compliance may rise with stringency, then, the potential for innovation offsets may rise even faster. Thus the *net* cost of compliance can fall with stringency and may even turn into a net benefit.

How Innovation Offsets Occur

Innovation in response to environmental regulation can take two broad forms. The first is that companies simply get smarter about how to deal with pollution once it occurs, including the processing of toxic materials and emissions, how to reduce the amount of toxic or harmful material generated (or convert it into salable forms) and how to improve secondary treatment... This sort of innovation reduces the cost of compliance with pollution control, but changes nothing else.

The second form of innovation addresses environmental impacts while simultaneously improving the affected product itself and/or related processes. In some cases, these "innovation offsets" can exceed the costs of compliance. This second sort of innovation is central to our claim that environmental regulation can actually increase industrial competitiveness.

Innovation offsets can be broadly divided into product offsets and process offsets. Product offsets occur when environmental regulation produces not just less pollution, but also creates better-performing or higher-quality products, safer products, lower product costs (perhaps from material substitution or less packaging), products with higher resale or scrap value (because of ease in recycling or disassembly) or lower costs of product disposal for users. Process offsets occur when environmental regulation not only leads to reduced pollution, but also results in higher resource productivity such as higher process yields, less downtime through more careful monitoring and maintenance, materials savings (due to substitution, reuse or recycling of production inputs), better utilization of by-products, lower energy consumption during the production process, reduced material storage and handling costs, conversion of waste into valuable forms, reduced waste disposal costs or safer workplace conditions. These offsets are frequently related, so that achieving one can lead to the realization of several others.

...

Innovation to comply with environmental regulation often improves product performance or quality. In 1990, for instance, Raytheon found itself required (by the Montreal Protocol and the U.S. Clean Air Act) to eliminate ozone-depleting chlorofluorocarbons (CFCs) used for cleaning printed electronic circuit boards after the soldering process. Scientists at Raytheon initially thought that complete elimination of CFCs would be impossible. However, they eventually adopted a new semiaqueous, terpene-based cleaning agent that could be reused. The new method proved to result in an increase in average product quality, which had occasionally been compromised by the old CFC-based cleaning agent, as well as lower operating costs (Raytheon, 1991, 1993). It would not have been adopted in the absence of environmental regulation mandating the phase-out of CFCs. Another example is the move by the Robbins Company (a jewelry company based in Attleboro, Massachusetts) to a closed-loop, zero-discharge system for handling the water used in plating (Berube, Nash, Maxwell and Ehrenfeld, 1992). Robbins was facing closure due to violation of its existing discharge permits. The water produced by purification through filtering and ion exchange in the new closed-loop system was 40 times cleaner than city water and led to higher-quality plating and fewer rejects. The result was enhanced competitiveness.

Environmental regulations may also reduce product costs by showing how to eliminate costly materials, reduce unnecessary packaging or simplify designs. Hitachi responded to a 1991 Japanese recycling law by redesigning products to reduce disassembly time. In the process, the number of parts in a washing machine fell 16 percent, and the number of parts on a vacuum cleaner fell 30 percent. In this way, moves to redesign products for better recyclability can lead to fewer components and thus easier assembly.

Environmental standards can also lead to innovation that reduces disposal costs (or boost scrap or resale value) for the user. For instance, regulation that requires recyclability of products can lead to designs that allow valuable materials to be recovered more easily after disposal of the product. Either the customer or the manufacturer who takes back used products reaps greater value.

These have all been examples of product offsets, but process offsets are common as well. Process changes to reduce emissions frequently result in increases in product yields. At Ciba-Geigy's dyestuff plant in New Jersey, the need to meet new environmental standards caused the firm to reexamine its wastewater streams. Two changes in its production process—replacing iron with a different chemical conversion agent that did not result in the formation of solid iron sludge and process changes that eliminated the release of potentially toxic product into the wastewater stream—not only boosted yield by 40 percent but also eliminated wastes, resulting in annual cost savings of $740,000 (Dorfman, Muir and Miller, 1992).[2]

Similarly, 3M discovered that in producing adhesives in batches that were transferred to storage tanks, one bad batch could spoil the entire contents of a tank. The result was wasted raw materials and high costs of hazardous waste disposal. 3M developed a new technique to run quality tests more rapidly on new batches. The new technique allowed 3M to reduce hazardous wastes by 10 tons per year at almost no cost, yielding an annual savings of more than $200,000 (Sheridan, 1992).

Solving environmental problems can also yield benefits in terms of reduced downtime. Many chemical production processes at DuPont, for example, require start-up time to stabilize and bring output within specifications, resulting in an initial period during which only scrap and waste is produced. Installing higher-quality monitoring equipment has

---

[2] We should note that this plant was ultimately closed. However, the example described here does illustrate the role of regulatory pressure in process innovation.

allowed DuPont to reduce production interruptions and the associated wasteful production start-ups, thus reducing waste generation as well as downtime (Parkinson, 1990).

Regulation can trigger innovation offsets through substitution of less costly materials or better utilization of materials in the process. For example, 3M faced new regulations that will force many solvent users in paper, plastic and metal coatings to reduce its solvent emissions 90 percent by 1995 (Boroughs and Carpenter, 1991). The company responded by avoiding the use of solvents altogether and developing coating products with safer, water-based solutions. At another 3M plant, a change from a solvent-based to a water-based carrier, used for coating tablets, eliminated 24 tons per year of air emissions. The $60,000 investment saved $180,000 in unneeded pollution control equipment and created annual savings of $15,000 in solvent purchases (Parkinson, 1990). Similarly, when federal and state regulations required that Dow Chemical close certain evaporation ponds used for storing and evaporating wastewater resulting from scrubbing hydrochloric gas with caustic soda, Dow redesigned its production process. By first scrubbing the hydrochloric acid with water and then caustic soda, Dow was able to eliminate the need for evaporation ponds, reduce its use of caustic soda, and capture a portion of the waste stream for reuse as a raw material in other parts of the plant. This process change cost $250,000 to implement. It reduced caustic waste by 6,000 tons per year and hydrochloric acid waste by 80 tons per year, for a savings of $2.4 million per year (Dorfman, Muir and Miller, 1992).

The Robbins Company's jewelry-plating system illustrates similar benefits. In moving to the closed-loop system that purified and recycled water, Robbins saved over $115,000 per year in water, chemicals, disposal costs, and lab fees and reduced water usage from 500,000 gallons per week to 500 gallons per week. The capital cost of the new system, which completely eliminated the waste, was $220,000, compared to about $500,000 for a wastewater treatment facility that would have brought Robbins' discharge into compliance only with current regulations.

At the Tobyhanna Army Depot, for instance, improvements in sandblasting, cleaning, plating and painting operations reduced hazardous waste generation by 82 percent between 1985 and 1992. That reduction saved the depot over $550,000 in disposal costs, and $400,000 in material purchasing and handling costs (PR Newswire, 1993).

Innovation offsets can also be derived by converting waste into more valuable forms. The Robbins Company recovered valuable precious metals in its zero discharge plating system. At Rhone-Poulenc's nylon plant in Chalampe, France, diacids (by-products that had been produced by an adipic acid process) used to be separated and incinerated. Rhone-Poulenc invested Fr 76 million and installed new equipment to recover and sell them as dye and tanning additives or coagulation agents, resulting in annual revenues of about Fr 20.1 million. In the United States, similar by-products from a Monsanto Chemical Company plant in Pensacola, Florida, are sold to utility companies who use them to accelerate sulfur dioxide removal during flue gas desulfurization (Basta and Vagi, 1988).

A few studies of innovation offsets do go beyond individual cases and offer some broader-based data. One of the most extensive studies is by INFORM, an environmental research organization. INFORM investigated activities to prevent waste generation—so-called source reduction activities—at 29 chemical plants in California, Ohio and New Jersey (Dorfman, Muir and Miller, 1992). Of the 181 source-reduction activities identified in this study, only one was found to have resulted in a net cost increase. Of the 70 activities for which the study was able to document changes in product yield, 68 reported yield increases; the average yield increase for the 20 initiatives with specific available data was 7 percent. These innovation offsets were achieved with surprisingly low investments and very short payback periods. One-quarter of the 48 initiatives with detailed capital cost information required no capital investment at all; of the 38 initiatives with payback period data, nearly two-thirds were shown to have recouped their initial investments in six months or less. The annual savings per dollar spent on source reduction averaged $3.49 for the 27 activities for which this information could be calculated. The study also investigated the motivating factors behind the plant's source-reduction activities. Significantly, it found that waste disposal costs were the most often cited, followed by environmental regulation.

...

Answering Defenders of the Traditional Model

Our argument that strict environmental regulation can be fully consistent with competitiveness was originally put forward in a short *Scientific*

American essay (Porter, 1991; see also van der Linde, 1993)...It has been warmly received by many, especially in the business community. But it has also had its share of critics, especially among economists (Jaffe, Peterson, Portney and Stavins, 1993, 1994; Oates, Palmer and Portney, 1993; Palmer and Simpson, 1993; Simpson, 1993; Schmalensee, 1993).

One criticism is that while innovation offsets are theoretically possible, they are likely to be rare or small in practice. We disagree. Pollution is the emission or discharge of a (harmful) substance or energy form into the environment. Fundamentally, it is a manifestation of economic waste and involves unnecessary, inefficient or incomplete utilization of resources, or resources not used to generate their highest value. In many cases, emissions are a sign of inefficiency and force a firm to perform non-value-creating activities such as handling, storage and disposal. Within the company itself, the costs of poor resource utilization are most obvious in incomplete material utilization, but are also manifested in poor process control, which generates unnecessary stored material, waste and defects. There are many other hidden costs of resource inefficiencies later in the life cycle of the product. Packaging discarded by distributors or customers, for example, wastes resources and adds costs. Customers bear additional costs when they use polluting products or products that waste energy. Resources are also wasted when customers discard products embodying unused materials or when they bear the costs of product disposal.[3]

As the many examples discussed earlier suggest, the opportunity to reduce cost by diminishing pollution should thus be the rule, not the exception. Highly toxic materials such as heavy metals or solvents are often expensive and hard to handle, and reducing their use makes sense from several points of view. More broadly, efforts to reduce pollution and maximize profits share the same basic principles, including the efficient use of inputs, substitution of less expensive materials and the minimization of unneeded activities.[4]

---

[3] At its core, then, pollution is a result of an intermediate state of technology or management methods. Apparent exceptions to the resource productivity thesis often prove the rule by highlighting the role of technology. Paper made with recycled fiber was once greatly inferior, but new de-inking and other technologies have made its quality better and better. Apparent tradeoffs between energy efficiency and emissions rest on incomplete combustion.

[4] Schmalensee (1993) counters that NO_x emissions often result from thermodynamically efficient combustion. But surely this is an anomaly, not the rule, and may represent an intermediate level of efficiency.

A corollary to this observation is that scrap or waste or emissions can carry important information about flaws in product design or the production process. A recent study of process changes in 10 printed circuit board manufacturers, for example, found that 13 of 33 major changes were initiated by pollution control personnel. Of these, 12 resulted in cost reduction, eight in quality improvements and five in extension of production capabilities (King, 1994).

Environmental improvement efforts have traditionally overlooked the systems cost of resource inefficiency. Improvement efforts have focused on *pollution control* through better identification, processing and disposal of discharges or waste, an inherently costly approach. In recent years, more advanced companies and regulators have embraced the concept of *pollution prevention*, sometimes called source reduction, which uses material substitution, closed-loop processes and the like to limit pollution before it occurs.

But although pollution prevention is an important step in the right direction, ultimately companies and regulators must learn to frame environmental improvement in terms of *resource productivity*, or the efficiency and effectiveness with which companies and their customers use resources.[5] Improving resource productivity within companies goes beyond eliminating pollution (and the cost of dealing with it) to lowering true economic cost and raising the true economic value of products. At the level of resource productivity, environmental improvement and competitiveness come together. The imperative for resource productivity rests on the private costs that companies bear because of pollution, not on mitigating pollution's social costs. In addressing these private costs, it highlights the opportunity costs of pollution—wasted resources, wasted efforts and diminished product value to the customer—not its actual costs.

...

A second criticism of our hypothesis is to point to the studies finding high costs of compliance with environmental regulation, as evidence that there is a fixed tradeoff between regulation and competitiveness. But these studies are far from definitive.

---

[5] One of the pioneering efforts to see environmental improvement this way is Joel Makower's (1993) book, *The E-Factor: The Bottom-Line Approach to Environmentally Responsible Business.*

Estimates of regulatory compliance costs prior to enactment of a new rule typically exceed the actual costs. In part, this is because such estimates are often self-reported by industries who oppose the rule, which creates a tendency to inflation. A prime example of this type of thinking was a statement by Lee Iacocca, then vice president at the Ford Motor Company, during the debate on the 1970 Clean Air Act. Iacocca warned that compliance with the new regulations would require huge price increases for automobiles, force U.S. automobile production to a halt after January 1, 1975, and "do irreparable damage to the U.S. economy" (Smith, 1992). The 1970 Clean Air Act was subsequently enacted, and Iacocca's predictions turned out to be wrong. Similar dire predictions were made during the 1990 Clean Air Act debate; industry analysts predicted that burdens on the U.S. industry would exceed $100 billion. Of course, the reality has proven to be far less dramatic. In one study in the pulp and paper sector, actual costs of compliance were $4.00 to $5.50 per ton compared to original industry estimates of $16.40 (Bonson, McCubbin and Sprague, 1988).

Early estimates of compliance cost tend to be exaggerated because they assume no innovation. Early cost estimates for dealing with regulations concerning emission of volatile compounds released during paint application held everything else constant, assuming only the addition of a hood to capture the fumes from paint lines. Innovation that improved the paint's transfer efficiency subsequently allowed not only the reduction of fumes but also paint usage. Further innovation in water-borne paint formulations without any VOC-releasing solvents made it possible to eliminate the need for capturing and treating the fumes altogether (Bonifant, 1994b). Similarly, early estimates of the costs of complying with a 1991 federal clean air regulation calling for a 98 percent reduction in atmospheric emissions of benzene from tar-storage tanks used by coal tar distillers initially assumed that tar-storage tanks would have to be covered by costly gas blankets. While many distillers opposed the regulations, Pittsburgh-based Aristech Chemical, a major distiller of coal tar, subsequently developed an innovative way to remove benzene from tar in the first processing step, thereby eliminating the need for the gas blanket and resulting in a saving of $3.3 million instead of a cost increase (PR Newswire, 1993).

Prices in the new market for trading allowances to emit SO_2 provide another vivid example. At the time the law was passed, analysts projected that the marginal cost of SO_2 controls (and, therefore, the price of an emission allowance) would be on the order of $300 to $600 (or more) per ton in Phase I and up to $1000 or more in Phase II. Actual Phase I allowance prices have turned out to be in the $170 to $250 range, and recent trades are heading lower, with Phase II estimates only slightly higher (after adjusting for the time value of money). In case after case, the differences between initial predictions and actual outcomes — especially after industry has had time to learn and innovate — are striking.

Econometric studies showing that environmental regulation raises costs and harms competitiveness are subject to bias, because net compliance costs are overestimated by assuming away innovation benefits. Jorgenson and Wilcoxen (1990), for example, explicitly state that they did not attempt to assess public or private benefits. Other often-cited studies that solely focus on costs, leaving out benefits, are Hazilla and Kopp (1990) and Gray (1987). By largely assuming away innovation effects, how could economic studies reach any other conclusion than they do?

Internationally competitive industries seem to be much better able to innovate in response to environmental regulation than industries that were uncompetitive to begin with, but no study measuring the effects of environmental regulation on industry competitiveness has taken initial competitiveness into account....

A number of studies have failed to find that stringent environmental regulation hurts industrial competitiveness. Meyer (1992, 1993) tested and refuted the hypothesis that U.S. states with stringent environmental policies experience weak economic growth. Leonard (1988) was unable to demonstrate statistically significant offshore movements by U.S. firms in pollution-intensive industries. Wheeler and Mody (1992) failed to find that environmental regulation affected the foreign investment decisions of U.S. firms. Repetto (1995) found that industries heavily affected by environmental regulations experienced slighter reductions in their share of world exports than did the entire American industry from 1970 to 1990. Using U.S. Bureau of Census Data of more than 200,000 large manufacturing establishments, the study also found that plants with poor environmental records are generally not more profitable than cleaner ones in the same industry, even controlling for their age, size and technology. Jaffe, Peterson, Portney and Stavins (1993) recently surveyed more than 100 studies and concluded there is little evidence to support the view that U.S. environmental regulation had a large adverse effect on competitiveness.

Of course, these studies offer no proof for our hypothesis, either. But it is striking that so many studies find that even the poorly designed environmental laws presently in effect have little adverse effect on competitiveness. After all, traditional approaches to regulation have surely worked to stifle potential innovation offsets and imposed unnecessarily high costs of compliance on industry (as we will discuss in greater detail in the next section). Thus, studies using actual compliance costs to regulation are heavily biased toward finding that such regulation has a substantial cost.[6] In no way do such studies measure the potential of well-crafted environmental regulations to stimulate competitiveness.

A third criticism of our thesis is that even if regulation fosters innovation, it will harm competitiveness by crowding out other potentially more productive investments or avenues for innovation. Given incomplete information, the limited attention many companies have devoted to environmental innovations and the inherent linkage between pollution and resource productivity described earlier, it certainly is not obvious that this line of innovation has been so thoroughly explored that the marginal benefits of further investment would be low. The high returns evident in the studies we have cited support this view. Moreover, environmental investments represent only a small percentage of overall investment in all but a very few industries.[7]

A final counterargument, more caricature than criticism, is that we are asserting that any strict environmental regulation will inevitably lead to innovation and competitiveness. Of course, this is not our position. Instead, we believe that if regulations are properly crafted and companies are attuned to the possibilities, then innovation to minimize and even offset the cost of compliance is likely in many circumstances.

---

[6] Gray and Shadbegian (1993), another often-mentioned study, suffers from several of the problems discussed here. The article uses industry-reported compliance costs and does not control for plant technology vintage or the extent of other productivity-enhancing investments at the plant. High compliance costs may well have been borne in old, inefficient plants where firms opted for secondary treatment rather than innovation. Moreover, U.S. producers may well have been disadvantaged in innovating given the nature of the U.S. regulatory process—this seems clearly to have been the case in pulp and paper, one of the industries studied by the Management Institute for Environment and Business (MEB).

[7] In paints and coatings, for example, environmental investments were 3.3 percent of total capital investment in 1989. According to Department of Commerce (1991) data (self-reported by industry), capital spending for pollution control and abatement outside of the chemical, pulp and paper, petroleum and coal, and primary metal sectors made up just 3.15 percent of total capital spending in 1991.

Designing Environmental Regulation to Encourage Innovation

If environmental standards are to foster the innovation offsets that arise from new technologies and approaches to production, they should adhere to three principles. First, they must create the maximum opportunity for innovation, leaving the approach to innovation to industry and not the standard-setting agency. Second, regulations should foster continuous improvement, rather than locking in any particular technology. Third, the regulatory process should leave as little room as possible for uncertainty at every stage. Evaluated by these principles, it is clear that U.S. environmental regulations have often been crafted in a way that deters innovative solutions, or even renders them impossible. Environmental laws and regulations need to take three substantial steps: phrasing environmental rules as goals that can be met in flexible ways; encouraging innovation to reach and exceed those goals; and administering the system in a coordinated way.

Clear Goals, Flexible Approaches

Environmental regulation should focus on outcomes, not technologies.[8] Past regulations have often prescribed particular remediation technologies—like catalysts or scrubbers to address air pollution—rather than encouraging innovative approaches. American environmental law emphasized phrases like "best available technology," or "best available control technology." But legislating as if one particular technology is always the "best" almost guarantees that innovation will not occur.

…Regulators must consider the technological capabilities and resources available at each stage, because it affects the likelihood that innovation will occur. With that in mind, the governing principle should be to regulate as late in the production chain as practical, which will normally allow more flexibility for innovation there and in upstream stages.

The EPA should move beyond the single medium (air, water and so on) as the principal way of thinking about the environment, toward total discharges or total impact.[9] It should reorganize around affected industry

---

[8] There will always be instances of extremely hazardous pollution requiring immediate action, where imposing a specific technology by command and control may be the best or only viable solution. However, such methods should be seen as a last resort.

[9] A first step in this direction is the EPA's recent adjustment of the timing of its air rule for the pulp and paper industry so that it will coincide with the rule for water, allowing industry to see the dual impact of the rules and innovate accordingly.

clusters (including suppliers and related industries) to better understand a cluster's products, technologies and total set of environmental problems. This will foster fundamental rather than piecemeal solutions.[10]

Seeding and Spreading Environmental Innovations

Where possible, regulations should include the use of market incentives, including pollution taxes, deposit-refund schemes and tradable permits.[11] Such approaches often allow considerable flexibility, reinforce resource productivity, and also create incentives for ongoing innovation. Mandating outcomes by setting emission levels, while preferable to choosing a particular technology, still fails to provide incentives for continued and ongoing innovation and will tend to freeze a status quo until new regulations appear. In contrast, market incentives can encourage the introduction of technologies that exceed current standards.

The EPA should also promote an increased use of preemptive standards by industry, which appear to be an effective way of dealing with environmental regulation. Preemptive standards, agreed to with EPA oversight to avoid collusion, can be set and met by industry to avoid government standards that might go further or be more restrictive on innovation. They are not only less costly, but allow faster change and leave the initiative for innovation with industry.

The EPA should play a major role in collecting and disseminating information on innovation offsets and their consequences, both here and in other countries. Limited knowledge about opportunities for innovation is a major constraint on company behavior. A good start can be the "clearinghouse" of information on source-reduction approaches that EPA

---

[10] The EPA's regulatory cluster team concept, under which a team from relevant EPA offices approaches particular problems for a broader viewpoint, is a first step in this direction. Note, however, that of the 17 cluster groups formed, only four were organized around specific industries (petroleum refining, oil and gas production, pulp and paper, printing), while the remaining 13 focused on specific chemicals or types of pollution (U.S. Congress, Office of Technology Assessment, 1994).

[11] Pollution taxes can be implemented as effluent charges on the quantity of pollution discharges, as user charges for public treatment facilities, or as product charges based on the potential pollution of a product. In a deposit-refund system, such product charges may be rebated if a product user disposes of it properly (for example, by returning a lead battery for recycling rather than sending it to a landfill). Under a tradable permit system, like that included in the recent Clean Air Act Amendments, a maximum amount of pollution is set, and rights equal to that cap are distributed to firms. Firms must hold enough rights to cover their emissions; firms with excess rights can sell them to firms who are short.

was directed to establish by the Pollution Prevention Act (PPA) of 1990. The Green Lights and Toxics Release Inventories described at the start of this paper are other programs that involve collecting and spreading information. Yet another important initiative is the EPA program to compare emissions rates at different companies, creating methodologies to measure the full internal costs of pollution and ways of exchanging best practices and learning on innovative technologies.

Regulatory approaches can also function by helping create demand pressure for environmental innovation. One example is the prestigious German "Blue Angel" eco-label, introduced by the German government in 1977, which can be displayed only by products meeting very strict environmental criteria. One of the label's biggest success stories has been in oil and gas heating appliances: the energy efficiency of these appliances improved significantly when the label was introduced, and emissions of sulfur dioxide, carbon monoxide and nitrogen oxides were reduced by more than 30 percent.

Another point of leverage on the demand side is to harness the role of government as a demanding buyer of environmental solutions and environmentally friendly products. While there are benefits of government procurement of products such as recycled paper and retreaded tires, the far more leveraged role is in buying specialized environmental equipment and services.[12] One useful change would be to alter the current practice of requiring bidders in competitive bid processes for government projects to only bid with "proven" technologies, a practice sure to hinder innovation.

. . .

Incentives for innovation must also be built into the regulatory process itself. The current permitting system under Title V of the Clean Air Act Amendments, to choose a negative example, requires firms seeking to change or expand their production process in a way that might impact air quality to revise their permit extensively, *no matter how little the potential effect on air quality may be.* This not only deters innovation, but drains the resources of regulators away from timely action on significant matters. On the positive side, the state of Massachusetts has initiated a program

---

[12] See Marron (1994) for a demonstration of the modest productivity gains likely from government procurement of standard items, although in a static model.

to waive permits in some circumstances, or promise an immediate permit, if a company takes a zero-discharge approach.

A final priority is new forums for settling regulatory issues that minimize litigation. Potential litigation creates enormous uncertainty; actual litigation burns resources. Mandatory arbitration, or rigid arbitration steps before litigation is allowed, would benefit innovation. There is also a need to rethink certain liability issues. While adequate safeguards must be provided against companies that recklessly harm citizens, there is a pressing need for liability standards that more clearly recognize the countervailing health and safety benefits of innovations that lower or eliminate the discharge of harmful pollutants.

Regulatory Coordination

Coordination of environmental regulation can be improved in at least three ways: between industry and regulators, between regulators at different levels and places in government, and between U.S. regulators and their international counterparts.

In setting environmental standards and regulatory processes to encourage innovation, substantive industry participation in setting standards is needed right from the beginning, as is common in many European countries. An appropriate regulatory process is one in which regulations themselves are clear, who must meet them is clear, and industry accepts the regulations and begins innovating to address them, rather than spending years attempting to delay or relax them. In our current system, by the time standards are finally settled and clarified, it is often too late to address them fundamentally, making secondary treatment the only alternative. We need to evolve toward a regulatory regime in which the EPA and other regulators make a commitment that standards will be in place for, say, five years; so that industry is motivated to innovate rather than adopt incremental solutions.

Different parts and levels of government must coordinate and organize themselves so that companies are not forced to deal with multiple parties with inconsistent desires and approaches. As a matter of regulatory structure, the EPA's proposed new Innovative Technology Council, being set up to advocate the development of new technology in every field of environmental policy, is a step in the right direction. Another unit in the EPA should be responsible for continued reengineering of the process of regulation to reduce uncertainty and minimize costs. Also, an explicit strategy is needed to coordinate and harmonize federal and state activities.[13]

A final issue of coordination involves the relationship between U.S. environmental regulations and those in other countries. U.S. regulations should be in sync with regulations in other countries and, ideally, be slightly ahead of them. This will minimize possible competitive disadvantages relative to foreign competitors who are not yet subject to the standard, while at the same time maximizing export potential in the pollution control sector. Standards that lead world developments provide domestic firms with opportunities to create valuable early-mover advantages. However, standards should not be too far ahead of, or too different in character from, those that are likely to apply to foreign competitors, for this would lead industry to innovate in the wrong directions.

...

Imperatives for Companies

Of course, the regulatory reforms described here also seek to change how companies view environmental issues.[14] Companies must start to recognize the environment as a competitive opportunity—not as an annoying cost or a postponable threat. Yet many companies are ill-prepared to carry out a strategy of environmental innovation that produces sizable compensating offsets.

For starters, companies must improve their measurement and assessment methods to detect environmental costs and benefits.[15] Too often, relevant

---

[13] The cluster-based approach to regulation discussed earlier should also help eliminate the practice of sending multiple EPA inspectors to the same plant who do not talk to one another, make conflicting demands and waste time and resources. The potential savings from cluster- and multimedia-oriented permitting and inspection programs appear to be substantial. During a pilot multimedia testing program called the Blackstone Project, the Massachusetts Department of Environmental Protection found that multimedia inspections required 50 percent less time than conventional inspections—which at that time accounted for nearly one-fourth of the department's operating budget (Roy and Dillard, 1990).

[14] For a more detailed perspective on changing company mindsets about competitiveness and environmentalism, see Porter and van der Linde (1995) in the *Harvard Business Review*.

[15] Accounting methods that are currently being discussed in this context include "full cost accounting," which goes a step further and attempts both to allocate costs more specifically and to include cost items beyond traditional concerns, such as indirect or hidden costs (like compliance costs, insurance, on-site waste management, operation of pollution control and future liability) and less tangible benefits (like revenue from enhanced company image). See White, Becker and Goldstein (1991), cited in U.S. Congress, Office of Technology Assessment (1994).

information is simply lacking. Typical is the case of a large producer of organic chemicals that retained a consulting firm to explore opportunities for reducing waste. The client thought it had 40 waste streams, but a careful audit revealed that 497 different waste streams were actually present (Parkinson, 1990). Few companies analyze the true cost of toxicity, waste, discharges and the second-order impacts of waste and discharges on other activities. Fewer still look beyond the out-of-pocket costs of dealing with pollution to investigate the opportunity costs of the wasted resources or foregone productivity. How much money is going up the smokestack? What percentage of inputs are wasted? Many companies do not even track environmental spending carefully, or subject it to evaluation techniques typical for "normal" investments.

Once environmental costs are measured and understood, the next step is to create a presumption for innovation-based solutions. Discharges, scrap and emissions should be analyzed for insights about beneficial product design or process changes. Approaches based on treatment or handling of discharges should be accepted only after being sent back several times for reconsideration. The responsibility for environmental issues should not be delegated to lawyers or outside consultants except in the adversarial regulatory process, or even to internal specialists removed from the line organization, residing in legal, government or environmental affairs departments. Instead, environmental strategies must become a general management issue if the sorts of process and product redesigns needed for true innovation are to even be considered, much less be proposed and implemented.

References

Acton, Jan Paul, and Lloyd S. Dixon, Superfund and Transaction Costs: The Experiences of Insurers and Very Large Industrial Firms. Santa Monica: Rand Institute for Civil Justice, 1992.

Amoco Corporation and United States Environmental Protection Agency "Amoco-U.S. EPA Pollution Prevention Project: Yorktown, Virginia, Project Summary," Chicago and Washington, D.C., 1992.

Basta, Nicholas, and David Vagi, "A Casebook of Successful Waste Reduction Projects," Chemical Engineering August 15, 1988, 95:11, 37.

Berube, M, J. Nash, J. Maxwell, and J. Ehrenfelds "From Pollution Control to Zero Discharge: How the Robbins Company Overcame the Obstacles," Pollution Prevention Review, Spring 1992, 2:2, 189-207.

Bonifant, B., "Competitive Implications of Environmental Regulation in the Electronics Manufacturing Industry," Management Institute for Environment and Business, Washington, D.C., 1994a.

Bonifant, B., "Competitive Implications of Environmental Regulation in the Paint and Coatings Industry," Management Institute for Environment and Business, Washington, D.C., 1994b.

Bonifant, B., and I. Ratcliffe, "competitive Implications of Environmental Regulation in the Pulp and Paper Industry," Management Institute for Environment and Business, Washington, D.C., 1994.

Bonson, N. C., Neil McCubbin, and John B. Sprague, "Kraft Mill Effluents in Ontario." Report prepared for the Technical Advisory Committee, Pulp and Paper Sector of MISA, Ontario Ministry of the Environment, Toronto, Ontario, Canada, March 29, 1988, Section 6, p. 166.

Boroughs, D. L, and B. Carpenter, "Helping the Planet and the Economy," U.S. News & World Report, March 25, 1991, 110:11, 46.

Clay, Don, "New Environmentalist: A Cooperative Strategy," Forum for Applied Reserch and Public Policy, Spring 1993, 8, 125-28.

DeCanio, Stephen J., "Why Do Profitable Energy-Saying Investment Projects Languish?" Paper presented at the Second International Research Conference of the Greening of Industry Network, Cambridge, Mass., 1993.

Department of Commerce, "Pollution Abatement Costs and Expenditures," Washington, D.C., 1991.

Dorfman: Mark H. Warren R. Muir, and Catherine G. Miller, Environmental Dividends: Cutting More Chemical Wastes. New York: INFORM, 1992.

Ehrlich, Paul, The Population Bomb. New York: Ballantine Books, 1968.

Freeman, A. Myrick, III, "Methods for Assessing the Benefits of Environmental Programs." In Kneese, A. V., and J. L. Sweeney, eds., Handbook of Natural Resource and Energy Economics. Vol 1. Amsterdam: North-Holland, 1985, pp. 223-70.

Gray, Wayne B, "The Cost of Regulation: OSHA, EPA, and the Productivity Slowdown," American Economic Review, 1987, 77:5, 998-1006.

Gray, Wayne B., and Ronald j. Shadbegian, "Environmental Regulation and Productivity at the Plant Level," discussion paper, U.S. Department of Commerce, Center for Economic Studies, Washington, D.C., 1993.

Hartwell, R. V., and L. Bergkamp, "Eco-Labelling in Europe: New Market-Related Environmental Risks?," BNA International Environment Daily, Special Report, Oct. 20, 1992.

Hazilla, Michael, and Raymond J. Kopp, "Social Cost of Environmental Quality Regulations: A General Equilibrium Analysis," Journal of Political Economy, 1990, 98:4, 853-73.

Jaffe, Adam B, S. Peterson, Paul Portney, and Robert N. Stavins, "Environmental Regulations and the Competitiveness of U.S. Industry," Economics Resource Group, Cambridge, Mass., 1993.

Jaffe, Adam B., S. Peterson, Paul Portney, and Robert N. Staving, "Environmental Regulation and International Competitiveness: What Does the Evidence Tell Us," draft, January 13, 1994.

Jorgenson, Dale W., and Peter J. Wilcoxen, "Environmental Regulation and U.S. Economic Growth," Rand Journal of Economics, Summer 1990, 21:2, 314-40.

Kalt, Joseph P., "The Impact of Domestic Environmental Regulatory Policies on U.S. International Competitiveness." In Spence, A.M., and H. Hazard, eds., International Competitiveness, Cambridge, Mass: Harper and Row, Ballinger, 1988, pp. 221-62.

King, A., "Improved Manufacturing Resulting from Learning-From-Waste: Causes, Importance, and Enabling Conditions," working paper, Stern School of Business, New York University, 1994.

Leonard, H. Jeffrey, Population and the Struggle for World Product. Cambridge, U.K.: Cambridge University Press, 1988.

Makower, Joel, The E-Factor: The Bottom-Line Approach to Environmentally Responsible Business. New York: Times Books, 1993.

Marron, Donald B., "Buying Green: Government Procurement as an Instrument of Environmental Policy," mimeo, Massachusetts Institute of Technology, 1994.

Massachusetts Department of Environmental Protection, Daniel S. Greenbaum, Commissioner, interview, Boston, August 8, 1993.

Meadows, Donella H., and Dennis L. Meadows, The Limits of Growth. New York: New American Library; 1972:

Meyer, Stephen M., Environmentalism and Economic Prosperity: Testing the Environmental Impact Hypothesis. Cambridge, Mass.: Massachusetts Institute of Technology, 1992.

Meyer, Stephen M, Environmentalism and Economic Prosperity: An Update. Cambridge, Mass.: Massachusetts Institute of Technology, 1993.

National Paint and Coatings Association, Improving the Superfund: Correcting a National Public Policy Disaster. Washington, D.C., 1992.

Palmer, Karen L. and Ralph David Simpson, "Environmental Policy as Industrial Policy," Resources, Summer 1993, 112, 17-21.

Parkinson, Gerald, "Reducing Wastes Can Be Cost-Effective," Chemical Engineering, July 1990, 97:7, 30.

Porter, Michael E, Competitive Advantage: Creating and Sustaining Superior Performance. New York: Free Press, 1985.

Porter, Michael E., The Competitive Advantage of Nations. New York: Free Press, 1990.

Porter, Michael E, "America's Green Strategy," Scientific American, April 1991, 264, 168.

Porter, Michael E, and Clans van der Linde, "Green and Competitive: Breaking the Stalemate," Harvard Business Review, September-October 1995.

PR Newswire, "Winners Announced for Governor's Waste Minimization Awards,"January 21, 1993, State and Regional News Section.

Oates, Wallace, Karen L. Palmer, and Paul Portney, "Environmental Regulation and International Competitiveness: Thinking About the Porter Hypothesis." Resources for the Future Working Paper 94-02, 1993.

Rappaport, Ann, "Development and Transfer of Pollution Prevention Technology Within a Multinational Corporation," dissertation, Department of Civil Engineering, Tufts University, May 1992.

Raytheon Inc, "Alternate Cleaning Technology." Technical Report Phase II. January-October 1991.

Raytheon Inc., J. R. Pasquariello, Vice President Environmental Quality; Kenneth J. Tierney, Director Environmental and Energy Conservation; Frank A. Marino, Senior Corporate Environmental Specialist; interview, Lexington, Mass., April 4, 1993.

Repetto, Robert, "Jobs, Competitiveness, and Environmental Regulation: What are the Real Issues?," Washington, D.C.: World Resources Institute, 1995.

Roy, M., and L. A. Dillard "Toxics Use in Massachusetts: The Blackstone Project," Journal of Air and Waste Management Association, October 1990, 40:10, 1368-71.

Schmalensee, Richard, "The Costs of Environmental Regulation." Massachusetts Institute of Technology, Center for Energy and Environmental Policy Research Working Paper 95-015, 1993.

Sheridan, J. H., "Attacking Wastes and Saving Money . . . Some of the Time," Industry Week, February 17, 1992, 241:4, 43.

Simpson, Ralph David, "Taxing Variable Cost: Environmental Regulation as Industrial Policy." Resources for the Future Working Paper ENR95-12, 1995.

Smith, Zachary A, The Environmental Policy Paradox. Englewood Cliffs, N.J.: Prentice Hall, 1992.

United States Environmental Protection Agency, "Multiple Pathways to Super Efficient Refrigerators," Washington, D.C., 1992.

U.S. Congress Office of Technology Assessment "Industry, Technology, and the Environment Competitive Challenges and Business Opportunities," OTA-ITE-586, Washington, D.C. 1994.

van der Linde, Class, "The Micro-Economic Implications of Environmental Regulation: A Preliminary Framework." In Environmental Policies and Industrial Competitiveness. Paris: Organization of Economic CoOperation and Development, 1993, pp. 69-77.

van der Linde, Class, "Competitive Implications of Environmental Regulation in the Cell Battery Industry," Hochschule St. Gallen, St. Gallen, forthcoming 1995a.

van der Linde, Claas, "Competitive Implications of Environmental Regulation in the Printing Ink Industry," Hochschule St. Gallen, St. Gallen, forthcoming 1995b.

van der Linde, Claas, "Competitive Implications of Environmental Regulation in the Refrigerator Industry," Hochschule St. Gallen, St. Gallen, forthcoming 1995c.

Wheeler, David, and Ashoka Mody, "International Investment Location Decisions: The Case of U.S. Firms," Journal of International Economics, August 1992, 33, 57-76.

White, A. L., M. Becker, and J. Goldstein, "Alternative Approaches to the Financial Evaluation of Industrial Pollution Prevention Investments," prepared for the New Jersey Department of Environmental Protection, Division of Science and Research, November 1991.

Do Corporate Global Environmental Standards Create or Destroy Market Value?

Glen Dowell, Stuart Hart, Bernard Yeung

46(8) MANAGEMENT SCIENCE 1059 (2000)

1.   Introduction

...

Led by MNEs [Multinational Enterprises], the affluent societies of the developed world account for more than 75% of the world s energy and resource consumption and create the bulk of the industrial, toxic, and consumer waste (Hart 1997). Environmentalists contend that MNEs are now engaging in flight to "pollution havens" by moving dirty operations to countries where regulatory standards are less stringent (Daly 1994). Through flight to pollution havens, MNEs can avoid expensive pollution controls, cut costs by recapitalizing old equipment, and continue to make products that are no longer considered environmentally acceptable in the more highly regulated markets of the developed world (Vernon 1992). Over time, it is claimed that these practices lead to a "race to the bottom" as poor nations and localities vie for plants and facilities that seek only to minimize cost and externalize environmental responsibility (Korten 1995).

While some MNEs clearly utilize such practices, it is unclear whether there is systematic advantage in racing to the bottom. There appear to be forces that encourage MNEs to integrate and standardize their environmental practices globally. Indeed, it may make business sense in some cases to adopt global standards that exceed those required by some local laws or regulations, especially when environmental laws and regulations become more stringent as an economy grows. By investing in state-of-the-art technology and processes in developing countries, MNE facilities may be able to achieve simultaneously world-class cost, quality, and environmental performance. In addition, MNE's may reap standardization benefits and other intangible advantages like positive reputation effects.

In this paper, we therefore seek an empirical answer to an intriguing and important question: Is firm value linked to an MNEs corporate environmental policy? Specifically, we examine whether adopting a single stringent corporate environmental standard enhances firm value compared to those MNEs defaulting to less stringent or poorly enforced host country standards. We find that firms adopting a stringent global environmental standard have higher market values...Our results have strong implications: Better firms appear to adopt higher environmental standards and pollute less. However, we cannot identify with our data any causal (time series) relationships between either past changes in environmental standards and current change in firm value, or past change in firm value and current change in environmental standards.

...

2.   Prior Research

A growing body of literature ties superior environmental performance to financial performance (e.g. Porter and van der Linde 1995, Hart 1995). For example, three recent studies link proactive environmental management to superior stock performance: Hamilton (1995), White (1995), and Klassen and McLaughlin (1996) all use event study methodology to demonstrate that (1) news of high levels of toxic emissions results in significant negative abnormal returns; (2) firms with strong environmental management practices have better stock price returns than firms with poor practices after a major environmental disaster, such as the Exxon Valdez accident; and (3) environmental performance awards result in significant positive abnormal returns. The first and second results indicate that investors expect that firms incur nontrivial costs for environmental cleanup and that these costs are lower for firms with better environmental records. The third result suggests that recognition of environmental performance has a positive reputation effect which possibly augments firm value.[1]

---

[1] The positive reputation effect may include not just investors' impressions of a firm's environmental performance; it may also include investors' impressions of a firm's management quality.

Feldman et al. (1996) analyze a sample of 300 large public companies in the United States to see if investments in environmental management lead to reduced risk, and if such risk reduction is valued by financial markets. Their findings suggest that investments in environmental management lead to substantial reduction in perceived risk of a firm, with an accompanying increase in a public company's stock price, of perhaps five percent.

Other scholars have examined the relationship between environmental and profit performance. Cohen et al. (1995), for example, demonstrate a strong correlation between environmental performance and firm profitability. Similarly, Hart and Ahuja (1996) present evidence indicating that efforts to prevent pollution and reduce emissions are positively associated with the "bottom line" (as measured by return on sales and return on assets) within one to two years of initiation, and that those firms with the highest emission levels stand to gain the most. Russo and Fouts (1997), in their study of 243 firms, find that environmental performance and return on assets (ROA) are positively linked, and that industry growth moderates this relationship, with returns to environmental performance higher for high-growth industries. Finally, Nehrt (1996) examines the relationship between timing and intensity of investment in pollution prevention and growth in profits within a sample of 50 pulp and paper companies. His results indicate a positive relationship between early movers in pollution prevention and profit growth.

While results are generally convergent, most empirical work to date has been restricted to MNEs in the United States or Western Europe where data are more available regarding environmental performance (e.g., Kennelly 1996). There has been some conceptual and case study treatment of MNE environmental performance in foreign contexts and developing countries (e.g., Korten 1995, Hart 1997), but little empirical research on this dimension has been conducted. The limited empirical work that has been done suggests that MNEs are more environmentally responsible than their local competitors in developing countries (Eskeland and Harrison 1997), but the evidence regarding MNE social performance is mixed (e.g., Zahra et al. 1993, Johnson and Greening 1994). We were unable to find any published empirical research focusing specifically on the question of how MNE international environmental standards, particularly their behavior in developing countries, affect firm market value. It is to that question that we now turn our attention.

3.   Theory

Arguments can be made on both sides of the question of whether a stringent global corporate environmental standard represents a competitive asset or liability for MNEs. Below, we articulate the major theoretical lenses on either side of the argument.

Global Environmental Standards as Altruistic Liability

Conventional economic logic suggests that, *ceteris paribus*, in countries where environmental regulation is either lax or not enforced, it is cheaper to operate than in countries where strict environmental regulations result in fines, liabilities, and administrative or legal action against polluters (Stewart 1993). For example, the annual cost of complying with environmental regulation in the United States now exceeds $125 billion, or about 2.1% of GDP. In most developing countries, environmental spending represents only a fraction of 1% of GDP (Jaffe et al. 1995).

Evidence also suggests that strict pollution control regulations in the United States may have an adverse impact on productivity (Gray and Shadbegian 1993), perhaps by forcing companies to commit resources and manpower to nonproductive uses such as environmental auditing, waste treatment, and litigation (Haveman and Christiansen 1981). Hence, when operating in countries with less stringent or poorly enforced environmental regulations, defaulting to local standards reduces costs.

Furthermore, by defaulting to local standards in countries with lax regulation or enforcement, companies may be able to recapitalize old equipment that is no longer acceptable in more regulated markets, thereby lowering costs even further. Companies can also market products in such countries that may be discouraged or even banned for environmental reasons in more regulated markets, thereby extending product life cycles and revenue streams (Vernon 1992, Korten 1995).

In short, there may be considerable financial penalties associated with overly general or constraining environmental policies in response to standardized criteria when it is not really needed or justified (Rondinelli and Vastag 1996). Overall the presumption is that defaulting to local standards is cost-saving, and that adhering to more stringent environmental standards where they are not required or enforced is wasteful. Firms that are altruistic in their attempts to achieve higher environmental standards when investing in low-standard countries are not serving their shareholders. The behavior hurts market value and may be a reflection of managerial idiosyncrasies.

Global Environmental Standards as Value-Adding Asset

A competing logic suggests that value-seeking investors may view defaulting to lower or poorly enforced local environmental standards as counterproductive to long-term profit performance. First, the cost savings associated with lower environmental standards may be exaggerated and may not even exist: MNEs often find that they have to pay for the remediation of environmental damages even if they are in full compliance with local regulations and requirements, often due to pressures from environmental interest groups or international organizations (e.g., World Bank). Such cleanup costs can be significant.

Second, in making new investments, a firm may find that moving downward from accustomed higher standards violates established corporate routines and is actually more costly than adhering to the higher standards, even in the absence of regulation. By specifying a single corporate standard, performance monitoring and evaluation costs might be reduced because a single set of values, specifications, and procedures can be deployed throughout the world, without the need to consider local deviations from the norm. Global standardization will also mean that production improvements made in one location can readily be transferred to all subsidiaries. Global strategies leverage the return on investment in improvements made in high environmental standard regions across all geographic locations (Prahalad and Doz 1987, Bartlett and Ghoshal 1989). Thus, adopting a single stringent environmental standard is consistent with pursuit of global competitive strategies by MNEs (Christmann 1998).

Third, while adequate environmental standards may not yet exist in many developing countries, it can be argued that in the not-too-distant future, standards will rise as income increases and people become more sensitive toward and concerned about environmental deterioration. This pattern of environmental regulation following GDP growth has already been observed among newly industrialized nations such as Taiwan, Korea, and Singapore (Grossman and Krueger 1995). In other words, there may be an important future benefit to adopting a single global standard if the productive life of capital extends beyond the period of lax or poorly enforced regulation.

When the environmental standards in developing countries improve with increases in per capita income, firms performing above current requirements will not need additional investment, while firms defaulting to the current minimums will need to reinvest to conform to the heightened requirements. A foresighted firm could take advantage of this by adopting higher environmental standards than are dictated by current regulations. MNEs are especially well-positioned in this regard: They can actually use the environment as a strategic competitive advantage by speeding up the process (e.g., by lobbying for tighter environmental regulations) and thus outcompete local firms with lesser financial means, knowledge, and capability.

Fourth, the presumption that polluting lowers production cost can be challenged. Putting aside the issue of regulatory stringency, there are other ways in which environmental standards may affect competitiveness. Specifically, not all environmental regulations affect firms' behavior in the same manner, and the form of environmental regulation can be an important determinant of business impact. For example, U.S. environmental regulations often mandate specific control or treatment technologies. These so-called "command and control" style regulations dictate that specific pollution control technologies be used, often at an exorbitant cost (Porter and van der Linde 1995).

However, in many cases, it is possible to reduce or eliminate pollution by making changes in the manufacturing or production process, rather than capturing pollutants for treatment or disposal at the "end-of-the pipe." Pollution and waste are reduced at the outset by a conscious effort to heighten resource efficiency. Many state-of-the-art technologies have high resource productivity. Such "eco-efficiency" can actually lower operating costs, rather than raise them (Porter and van der Linde 1995, Hart and Ahuja 1996).

Finally, there may be fringe benefits associated with adhering to higher environmental standards. By committing to standards that exceed those of the host country, the company might benefit from heightened employee morale and thus productivity (Romm 1993). Adopting an internal corporate environmental standard ahead of legal requirements avoids special interest group pressures and may result in positive reputation effects for the firm, improving its public image relative to competitors.

These considerations suggest that a firm defaulting to lower or poorly enforced local environmental standards may be overlooking both tangible and intangible benefits associated with conforming to a higher global standard. Firms conforming to a higher global environmental standard may find that the strategy enhances value.

Value Creation or Destruction?

The conflicting nature of the above arguments suggests that the relationship between corporate environmental standards and firm value is an empirical question. We therefore investigate two questions:

1. Are MNEs which exceed local environment standards (those adopting higher global standards) higher- or lower-value firms? Is adhering to higher global environmental standards associated with higher market value or does it represent a nonproductive use of assets and a drag on market value?

2. Is there a detectable lead-lag relationship between firm value and environmental standards? In other words, do changes in environmental standards cause changes in market value or visa versa?

4.   Methods

Sample

The sample of firms for this study was drawn from the U.S. Standard and Poor's 500 list of corporations. Although this population of firms is clearly biased towards the largest firms, this was not deemed to be a problem because MNEs were our target sample and the S&P 500 contains largely MNEs. Our sample period was from 1994 to 1997...

Two screens were applied in selecting firms. First, only those MNEs involved in manufacturing or mining (SIC codes between 2000 and 3999) were selected because the main research variable, corporate environmental standards, was most salient to these firms. Second, only those MNEs with production operations in countries with GDP per capita below $8,000 (1985 dollars) were included in the study. Evidence suggests that concern for and activity in environmental regulation decreases dramatically for countries with per capita income levels below $8,000 (Grossman and Krueger 1995). Sampling on this dimension therefore allows us to insure that there is a difference between those firms that default to local standards and those that adopt a global standard. After applying these two screens to the population, we ended up with eighty-nine firms, which were drawn from fifteen two-digit SIC codes....

6. Discussion

Our finding that adopting stringent global environmental standards is positively associated with a higher firm value is open to several possible interpretations. First, it may be that private valuations internalize environmental externalities: The less negative externalities a firm imposes, the higher the firm value. Second, it is possible that adopting stringent environmental standards is actually more profitable than defaulting to lower or poorly enforced local environmental standards. Finally, poorly managed and less competitive firms may tend to adopt lower environmental standards. In this section, we discuss each of these interpretations.

Internalization of Externalities

The first interpretation is based not only on our data, but also on the results of other studies (e.g., Hamilton 1995, White 1995, Klassen and McLaughlin 1996). All these results suggest that investors incorporate potential environmental problems and liabilities into their pricing of companies. In developed economies with strong regulatory regimes, the mechanism exists to support this observation: The institutional and legal systems support the public's rights to a clean environment so that polluters have to pay for their environmental damage. Hence, firms that have higher potential environmental liabilities realize lower market values.

The focus of this study (developing countries), however, involves locations where environmental regulations are lax or property rights to a clean environment are poorly enforced. In these contexts, other mechanisms must be at work. One possible mechanism for the internalization of externalities under these circumstances is as follows: Interest groups and nongovernmental organizations expose unsound corporate environmental practices, raise consumer awareness, and put pressure on governments to discipline polluters even if the pollution is in overseas locations. Through these means poor environmental performance is translated into bad public image, lower consumer goodwill, and ultimately, lower firm value.[13] Aware of this disciplinary effect, far-sighted managers conscious of firm value opt to maintain a high level of environmental practice, even where regulations do not require it.

Bottom-line Benefits

There appear to be economic implications of adopting high environmental standards that extend beyond the negative or "disciplinary" effects associated with poor environmental performance discussed above. In fact, the smallest coefficient for ED2...indicates that firms adopting their own stringent global environmental standards have a Tobin's q that is approximately 1.002 higher than those using U.S. standards abroad. Given the mean value of firm tangible assets in our sample, 1.002 represents more than $8.6 billion per firm. If we use the average of the regression coefficients for ED2 in Table 4, the number increases to $10.4 billion per firm. Even company estimates of the cost (including punitive damages) of the largest environmental cleanup in history (the Exxon Valdez accident) are less than $8 billion (*The Lamp* 1999). The magnitude of the value increase associated with higher environmental standards thus represents more than just the monetarization of negative externalities.

We therefore advance our second interpretation: Adopting stringent environmental standards is more profitable than defaulting to lower or poorly enforced local environmental standards. This interpretation is consistent with other studies (e.g., Cohen et al. 1995, Hart and Ahuja 1996, Russo and Fouts 1997), all of which suggest a higher level of profitability associated with better environmental practices and efforts to reduce emissions and waste.

We need to be careful, however, in explaining how stringent environmental standards might raise profit performance. Two possible

---

[13] For example, *The Economist* (July 20, 1996; "The fun of being a multinational") reported that:In Malaysia, a $5.5 billion hydroelectric dam to be built by a consortium including ABB Asea Brown Boveri, a Swiss-based multinational, is being attacked by local people and western environmental groups for destroying rainforest. The average oil baron or mining boss might once have shrugged off such events as little local difficulties. Some even relished a brawl. Nowadays, they recognise that the stakes are higher. It is not only the prospect of consumer boy cotts that worries them. In addition, staff morale can suffer (many Shell employees opposed the sinking of the Brent Spar), political contacts can be upset (Nelson Mandela denounced Shell's behaviour in Nigeria) and worst of all sanctions can be imposed (the state of Massachusetts recently banned contracts with firms doing business in Myanmar).

mechanisms apply. First, it may be that adopting the latest technologies and equipment increases productivity, and that is what makes the investment worthwhile. Better environmental practices are embedded in the latest technologies as a result of pressures from interest groups and governments in developed countries. From this perspective, the contribution of high environmental standards to bottom-line performance is "coincidental": The effect would not be present were it not for societal pressures to develop more environ-mentally friendly technologies and equipment. One would expect early movers to see the biggest gains from such investments, as Nehrt (1996) reports. Over time, companies not able to keep up with the investments would evidence erosion in bottom-line performance and firm value.[14]

A second, internally driven mechanism may also be at work, however. Firms that adopt high environmental standards are those that strive for eco-efficient production systems. The conscious policy to pursue technologies and processes that increase the *resource* productivity of their operations has a positive result for the bottom line.[15]

Low Performers Race to the Bottom

…One can…interpret our results as suggesting that "quality" firms adopt high environmental standards independent of local requirements, and generate less pollution, while lower-quality firms engage in a "race to the bottom," as a means of gaining short term financial advantage. High "quality" firms are typically more focused on corporate goals and competitive position. The application of a stringent global environmental standard may be indicative of a desire to build organizational awareness amongst all affiliates, of company policies and practices. It may also be an indicator that a company, as an industry leader, aims to stay on top in all aspects of its business.

There are still other possible explanations for the linkage between firm quality and firm environmental standard. For example, it is possible that

---

[14] However, this is not a typical "equilibrium" perspective. At equilibrium, the value of the above investment should reflect the value of cash flow and thus should not affect Tobin's *q*.

[15] An extension of our argument is that developing countries offer particularly attractive locations to experiment with such "clean technology" because they are not subject to the same level of costly "command and control" regulation that is found in developed economies such as the United States. Indeed, under these circumstances, it may be possible for firms to jointly optimize cost, quality, and environmental performance.

better firms have the foresight to plan for the future: They see the importance of applying high environmental standards even where not required because the standards will increase as a region grows and develops. It is also possible that higher-quality firms simply have the resources to invest in higher environment standards. They use environmental performance as a competitive weapon against other firms with fewer resources or means to keep up.

7.   Conclusion

This paper refutes the idea that adoption of global environmental standards by MNEs constitutes a liability that depresses market value. On the contrary, the evidence from our analysis indicates that positive market valuation is associated with the adoption of a single stringent environmental standard around the world.

Our results imply that private valuations may incorporate negative environmental externalities, even if the externalities take place in countries with lax environmental regulations and poorly protected environmental property rights. In addition, adopting stringent environmental standards may actually be more profitable than defaulting to lower local environmental standards. This may be a by-product of pressures in the developed world to make new technologies and equipment more environmentally friendly. It may also be that environmentally conscious firms are more diligent in reducing waste and improving resource productivity.

The notion that MNEs, as a group, pursue the lowest environmental standards and create a "race to the bottom" among developing countries desperate for foreign investments is not substantiated by the data. The most common corporate environmental practice in our sample is the opposite: adopting a stringent internal standard globally. We do not, however, suggest that the race to the bottom does not exist. In fact, our findings also suggest that companies with lower market values tend to pursue lower environmental standards. Perhaps these companies opt to default to host country standards because they lack the means to make the investment in environmentally superior technology worldwide. They may also be less well-run companies focusing on short-term cost savings. This might include, but is certainly not limited to, strategies such as recapitalizing old production assets, extending obsolete product life cycles, and exploiting low labor costs.

From a public policy standpoint, then, there are clear implications regarding these results: Developing countries may indeed attract foreign investment by lowering environmental standards, but the type of companies they attract by doing so will be weaker (and more pollution-intensive) firms not investing in state-of-the-art plants and equipment. After a temporary presence marked by the exploitation of the lower or poorly enforced host country standards, these companies may well end up fodder for those globally competitive firms which have adopted worldwide environmental standards and are reaping the competitive and market benefits of that policy. Thus, developing countries may be best served by promoting aggressive environmental objectives combined with a willingness to work collaboratively with the world's leading MNEs to define and implement policies that facilitate "win-win" environmental solutions.

The most important conclusion suggested by our results is that higher "quality" firms...appear to pollute less. Future research should examine this relationship in greater depth. Two future directions appear evident. First, our study was constrained by data availability. Future research should supplement the current data with more variables, including firm reputation, more detailed information on firms' actual environmental practices and performance, and a longer time series. Second, future work should aim to identify why firms adopt higher environmental standards. While we have proposed several plausible explanations here, examination of their validity awaits further research.

References

Bartlett. C., S. Ghoshal. 1989 *Managing Across Borders*. Harvard Business School Press, Boston, MA.

Caves, Richard E. 1996 *Multinational Enterprise and Economic Analysis*, 2nd ed. Cambridge University Press, New York

Christmann, P 1998, Environmental strategies of multinational chemical companies. Global integration or national responsiveness Working paper, University of Virginia, Charlottesville,VA.

Cohen, M , S. Fenn, J Naimon. 1995 *Environmental and Financial Performance*. IRRC, Washington, DC

Daly, H 1994. Fostering environmentally sustainable development: Four parting suggestions for the World Bank. *Ecological Econom.* 10 183-187

Eskeland, G., A. Harrison. 1997. Moving to greener pastures? Multinationals and the pollution haven hypothesis. Policy Research Working Paper 1744. The World Bank, Washington, DC.

Feldman, S., P. Soyka, P. Ameer. 1996. *Does Improving a Firm's Environmental Management System and Environmental Performance Result in a Higher Stock Price?* ICF Kaiser, Washington

Gladwin, T., J. Kenelly, T. Krause. 1995. Shifting paradigms for sustainable development: Implications for management theory and research. *Acad. Management Rev.* 20 874-907.

Gray, Wayne B., Runs 1. Shudhogian. 19-13. Environmental regulation and manufacturing productivity at the plant level, Discussion paper, U S. Department of Continence, Center for Economic Studies, Washington, D.C.

Greider, W. 1997. *One World, Ready or Not.* Simon and Schuster, New York

Grossman, C. A. Krueger. 1995. Economic growth and the environment. Quart. 7. Econom. 110(2) 353-377.

Hamilton, J 1995. Pollution as news: Media and stock market reactions to the Toxics Release Inventory data. J Environment. *Econom. Management Rev.* 28 98-113

Hart, S. 1995 A natural-resource-based view of the firm. *Acad.* Management *Rev.* 20 986-1014.

_____ 1997. Beyond greening: Strategies for a sustainable world. *Harvard Bus. Rev.* 75(1) 67 76.

_____, G. Ahuja. 1996. Does it pay to be green? An empirical examination of the relationship between emission reduction and firm performance Bus. Strategy *and the* Environment 5 30-37.

Haveman, R.. C. Christiansen. 1981 Environmental regulations and productivity growth. H. Peskin, P Portney, A. Kneese, eds. *Environmental Regulation and the US Economy.* Resources for the Future, Washington, DC.

Hawken, P. 1993 *The Ecology of Commerce.* HarperBusiness, New York.

Jaffe, A., S. Peterson, P. Portney, R., Stavins. 1995. Environmental regulation and the competitiveness of U. S. manufacturing What does the evidence tell us? *J Econom. Literature* 32 132-163.

Johnson. R., D. Greening. 1994. Relationships between corporate social performance, financial performance, and firm governance. *Acad. Management* Best *Paper Proc.* Dallas, TX 314-318

Kenelly, J 1996. The relationship of level of multinationality and institutional ownership of US firms and their social and environmental performance. Ph.D. Dissertation, Stern School of Business, Now York University, New York.

Kiassen, R., C. McLaughlin. 1996 The impact of environmental management on firm performance. *Management Sci.* 42 1199-1214.

Kogut, B. 1983. Foreign direct investment as a sequential process. C. Kindleberger, U. Audreresch. eds. *The Multinational Corporation in the 1980s.* MIT Press, Cambridge. MA. 38-56.

Korten. D. 1995. *When Corporations Rule The World.* Berrett-Koehler Publishers, San Francisco. CA.

The Lamp. 1999. Prince William Sound Revisited Spring.

Lindenberg. E. B., S. A. Ross. 1981. Tobin a q ratio and industrial organization. *J. Bus.* 54 (January) 1-32.

Morck, R. K., B Y. Young. 1991. Why investors value multinationality. 7. *Bus.* 64 (April) 165-187.

_____, _____.1992. Internalization: An event study test. *J Internat Econont.* 33 41-56.

_____, _____.1998. Why firms diversify: Internalization vs. agency behavior. Mimeo. March.

Nehrt. C. 1996. Timing and intensity effects of environmental investments. *Strategic Management J.* 17 535-547.

Porter, M., C. van den Linde. 1995. Green and competitive. Ending the stalemate. *Harvard Bus Rev.* 73 120-134.

Prahalad, C. K., Y. Doz. 1987 The Multinational Mission. Free Press, New York.

Rondinelli D., C. Vastag. 1996. International environmental standards and corporate policies: An integrative framework *California Management Rev.* 39(1) 106-122.

Romm, J. 1993. *Lean* and Clean Management. Free Press, Ness York.

Rugman. Alan M.. Alain Verbeke. 1998. Corporate strategies and environmental regulations: An organizing framework. *Strategic Management* 1, 19 363-375.

Russo, M., P. Fonts. 1997. A resource-based perspective on corporate environmental performance and profitability. *Acad. Management J* 40 534-559.

Stewart, R 1993. Environmental regulation and international competitiveness. Y*ale law J.* 102 2039-2106.

United Nations Commission on Trade and Development (UNCTAD). 1995 *World Investment Report.* United Nations Geneva, Switzerland.

Vernon, R 1992. Transnational corporations: Where are they coming from, where are they headed? *Transnational Corporations* 1(2) 7-35.

White, H. 1980. A heteroskedastic-consistent covariance matrix estimator and a direct test for heteroskedasticity. *Econometrica.* 48 (4) 817-838.

White,M. 1995. Does it pay to be green? Corporate environmental responsibility and shareholder value. Working paper University of Virginia, Charlottesville, VA.

Wolfensohn. J. 1997. Speech at the Global Knowledge Conference, Toronto, Ontario. June 18.

Zebra, S., B. Oviatt, K. Minyard. 1993. Effects of corporate ownership and board structure on corporate social responsibility and financial performance. *Acad. Management Best Paper Proc.* Atlanta, GA 336—340

Environmental Enforcement and Compliance and Its Role in Enhancing Competitiveness in Developing Countries

Lawrence Pratt & Carolina Mauri

7TH INECE CONFERENCE PROCEEDINGS (Forthcoming 2005).

...

II.   Perceptions of Environment and Competitiveness

Historically, in developing regions such as Latin America, many in the private sector (as well as in government) have believed that improving environmental performance has only negative effects on the countries' ability to improve competitiveness. The traditional view argues that: increased costs to firms to upgrade technology and treat externalities hurt firm level cost-competitiveness in the international marketplace, stringent national environmental standards encourage companies to invest in countries with less stringent standards, the costs to governments of enforcing environmental legislation could be better used elsewhere, and, improved environmental performance is a "luxury" for wealthier countries that poor countries cannot afford.

While there is a certain logic to the arguments, and in certain cases all can be true, the experience of firms and countries over the past decade has led to deeper understanding of how environmental performance relates to the more traditional economic policy goals of nations — such as furthering trade relationships and improving firm competitiveness. This new experience has shown that the issues are much more complex than we had imagined, and that the traditional view is, at a minimum, overly simplistic, and at the limit largely incorrect in the context of most developing countries.

We now know that there are strong positive relationships between good environmental performance and increased country and firm competitiveness. These newly understood relations have important implications for integrating environmental policy (and its effective implementation and enforcement) across many aspects of national policy-making and programs. The following three sections of the paper attempt to articulate the arguments for the positive relationships. The two following sections examine in more detail the potential role of E&C [enforcement and compliance] strategies and programs and considerations for developing country policy-makers.

III.   Firm Level Competitiveness

...

At the firm level, there are clear links between higher levels of environmental performance and improved competitiveness. Many are well known and well-documented, others are anecdotal or simply believed by business people and researchers to be relevant, pending more empirical research.

Costs and Competitiveness

First, the cost differential between environmentally "sound" and environmentally "unsound" products is a relatively small component of the cost structure for most companies. In the United States, arguably the country with the most expensive environmental regulatory system with which to comply, the average costs of compliance with all environmental regulation has been estimated at less than one percent of total costs....

Second, producing with less waste is usually more profitable. Waste products are, by definition, raw materials that enter into a process which are not used in the final product. Eliminating the waste streams by incorporating them into the product, reusing them or recycling them are always more profitable alternatives to treating the product for disposal (and usually more profitable than throwing the product away untreated)....

New Understanding of Opportunities

The other manner in which the traditional view of environmental costs is being challenged is through increasing opportunities for realizing market value from improved environmental performance. Globalization, increased connectivity, and changes in stakeholder expectations of firm's behavior are creating opportunities for firms to increase value for consumers, business customers and investors. (Pratt 2000, SustainAbility 2002).

Relating to Firm Business Opportunities

Efficiency.

As discussed above, there are very good opportunities for firms to invest in making their production processes more efficient, and their products more valuable per unit of energy and raw materials usage. Investments in energy and material efficiency can be highly profitable and can increase long-term competitiveness for many firms. In developing countries, particularly those of Latin America, there are outstanding opportunities for investment. High costs of capital (due to macroeconomic factors), a historic scarcity of investment capital and a tradition of relatively closed economies (limiting much cost competition) have led to underinvestment in new technology and allowed processes to be considerably less efficient than global competitors. As these economies open there will be increasing need to improve efficiency and ample opportunities to move to cleaner, more-efficient production technology. Fortunately, greater macroeconomic stability should allow investment costs to be more manageable permitting increased investment.

E&C programs can play an important role in improving efficiency in a number of circumstances. Where regulatory systems push firms toward higher levels of performance (such as more stringent effluent standards), E&C programs can be structured to allow companies to pursue a variety of options for achieving the regulatory goals. For example, gains in process efficiency are almost always competitiveness enhancing while investments in pollution control technology rarely are. Another important area is in advancing environmental goals in sectors that are highly competitive locally. There are many cases where many actors in a given industry all want to pursue more environmentally-sound production paths, but no single actor is willing to go first for fear of the others gaining an advantage by not following the same path.[1]

Adapting to trends toward more environmentally sound products.

Trends in consumer markets and "business to business" markets are rewarding firms with environmentally superior products and services and increasingly rejecting products that are lacking in certain attributes. For example, in markets for foodstuffs, organic and other "sustainable" agricultural products are growing rapidly as market segments. Organic sales alone represent over $20 billion of sales in each the US and Europe, and now account for about 2% of the total food market. While still relatively small, historic growth rates of around 20% per year (versus less than 2% for conventional foodstuffs) make it a very interesting market. Developing countries have outstanding potential to take advantage of these opportunities (due to lower labor costs, and frequently favorable climatic conditions).

In business to business relations, entire industries are moving to ensure that their products incorporate environmental aspects. The ISO14001 environmental management systems standard has proven to be the preferred vehicle for "B to B" environmental relationships. ISO14001 is now a "de facto" requirement for most of the value chains supplying the electronics and automobile industries and will likely take on similar importance in other industries.

Trends in forestry products (for sustainably managed timber sources) and fisheries (for more responsible capturing practices) and a number of other industries are indicative of the strength of these trends.

...

Innovation.

There is strong evidence from a number of industries of increased product and process innovation emerging as a result of stringent environmental standards....

---

[1] A well known case is the Costa Rican coffee processing sector. A voluntary agreement among all firms and the Environment Ministry permitted all companies to simultaneously pursue very large reductions in biological oxygen demand without risk.

There is little doubt that the success of industries such as the air emissions reduction industry that emerged in California was a direct result of a "home-grown" response to that state's stringent air emissions standards. Similarly, it is clear that Sweden's domination of the cellulose pulp processing industry is due to the extremely efficient production machinery developed in Sweden to meet that country's demanding air, water and waste standards.

...

The relevant point for E&C programs in this area is that compliance, per se, does not stifle innovation. However, it is clear that regulatory regimes can either stifle [or] encourage innovation depending on a number of characteristics discussed later in the paper.

Relating to Stakeholder Issues

Perhaps the greatest change in the environment-competitiveness relationship has been the increasing number of different stakeholders taking an interest in firm-level performance. Increased awareness of the negative consequences of poor environmental performance, increased speed of communications, and increased empowerment of communities and civil society in general have led to greater interest and involvement, and have increased the risks of weak environmental performance. Much of the risk is tied to the effectiveness of a country's regulatory system and its E&C mechanisms.

Social license to operate/Avoidance of Direct Action

...

E&C play a critical role in this sphere. Fair and conscientious application of environmental standards strengthens the legitimacy of a regulatory regime. If rules are unclear or not clearly understood, E&C can "save the day" by stepping in to clarify the conflict. Conversely, where rules are clear failure of an E&C effort to lead to a just outcome (or a perceived just outcome) can undermine confidence and negate the effectiveness of the regulatory system.

Regulatory risk.

Without clear and clearly enforced standards (particularly regarding emissions parameters), firms face a great deal of risk. Citizen complaints or arbitrary or capricious action by officials can lead to sanctions (in Latin America temporary closure is the most common sanction). A more sophisticated and stable system increases predictability and transparency and greatly reduces the risk of regulatory action. E&C is the interface between the rules themselves and the firms that are obliged to implement them. If this function is fulfilled in a consistent and transparent way, firms benefit from lower costs (they understand what is expected of them and focus on that) and lower risk (of misunderstandings or arbitrary actions).

Risk for financiers

...

E&C professionals should consider strategies for working with the financial sector to help finance practitioners understand the obligations their clients face and determine strategies for ensuring that risks to the company (and by extension their financiers) are managed effectively.

Evidence

The most compelling support for positive links between environmental performance and firm level competitiveness come from changes evident in the financial markets. Today, roughly one seventh of all globally invested funds include specific exclusions (called "filters" or "screens") for a number of sectors seen as objectionable or "unethical" (such as arms, nuclear energy, tobacco, gambling). This is in response to demand from individual and institutional investors (such as pension funds) who prefer not to have their savings and investments used to finance those industries. From 1996 to 1999 total assets in "screened" funds grew 80% during the past three years, compared to just over 40% for the rest of the market. (Social Investment Forum 1999)

A number of financial organizations are testing the theory that sound environmental performers are also superior financial performers by building mutual funds that include only companies that pass relatively high "filters" for environmental and social performance. Because these funds are new and relatively small (total market capitalization of all the funds is only US$1 to US$2 billion), it is too early to draw conclusions, but results thus far are encouraging. A 1998 comprehensive review of these funds showed that they were performing well against established benchmark indexes. (Ganzi 1998) Most of the funds also showed a much faster rebound from the stock market crash of 2000 and 2001 (author's review). A detailed study by ABN/AMRO, a leading Dutch financial institution concluded that while the case cannot yet be made for superior performance of sustainability-based investment funds, performance is at a minimum as good for ethically oriented portfolios including environmental ones. (ABN/AMRO 2001)

...

As noted previously, most of the data to support links between superior environmental performance and improved competitiveness are based on industry observations and case studies. However, empirical research on environmental performance and capital markets shows that the most successful and valuable multinational firms are those that adhere to the highest environmental standards.(Dowell and Hart 1998) The authors researched the relationship between firm value creation and the stringency of internal company environmental standards for over 500 publicly traded, U.S.-based multinationals in non service sectors. The study found that multinationals that have internal worldwide standards higher than any individual countries' standards are those with the highest levels of value creation. In contrast, firms that adhere to the lowest standards in the countries in which they operate are those with the lowest value.

...

III.   Trade and Environment

Nearly every developing country in the world is pursuing economic strategies that feature export-led economic growth. Environmental performance is critical in at least two dimensions of these economic strategies.

Import Requirements and restrictions

Most industrialized countries already have in place stringent rules regarding the environmental attributes of products entering their borders (limitations on chemical residues, types of plastics used, even packaging materials). In addition, international trade rules allow countries to restrict imports of products that are produced using certain processes that are deemed harmful (such as those that harm endangered species). To realize the potential from export-led growth, countries (and companies operating in them) must ensure that their products meet both the standards required by the destination market as well as those conditions established by exporting country. In addition, they must pay increasing attention to the manner in which export products are harvested and produced to ensure adherence to more stringent process-based requirements.

For the natural resource-based economies of most developing countries, this issue underlines the importance of regulatory programs and sound E&C initiatives in areas such as agricultural chemicals and pesticides, marine and coastal resources (particularly marine mammals, turtles, wetlands and mangroves), and endangered species protection. A limited number of "problems" identified in industrialized countries can ruin an entire industry, even if the failures are from only one firm. For example, Guatemala's berry industry has been destroyed twice in the past ten years due to an embargo on exports to the United States (imposed by the U.S. due to Guatemala's failure to adequately manage chemical and biological risks affecting the berries' quality). In both cases, more serious attention to chemical use and biological contamination would have eliminated the problem. A small number of containers of Chilean grapes found to have unacceptably high levels of pesticide for the U.S. market led to an embargo of all Chilean grapes for a lengthy period.

Other cases can be found, and trade rules at an international level are moving toward allowing countries greater latitude to restrict imports based on undesirable environmental criteria. (IISD 2002) Tropical timber is an interesting example. Due to an agreement of the International Tropical Timber Organization, international trade rules now allow any WTO member country to prohibit the importation of wood or wood products that are not certified as coming from sustainable sources. While it is not yet in any country's interest to exercise this right, WTO rules allow the restriction to be implemented at any time. The key for developing countries to protect their timber exports is to put in place programs (with appropriate compliance assurance mechanisms) that promote sustainable forest management and reduce the likelihood of any of their exports being rejected for lack of certification.

Trade Policy and Strategy

Most developing countries are pursuing closer trading relationships with the U.S. and Europe, primarily in the form of free trade agreements. In the case of the United States in particular it is clear that environmental issues are a critical component of reaching the agreement. Concerns in the United States regarding trading partners' environmental and labor performance are considered to be the most serious political obstacles to furthering trade agreements.

The North American Free Trade Agreement (NAFTA, between the U.S., Canada and Mexico) included an entire parallel agreement obliging the countries to undertake a wide variety of activities to strengthen environmental performance, resource management, and cooperation. This agreement is largely responsible for a wholesale change in Mexico's environmental laws, regulations and approach toward more sound environmental management. Both the obligations of the agreement and a sophisticated understanding of the competitive implications of environmental performance for Mexican exporters have led to dramatic improvements in many areas.

Responsible environmental standards and the ability and will to enforce them are part of the "price of admission" to closer trading ties with the U.S. It is clear in all of the post-NAFTA trade agreement processes (with Chile, Singapore, Jordan and the Central American nations) that the U.S. expects all of its trading partners to have in place laws, rules, administrative structure and E&C programs necessary to ensure responsible environmental performance, and that it will sanction its trading partners if their enforcement and compliance systems do not ensure that the rules are followed.

...

E&C's role is critical. The United States in particular looks frequently to E&C indicators to assess whether or not countries are taking appropriate action to ensure compliance with the environmental laws and regulations. For this reason, Latin American countries' E&C programs will likely be in the "spotlight" of any potential disagreements or disputes.

III. Business Climate

...

Each year since 1992, the World Economic Forum has published annual assessments of countries' competitiveness including rankings. In 1997, the WEF began including a number of environmental variables in recognition of an emerging understanding of the relationship between environmental performance and the development path of countries.

Today, the WEF environmental determinants of business climate and the subsequent rankings comprise one of the 11 "chapters" of the analysis and rankings. The issues assessed, analyzed and ranked are:

-     Stringency of air, water, waste disposal, chemical and overall environmental regulation,

-     Speed of adoption and enacting of environmental rules

-     Level of government priority to enacting international environmental regulations

-     Clarity and stability of regulations

-     Flexibility offered by system and authorities to meet required obligations

-     Consistency and fairness of environmental enforcement

-     Perceptions of effect of compliance on firm competitiveness

-     Extent of public-private cooperation to reach environmental gains

-     Prevalence of environmental management systems

The critical issue for policy-makers is that a very "mainstream" business policy organization is completely convinced of the positive linkages between environmental performance and a healthy competitive business climate. Countries seeking to improve their ranking (which is seen internationally as an important barometer of economic development potential) will need to take these criteria into account when working to strengthen their business climate.

A 2001 analysis of the results of the indicators reached an important conclusion:

"..the quality of a nation's environmental regulatory regime is strongly and positively correlated with its competitiveness.." (page 95) and continues:

"...The analysis provides considerable empirical evidence that cross-country differences in environmental performance are associated with the quality of the environmental regime in place. We find that the rigor and structure of the environmental regulations have particular impact, as does emphasis on enforcement."

...

For developing countries, this provides a very strong competitiveness and business-climate case for advancing more stringent regulatory structures, and for developing much greater capacity to ensure compliance with established laws and regulations.

It is important to note that E&C plays a direct or indirect role in nearly every one of the key environmental business climate factors. Some are direct – such as perceived consistency and fairness, and the level of public and private cooperation. Others are indirect – for example, the stringency of regimes (in particular in developing countries stringency is very much related to actions taken by E&C programs), flexibility, and perceived benefits on competitiveness.

IV.   The Role of E&C in Promoting Competitiveness

There is strong evidence that improved environmental performance is positively correlated with increased competitiveness. Further, we understand from experience in both rich countries and developing countries that environmental performance in the economy in general is largely a function of stringency of the environmental regulatory regime and of the seriousness of E&C efforts and programs. At the firm level, companies are frequently rewarded in the market place by improved environmental performance.

Experience in developing countries has shown that without effective E&C, progress toward national environmental goals will be limited. There is evidence that effective environmental E&C systems (based on fundamentally sound regulatory structures) can play an important role in encouraging firms to improve environmental performance, which can strengthen broader competitiveness-related goals at the national level.

...One of the challenges in using E&C as a tool to strengthen competitiveness is that E&C, by virtue of its role in an overall environmental regime, is a function of the policies and rules set out by the country. It is hard for E&C efforts alone to compensate for deficiencies in the laws and regulations. If the overall regulatory regime is misguided in this regard, then E&C will likely have little or no positive competitive impact.

...

Compliance and enforcement can also have neutral or even negative effects on competitiveness. Enforcement of rules that do not assist local companies in realizing environmental benefits will not improve competitiveness (thought it may not harm it either). In some cases, countries must enforce rules to achieve social and environmental goals that are not may harm the competitiveness of companies (footnote, refer to section on goals of national regimes). Also, uneven, unpredictable or inconsistent compliance and enforcement sends mixed signals, allow firms to gain short term advantages over local competitors through non-compliance.

...

VI.   Considerations for Developing Countries

As in many areas of environmental policy, implementation in developing countries implies a great number of challenges. Among the most relevant ones to be considered include:

> ➤   Relatively immature regulatory systems

> ➤   Limited national budgets leading to weak (underfunded, understaffed) institutions.

> ➢ Lack of understanding of how environmental performance relates to competitiveness

> ➢ Predominance of traditional views among private sector and government officials emphasizing "costs" of environmental performance

> ➢ Unique natural resource bases that present different challenges and reduce the possibility of "cut and paste" strategies from the U.S. and E.U.

A consensus "laundry list" of attributes of an overall environmental regime capable of enhancing competitiveness would include:

> ➢ Clear and stable rules based on a sound legislative mandate

> ➢ Clear and clearly delineated obligations for regulated community and other societal actors

> ➢ Clear performance parameters for regulated community (numeric, unequivocal)

> ➢ Mechanisms that drive and support the development of related industries and infrastructure (this allows for cost-effective waste management, a deep market for production equipment and control technologies, and other items),

> ➢ Rules designed to force companies to internalize the costs of low levels of environmental performance and which reward companies that reduce their externalities on the society

> ➢ Long-term goals that avoid technological "lock-in" (permitting technological revolution, rather than just evolution to meet increasingly stringent standards)

> ➢ That allow the regulated community certain flexibility in choice of solution to reach regulatory goals.

> ➢ Emphasis on solutions that reduce waste (materials, water and energy) rather than seek to treat it.

> ➢ Goals that push firms toward global product and process standards and the expectations of international trading partners.

> ➢ Structures that permit cost-effective E&C (burdens of proof, standards)

> ➢ Clear and simple legal procedures for the regulated community which reduce paperwork and time and effort interacting with authorities.

...

One particular advantage in most developing countries at this time is that their regulatory systems are still relatively immature. The immature systems may permit greater latitude to improve them through regulation or decree, and more specifically they may allow E&C professionals to "simulate" more ideal attributes through their policies, strategies and programs.

The most pressing question for E&C planners in a given country is to what extent the current systems and rules grant the degrees of freedom necessary to engage in competitiveness-enhancing activities? Only detailed country-by-country analysis can answer this question and develop recommendations for expanding the space in which E&C programs can engage in these issues.

Sources

ABN/Amro, "Title", ABN/AMRO, Amsterdam, 2001.

Dowell, Glenn, Stuart Hart and Bernard Yeung. "Do Corporate Global Environmental Standards Create or Destroy Market Value?" *Management Science*, June 1998.

Environmental Law Institute, "Innovation, Cost and Environmental Regulation: Perspectives on Business, Policy and Legal Factors Affecting The Cost of Environmental Compliance," Environmental Law Institute, Washington, DC 1999.

Esty, Daniel C. and Michael E. Porter, "Chapter 2.1 Ranking National Environmental Regulation and Performance: A Leading Indicator of

Future Competitiveness?" in *The Global Competitiveness Report 2001-2002*. World Economic Forum and Harvard University. Oxford University Press. 2001.

Ganzi, John, S. Buffet and R. Dunn, "A Review of Publicly Available Funds that Focus on Financial and Environmental Performance." A report by the Environment and Finance Enterprise for the U.S. Environmental Protection Agency, November 1998.

Jaffe, Adam et al. (1995). "Environmental Regulation and the Competitiveness of US Manufacturing: What Does the Evidence Tell Us?" Journal of Environmental Literature, Vol. XXXIII March 1995.

IISD, "Name", *Bridges*, No. XX, Geneva, 2002.

Panayotou, Theodore, editor, *The Environment for Central American Competitiveness*, Harvard University Press, Boston, 2000.

Porter, Michael E. *The Competitive Advantage of Nations*, Free Press, New York, 1998.

Porter, M.E. (1991), "America's green strategy," *Scientific American* 264,168.

Porter, M.E. and C. van der Linde (1995), "Toward a new conception of the environment competitiveness relationship," *Journal of Economic Perspectives* 9(4), 97-118.

Pratt, Lawrence P., "Rethinking the Private Sector-Environment Relationship in Latin America," Background Paper for the Seminar on the "New Vision for Sustainability:
Private Sector and the Environment" IDB/IIC Annual Meeting of the Board of Governors
New Orleans, Louisiana, March 25, 2000.

Social Investment Forum, *1999 Report on Socially Responsible Investing Trends in the United States*, November 4, 1999.

SustainAbility, "Developing Value: The Business Case for Sustainability in Emerging Markets," SustainAbility and IFC, London, 2002.

UBS, general information on investment funds at <u>http://www.ubs.com/ e/globalam/emea/switzerland/funds/ecoperformance.html</u>, January 23, 2004.

Win–win opportunities and environmental regulation: testing of porter hypothesis for Indian manufacturing industries

M.N. Murty, S. Kumar

67 JOURNAL OF ENVIRONMENTAL MANAGEMENT 139 (2003)

1.   Introduction

...The objective of this paper is to study the effect of environmental regulation relating to water pollution by the manufacturing industry in India on the productive efficiency of firms. The panel (time series-cross-section) data of 92 water-polluting firms for three year period 1996–99 are used to test the Porter hypothesis.

4.   Results

...

...The more the industry comply with the regulation the more efficient it becomes. This result supports the Porter hypothesis. The positive (negative) sign of the coefficient of time implies an increase (decrease) of technical inefficiency over time. Water conservation results in the saving of costs to the industry and thus contributes to an increase in productive efficiency. There may be potential complementarities between production of conventional output and a reduction of pollution loads. With the abatement technologies involving process changes as opposed to the end of pipe treatment, the cost of jointly producing conventional output and clean environment may be lower than the cost of producing them separately. Such complementarities might arise, for example, from cost savings associated with recovered or recycled effluents and reuse of waste water. The proponents of the Porter hypothesis argue that complementarities between environmental activities and conventional production combined with the induced innovations associated with environmental requirement can partially offset or actually exceed the direct expenditures associated with environmental protection.

5.   Conclusion

The approach used in this paper has the advantage in simultaneously measuring efficiency and determining the factors affecting it. Many of the empirical studies about the affect of environmental regulation on the productive efficiency of firms show that the regulation makes the firms less efficient. However, there are a few studies showing the opposite, the study reported in this paper being one of them.

The environmental regulation could provide incentives to the firms for the innovation and resource conservation in the environmental management. To study this problem we require firm specific panel data on the production and environmental management practices of firms. This paper uses firm specific data for 3 years for a sample of 92 water polluting firms in India. The Porter hypothesis about the possibility of win–win opportunities for the firms subjected to environmental regulation is tested for the Indian water-polluting industry. This is done by estimating the output distance function jointly with the equation explaining the relationship between technical inefficiency and indices of environmental regulation and water conservation and the time variable. The main empirical result is that the technical efficiency of firms increases with the intensity of environmental regulation and the water conservation efforts. This result supports the Porter hypothesis about environmental regulation.

The win–win opportunities from the environmental regulation could be found more in some industries and less in others. Similar studies for specific industries could help us to identify the industries with no such opportunities so that the monitoring and enforcement could be directed to those industries in which incentives are absent. Given the very high monitoring and enforcement cost of environmental regulation, this could result in the significant cost savings.

...

AFTERWORD

Making Law Work has drawn from a wide range of sources to present a selection of the best literature relating to environmental compliance and enforcement. The articles excerpted for the book represent a diverse set of disciplines and address a broad range of the issues in the compliance field. They show how the field is evolving to meet the challenges of environmental protection and sustainable development.

Increasingly, the world is recognizing that we need a stronger and more global rule of law, with stronger and more global compliance and enforcement efforts, if we are to curb the excesses of globalization — including excesses of pollution, excesses from natural resource exploitation, and other adverse environmental impacts. Together, they are the foundation for good governance and ultimately for sustainable development.

If our global environmental governance systems are to improve, actors of all types – individuals, NGOs, the media, businesses, certifiers, lawyers, scientists, financial markets, regulators, legislators, courts, networks, negotiators, international tribunals, development banks – and at all levels – local, national, regional, supranational, international – must participate in assuring compliance with environmental law and promoting sustainable development.

Multilateral Environmental Agreements provide a critical start to international environmental governance, but to be effective they need to be implemented at the national level, and compliance with them ensured. This requires sufficient resources and sufficient political will. However, MEAs today are mostly insufficient; their efforts must be strengthened.

To make better progress towards our sustainable development goals through MEAs, we need to improve our data gathering efforts and ensure that the data we gather is used to develop more effective regimes. We also need to ensure that our experiences with and information about different approaches to implementing MEAs are exchanged and shared, creating a pool of knowledge about possible approaches from which the most appropriate one for a given set of circumstances can be chosen.

We need a strong enforcement and deterrence framework, with cooperative approaches and robust compliance assistance for weaker States as well as small and medium-size enterprises. We need policies designed to promote both competitiveness and compliance. We need to foster the internalization of sustainable development and law compliance norms, and construct laws that draw on our deepest values and principles.

We need to build the framework of equitable, strong, and effective laws to manage humanity's interaction with the Earth and build a fair and sustainable society – a society that protects and manages the environment and natural resources for future generations, alleviates poverty, and promotes appropriate economic, social, and cultural development.

With this book, INECE provides empowering knowledge, insights, and strategies concerning the issues critical to fostering a culture of compliance.

Not every idea presented in this book is appropriate for all actors. In some developing countries and countries in transition, getting the basic institutional and administrative infrastructure in place – good governance, the rule of law, and the elimination of corruption – might be the principal issue to attend to before the others discussed in this book are even an option. Developed countries might be too embedded in a current path of regulation to completely change course, although they still can modify procedures and structures when international experience has shown alternatives to be more effective. Regardless of the particular circumstances facing developed and developing countries, these cannot be excuses for inaction.

Time is short. We have a moral and ethical responsibility to meaningfully address and to reverse the continuing deterioration of the global environment. As Klaus Toepfer notes in his Preface, we *can* still choose a sustainable future, but to do so we must learn from the successes and failures of the past and present.

And then we must act to make law work.

> Ladislav Miko
> Deputy Minister
> Czech Ministry of Environment
>
> Director Designate
> Directorate B: Protecting the Natural Environment
> Environment DG
> European Commission
>
> Spring 2005

About the Editors

Durwood Zaelke is the founding Director of the Secretariat for the International Network for Environmental Compliance & Enforcement (http://www.inece.org); the founder of the Institute for Governance & Sustainable Development in Washington, DC and Geneva; the co-founder (with Dr. Oran Young and Matthew Stilwell) of the *Program on Governance for Sustainable Development* at the University of California, Santa Barbara's Bren School of Environmental Science & Management; the founder of the Center for International Environmental Law; and the founder of the *International & Comparative Environmental Law Program* at the Washington College of Law at American University law school (http://www.wcl.american.edu/environment/llm.cfm). In addition to the Bren School of Environmental Science & Management at the University of California, Santa Barbara and American University law school, he has taught at Yale Law School, Duke Law School, and Johns Hopkins. His textbook, INTERNATIONAL ENVIRONMENTAL LAW & POLICY (Foundation Press 2nd ed. 2002) (with Hunter & Salzman), is the leading text in its field. Mr. Zaelke also is the Resident Managing Partner in the Washington, D.C. office of Zelle, Hofmann, Voelbel, Mason & Gette, LLP (http://www.zelle.com), specializing in corporate strategies for enhancing competitiveness through sustainable development, as well as the resolution of complex disputes.

Donald Kaniaru is the Managing Partner of Kaniaru & Kaniaru Advocates, in Nairobi, Kenya. A lawyer and advocate by training, he formerly served as the Director of the Division of Environmental Policy Implementation and as Director of the Division on Environmental Conventions with UNEP. He worked with UNEP for over 28 years and continues to serve as Special Legal Adviser to the Executive Director, UNEP. He is a member of the Law Society of Kenya, the East African Law Society, the British Institute of Public and Comparative Law, the IUCN Commission on Environmental Law, and the International Council of

Environmental Lawyers (ICEL), for whom he serves as representative to the UN in Kenya. He is a Trustee of the Center for International Environmental Law in Washington, DC and is an appointed member of the ICIPE Governing Council.

Eva Kružíková is the co-founder and Director of the Institute for Environmental Policy in the Czech Republic; is the former head of the Legislation and International Relations departments of the Czech Ministry of Environment, a ministry she was instrumental in establishing; has served as a member of the Environmental Advisory Council for the European Bank for Reconstruction and Development; and previously served as National Expert to the Commission of the EC, DG XI. She is an advisor to the Minister of Environment of the Czech Republic and a member of numerous national and international professional committees, including the Legislative Council of the Czech Government, the Compliance Committee of the Aarhus Convention, the IUCN's Commission on Environmental Law, and the International Council for Environmental Law. She is an Associate Professor of Environmental Law and teaches the course on EU environmental legislation at the Faculty of Humanities, Charles University, Prague. She has also been a visiting professor at the College of Law, Florida State University, USA, teaching a course on EU environmental legislation in 1999, 2001, and 2005.

About the Institute for Governance and Sustainable Development & Affiliated Organizations

The Institute for Governance & Sustainable Development (IGSD) was founded in 2002 to expand knowledge of the role institutions play in causing and confronting the challenges of sustainable development and to enhance the effectiveness, inclusiveness, and accountability of institutions that manage the complex interdependencies between society, economy, and environment. With offices in Washington, DC, and Geneva, the Institute aims to deepen understanding of the challenges of governance for sustainable development and their potential solutions through basic and applied research and analysis with an emphasis on empirical data; to strengthen the capabilities of others in civil society, the private sector, government, and intergovernmental organizations to enhance institutions through teaching, training, and capacity building; and to enhance the practice of governance for sustainable development by advising partners in civil society, the private sector, government, and intergovernmental organizations on specific issues of reform, and through its own advocacy of better policies and institutions. Durwood Zaelke serves as the President of the Institute, which serves as the Secretariat for INECE. For more information, email zaelke@inece.org.

The International Network for Environmental Compliance and Enforcement (INECE) was founded by the Dutch and United States environmental agencies in 1989, and now comprises more than 4,000 enforcement and compliance practitioners from government, non-government organizations, and international organizations in over 120 countries. INECE contributes to a healthy and clean environment, sustainable use of natural resources, and the protection of ecosystem integrity by ensuring effective compliance with and enforcement of environmental laws. INECE's goals are to raise awareness of the importance of compliance and enforcement, develop networks for enforcement cooperation, and strengthen capacity to implement and enforce environmental requirements. INECE is dedicated to strengthening both cross-border and internal domestic cooperation among professionals who work on environmental compliance and enforcement – investigators, prosecutors, regulators, parliamentarians, judges, and NGOs. A central INECE project is to develop indicators to measure environmental compliance and enforcement, so as to provide reliable, harmonized, and easily understandable information to help public agencies manage performance – by monitoring their activities and measuring their results – to determine which strategies are most effective and most efficient. INECE also offers a course on *The Principles of Environmental Enforcement* and maintains extensive Web resources for practitioners to share ideas and learn from topic-specific forums, news, digital libraries, interactive discussions, and fully searchable databases. Through its International Conferences, INECE presents practitioners from around the world with the opportunity to acquire the knowledge and to build the long-term relationships needed to tackle the challenges of environmental compliance and enforcement. In addition to the Dutch and U.S. environmental agencies, INECE receives additional support from the United Nations Environment Programme (UNEP), the World Bank, the Organisation for Economic Co-operation and Development (OECD), the European Commission, Environment Canada, the Environment Agency (England and Wales), the Czech Republic, and other governments. Durwood Zaelke is the Director of the INECE secretariat. For more information, see www.inece.org or email inece@inece.org.

The Program on Governance for Sustainable Development at the University of California, Santa Barbara's Bren School of Environmental Science & Management, encourages a systematic effort of scholarship, research, and other activities aimed at designing and implementing better governance systems. Directed by Matthew Stilwell, Oran Young, and Durwood Zaelke, the GSD Program is designed to address the big picture – how we should govern the interaction between the natural system and the human system. The GSD Program promotes multi-disciplinary research and facilitates efforts to pool the knowledge of dynamic and innovative thinkers in political and social science, law, economics, physical science, and related disciplines on specific problems of governance, while helping to educate future leaders through graduate courses and supervision of Ph.D. students and interns. For more information, see http://fiesta.bren.ucsb.edu/~gsd/ or email info@gsdprogram.org.